Hebraica Veritas?

JEWISH CULTURE AND CONTEXTS

Published in association with the Center for Advanced Judaic Studies of the University of Pennsylvania

David B. Ruderman, Series Editor

Advisory Board
Richard I. Cohen
Moshe Idel
Deborah Dash Moore
Ada Rapoport-Albert
David Stern

A complete list of books in the series is available from the publisher.

Hebraica Veritas?

Christian Hebraists and the Study of Judaism in Early Modern Europe

Edited by
Allison P. Coudert and Jeffrey S. Shoulson

PENN

University of Pennsylvania Press
Philadelphia

Publication of this volume was assisted by a grant from the Martin D. Gruss Endowment Fund of the Center for Advanced Judaic Studies, University of Pennsylvania.

Copyright © 2004 University of Pennsylvania Press
All rights reserved
Printed in the United States of America on acid-free paper

10 9 8 7 6 5 4 3 2 1

Published by
University of Pennsylvania Press
Philadelphia, Pennsylvania 19104-4011

Library of Congress Cataloging-in-Publication Data

Hebraica veritas? : Christian Hebraists and the study of Judaism in early modern Europe / edited by Allison P. Coudert and Jeffrey S. Shoulson.
   p. cm. — (Jewish culture and contexts)
   Includes bibliographical references and index.
   ISBN 0-8122-3761-7 (cloth : alk. paper)
   1. Hebraists, Christian—Europe—History—Congresses. 2. Judaism—Study and teaching (Higher)—History—Congresses. 3. Jews—Europe—Intellectual life—Congresses. 4. Jewish learning and scholarship—Europe—History—Congresses. 5. Christianity and other religions—Judaism—Congresses. 6. Judaism—Relations—Christianity—Congresses. I. Coudert, Allison, 1941– II. Shoulson, Jeffrey S. III. Series.

PJ4509.H4 2004
296'.07'04—dc22
                                                                            2003070529

To Richard Popkin and in memory of Smadar Heyd

Contents

Preface   ix
David B. Ruderman

Introduction   1
Allison P. Coudert and Jeffrey S. Shoulson

PART I   NEGOTIATING DIALOGUE

1. Polemic and Exegesis: The Varieties of Twelfth-Century Hebraism   21
Michael A. Signer

2. Man as the "Possible" Entity in Some Jewish and Renaissance Sources   33
Moshe Idel

3. Jews, Humanists, and the Reappraisal of Pagan Wisdom Associated with the Ideal of the *Dignitas Hominis*   49
Fabrizio Lelli

4. The Mechanics of Christian-Jewish Intellectual Collaboration in Seventeenth-Century Provence: N.-C. Fabri de Peiresc and Salomon Azubi   71
Peter N. Miller

5. John Selden's *De Jure Naturali . . . Juxta Disciplinam Ebraeorum* and Religious Toleration   102
Jason P. Rosenblatt

6. Censorship, Editing, and the Reshaping of Jewish Identity: The Catholic Church and Hebrew Literature in the Sixteenth Century   125
Amnon Raz-Krakotzkin

PART II IMAGINING DIFFERENCES

7   Skepticism and Conversion: Jews, Christians, and Doubters in *Sefer ha-Nizzahon*   159
    Ora Limor and Israel Jacob Yuval

8   Reassessing the "Basel-Wittenberg Conflict": Dimensions of the Reformation-Era Discussion of Hebrew Scholarship   181
    Stephen G. Burnett

9   Polemical Ethnographies: Descriptions of Yom Kippur in the Writings of Christian Hebraists and Jewish Converts to Christianity in Early Modern Europe   202
    Yaacov Deutsch

10 The "Jewish Quaker": Christian Perceptions of Sabbatai Zevi as an Enthusiast   234
    Michael Heyd

11 Colliding Visions: Jewish Messianism and German Scholarship in the Eighteenth Century   266
    Nils Roemer

12 Five Seventeenth-Century Christian Hebraists   286
    Allison P. Coudert

List of Contributors   309

Index   313

Acknowledgments   317

Preface

David B. Ruderman

As early as 1996, Moshe Idel and Gedalia Stroumsa of the Hebrew University, Anthony Grafton of Princeton University, and I had discussed the possibility of devoting an entire year of study at the University of Pennsylvania's Center for Advanced Judaic Studies to the subject of Christian Hebraism in early modern Europe. The topic was one of great significance, which had been relatively neglected by modern scholarship. Here would be a chance to bring together scholars of Jewish history, literature, and thought with scholars of the Renaissance, Reformation, and Christian thought in general. Here, too, would be an opportunity to energize a field of tremendous import to both Jewish and Christian history, and to the connection between the two.

With the help of my three distinguished colleagues, a proposal was prepared and submitted to the advisory committee of the center, and in the fall of 1999 a working group on Christian Hebraism convened in Philadelphia. Our numbers included scholars from the United States, Israel, and Europe, both senior and junior, and from a wide variety of academic and personal backgrounds. This was indeed an enterprise marked by humanistic virtue. The participants were positive, generous, and open to the different approaches represented within the group; the topic was addressed with enormous commitment; and the weekly seminars and the culminating conference were joyous occasions of intellectual stimulation and dialogue based on mutual respect and friendship. Those who joined in the year's activities were transformed by these ongoing and fruitful interactions, and the present volume is the end result of that truly special year.

It is a great personal pleasure to thank all the fellows and regular guests who participated in the group, both those who are included in this volume and those who were unable to contribute to it. The editors, Allison Coudert and Jeffrey Shoulson, worked responsibly and tirelessly to shape a year's conversation into a coherent book. Jerome Singerman, humanities editor of the University of Pennsylvania Press, offered his usual intelligent advice.

One of the high points of the year was the appearance of Richard Popkin. Professor Popkin is the doyen of the study of Christian Hebraism, and it was an honor to have him at our final colloquium to offer a survey of the field over the past half century. It is only fitting that we dedicate this volume to him, to the life's work that he continues to enjoy, and to the impact he has had on the work of every scholar who was a part of our collective enterprise. It is with sadness that we dedicate the volume, too, to Smadar Heyd, of whose tragic and premature death the editors and fellows learned just as this book was nearing completion. Artist, art historian, writer, and editor, Smadar was the wife of Michael Heyd, one of our key participants, and she was a full partner with Michael in the exhilarating experience of the year. Among her many contributions was the preparation of the artwork for a Passover seder for the center's fellows, a remarkable learning experience for all present. She is sorely missed by those who came to appreciate her gentle and sweet presence.

Introduction

Allison P. Coudert and Jeffrey S. Shoulson

The essays in this volume deal with the important but too often neglected subject of Christian Hebraists and their Jewish contemporaries, who acted variously as collaborators, mediators, and adversaries. The encounter between Jews and Christians had an important impact on both sides of the religious divide. On the one hand, it was an essential element in shaping each group's self-perception and sense of otherness (consequently contributing to the emergence of the modern study of cultural anthropology, comparative religion, and Jewish Studies); on the other, it challenged traditional religious beliefs, fostering the skepticism, toleration, and irreligion conventionally associated with the Enlightenment. By no means the first scholars to study the effect of Jewish scholarship on the Christian intellectual community of medieval and early modern Europe, the contributors to this collection depart from their important predecessors, historians like Jerome Friedman, Gareth Lloyd Jones, and Frank Manuel, by featuring the centrality of *exchange* and *interaction* between Jews and Christians.[1] This is especially important for the early modern period when Christians for the first time put the study of Hebrew on an equal footing with the study of Latin and Greek. The increased interest in Hebraica and Judaica was largely the result of Renaissance Humanist scholarship and Reformation controversies over the accuracy and reliability of the Hebrew text. Both had complex and in many instances unintended repercussions not only for the various confessional denominations within European Christianity but also for European Jews and Judaism.

In recent years there has been a profound rethinking of Jewish-Christian relations in medieval and early modern Europe and a growing interest in integrating Jewish history within the context of European history as a whole. Instead of envisioning Jewish and Christian cultures as discrete entities largely developing in isolation from each other—the paradigm favored by Heinrich Graetz and Gershom Scholem, especially in the case of Ashkenazic Jews—modern scholars have focused on the complex interaction between Christians and Jews as both communities reacted to the manifold changes that marked the transition from the medieval to the early modern and modern worlds.[2]

While earlier scholarship was preoccupied with investigating relations between Jews and Christians primarily in terms of persecution and toleration, these categories have now given way to more nuanced studies describing the varied relationships in specific periods and places. Starting with Salo Baron, the "lachrymose" view of Jewish history,[3] which reads history backward from the Holocaust and sees it as a continuous series of persecutions, has been largely rejected. And although a number of historians have identified various "turning points" in the Middle Ages, when they believe the relative security and toleration of Jews gave way to increasing hostility, the very search for such turning points has come into question. So too have monocausal explanations for the alleged worsening of the situation of European Jewry—be they in terms of the Crusades,[4] the Fourth Lateran Council's promulgation of the doctrine of transubstantiation,[5] the Christian attack on the Talmud,[6] the rise of the mendicant orders,[7] usury,[8] apocalypticism,[9] scholastic rationalism,[10] or the consolidation of political power.[11] John Van Engen suggested in 1985 that it was futile for historians to look for any continuous process of evolution during the medieval period: "Historians must accept that there were periods of sporadic change, when a pattern of advance or regression is not perceptible, periods of discernible change whether for good or ill, and periods of relative stability, without the whole necessarily fitting into a continuing evolutionary process."[12] The current suspicion of the teleological historiography of "grand narratives" and the emphasis on local history characteristic of European historians in general has clearly been incorporated into more recent Jewish historiography as well. David Nirnberg emphasizes the futility of trying to discover patterns of violence and persecution in medieval Europe in relation to all groups, including Jews. He stresses the need for microhistories investigating the specific geographical and political settings in which violence occurs and argues that the persecution of Jews must be seen in relation to the violence routinely endured by peasants, religious dissidents, and anyone who stood in the way of predatory rulers.[13] The same reluctance to read Jewish-Christian relations in terms of any one set of ongoing patterns also characterizes the work of early modern historians. This is not to deny that there were broad patterns of violence resulting in the expulsion of Jews in medieval and early modern Europe but to claim that violence was not an inevitable and inevitably recurring aspect of Jewish-Christian relations. But this still leaves historians with the dilemma astutely identified by Heiko Oberman: even if we reject the Holocaust as inevitable, we are nevertheless so haunted by it that we condemn or excuse the actions and beliefs of historical figures in its glaring light.[14]

While the suffering of Jews is certainly a legitimate topic, what increasingly interests scholars is the resilience of individual Jewish communities in the face of selective exploitation and expulsion. What, in fact, accounts for their long-term survival? Under what conditions and in what ways did they manage to survive and in some places prosper in the myriad and diverse microcultures that made up medieval and early modern Europe? The very idea that Europe can be described as "Christian" has been challenged by historians who emphasize the wide diversity of beliefs and practices among different groups and classes, and the persistence of pagan and magical elements that cut across ethnic and religious lines.[15] Indeed, alongside the current rethinking of the Jewish presence in medieval and early modern European history, scholars have also begun to incorporate the discussion of Islam, not merely as the perennial Christian enemy but as an ongoing presence *within* European culture before, during, and after the Crusades and *Reconquista*.[16] The instability of Christian and Jewish identity in the medieval and early modern periods makes it that much more difficult to postulate broad generalizations about Christian attitudes toward Jews or Jewish attitudes toward Christians. While it is an undoubted truth that an individual's identity is shaped by his or her perception of others,[17] the definition of "otherness" constantly changed over time. The world of Hugh of St. Victor was not the world of Luther or Sabbatai Sevi, and the identities of Jews and Christians inhabiting these different worlds were necessarily different. Therefore, while the concept of the "other" is useful when investigating the relations between Jews and Christians, it needs to be formulated in broad terms that take into account the ways each community reacted to the specific beliefs, practices, and institutions of the other and the way these reactions shaped and reshaped stereotypes.

Jews were "rooted" in Europe. However much they saw themselves as being in exile, they had what Yosef Yerulshalmi describes as "the sentiment in exile of feeling at home."[18] Jews and Christians interacted in villages, towns, marketplaces, courts, universities, and later in those printing houses that published Hebrew texts and the work of the Christian Hebraists who are the subject of this volume. While Jews were largely prohibited from owning land and barred from most professions except money lending, they practiced many trades patronized by Christians, and they were particularly valued as physicians.[19] The extent of the interaction between Jews and Christians is reflected in the prohibitions issued by church councils: Christians were not to eat with or marry Jews; Jews were prohibited from owning slaves and acting as tax collectors or judges.[20] The reason Innocent III wanted Jews distinguished by special clothing was so that Christians would not knowingly or unknowingly associate with them, which implied they were doing just that. Jews and Christians celebrated their religious culture in public ceremonies viewed by the members of both groups. "Cultural feedback" was thus a fact of life, working in both directions. In such an atmosphere, the alienation produced by the awareness of alterity is always balanced by the familiarity of mutual recognition. As Freud would observe several centuries later, the *unheimlich* is so powerful a psychological and social force precisely because it contains within it the *heimlich*.

Newer approaches to Jewish-Christian relations examine this feedback and relate it to the dynamics common to both groups, faced as they were with the growing centralization of political and religious power, the emergence of new forms of spirituality, changing concepts of personal, religious, and national identity, and the profound economic and cultural changes accompanying Europe's increasing involvement in the world at large. Jews and Christians were affected—to different degrees, to be sure—by the same currents in politics, economics, scholarship, and science.[21] These new studies provide the rationale for a more flexible approach to Jewish-Christian relations in medieval as well as early modern Europe that allows for the possibility of mutual influences, direct or indirect, polemical or assimilationist. In this regard, a number of historians have demonstrated the way Jews and Christians reconfigured their traditions in response to developments in the other community.[22] This, in turn, has occasioned historians to reevaluate evidence dealing with several key questions. How successful were Christian efforts to convert Jews? Did the conversion and assimilation of Jews into Christian culture proceed smoothly, or did it produce a hostile reaction on the part of envious or suspicious Christians? Were there significant numbers of resistant Jewish converts, who secretly retained their Jewish identity, or were these so-called Marranos the creation of paranoid Christians and Christian institutions such as the Inquisition? Is it appropriate to describe Christian hostility toward Jews in medieval and early modern Europe as anti-Judaism on the grounds that this hostility was purely religious, or is it appropriate to use the term *antisemitism*, which, although anachronistic, correctly identifies the racial dimension of Christian hostility in these earlier periods? And finally, what, if any, effect did the conversion and assimilation of Jews have on Christian culture in general?

It is the purpose of the present volume to contribute further to the newer approaches to Jewish-Christian relations described above and to address some of these larger issues especially in terms of the early modern period. The essays included are all concerned with the cultural, social, and intellectual interaction of Jews and Christians in such areas as travel, trade, teaching, translating, and printing, and they investigate the consequences of this interaction for both communities and Western civilization at large. While the kinds of relationships between Jews and Christians characteristic of the medieval period continued to exist, new developments complicated these relationships and led in some cases to an intensification of the opposing currents of assimilation and hostility. In terms of assimilation, printing, trade, and travel brought many Christians and Jews into closer contact than ever before, be it face to face or on the printed page. The kind of scholarship and search for the *prisca theologia*—an idealized, pristine wisdom often attributed to prehistoric Adam—characteristic of the Renaissance Humanism of Pico della Mirandola and others emphasized the centrality of texts and the importance of Hebrew in addition to Latin and Greek, and led Christians to patronize Jewish scholars. The growing interest in magic and the Kabbalah further encouraged Christians to study Hebrew under the tutelage of Jewish intellectuals and led to a greater awareness of the diversity of Jewish culture and beliefs. During the Renaissance and early modern period, new institutions for Jewish-Christian interaction developed as universities and medical schools became more open to Jews. Printing shops specializing in the publication of Hebrew, Syriac, Aramaic, and biblical texts provided another important place for intellectual exchange as Jews filled the role of copyists, typesetters, proofreaders, and even censors.

Early modern scholars are as divided as their medieval counterparts on how to assess the effects and significance of these new opportunities for contact and exchange. The "lachrymose" view of history colors the work of historians who treat the early modern period as an extension and intensification of the hostility they see as characteristic of the later Middle Ages. In the estimation of these scholars the medieval image of the Jew as a sorcerer and minion of the devil was preserved in Catholic thought and reinforced in the writings of many Lutherans and Calvinists intent on converting Jews or expelling them altogether. They see antisemitism as an important aspect of what German historians describe as the growth of "communalism" within rural and urban communities during the fifteenth and sixteenth centuries. They contend that the continual expulsions of Jews from major centers of European culture and commerce resulted in their becoming more marginalized than ever since they were effectively barred from the economic, cultural, and intellectual developments that occurred from the Renaissance to the eighteenth century.[23]

In recent years this view has been vigorously contested. A number of historians argue that the Renaissance marks a positive change in the relation between Christian and Jews inasmuch as Humanism and the quest for the *prisca theologia* led not only to a greater appreciation of Hebrew texts but also to the ecumenical belief that all traditions shared part of one primeval truth, which began with Judaism.[24] In *European Jewry in the Age of Mercantilism* Jonathan Israel emphasizes the reintegration of Jews into Western Europe as newer political philosophies advocating mercantilism encouraged rulers to appreciate the practical interests of the state and the financial advantages that Jews could provide. He stresses the positive effects this had on Jewish social and economic life until the early eighteenth century when European rulers adopted more protectionist policies that reduced the importance of Jewish international trading networks.[25] Moshe Idel has discussed the positive aspects of the expulsion of Jews from Spain, highlighting Jewish relocation in other parts of Christian Europe and the consequent revitalization of Jewish intellectual life that occurred as different schools of thought in philosophy and Kabbalah interacted.[26] He points out the effect this had on stimulating Christian thought as well,[27] a theme that he continues to emphasize in his essay in the present volume. Alexander Altmann, Richard Popkin, David Katz, David Ruderman, J. van den Berg, Ernestine van der Wall, Matt Goldish, Hava Tirosh-Rothschild, and Silvia Berti have all provided further examples to demonstrate the substantial interaction between Christian and Jewish scientists, philosophers, and intellectuals in the early modern period.[28]

Negotiating Dialogue

The first six essays in this volume deal with these important aspects of Jewish-Christian relations. Always aware of the tensions that continually threatened to erupt into full-blown hostilities, the essayists have emphasized the efforts—on both Jewish and Christian sides—to forge some form of dialogue that bespeaks the potential (if not the reality) of mutual respect. We have titled this section "Negotiating Dialogue" to underscore the tenuousness of these exchanges while simultaneously highlighting that conversations did indeed develop.

Michael Signer's essay offers an overview of twelfth-century Christian Hebraism that reveals its limitations and sets the scene for the enormous advances made during the Renaissance and early modern period. Signer distinguishes what he calls "cultural Hebraism" from "lexical Hebraism." While the cultural Hebraist exhibited a general interest in the Hebrew language and postbiblical Hebrew literature, he had no firsthand knowledge of either but relied on Jewish informants. The "lexical Hebraist," on the other hand, did possess first hand knowledge of Hebrew and at least some Hebrew texts. According to Signer there were very few lexical Hebraists in the twelfth century. The kind of textual scholarship that flourished among Renaissance and early modern Christian Hebraists began only in the thirteenth century with the rise of the mendicant orders.

The increasing interaction between Christian and Jewish scholars during the Renaissance and the ramifications this had for Christians is stressed in Moshe Idel's essay. He makes the provocative suggestion that the Renaissance notion of the dignity of man did not originate among Italian Humanists in Renaissance Italy but arose from Jewish sources in medieval Spain. His essay emphasizes the essential role Jewish intellectuals played in the emergence of the field of Christian Hebraism and the important ways in which Christian patronage of Jews affected both communities. Pico della Mirandola could never have incorporated elements of the Jewish Kabbalah into his eclectic philosophy had it not been for his Jewish teachers Yohanan Alemanno and the converted Jew Flavius Mithridates.

Fabrizio Lelli offers another example of the exchange of cultural motifs between Jews and Christians in Renaissance Italy. He analyzes the new and positive ways in which Italian Humanists viewed biblical figures and shows how contemporary Jews adopted these same interpretations to express their identity. Peter Miller provides an example of the fruitful exchange of ideas that occurred between Jews and Christians in the early modern period. He reconstructs the intellectual collaboration of an otherwise unknown Jewish rabbi, Salomon Azubi, and the renowned seventeenth-century scholar Nicolas-Claude Fabri de Peiresc. His description of their encounters reveals that mutual respect and forbearance could be an aspect of Jewish-Christian interaction. What Miller emphasizes is not the extraordinary nature of this collaboration between an abbé commendataire and a rabbi but its very ordinariness, and he demonstrates the significance of this kind of collaboration in terms of changing patterns of scholarship. By analyzing the issues discussed by the two men, he reveals the contribution Christian Hebraism made to the emerging study of comparative religion and cultural anthropology.

In his essay on John Selden's *De jure naturali . . . juxta disciplinam ebraeorum*, Jason Rosenblatt provides further evidence that the engagement of Christians with Jews and Jewish texts could lead to a greater sympathy between the two groups and contribute to emerging ideas of ecumenism and tolerance. Admittedly, Selden's evenhanded approach to rabbinic texts was the exception among Christian scholars rather than the rule; but as Rosenblatt argues, it did influence some of Selden's younger contemporaries in the direction of liberalism and inclusiveness, and it provided them with striking examples of Jewish charity toward non-Jews. Selden's acceptance of the validity of the so-called Noachide precepts and the equation he drew between them and Roman and natural law effectively built a bridge between different cultures and communities, thus contributing to new comparative approaches to history.[29]

While the essays discussed above deal primarily with instances of personal and intellectual exchanges between Jews and Christians, Amnon Raz-Krakotzkin's contribution posits the Hebrew printing shop as an important institutional meeting place for Jews, Christians, and Conversos. Raz-Krakotzkin makes the important point that even the censorship that invariably accompanied the publication of Hebrew texts was not always negative but could have the positive effect of muting or eliminating polemical passages, thereby making it easier for each community to approach the texts of the other. His essay's argument is consistent with those of scholars who reject the view that the

Counter-Reformation led to a decline in Jewish culture. He suggests instead that Jews played a more important, autonomous, and positive role in censorship than has been generally recognized. In his view the period of the Counter-Reformation released new cultural energies fostering the notion of the Jewish autonomous identity that became a hallmark of modernity. He makes the further provocative suggestion that modern Jewish historiography has in certain cases followed in the footsteps of Counter-Reformation censors in defining Jewish identity as an autonomous culture that developed apart from Jewish-Christian polemics but shared the same cultural and moral values as the dominant Christian culture.

The generally positive nature of the Jewish-Christian relations described in the aforementioned essays is especially interesting in terms of the growing intolerance of the Reformation and early modern periods. Heiko Oberman argues that the sixteenth century marks a "new peak of anti-Judaism" because heightened religious fervor, social unrest, and millenarianism combined to emphasize the Jews as hated allies of ruling elites and diabolical obstacles to an imminent apocalypse.[30] Not all scholars, as we have seen, agree with this bleak assessment, which once again underlines the difficulty of making comprehensive statements about Jewish-Christian relations over any period of time or across geographical areas and religious divisions. A number of scholars have in fact taken a contrary position and argued that millenarianism was actually beneficial to Jews inasmuch as it encouraged Christians to see Jews as human beings and potential converts, and not the hated "other."[31] But liking Jews solely as potential Christians is hardly toleration as we know it. Furthermore, it appears that during the early modern period increasing numbers of Christians began to doubt that Jews would convert or, if they did, that they could ever shed their intrinsic Jewishness.[32] R. Po-chia Hsia has also detected a turn for the worse during the same period, especially among Lutherans, but for different reasons. As Christian attitudes toward Jews became "disenchanted" and stripped of their sacramental and magical character, new forms of antisemitism emerged that were overtly racist.[33]

Imagining Differences

Given the degree of dissension among scholars, perhaps the only generalization that can be made about Jewish-Christian relations in the early modern period is that there was a clear ambivalence in Christian attitudes toward Jews. The essays in the second half of this volume take up various aspects of the fraught Christian impulse to imagine Jews and Judaism as both unavoidably different and potentially assimilable. Somewhat paradoxically, it was the growing intolerance characteristic of Reformation and Counter-Reformation Europe that had the greatest effect on transforming Jewish-Christian relationships from what they had been in the Middle Ages. The hardening of religious lines through increasing confessionalization destroyed the illusion of a united Christendom and vitiated the ideal of a single religious truth. Forced conversions among Jews and Reformation and Counter-Reformation conflicts among Christians effectively undermined the traditional connection between national, religious, and personal identity for many Jews and Christians alike. As a number of scholars have pointed out, the Conversos were paradigmatic of what has been called a "Marrano" mentality. They experienced both sides of the religious divide and in certain instances combined aspects of the two traditions in bizarre ways. Kaplan, Yerulshalmi, Popkin, and others provide extraordinary vignettes of the way Conversos and Marranos often straddled the religious divide and joined together elements from the opposing traditions, if they did manage to stay on one side or the other. The case of reconverted Conversos wearing hair shirts is perhaps the most extraordinary example of the kind of dual allegiance fostered, in effect, by intolerance.[34] Popkin has been especially concerned with emphasizing the contribution of Conversos to the growing skepticism, relativism, deism, and atheism that emerged in the early modern period and characterizes one strand of Enlightenment thought.[35] This is not to argue that all Conversos were skeptics. Many did successfully reconvert to Judaism, but their reconversion was aided by a new kind of Jewish literature especially directed at Jews contemplating conversion to Christianity or wishing to return to the Jewish fold. In many cases this literature was written by Conversos who had themselves returned to Judaism. They therefore knew Christianity from the inside. They spoke the same idiom as Christians, educated as they were in Christian schools and universities, and they could consequently tailor their arguments specifically to refute Christian claims. These texts were enormously important not only in educating Jews contemplating conversion to Christianity and Conversos contemplating reconversion to Judaism but also for the effect they had on Christians. They presented Judaism in a self-censored, reasonable way while at the same time offering a defense of Judaism with an implied or, in some cases, overt criticism of Christianity. These sources helped to undermine Christian beliefs.[36]

One of the major Jewish texts to fit such a description was Yom Tov Lippman Mulhausen's *Sefer ha-Nizzahon*, described in Ora Limor and Israel Yuval's essay. Written in the earliest stages of the transition into early modernity (c. 1400), this text played an important part in subsequent early modern Christian polemics against Judaism. But as Limor and Yuval argue, the text is equally important as an example of a new kind of Jewish polemical reaction to Christianity predicated on considerable knowledge of Christian theology and borrowings from Christian philosophical and rhetorical traditions. The text provides evidence that Lippman interacted with Christians through daily contacts, conversations, and disputations. Limor and Yuval contend that Lippman realized that the traditional arguments of halakhic Judaism were powerless in the face of the newer philosophical and rational arguments of Christian theologians with university training. Consequently, he developed a new rational form of argument that incorporated Christian approaches. His work is a further instance of the kind of "feedback" between the two communities.

Stephen Burnett's essay on Christian Hebraism among Reformation Protestants underscores the tensions in the disparate and often-conflicting views of Jews and Judaism held by Christians of different confessional affiliations. It is undeniable that the initial drive to go back to the original Hebrew text of the Bible in order to circumvent corrupt Catholic traditions sparked a remarkable growth in Christian Hebraism among Protestants, but the spread of Hebrew studies provoked increasing conflict over the utility of Jewish scholarship for biblical interpretation. As Protestants became more proficient in Hebrew, they increasingly relied on each other as teachers rather than actual Jews, except in the case of the small number of Christians interested in the Kabbalah, who continued to seek out Jewish tutors. There was therefore a distancing of Protestant Christian Hebraists from Jews in terms of personal relationships. As a result, the most important role that professing Jews played in Reformation Hebrew studies was not as tutors but as Hebrew printers and authors. Burnett points out that the production and consumption of Hebrew texts was of crucial importance for the growth of Christian Hebraism, but the very growth of Christian Hebraism caused resistance on the part of many Protestant scholars, foremost among whom was Luther.[37]

In his essay on Christian ethnographies of Jews, Yaacov Deutsch also documents the ambiguous and often hostile attitudes toward Jews in the early modern period. He rejects the term *Christian ethnographies* put forward by R. Po-chia Hsia on the grounds that the objectivity one expects from ethnographies is conspicuously absent from these texts.[38] Thus if one is to use the term *ethnography,* it must be preceded by *polemical* because these works routinely dwell on what the authors perceive to be the anti-Christian, ridiculous, and superstitious nature of Jewish rituals and beliefs. Deutsch contends that there is a perceptible difference between ethnographies written by Jewish converts to Christianity and those written by Christians. While the first group tends to emphasize the anti-Christian nature of Jewish practice, the second concentrates on its superstitious and absurd character. This latter tendency becomes dominant in the late seventeenth and eighteenth centuries and fits in with the Enlightenment critique of religion in general and Judaism in particular. To further discredit Jews and Judaism, Christian authors emphasized the difference between biblical and rabbinic Judaism. This distinction was first made in the Middle Ages, but Deutsch argues that in the early modern period it becomes part of a systematic attempt to dissociate contemporary Judaism from its scriptural roots and so discredit it.

Michael Heyd's essay on Christian reactions to Sabbatai Sevi highlights the complexity of the religious situation and the way this could in certain instances lead to an alliance between Christians and Jews, even when the predominant relationship was adversarial. Along with a number of scholars, Heyd rejects Scholem's contention that the Sabbatian movement was primarily an autonomous Jewish affair. The sources Heyd cites show that a number of Christians were aware of the influence Christian millenarianism had on Sabbatianism. Heyd argues that the identification of Sabbatai Sevi with the Quaker James Nayler in several Christian pamphlets reveals that the authors recognized the common threat millenarian enthusiasm posed for both religions. While in no way denying the polemical intent of Christian reports on Sabbatai Sevi, he contends that establishment Christians did evince some kind of fellow feeling for their rabbinic counterparts in the face of a common enemy. Heyd's evaluation of millenarianism is original; instead of concentrating on what Christian millenarians thought of Jews, he is concerned with the views of anti-millenarian Christians and their sympathetic response to like-minded, anti-millenarian Jews.

Modern scholars have recognized that early modern messianism and apocalypticism, in both Christian and Jewish manifestations, were profoundly linked to developments in the historical and political thought of the period. Nils Roemer's essay picks up on many of the issues raised in Heyd's analysis of the Sabbatian movement, revealing how writers of the German Enlightenment who proposed a newly secularized model of historical progress did so by positioning themselves in opposition to what was rendered—explicitly or implicitly—as an outmoded Jewish messianism. Revising Karl Löwith's highly influential account of the intimate connection between modern philosophies of history and Christian eschatology, Roemer asserts that the *Aufklärung* conception of historical progress and salvation displaced Jewish messianism by rendering it as outdated and lacking a spiritual dimension. Instead of a religious challenge, the "Jewish question" became primarily a social one about cultural improvement and political integration.

Many Christians experienced a similarly divided religious identity as a consequence of the religious wars endemic to the early modern period and the doctrine of *cuius regio eius religio*—the power of the ruler to determine the religion of his subjects. Forced to convert, and in some cases, reconvert from various forms of Protestantism to Catholicism or vice versa, some Christians simply opted out of institutional religion altogether. Ernst Benz and Lezek

Kolakowski have illustrated the kind of religious no-man's land in which these Christians found themselves.[39] They were, to use Kolakowski's memorable phrase, *Chrétiens sans église*, who in many respects shared the crisis of identity and rootlessness experienced by many Conversos, whom Kaplan has described as "Jews without Halakhah."[40] To these alienated Jews and Christians one must add the mainly Calvinist refugees banished from France and other parts of Europe, who made up what has been called the Third Reformation. Forced into exile, these Protestants reinterpreted the relation of church and state and reread the Scriptures in the light of their own enforced exile. A salient characteristic of this group was a new attitude toward Judaism and an appreciation of the parallels between the persecution of Christians and the diaspora of the Jews.[41]

But while the intolerance of the early modern period sparked a reaction that laid the foundation for the Enlightenment critique of religious particularism and contributed to the movement for toleration and ecumenism, it is undeniable that most Jews and Christians remained within their own particular denominations. In many cases those who remained drew sharper lines than ever between themselves and other religious communities. This complex religious situation and the way it was reflected in contacts between Jews and Christians is the subject of Allison P. Coudert's essay. She analyzes the diverse reactions of a group of Christian Hebraists to the conversion of one of their number, Johan Peter Späth, to Judaism. They range from horror to indifference and reveal the same opposing responses of assimilation and increased hostility characteristic of Jewish-Christian relations from the twelfth century on. But these diverse reactions demonstrate the important effect that religious conflict had in separating religion from politics and hence in fostering the process of secularization.

From antiquity to the present Jewish-Christian encounters have played a key role in defining attitudes toward personal, national, and religious identity in Western culture. These definitions, in turn, involved debates about history, religion, morality, and truth in general. The work of the Christian Hebraists described in this volume impinged on all these highly sensitive areas; they were linguists and textual critics, and their work highlighted the ambiguous role played by language and texts in transmitting natural and divine truth. The subject of Christian Hebraism is therefore not peripheral to European history but one that has direct relevance to understanding the intellectual changes and challenges characterizing the transition from the ancient to the modern world. This is nowhere more true than in the early modern period, when many of the concepts underpinning modern Western secular society came into existence.

Notes

1. Christian Hebraica has come in and out of focus in the work of intellectual and cultural historians of early modern Europe of the past half century. Three of the most important studies of the subject in recent years—and in many ways the progenitors of this volume—are Jerome Friedman, *The Most Ancient Testimony: Sixteenth-Century Christian-Hebraica in the Age of Renaissance Nostalgia* (Athens: Ohio State University Press, 1983); Gareth Lloyd Jones, *The Discovery of Hebrew in Tudor England: A Third Language* (Manchester: Manchester University Press, 1983); and Frank E. Manuel, *The Broken Staff: Judaism through Christian Eyes* (Cambridge: Harvard University Press, 1992).

2. See, for example, Hava Tirosh-Rothschild, "Jewish Culture in Renaissance Italy: A Methodological Survey," *Italia* 9 (1990): 63–96; David B. Ruderman, "The Italian Renaissance and Jewish Thought," in *Renaissance Humanism: Foundations, Forms, and Legacy*, ed. A. Rabil Jr. (Philadelphia: University of Pennsylvania Press, 1988), 382–433.

3. Salo W. Baron, "Graetz and Ranke: A Methodological Study," in *History and the Jewish Historian: Essays and Addresses* (Philadelphia: Jewish Publication Society, 1964), 271–72.

4. Israel Yuval, "Vengeance and Damnation, Blood and Defamation: From Jewish Martyrdom to Blood Libel Accusations," *Zion* 58 (1993): 33–90. In an essay in the 1994 fascicle of *Zion* devoted to Yuval's essay, Mary Minty takes up the issue of Christian awareness of the Jewish martyrdoms of 1096: "Kiddush Ha-Shem in German Christian Eyes in the Middle Ages," *Zion* 59 (1994): 209–66.

5. Gavin Langmuir, *Toward a Definition of Anti-Semitism* (Berkeley and Los Angeles: University of California Press, 1990).

6. Amos Funkenstein, "Changes in the Patterns of Christian Anti-Jewish Polemics in the Twelfth Century," in *Perceptions of Jewish History* (Berkeley and Los Angeles: University of California Press, 1993), 172–219.

7. Jeremy Cohen, *The Friars and the Jews: The Evolution of Medieval Anti-Judaism* (Ithaca: Cornell University Press, 1982).

8. Lester K. Little, *Religious Poverty and the Profit Economy in Medieval Europe* (London: P. Elek, 1978).

9. Richard Landes, *Relics, Apocalypse, and the Deceits of History: Ademar of Chabannes, 989–1034* (Cambridge: Harvard University Press, 1995).

10. Anna Sapir Abulafia, *Christian and Jews in the Twelfth-Century Renaissance* (London: Routledge, 1995).

11. R. I. Moore, *Formation of a Persecuting Society: Power and Deviance in Western Europe, 950–1250* (Oxford: Basil Blackwell, 1987). For an overview and evaluation of these theories, see Robert Chazen, *Medieval Stereotypes and Modern Antisemitism* (Berkely and Los Angeles: University of California Press, 1997); and David Berger, "From Crusades to Blood Libels to Expulsions: Some New Approaches to Medieval Antisemitism," in *Second Annual Lecture of the Victor J. Selmanowitz Chair of Jewish History, Touro College* (New York: Touro College, 1997), 1–29.

12. John Van Engen, "Christian Middle Ages as an Historiographical Problem," *American Historical Review* 91 (1985): 519–52.

13. David Nirnberg, *Communities of Violence* (Princeton: Princeton University Press, 1996).

14. Heiko Oberman, "Three Sixteenth-Century Attitudes towards Judaism: Reuchlin, Erasmus, and Luther," in *Jewish Thought in the Sixteenth Century*, ed. B. D. Cooperman (Cambridge: Harvard University Press, 1983), 327: "We are still so haunted by a nightmare which continues to be daylight reality, that in our field it is hard to find a middle ground between aggressive accusations and escapist apologies. If the historian's first task be to act as the final advocate for the dead, it is nearly impossible for him to distinguish between his role and his conscience; if the historian's second task be to act as public prosecutor, it is nearly impossible for him not to judge the past in order to prevent recurrence in the future. And worst of all, if it is true that both tasks, the advocate's and prosecutor's, presuppose a careful hearing of the sources as the witnesses, it requires a more-than-human effort not to follow the relativizing escape route of 'attenuating circumstances'—attenuating for a single man like Martin Luther or for all northern Europe's hesitant historians of tolerance, said to be the finest fruit of Renaissance humanism."

15. Van Engen, "Christian Middle Ages," 533: "Few medieval historians speak with any confidence of some common ideal animating all of medieval Christianity irrespective of particular places, times, schools, orders, and authors." For the diffusion of non-Christian pagan and magical practices, see Carlo Ginzburg, *The cheese and the worms: The cosmos of a sixteenth-century miller,* trans. John and Anne Tesdeschi (Baltimore: Johns Hopkins University Press, 1980); idem, *The night battle: Witchcraft and agrarian cults in the sixteenth and seventeenth centuries,* trans. John and Anne Tedeschi (Baltimore: Johns Hopkins University Press, 1983); idem, *Ecstasies: Deciphering the witches' Sabbath* (New York: Pantheon, 1991); Keith Thomas, *Religion and the Decline of Magic* (New York: Charles Scribner's Sons, 1971).

16. See, for example, Yvonne Yazbeck Haddad and Wadi Zaidan Haddad, eds., *Christian-Muslim Encounters* (Gainesville: University Press of Florida, 1995); Khalil I. Semaan, ed., *Islam and the Medieval West: Aspects of Intercultural Relations* (Albany: State University of New York Press, 1980); John Victor Tolan, ed., *Medieval Christian Perceptions of Islam* (New York: Garland, 1996); Minou Reeves, *Muhammad in Europe: A Thousand Years of Western Myth-Making* (New York: New York University Press, 1999); Toby E. Huff, *The Rise of Early Modern Science: Islam, China, and the West* (Cambridge: Cambridge University Press, 1993); David R. Blanks and Michael Frassetto, eds., *Western Views of Islam in Medieval and Early Modern Europe: Perceptions of the Other* (New York: St. Martin's Press, 1999).

17. See, for example, the way Ruth Mellinkoff uses the concept of "otherness" to illuminate themes in the history of art and to identify specific scenes and characters in *Outcasts: Signs of otherness in northern European art of the late Middle Ages* (Berkeley and Los Angeles: University of California Press, 1993). See also Michael Ragussis, *Figures of Conversion: "The Jewish Question" and English National Identity* (Durham, N.C.: Duke University Press, 1995); and James Shapiro, *Shakespeare and the Jews* (New York: Columbia University Press, 1996).

18. Yosef Yerulshalmi, "Exile and Expulsion in Jewish History," in *Crisis and Creativity in the Sephardic World, 1391–1648,* ed. B. R. Gampel (New York: Columbia University Press, 1997): 3–23.

19. Harry Friedenwald, *The Jews and Medicine* (Baltimore: Johns Hopkins University Press, 1994); Joseph Shatzmiller, *Jews, Medicine, and Medieval Society* (Berkeley

and Los Angeles: University of California Press, 1994); and John M. Efron, *Medicine and the German Jews: A History* (New Haven: Yale University Press, 2001).

20. Amnon Linder, ed. and trans., *Jews in the Legal Sources of the Early Middle Ages* (Detroit: Wayne State University Press, 1997).

21. See, for example, the essays in Michael A. Signer and John Van Engen, eds., *Jews and Christians in Twelfth-Century Europe* (Notre Dame: University of Notre Dame Press, 2001).

22. A good example of this kind of reconfiguration is discussed in Ivan Marcus, *Rituals of Childhood* (New Haven: Yale University Press, 1996).

23. Joshua Trachtenberg, *The devil and the Jews: The medieval conception of the Jew and its relation to modern antisemitism* (New Haven: Yale University Press, 1944); H. A. Oberman, *The roots of antisemitism in the age of Renaissance and Reformation*, trans. James I. Porter (Philadelphia: Fortress, 1984); H. A. Strauss, "Juden und Judenfeindschaft in der frühen Neuzeit," in *Antisemitismus: Von der Judenfeindschaft zum Holocaust*, ed. Herbert A. Strauss and Norbert Kampe (Frankfurt: Campus Verlag, 1985), 66–88; E. L. Ehrlich, "Luther und die Juden," in *Antisemitismus*, 47–65; Robert von Friedeburg, "Village Strife and the Rhetoric of Communalism: Peasant and Parson, Lords and Jews in Hesse, Central Germany, 1646–1672," *Seventeenth Century* 7 (1992): 201–26.

24. Chaim Wirszubski, *Pico della Mirandola's Encounter with Jewish Mysticism* (Cambridge: Harvard University Press, 1989); F. Secret, *Les Kabbalistes Chrétiens de la Renaissance* (Paris: Dunod, 1964); D. P. Walker, *The Ancient Theology: Studies in Christian Platonism from the Fifteenth to the Eighteenth Centuries* (London: Duckworth, 1972); idem, "The Prisca Theologia in France," *Journal of the Warburg and Courtauld Institutes* 27 (1954): 204–59.

25. Jonathan Israel, *European Jewry in the Age of Mercantilism* (Oxford: Clarendon, 1985).

26. Idel, "Encounters between Spanish and Italian Kabbalists in the Generation of the Expulsion," in *Crisis and Creativity in the Sephardic World*, ed. B. R. Gampel (New York: Columbia University Press, 1997), 189–222; idem, "Religion, Thought, and Attitudes: The Impact of the Expulsion on the Jews," in *Spain and the Jews: The Sephardic Experience, 1492 and After*, ed. E. Kedourie (London: Thames and Hudson, 1992), 123–39.

27. Idel, "Jewish Kabbalah and Platonism in the Middle Ages and Renaissance," in *Neoplatonism and Jewish Thought*, ed. L. E. Goodman, Studies in Neoplatonism: Ancient and Modern 7 (Albany: State University of New York Press, 1992); idem, "Magical and Neoplatonic Interpretations of the Kabbalah in the Renaissance," in *Jewish Thought in the Sixteenth Century*, ed. Cooperman, 186–242.

28. Alexander Altmann, "Lurianic Kabbalah in a Platonic Key: Abraham Cohen Herrera's *Puerta del Cielo*," *Hebrew Union College Annual* 53 (1982): 317–52, reprinted in *Jewish Thought in the Seventeenth Century*, ed. I. Twersky and B. Septimus (Cambridge: Harvard University Press, 1987), 1–38; Richard H. Popkin, "Jewish Anti-Christian Arguments as a Source of Irreligion from the Seventeenth to the Early Nineteenth Century," in *Atheism from the Reformation to the Enlightenment*, ed. M. Hunter and D. Wooton (Oxford: Oxford University Press, 1992), 159–81; idem, "Jewish Messianism and Christian Millenarianism," in *Culture and Politics*, ed. Perez Zagorin (Berkeley and Los Angeles: University of California Press, 1980), 67–90; idem, "The Jews of the Netherlands in the Early Modern Period," in *In and Out of the Ghetto: Jewish-Gentile Rela-*

tions in Late Medieval and Early Modern Germany, ed. R. P. Hsia and H. Lehmann (New York: Cambridge University Press, 1995), 311–16; Richard H. Popkin and Gordon M. Weiner, eds., *Christian-Jews and Jewish-Christians* (Dordrecht, Neth.: Kluwer, 1994); David S. Katz, "The Abendana Brothers and the Christian Hebraists of Seventeenth-Century England," *Journal of Ecclesiastical History* 40 (1989): 28–52; idem, *Philo-Semitism and the Readmission of the Jews to England, 1603–1655* (Oxford: Oxford University Press, 1982); idem, *Sabbath and Sectarianism in Seventeenth-Century England* (Leiden: E. J. Brill, 1988); David B. Ruderman, "The Italian Renaissance and Jewish Thought," in *Renaissance Humanism: Foundations, Forms, and Legacy*, ed. Rabil, 382–433; idem, *Jewish Thought and Scientific Discovery in Early Modern Europe* (New Haven: Yale University Press, 1995); idem, *Kabbalah, Magic, and Science: The Cultural Universe of a Sixteenth-Century Jewish Physician* (Cambridge: Harvard University Press, 1988); J. van den Berg and Ernestine G. E. van der Wall, eds., *Jewish-Christian Relations in the Seventeenth Century: Studies and Documents* (Dordrecht, Neth.: Kluwer, 1988); Matt Goldish, *Judaism in the Theology of Isaac Newton* (Dordrecht, Neth.: Kluwer, 1996); Hava Tirosh-Rothschild, *Between Worlds: The Life and Thought of Rabbi David ben Juda Messer Leon* (Albany: State University of New York Press, 1991); Silvia Berti, "At the Roots of Unbelief," *Journal of the History of Ideas* 56 (1995): 555–75.

29. The seven Noachide precepts are described in Sanhedrin (56a–b) as follows: 1) the prohibition against idolatry and 2) blasphemy, 3) an injunction to establish a legal system, 4) commandments against bloodshed, 5) an enumeration of sexual sins, 6) a prohibition against theft, 7) an injunction against cutting flesh from a living animal.

30. Oberman, "Three Sixteenth-Century Attitudes towards Judaism," 324.

31. Katz, *Philo-Semitism and the Readmission of the Jews*. See also Jeffrey Shoulson, *Milton and the Rabbis: Hebraism, Hellenism, and Christianity* (New York: Columbia University Press, 2001) for the discussion of a specific case, that of the English poet and polemicist John Milton, in which Jewish distinctiveness elicits a profound ambivalence as it informs evolving notions of election, Calvinist or otherwise.

32. Jerome Friedman, *The Most Ancient Testimony: Sixteenth-Century Christian Hebraica in the Age of Renaissance Nostalgia* (Athens: Ohio State University Press, 1983). Speaking of the failure of the movement to readmit Jews to England in his article "The Jew in Seventeenth-Century Protestant Thought," *Church History* 46 (1977): 63–79, Robert Healey comments: "The readmission movement failed because not enough English believed that the Jews were future Christians and harbingers of the millennium" (77). In "The Beginning of the Change in the Attitude of European Society towards the Jews," *Scripta Hierosolymitana* 7 (1961): 193–219, S. Ettinger makes the further sobering point that "those who spoke in favor of the Jews did not actually believe in the permanence and future of human political society" (202).

33. The term *disenchanted* appears in R. P. Hsia, *The Myth of Ritual Murder: Jews and Magic in Reformation Germany* (New Haven: Yale University Press, 1988), 131ff. For a further discussion of the emerging racist stereotyping of the Jews, see Hsia, "The Usurious Jew: Economic Structure and Religious Representations in an Anti-Semitic Discourse," in *In and Out of the Ghetto: Jewish-Gentile Relations in Late Medieval and Early Modern Germany*, ed. Hsia and Lehmann.

34. Yosef Kaplan, *The Story of Isaac Orobio de Castro*, trans. Raphael Loewe, Littman Library of Jewish Civilization (New York: Oxford University Press, 1989).

35. Richard H. Popkin, *The History of Scepticism from Erasmus to Spinoza*, rev. ed. (Berkeley and Los Angeles: University of California Press, 1979).

36. Yosef Kaplan, *From Christianity to Judaism;* Richard H. Popkin, "Jewish Anti-Christian Arguments as a Source of Irreligion from the Seventeenth to the Early Nineteenth Century," in *Atheism from the Reformation to the Enlightenment,* ed. M. Hunter and D. Wooton (Oxford: Oxford University Press, 1992), 159–81; Silvia Berti et al., eds., *Heterodoxy, Spinozism, and Free Thought in Early-Eighteenth-Century Europe: Studies on the Traité des trois impostures* (Dordrecht, Neth.: Kluwer, 1996).

37. Martin Friedrich argues that by the seventeenth century Lutherans had no real respect or appreciation for Jews and little concern with missionary activities because they thought it fruitless. See his *Zwischen Abwehr und Bekehrung: Die Stellung der deutschen evangelischen Theologie zum Judentum im siebzehnten Jahrhundert,* Beiträge zur historischen Theologie (Tübingen, Ger.: J. C. B. Mohr, 1988), n. 72. Elisheva Carlebach takes a more positive view of Lutheran missionizing efforts although she does point out the difficulties Jewish converts had in persuading Christians that their conversions were genuine. See Carlebach, *Divided Souls: Converts from Judaism in Germany, 1500–1700* (New Haven: Yale University Press, 2001).

38. R. P. Hsia, "Christian Ethnography of Jews in Early Modern Germany," in *The Expulsion of the Jews: 1492 and After,* ed. R. B. Waddington and A. H. Williamson (New York: Garland, 1994), 223–35.

39. Ernst Benz, "La Kabbala Chrétienne en Allemagne du xvi au xvii siècle," in *Kabbalistes Chrétiens,* ed. Antoine Faivre and F. Tristan, Cahiers d'Hermetisme (Paris: Editions Albin Michel, 1979), 89–109; L. Kolakowski, *Chrétiens sans église* (Paris: Gallimard, 1969).

40. Kaplan, *From Christianity to Judaism.*

41. Trevor-Roper, "The Religious Origins of the Enlightenment," in *The Crisis of the Seventeenth Century: Religion, the Reformation, and Social Change* (New York: Harper and Row, 1968); Oberman, "Three Sixteenth-Century Attitudes towards Judaism," 349ff.

PART I

Negotiating Dialogue

1
Polemic and Exegesis: The Varieties of Twelfth-Century Hebraism

Michael A. Signer

Within the context of Christian Hebraism in the early modern period, the twelfth century in Northern Europe can serve only as a prologue. When one studies the work of twelfth-century Christians who had an interest in the "Hebrew truth," one discovers that they limited their focus to the sphere of biblical studies. There were no reference books or bilingual dictionaries in Latin or the vernacular that would have provided access to an aspiring scholar who wanted to engage in the study of Hebrew language—biblical or post-biblical—independently. It would seem that in the years between 1109 (Stephen Harding) and the 1190s (Alan of Lille) any interest in Hebrew language or traditions forced Christians into contact with members of the Jewish community who were faithful to their tradition or had recently converted to Christianity. With the exception of Petrus Alfonsi—who is beyond the scope of this essay—the Jews (*Hebrei*) who are inscribed into the writings of Christian authors were actual living Jews.[1] Christians sometimes encountered learned Jews, but there is some evidence that they also spoke with Jews who did not provide the highest level of scholarship.

The emphasis on contact with living Jews that appears to constitute the core of Christian Hebraism during the twelfth century is an effort to balance an argument central to the important book by Jeremy Cohen, *Living Letters of the Law: Ideas of the Jew in Medieval Christianity*. In the introduction Cohen explains that he examines key chapters in the earlier history of the "hermeneutical Jew"—that is, the Jew as constructed in the discourse of Christian theology, and above all in Christian theologians' interpretation of Scripture.[2] Cohen's focus is on the "images" of the Jew as constructed in the writings of Christian theologians from Augustine through the Friars. From his perspective the Augustinian theological construction of the place of Jews in the economy of salvation shaped the writings of later theologians. As the textual tradition of the early Christian authors came under the critical methods of medieval scholars, the "hermeneutical Jew" met the "real," or "living," Jew. These Jews who lived in proximity to Christian centers of learning could impart their knowledge of Hebrew, and their Christian "students" would be left to discern what they would use from those exchanges in order to develop their own theological and exegetical works. The living Jew constituted more than a literary trope as the basis for Christian apologetics. For a small but significant group of Christians it became increasingly important to seek out Jewish interlocutors in order to develop their own internal Christian theological writings.

The efforts by twelfth-century Christian scholars to use the Hebrew language for interpreting the Old Testament may be described as "cultural" and "lexical" Hebraism. The distinction between these two terms is based on whether the Christian scholar had independent access to reading Jewish exegesis in Hebrew or was dependent upon his Jewish interlocutor. Cultural Hebraism, the dependence upon conversation with a living Jew, is based on the work of Beryl Smalley, who was one of the first modern investigators to use the term *Hebraist* to describe the writings by the twelfth-century scholar, Andrew of St. Victor.[3] She discovered that when Andrew provided explanations of the vocabulary and actions in the biblical text, his Jewish interlocutors, whom he called "Hebrei," were transmitting explanations that had parallels in the writings of Jewish scholars such as Rabbi Solomon ben Isaac of Troyes, Rabbi Joseph Kara, and Rabbi Samuel ben Meier of Ramerupt. Smalley never made the claim that Andrew could read these sources independently. However, she considered him a "Hebraist" because of his singular focus on explaining the Old Testament without reference to standard topoi of the Christian tradition. In the concluding chapter of *The Study of the Bible* she describes the important role played by medieval Jews in the development of Christian notions of the literal sense: "The Jew appealed to him [the Christian scholar] as a kind of telephone line to the Old Testament. Here was a people which spoke the language of Moses and observed the Law and had a vast store of traditions about Bible history. . . . So in his dealings with the Synagogue [in our case the direct conversation with the living Jew] he abstracted his disapproval of the present day representatives for his veneration for its past."[4] In this vivid description Smalley argues for what I call "cultural Hebraism," which describes the broad interest of some Christians in both the Hebrew language and postbiblical Hebrew literature. To qualify as a "cultural Hebraist," it is sufficient for the Christian scholar to seek information from a living Jew with no requirement of independent access to the Hebrew language. The ability to control Hebrew grammar or read texts in biblical or rabbinic Hebrew is subordinate to the utilization of the information transmitted by Jews. The cultural Hebraist had no need to determine whether the Jew transmitted his tradition from the Hebrew text of the Bible or the Talmud or even if he offered an explanation by one of the contemporary Jewish exegetes like Rashi, whose works were expressed orally or in writing. The word spoken by the Jew himself becomes the authoritative interpretation of any difficult passage in the Old Testament, the *Hebraica Veritas*.

"Lexical Hebraism" is predicated on the independent ability of the Christian to read biblical and postbiblical texts. Avrom Saltman, based on his own descriptions of Christian Hebraism, set this higher standard. He would consider only those Christian authors who had independent knowledge of the Hebrew language—particularly postbiblical Hebrew.[5] By this higher standard there would be very few Christian Hebraists until the thirteenth century and the rise of the mendicant orders.[6] The remainder of this chapter steers a middle course between "cultural" Hebraism and the more stringent standards of "lexical" Hebraism, collapsing the two distinct categories into one subtle and flexible type that would allow an evaluation of Christian Hebraists along more of a continuum moving from cultural to lexical Hebraism.

As a heuristic device to demonstrate the degree and kind of Hebrew knowledge possessed by such important medieval Christian theologians as Stephen Harding, Nicolas Manjacoria, Hugh and Andrew of St. Victor, Herbert of Bosham, and the anonymous author of the *Ysagoge in Theologiam*, it is useful to employ the categories developed by Hugh of St. Victor in his *Didascalicon*, where he describes the various approaches to understanding the biblical text.[7] First we shall describe the efforts by each of these exegetes to understand the words of the Latin Vulgate as a translation from the Hebrew—what Hugh of St. Victor terms the *littera*, or lexical meaning. Then we shall observe the ways that these Christian exegetes put words into the context of sentences or units of narrative—what Hugh would call the *sensus*. Finally, we will attempt to determine if the Hebrew text itself or the tradition that Jews transmitted to their Christian interlocutors had any influence on in their determination of the *sententia*—the term Hugh uses to refer to the meaning of the Old Testament text in light of the Christian economy of salvation.

We begin with the colophon of the letter of Stephen Harding, Abbot of Citeaux, where he described his project to produce an accurate text of the Latin Vulgate.[8] Stephen found precedents for his own efforts in the work of Carolingian scholars like Hrabanus Maurus, who attempted to transmit the heritage of patristic commentary, and in the work of Alcuin and Theodulf, who tried to provide a uniform text of the Latin Bible.[9] Both Hrabanus Maurus and Theodulf employed the efforts of contemporary Jews in their enterprises.[10] The work of Sigembert of Gembloux provides further evidence that Christians turned to Jews to help them in their interpretations of the biblical text. Only a few years before Stephen Harding's project he was described as "most dear to the Jews because he was expert (*peritus*) in distinguishing the text of the Latin based on the Hebrew bible by Jerome from the other versions such as the Septuagint."[11] To produce a "corrected text" of the Latin Bible required a scholar who was willing to excavate what lay beneath the Bible that lay before him. The turn to the Hebrew translation of Jerome, often called "Hebrew Truth" (*Hebraica Veritas*), was also a turn to those people who transmitted the Hebrew tradition.

Harding made his recourse to living Jews explicit when he explained that his motivation for the project was the discrepancy that existed between the Latin versions and the Hebrew Truth translated by Jerome. He therefore consulted (*adivimus*) with some Jews, *inquiring of them* (questioning them) in French (*lingua romana*) concerning those places in Scripture where the translations differed. Harding inserted their translations into his own Bible. What is remarkable in Harding's letter is that he describes the actual scene as the Jews "went through their books in our presence" (*revolventes . . . coram nobis*) and explained the Hebrew and Aramaic writings in French. He concludes that "the Jews did not find many of the words or verses that had disturbed us in the diverse Latin texts that we had before us." As a result of these oral consultations, Harding removed all the passages where the Latin diverged from the Hebrew.[12] It seems clear that Harding was not a lexical Hebraist himself. He could not read the text of the Hebrew independently of the presence of Jewish interlocutors. However, Harding's efforts mark a significant continuity with the patristic period. He followed the pattern established by Jerome, who had consulted with Jews. He was willing to ascribe to the Jews and their version of the scriptural text a greater measure of accuracy than the Latin texts he had available to him.

Writing in the mid-twelfth century, Nicolas Manjacoria, a Cistercian at the Abbey of Three Fountains, shared Harding's concern for improving the quality of the biblical text.[13] His efforts focus exclusively on the Psalter, the liturgical text and one that had caused Jerome himself no end of trouble because of the diverse textual traditions. In the prefaces to his three commentaries Nicolas indicates that he consulted with learned Jews (*dissertores*). On one occasion he praises a "certain Hebrew" from Spain who was "learned" (*eruditus*) in many languages. He also described his discussions with one Jew about a Psalter that he had brought along with him from Monte Cassino.[14] This discussion prompted Nicolas to express his desire to learn Hebrew. However, there is no indication in the commentaries themselves that he ever reached the level of reading either biblical or postbiblical Hebrew texts independently.

Both Harding and Manjacoria form a bridge between Carolingian scholars and the efforts by the mendicant orders in the thirteenth century to provide the best (I hesitate to use the word *critical*) text of the Vulgate. Carolingians and their twelfth-century heirs were cultural Hebraists. However, they manifested a desire to focus on the Hebrew language as a significant tool for analyzing the biblical text. We shall have to wait until the thirteenth century for a lexical Hebraist like Thibaud of Sezannes to engage in textual criticism of the Scriptures based upon his independent ability to work with the Hebrew language.[15]

At the Abbey of St. Victor in Paris we find more solid evidence linking thirteenth-century Hebraists to their twelfth-century forerunners.[16] Hugh of St. Victor and his pupil Andrew made efforts not only to understand the lexical dimensions of the Hebrew Bible (*littera*) but also to utilize lexicography and etymology as the fundamental tools for developing an interpretation of biblical words or verses within the context of larger units of narrative within the whole canon of Christian Scripture. Both of them were interested in the sequence of the narrative in the Old Testament (*historia*) because that very sequence formed the foundation of the greater Christian allegorical interpretation—a demonstration of the continuity between the Old and the New Testaments.[17]

Hugh sets out his intellectual plan in his *Didascalicon* and in the preface to his notes on the Octateuch, *De Scripturis et scriptoribus sacris*.[18] Andrew is less explicit about his theoretical framework, but his commentaries indicate that he also understood his task as more than providing "the best text."[19] Both scholars focus on a careful analysis of the language in the Old Testament based on the Christian tradition supplied by Jerome or Bede as well as the information they derive from Jews in their own era.

In his *Notulae* on the Pentateuch, Hugh provides a number of glosses where transcriptions of Hebrew words are inserted into the commentary. There are more than sixty references in the *Notulae* to Jews (*Hebrei*).[20] Many of these references correlate with explanations in rabbinic literature or in the commentaries by Rashi.[21] Hugh follows the tradition of Jerome and Augustine in preferring the Hebrew text of the Old Testament to the Septuagint. He repeats the patristic argument that the Jews deliberately omitted explicit references to the Trinity when making the Greek translation lest they lead Ptolemy and the pagans into thinking that there are many Gods or that the Hebrew Bible comports with Platonic philosophy.[22] Did these forays by Hugh into Jewish explanations of the *littera* and *sensus* affect his interpretation of the deeper meaning of the text (*sententia*)? More research is required to establish such a connection, but we can say that in the *Notulae* there is a very narrow range of passages that Hugh permits as the foundation for Christological reading: he denies the tradition that the binding of Isaac on Mount Moriah occurred at the place where Christ was crucified, nor does he describe Melchizedek as a type of Christ.[23] Hugh then moves toward a broader horizon for the use of Jewish interlocutors than simply a resource for etymology and translation. The

Jews become his guides to establishing a plain meaning of narrative (*historia*) in the Hebrew Bible.

Andrew advances on Hugh's project. During the latter part of his career, 1153 to 1163, he wrote commentaries on the prophetic and wisdom books. In these commentaries he makes more frequent reference to his Jewish postbiblical material than his teacher.[24] There are frequent references to "the Jews say" (*Iudei dicunt*) or "my Jew told me" (*Hebreus meus dicit*).[25] It is also clear that Andrew obtained his information from Jews by conversing with them in Old French. We are able to determine this because the Old French glosses in his commentaries match those in Rashi or in Old French Jewish dictionaries.[26] At times he indicates that his Jewish interlocutors may be improvising an explanation on the spot: for example, he writes "as the Jews determined" (*ut arbitrantur Hebrei*).[27] But if Andrew did not know Hebrew, he reveals considerable sensitivity for its linguistic idiosyncrasies in his commentaries. He writes about the *waw* conversive and makes statements about the ways that Hebrew expresses itself with phrases like "according to idiomatic Hebrew" (*idioma linguae hebraicae*) and "according to the Hebrew way of speaking" (*consuetudo hebraice locutionis*).[28] Andrew also has an ethnographic eye: he describes Jewish mourning practices and points out that the Jews do not consider anyone from the nations as their kin. He also knows that Jews identify Christians with Esau.[29] Andrew seems to have been swayed by Jewish interpretations of the virgin passage in Isaiah 7 and the suffering servant passage in Isaiah 53.[30] However, a careful reading of his comments as well as some of his other remarks about "open prophecies of Christ" indicates that while Jewish interlocutors could be "heard" in shaping Andrew's understanding of the Hebrew Bible, their voices ultimately could not contradict the claim that Jesus was indeed the Christ or the Christian understanding of the history of salvation.

We turn now to Herbert of Bosham, whom Beryl Smalley called "Andrew's most apt pupil."[31] Herbert studied in Paris at midcentury and edited Peter the Lombard's commentary on the Psalter.[32] After serving in the entourage of theologians surrounding Thomas Becket in England, he ended his career in the Cistercian Abbey in Pontigny, where he composed a commentary on the *Psalterium iuxta hebraicam* that exists in a single manuscript.[33] Raphael Loewe published the preface and parts of the commentary and joined Smalley in praising the unique focus of the commentary on the plain meaning of the Psalter, declaring that Herbert was capable of reading Rashi on his own.[34] A recent study of the full commentary has confirmed some of Loewe and Smalley's research.[35] Herbert seems to be the first twelfth-century example of both a cultural and a lexical Hebraist. His commentary anticipates the efforts of Nicolas of Lyra. Like Lyra, Herbert makes use of Rashi for his own purposes. His procedure is to contrast the Christian tradition of exegesis (*ecclesiastici*) with the "learned Jews" (*litteratores Hebraici*). Herbert developed a method for determining those psalms where David explicitly refers to Christ and those where the psalm refers to an event in history of biblical Israel. On many occasions Herbert simply allows the weight of the Christian tradition to determine that David is speaking of Jesus. There are other psalms where Herbert adopts a critical stance toward the historical explanation of his Jewish teacher (*litterator*)—precisely when the teacher indicates that the ancient rabbis (*Hebrei antiqui*) believed that the psalm referred to the Jewish messiah.[36] In the commentary by Herbert the word and *sensus* do have an effect on the deeper meaning. Herbert argues that there is a middle ground: Jesus has filled the role of the messiah in part (*ex parte impletum*) while the Jews still await their messiah. However, it is Jesus who will ultimately come and redeem both Jews and Christians as Saint Paul has indicated in his epistle to the Romans.[37]

In the anonymous *Ysagoge in Theologiam,* published by A. M. Landgraf and identified as deriving from the school of Abelard, there is a variety of Christian Hebraism that goes beyond the genre of biblical commentary to that of theological exegesis.[38] This collection of theological authorities (*Sententiae*) belongs to the "scholastic" attempt to present Christian theology as a system.[39] In the midst of its presentation of Creation, the Fall, and God's remedies for humankind one encounters a macaronic text with Hebrew characters, transliterations, and Latin translations of the Hebrew text of the Bible that are more literal than Jerome's. The Hebrew characters are integral to the text rather than added by a later hand. They illustrate the author's conviction that Hebrew is the mother of all languages and that the law and prophets transmit the foundations of theology, which were translated into Greek and Latin at a later period.[40] The author utilizes the same rationale as Hugh of St. Victor for the lack of direct reference to the Trinity in the Old Testament: so as not to mislead Ptolemy and the pagans. In the process of putting forward these arguments the *Ysagoge* calls upon Christians to recall Jews from their error just as Jesus was sent to the lost sheep of Israel.[41]

In his description of the mechanics of transliteration the anonymous author sets forth the distinct vowel sounds of Hebrew and those graphemes that have no equivalent in the Latin language.[42] As an ironic twist to his argument that the division of languages began with the tower of Babel, the author asserts, "Hebrew descends from right to left while Greek and Latin climb from left to right so that the downfall of the Jews prefigures the rise of the nations."[43] The *Ysagoge* then proceeds to set forth a standard set of Old Testament references that are interpreted within the framework of Christian theological tradition.[44] In this way the *Ysagoge* brings the Hebrew *littera* into the Christian *sensus* and *sententia*. In this particular work, lexical Hebraism overshadows cultural Hebraism in anticipation of the work of the mendicant orders of the thirteenth century.

This brief survey of twelfth-century Christian authors indicates that the Hebrew language and the Jewish tradition were an object of Christian curiosity. The development of theological inquiry in all ecclesiastical institutions, the monastic schools, the new open school of the Augustinian canons of St. Victor Abbey in Paris, and the schoolrooms of Paris all shared an interest in Hebraism. Erudition and the appreciation of antiquity were part of the cultural advancement of that era. Urbanization and advances in theological inquiry led to increasing opportunity for contact between Jews and Christians, and it is clear that Christians and Jews did come into greater contact as Christians became more organized in their study of the biblical text.[45] It was the hope of many twelfth-century masters that they were both imitating the fathers and moving forward. Jerome's appreciation for the Hebrew language was reinforced by Saint Augustine's notion that Hebrew was the original language and the language spoken by God. However, Augustine urged caution in accepting anything more than a simple lexical explanation from the Jews. Because they had not "seen" Christ, their explanations were not in agreement with the rule of faith.[46] In twelfth-century Christian Hebraism we have discerned that the boundaries set by the bishop of Hippo were not ignored, but that the Hieronymian tradition permitted a broader horizon for creative scholarship.

Notes

1. On Petrus Alfonsi and his interest in Hebrew, see John Tolan, *Petrus Alfonsi and His Medieval Readers* (Gainesville: University Press of Florida), 12–26, 115–19.

2. Jeremy Cohen, *Living Letters of the Law: Ideas of the Jew in Medieval Christianity* (Berkeley and Los Angeles: University of California Press, 1999), 3.

3. Beryl Smalley, "Andrew of St. Victor, Abbot of Wigmore: A Twelfth-Century Hebraist," *Recherches de théologie ancienne et médiévale* 10 (1938): 358–73. She expanded this research in her now-classic book, *The Study of the Bible in the Middle Ages* (Oxford: Oxford University Press, rev. ed., 1952). Although she knew no Hebrew herself, Smalley sought the help of L. Rabinowitz and later Herbert and Raphael Loewe (*Study of the Bible*, 362).

4. Smalley, *Study of the Bible*, 362.

5. Pseudo-Jerome, *Quaestiones on the Book of Samuel*, ed. Avrom Saltman (Leiden, Neth.: Brill, 1975), 44–49.

6. On Hebraism among the mendicant orders, see Jeremy Cohen, *The Friars and the Jews* (Ithaca: Cornell University Press, 1984) and *Living Letters of the Law;* Gilbert Dahan, *Les intellectuels chrétiens et les juifs au moyen age* (Paris: Cerf, 1990), 239–70, 423–510. The most comprehensive survey of Christian Hebraism by mendicants is Ch. Merchavya, *The Church versus the Talmudic and Midrashic Literature, 500–1248* (in Hebrew) (Jerusalem: Mossad Biglik, 1970). See also Deeana Copeland Klepper, "Nicho-

las of Lyra and Franciscan Interest in Hebrew Scholarship," in *Nicholas of Lyra: The Senses of Scripture*, ed. Philip Krey and Lesley Smith (Leiden, Neth.: E. J. Brill, 2000).

7. *The Didascalicon of Hugh of St. Victor: A Medieval Guide to the Arts*, translated from the Latin with an introduction and notes by Jerome Taylor (New York: Columbia University Press, 1968), bk. 6, ch. 8–12, 147–51.

8. The text of Stephen's letter is in J. P. Migne, *Patrologia Latina* 166: 1375–76 (hereafter *PL*). The text also appears in H. Denifle, "Die Handschriften der Bibel-Correctorien des 13. Jahrhunderts," *Archiv für Literatur und Kirchengeschichte* 4 (1888): 267–78. On Stephen Harding's biblical studies, see J. P. P. Martin, "Saint Etienne Harding et les premiers recenseurs de la Vulgate latine, Theodulfe et Alcuin," *Revue des sciences ecclésiastiques* 54 (1886): 511, 55 (1887): 5, 92, 213; David Kaufman, "Les Juifs et la Bible de l'abbé Étienne de Citeaux," *Revue des études juives* 18 (1889): 131–33.

9. On biblical studies in the Carolingian period, see Raphael Loewe, "The Medieval History of the Latin Vulgate," in *Cambridge History of the Bible*, vol. 2, *The West from the Fathers to the Reformation* (Cambridge: Cambridge University Press, 1969), 102–54. Christian Hebraism in this period is discussed in Matthias Thiel, *Grundlagen und Gestalt der Hebräischkenntnisse des Frühen Mittelalters* (Spoleto: Centro Italiano di Studi sull'alto Medioevo, 1973).

10. On Hrabanus Maurus and his knowledge of Hebrew, see B. Blumenkranz, *Les Auteurs chrétiens latins du moyen age sur les juifs et le judaisme* (Paris: Le Haye, 1963), 174; Merchavya, *Church versus Talmudic and Midrashic Literature*, 55–57; M. Rissel, *Rezeption antiker und patristischer Wissenschaft bei Hrabanus Maurus* (Bern: Peter Lang, 1976). For the Hebraism of Theodulf, see Avrom Saltman's introduction to Pseudo-Jerome, *Quaestiones on the Book of Samuel*, 1–29; L. Delisle, "Les Bibles de Theodulfe," *Bibliothéque de l'École des Chartes* 40 (1879): 5–47; E. Power, "Corrections from the Hebrew in the Theodulfian Manuscripts of the Vulgate," *Biblica* 5 (1924): 233–58.

11. Cited in Beryl Smalley, *Study of the Bible* (79) from Godescalc, *Gesta Abbatum Gemblacensium*, *PL* 160, 641.

12. Gilbert Dahan, *L'exégèse chrétienne de la Bible en Occident médiévale* (Paris: Cerf, 1999), 167–71.

13. A. Wilmart, "Nicolas Manjacoria, cistercien à Trois-Fontaines," *Revue bénédictine* 33 (1921): 136–43; A. Vaccari, "I tre salteri di san Girolamo al vaglio di Nicolo Maniacoria," in *Scritti di erudizione e di filologi*, vol. 2 (Rome: Edizioni di storia e letteratura, 1958), 53–74; R. Weber, "Deux prefaces au Psautier due à Nicolas Maniacoria," *Revue bénédictine* 63 (1953): 3–17; R. Weber, "Un Nouveau manuscrit de la revision du Psautier "Juxta Hebraeos" due à Nicolas Maniacoria," *Revue bénédictine* 85 (1975): 402–4. For a summary of these articles, see Dahan, *L'exégèse chrétienne de la Bible*, 171–75.

14. V. Peri, "Correctores immo corruptores: Un saggio di critica testuale nella Roma del XII secolo," *Italia medioevale e umanistica* 20 (1977): 19–125.

15. Denifle, "Die Handschriften," provides a survey of thirteenth-century Bible "correctoria," and Dahan surveys more recent scholarly developments in *L'Éxégèse chrétienne de la Bible*, 175–238.

16. Beryl Smalley outlines the content and purpose of the exegetical writings by Hugh, Andrew, and Richard of St. Victor in *Study of the Bible*, 83–195. Smalley supplies the majority of references used in this chapter. A. Grabois gives a broad sketch of biblical studies within the context of intellectual developments in twelfth-century France in

"The Hebraica Veritas and Jewish-Christian Intellectual Relations in the Twelfth Century," *Speculum* 50 (1975): 613–34.

17. Hugh's biblical hermeneutics are described by Patrice Sicard, *Hugues de Saint-Victor et son École* (Tunhout, Belg.: Brepols, 1991), 74–80; Dominique Poirel, *Hugues de Saint-Victor* (Paris: Cerf, 1998), 65–81; and Rebecca Moore, *Jews and Christians in the Life and Thought of Hugh of St. Victor* (Atlanta: Scholars Press, 1998), 57–60.

18. The *Didascalicon* sets out the approach to Scripture in book 6. No modern edition exists for the *De Scriptoribus*. The text is in *PL* 175:9–28D. Grover Zinn, "The Influence of Augustine's *De doctrina Christiana* upon the Writings of Hugh of St. Victor," in *Reading and Wisdom: The De Doctrina Christiana of Augustine in the Middle Ages*, ed. Edward A. English (Notre Dame: University of Notre Dame Press, 1995), 48–60 studies the *De Scripturis* as an introduction to the *Notulae* on the Pentateuch.

19. Rainer Berndt supplies an exhaustive study of Andrew of St. Victor's text of the Bible in *André de Saint-Victor (+1175), exégète et théologien* (Turnhout, Belg.: Brepols, 1991), 108–63.

20. H. J. Pollitt indicates that the Hebrew letters constitute part of a revision of the *Notulae* in "Some Considerations on the Structure and Sources of Hugh of St. Victor's Notes on the Octateuch," *Recherches de théologie ancienne et médiévale* 33 (1966): 5–38. Moore summarizes the positions of scholars on Hugh's ability with Hebrew in *Jews and Christians*, 79, fn. 8. The scholarly disagreement about whether the Hebrew transcriptions originate with Hugh will hopefully be resolved in the dissertation currently in progress by Montserrat Leyra at Hebrew University.

21. In *Jews and Christians* (80–92) Moore provides a summary of previous correlations made by Beryl Smalley and Hermann Hailperin in "Jewish Influence on Christian Biblical Scholars in the Middle Ages," *Historia Judaica* (1942): 163–74.

22. Hugh of Saint Victor, *Adnotationes in Pentateuchon*, *PL* 175:32D. The problem of the Septuagint as a point of contention between Jerome and Augustine is described in my article "From Theory to Practice: The *De Doctrina Christiana* and the Exegesis of Andrew of St. Victor," in *Reading and Wisdom: The De Doctrina Christiana of Augustine in the Middle Ages*, ed. English, 84–98.

23. Hugh of Saint Victor, *Adnotationes*, *PL* 175:51. For commentary on this passage, see Smalley, *Study of the Bible*, 99–100; and Moore, *Jews and Christians*, 86, 106–8.

24. The most complete treatment of Andrew is Berndt, *André de Saint-Victor*. This monograph may be supplemented by *Andreae de Sancto Victore, Expositionem in Ezechielem*, ed. M. A. Signer, Corpus Christianorum Continuatio Medievalis 53E (Turnout, Belg.: Brepols, 1991), ix–xxxvii; idem, "*Peshat, Sensus Litteralis*, and Sequential Narrative: Jewish Exegesis and the School of St. Victor in the Twelfth Century," in B. Walfish, ed., *The Frank Talmage Memorial Volume* (Haifa, Isr.: Haifa University Press, 1993), 1: 203–16; idem, "Andrew of St. Victor's Anti-Jewish Polemics" (in Hebrew), in *The Bible in the Mirror of Its Interpreters*, ed. Sara Japhet (Jerusalem: Magnes Press, 1993), 412–20.

25. Signer, ed., *Expositio in Ezechielem*, xxviii–xxxii; William McKane, *Selected Christian Hebraists* (Cambridge: Cambridge University Press, 1989), 42–75; R. Berndt, "Les interprétations juives dans le 'Commentaire de l'Heptateuque' d'André de Saint Victor," *Recherches Augustiniennes* 24 (1989): 199–240.

26. Signer, ed., *Expositio in Ezechielem*, xxii and the bibliography in the footnotes. Further evidence of an Old French background to Andrew and the school of Rashi may be found in my article, "Restoring the Narrative: Jewish and Christian Exe-

gesis in the Twelfth Century," in *Reverence for the Word*, ed. Jane McAuliffe (Oxford: Oxford University Press, 2002), 139–65.

27. Signer, ed., *Expositio in Ezechielem* to Ezechiel 9:1, 46 (lines 4–5).

28. Ibid., xxii–xxv.

29. Ibid., xxx–xxxii.

30. Berndt, *André de Saint-Victor*, 294–311.

31. Smalley, *Study of the Bible*, 179.

32. The Epistles and first half of the Psalter are in Trinity College Cambridge MSS. B 5, 6, 7 and B 5.4; the second half of the Psalter is in Bodleian Library MS. Auct. E infra 6.

33. *Psalterium cum commento H. de Bosham* (St. Paul's MS 2).

34. See Beryl Smalley, "A Commentary on the *Hebraica* by Herbert of Bosham," *Recherches de théologie ancienne et médiévale* 18 (1951): 29–65; the second and third editions of her *Study of the Bible in the Middle Ages* (Notre Dame: University of Notre Dame Press, 1978); and her book, *The Becket Conflict and the Schools* (Totowa, N.J.: Rowan and Littlefield, 1973). See also Raphael Loewe, "Herbert of Bosham's Commentary on Jerome's Hebrew Psalter," *Biblica* 34: 44–77, 159–92, 275–298.

35. Deborah L. Goodwin, "A Study of Herbert of Bosham's Commentary on the Psalms (ca. 1190)" (Ph.D. diss., University of Notre Dame, 2001). Goodwin's investigations indicate that Herbert utilized Rashi's commentary on the Psalter but that one still cannot state definitively whether Herbert read the Hebrew by himself or had a Jewish interlocutor.

36. Deborah L. Goodwin, "*Ibimus Vobiscum:* Messianic Psalms in the Commentary of Herbert of Bosham," unpublished paper presented at the International Congress of Medieval Studies, 6 May 2000.

37. Folio 102r (from Psalm 86:4) where the text reads, "Adeo eciam quod exortantes se invicem et explorantes qui sint de israelitis et dominum scientibus; adducent in ierusalem; offerentes eos quasi donum domino. Iuxta quod scriptum est *Et adducent omnes fratres vestros* [illegible superscript] *de cunctis donum domino* [Is. 66:20] et al. *In diebus illis in quibus apprehendent fimbriam? viri judei dicentes Ibimus vobiscum. Audivimus enim quod deus vobiscum est* [Zech. 8:23]. Judei; istud sub messia suo expectavit futurum. Ecclesiastici vero iam vident per christum et per apostolos ex parte impletum; in fine vero conplendum quando omnis israel salvabitur." Transcription by Deborah Goodwin.

38. Arthur Landgraf, *Écrits Théologiques de l'École d' Abélard: Textes Inédits*, Spicilegium Sacrum Lovaniense Études et Documents, vol. 14 (Louvain, Belg.: Spicilegium Sacrum Lovaniense, 1934), 64–285.

39. The theology and structure of the *Ysagoge* is treated by Landgraf in his introduction, *Écrits*, xlvi–xlviii, and H. Cloes, "La systématization théologique pendant la première moitié du XIIe siècle," *Ephemerides Theologicae Lovanienses* 23 (1959): 277–329. See also David E. Luscombe, *The School of Peter Abelard*, Cambridge Studies in Medieval Life and Thought, 2d ser., vol. 14 (Cambridge: Cambridge University Press, 1969), 236–44; and Dahan, *Les intellectuels chrétiens*, 445–48.

40. The Hebrew citations have been analyzed by J. Fischer, "Die hebräischen Bibelzitate des Scholastikers Odos," *Biblica* 16 (1934): 50–93, and supplemented by Landgraf in the footnotes to his edition.

41. Landgraf, *Ysagoge*, 126–29.

42. Ibid., 128–29 with notes.

43. Ibid., 128. "Sed quoniam lingua Hebraica a dextro in sinistrum descendit, sicut e contra tam greca quam Latina a sinistra in dextram scandit, ut et Iudeorum lapsus et Gentium figuretur surrectio, retrograde legendus erit versus latinus suppositum sibi exponens hebreum."

44. For an index of the biblical passages, see H. Schreckenberg, *Die christlichen Adversus-Judaeos-Texte, 11.–13. Jh.* (Frankfurt: Peter Lang, 1998), 159–62.

45. For descriptions of twelfth-century scholarly study and the interaction between Jews and Christians, see Michael A. Signer and John H. Van Engen, *Jews and Christians in the Twelfth Century* (Notre Dame: University of Notre Dame, 2001).

46. The influence of the Jerome-Augustine correspondence about *Hebraica Veritas* constitutes an important element in the history of Christian Hebraism. I have indicated some of its effect in my article "From Theory to Practice: The *De doctrina christiana* and the Exegesis of Andrew of St. Victor," in *Reading and Wisdom: The De doctrina christiana of Augustine in the Middle Ages*, 84–98.

2

Man as the "Possible" Entity in Some Jewish and Renaissance Sources

Moshe Idel

What Is New in Renaissance Anthropology?

The role played by new approaches to the nature of man and his actions in Renaissance thought is well known. One of the most comprehensive descriptions of the novelty of Renaissance anthropology is that of Dame Frances A. Yates. Emphasizing the medieval fascination with mental operations, she detected a dramatic shift in the attitude toward action on the part of key Renaissance thinkers: "Fundamentally, the Greeks did not want to operate. They regarded operations as base and mechanical, a degeneration from the only occupation worthy of the dignity of man, pure rational and philosophical speculation. The Middle Ages carried on this attitude in the form that theology is the crown of philosophy and the true end of man is contemplation."[1] According to Yates's diagnosis, the change toward a much greater activism was related to "the religious excitement caused by the rediscovery of the *Hermetica*, and their attendant Magia; in the overwhelming emotions aroused by Cabala and its magico-religious techniques. It is magic as an aid to gnosis which begins to turn the will in the new direction. . . . Thus 'Hermes Trismegistus' and the Neoplatonism and Cabalism associated with him, may have played during his period of glorious ascendance over the mind of western man a strangely important role in the shaping of human destiny."[2] Although this emphasis on the hermetic contribution to both Pico della Mirandola's and Marsilio Ficino's thought has been recently questioned,[3] Yates's highlighting of the importance of the ascent of the ideal of action in the Renaissance has remained, to the best of my knowledge, unchallenged.

In what follows, I shall argue that a description of the Middle Ages as uniformly displaying a mentalistic orientation is problematic. Yates's view more aptly describes those elite approaches that emerged under the aegis of varieties of Aristotelian thought, as we can see from Christian, Muslim, and Jewish theological literature. In other speculative corpora, which were dominated by astral thought and neoplatonic and theosophical-theurgical views, action (especially ritualistic action) is much more important. Since these two types of approaches were available to many Renaissance thinkers, an explanation of the genesis of the new anthropology may lie in more than a movement away from medieval mentalism. The status of mentalistic approaches in the Middle Ages was, at least in the overall picture of Judaism, much more fragile than we normally imagine. For example, more supercommentaries were written on R. Abraham ibn Ezra's practical exegesis in his Commentary on the Pentateuch than on Maimonides's philosophically abstract *Guide for the Perplexed*.[4] Nor was the astro-magical propensity of ibn Ezra criticized so drastically and in such a dramatic manner as Maimonides was. R. Yehudah ha-Levi's *Kuzari*, characterized by a sacramental approach to religion so different from Maimonides's understanding, had an ongoing impact on medieval Jews of various convictions. Among the medieval commentaries, some of the most widespread interpreted Maimonides as if he were a mystic.[5] Yates's thesis, which grants new roles to kabbalistic literature in the development of the ontology, epistemology, and anthropology of the late fifteenth and sixteenth centuries, has recently been extended to the sixteenth and seventeenth centuries by Allison Coudert.[6] In fact, what seems to emerge from the studies mentioned above is the movement of certain theories, some of which originated in the Middle Ages or far earlier, from the margins of thought to the intellectual center, which then leads to their dissemination among audiences previously unacquainted with more activistic and optimistic views of human nature. Indeed, the Renaissance attitude toward man as expressed by Ficino and especially Pico has an interesting parallel in the emphasis on theurgy and magic characteristic of Kabbalah in the late fifteenth and sixteenth centuries.[7] I shall return to some other aspects of Yates's thesis at the end of this article, although from another point of view.

Two Spanish Traditions

Early in the twelfth century the Spanish Arab philosopher Ibn al-Sid al-Batalyawsi (1052–1127) wrote a philosophical treatise titled *The Imaginary Circles* (*Kitab al-Hadaiq* in Arabic and *Sefer ha-'Aggulot ha-Ra'yoniyot* in Hebrew),[8] in which he emphasizes the "contingent" nature of man:

And I told you by way of admonition: Repent! . . . And the fact that man belongs to [the category of] the contingent [or possible] is [as follows]: he is one form of the [numerous] forms whose substratum is the *hyle*, and onto the *hyle* stands the nature of contingency, because it sometimes receives a form and sometimes it is stripped of it; and the form will be sometimes *in potentia* and sometimes *in actu*; and without the existence of the *hyle*, the nature of the contingency[9] would disappear and things would exist only in two modes, the necessary and the impossible.[10]

As has been shown in several studies, this book was very influential in medieval and Renaissance Jewish literature.[11] I had the opportunity to deal with this passage, along with some others from the same book, elsewhere in connection with their possible influence on Pico via R. Yohanan Alemanno.[12] Here I would like to deal with some additional instances of the influence of this text in Spain as a possible background for the emergence of the positive view of man in the Florentine Renaissance.

The description of man as "contingent" recurs, apparently under the impact of the above passage, in a discussion of R. Nissim Gerondi, a mid-fourteenth-century Catalan author who had a significant impact on Jewish thought. In his first sermon he writes that "man, because of his being contingent, is similar to animals or worse than them, in accordance to his rebellion. This is why a certain day has not been specified [in the Bible] in his case. But he is the last composite, so as to remove [him] from the deficient bodies [and] to bring him close to the perfect ones, which are the celestial bodies, so that he may be more worthy of persistence and the life granted to him."[13] The crucial term that corroborates the affinity between this passage and al-Batalyawsi is the description of man as *'efshar*. The term *last composite* (*ha-murkkav ha-'aharon*) was current in the twelfth and thirteenth centuries and is simply another way to describe man as a microcosm.[14] We shall return to this issue below. Man is, accordingly, posited at the midpoint between the lower and higher worlds, and he may move from one world to another since no specific day among the six days of Creation has been specified in the case of his creation, which is to say that unlike every other creature, man has not been endowed with a specific essence, or *telos*. In the early fifteenth century a paraphrase of the discussion of man as "contingent" is found in R. Moses ibn Haviv's commentary on R. Yeda'yah Bedershi's *Behinat 'Olam*, which was written in Spain.[15] In the mid-fifteenth century another Spanish thinker, R. Abraham Bibago, betrays a substantial affinity to the view of al-Batalyawsi quoted above. In his sermon *Zeh Yenahameni* and to a certain extent also in his much more influential *Sefer Derekh 'Emunah* he adopted some of al-Batalyawsi's views.[16] For example, he includes the idea that man is "contingent" (*me-hoq ha-'efshar*)[17] and that he is the median being who links the lower and higher worlds.[18]

Let me turn from the philosophical to the kabbalistic anthropological tradition that developed in Spain in the context of al-Batalyawsi's book. In what was destined to become a classic of Kabbalah in the following century, an older contemporary of Bibago, a Kabbalist called R. Shem Tov ben Shem Tov, wrote:

Man is by necessity one in [his] humanity[19] no more. Behold, the ancients called it microcosm, and the entire, comprehensive world is one, because the great sphere is one, and it is all the spheres and zodiac-signs and stars, all are linked and combined with each other. It [the highest sphere] is [found] within the supernal entities, and the supernal entities within even higher entities, until the first cause, which is the supernal soul of the entire universe . . . and all are truly one world. And when man is comprehensive, he is one in his humanity, and he has different actions because his spiritual faculties correspond to the supernal powers, and it is not surprising that since he is connected to them his parts and actions are directed toward the supernal parts and actions. And when a good act will arise in his soul, a good act will arise [on high], and when a bad act will arise it will stir up a bad act. The truth is that this is the intention of the Torah when it is said: "Behold the man is become like one of us, knowing good and evil and now what if he put forth his hand" [Gen. 3:22], namely that this man has a power to comprise all the things and he is like a *hyle*, which [is capable of] clothing itself[20] in all the forms.[21]

The entire text should be understood as follows: each lower realm is included in the higher so that everything is encompassed by the first cause, which is also the most comprehensive being. This comprehension of everything within the highest realm transforms everything into a unified universe. Because of the correspondence between man's structure (the microcosm) and the greater world (the macrocosm) everything is found in man and he is conceived of as one universe.[22] By becoming comprehensive, every human being becomes similar to every other, and this comprehensiveness is the unifying factor that transforms different men into what is then described as "one humanity." The comprehensiveness is not only a matter of structural correspondences but also of sympathetic influences. By virtue of the precise parallelism between the macrocosm and the microcosm, every human act resonates on the cosmic level. This conviction reflects theurgical and magical understandings of Kabbalah, which become even more evident from the late fifteenth century in both Spanish and Italian Jewish texts.[23]

Let me analyze the Hebrew phrase preceding the description of man as *hyle*: *yesh bo koah likhlol kol ha-'inyanim, ve-hu' kmo hyuli lilbosh kol ha-tzurot*. This is an Aristotelian description of *hyle* and forms. Countless medieval discussions describe *hyle* as accepting different forms. However, in this passage the characteristic of *hyle* is analogous to the human capacity to adopt all the forms. Unlike *hyle*, man is able to receive even the form of the divine, as the biblical verse suggests. Indeed, in a variety of kabbalistic texts beginning in the early thirteenth century there is a description that approximates a formulation found in the text quoted above: "Man is comprised of all spiritual things," which means in those contexts that the ten *sefirot* also comprise the human constitution.[24] The same idea occurs in another anonymous kabbalistic text: "'And He created man in His image' [Gen. 1:26]. You already know that all the spiritual things are comprised in man, and this is reason why he is a world in itself and perfected and prepared from '*Ein Sof*, which is the reason for his existence."[25] The vision of man as a world in himself is quite interesting. Indeed, the expression "the world of man" is not a new one: it occurs in R. Abraham Abulafia's writings,[26] and earlier in R. Abraham bar Hiyya, one finds the expression '*olam 'adam ha-rishon*.[27] Such an expression occurs also in R. Yohanan Alemanno's *Hei ha-'Olamim*.[28] Moreover, in Abraham Abulafia it is also possible to find expressions according to which man comprises the ten *sefirot* though the meaning of "the world of man" differs from the meaning it has been given in the theosophical Kabbalah.[29] Moreover, the emphasis in the theosophical Kabbalah is much more on the theurgical element than on the structural one. We learn this from an influential text by R. Menahem Recanati, which had been translated into Latin and was known to Pico: "Since man is comprised of all the essences, his power is great and so is his perfection when he directs his intention and knowledge to draw downwards and cause the emanation out of the 'Nought of Thought.'"[30]

To return to R. Shem Tov, the fact that the description of man as hylic is presented as the meaning of the biblical verse suggests the possibility that this Kabbalist, one of the most antiphilosophical authors among the Kabbalists, considered it to be a Jewish concept. In this quotation, man, perhaps Adam, is envisaged as a dynamic microcosm whereas some lines before the above passage he is envisioned in terms of a static microcosm, and this view is attributed to the ancients. Thus, at least in the case of this fifteenth-century Kabbalist, the influence of the two views of man as a static and a dynamic microcosm is conspicuous.[31]

What seems to be new in the last passage, in comparison to *The Imaginary Circles*, is the fact that the hylic nature of man is presented as including the potentiality of becoming like God. According to al-Batalyawsi, this is totally impossible because man's intellect can reach only up to the Agent Intellect, which is a cosmic intellect different from God.[32] Moreover, unlike the Muslim thinker, the Kabbalist explicitly identifies the cosmic soul with God, apparently following a view adduced in R. Yehudah ha-Levi's *Kuzari*.[33] In other words, R. Shem Tov combined the Aristotelian theory of *hyle* when applied to man, as expressed in al-Batalyawsi, with a neoplatonic theory of the universe and the kabbalistic vision of man as comprising the sefirotic world. From the theosophical-theurgical Kabbalah he drew the activist, dynamic view of man, which is absent in the philosophical approach since it is more cosmologically and noetically oriented. Indeed, a Plotinian vision of the soul as having its supernal source on high while in this world constitutes the explanatory framework for the impact of lower acts on higher realms. The soul is envisaged as a branch that emanates from a supernal root.[34] On the other hand, by dint of the comparison with the first cause, the soul is to be understood as encompassing the body, an idea that is also reminiscent of neoplatonic views. Although we do not know much about the circle in which R. Shem Tov studied,[35] it would be plausible to understand the above passage against a primarily neoplatonic and theosophical background. It is possible to refer to an additional background as well, which, though more vague, may also be pertinent for our discussions. As mentioned earlier, R. Shem Tov was one of the most antiphilosophical Kabbalists in the history of Kabbalah in Spain. He repeatedly criticized philosophy, including Jewish medieval philosophy. His critical approach is reminiscent of other major critics such as his contemporary, the philosopher Don Hasdai Crescas, who may be classified among the intellectual critics of philosophy who analytically addressed major philosophical issues like space, time, and infinity in order to propose alternative solutions.[36] Unlike him, however, R. Shem Tov was solely interested in the problems created by philosophical approaches to religious matters. His solution is, naturally, not provided by a different philosophy but by the kabbalistic traditions he studied in books. Along the same lines, though from a different point of view, another Kabbalist (or circle of Kabbalists) active around 1470 in Spain offered a very sharp critique of philosophy, sciences, and Christianity, based on the assumption that divine and angelic revelations provided them with kabbalistic alternatives.[37]

As far as we know, the *Sefer ha-'Emunot* did not exercise any discernible influence on the development of Kabbalah in the second half of the fifteenth century though from the 1530s it had a considerable impact.[38] Thus it would be inappropriate to claim that the above passage influenced late fifteenth-century thought in Italy either among Jews or Christians. However, despite this obvious fact, the above text may demonstrate that some developments that occurred in Spain anticipated some aspects of what is conceived of as a specifically Renaissance type of anthropology. On the basis of an analysis of the sources of these passages, I believe they are completely independent of late fifteenth-century Florentine influences.[39] The more plausible assumption may be that there were some intermediaries between the variety of Jewish Spanish speculative literature I have discussed and the Christian thinkers in Florence.

R. Yohanan Alemanno and Pico della Mirandola

The paramount power of man is part and parcel of many trends in Kabbalah, and we have already seen an example of such an emphasis on man as a microcosm with the power to influence the macrocosm. Especially important in this context is the figure of the biblical Enoch, sometimes described as a mystical figure who ascends on high, in other cases understood in hermetic terms as the link between the lower and the higher worlds. This view had a considerable effect on Jewish Renaissance literature.[40] One of the inheritors of some of those trends was R. Yohanan Alemanno, a late fifteenth-century thinker, active for some years in Florence and acquainted with Pico della Mirandola.[41] As someone who had a profound interest in magic, both natural and demonic, Alemanno viewed the possibility of influencing the world as the highest human activity. Consequently, he reserved the study of magic for the most advanced level in his ideal curriculum.[42] Moreover, in his commentary on the Song of Songs, *Hesheq Shlomo*, he describes the achievement of King Solomon (the ideal king, according to Alemanno) as consisting of two levels: the magical, to be addressed immediately below, and a higher level dealing with forms of cognition:[43] "The first is the rank to which he ascended in the book entitled *Sefer Raziel*,[44] attributed to him . . . to ascend to the deed to change[45] the entire world according to his will, so that the lower entities are subjugated to him, to innovate miracles and wonders, just as the body of man is subjugated by the powers of the soul to do what he wants."[46] Alemanno resorts to a way of thought similar to R. Shem Tov: the ability of humans to influence the universe may be understood in terms of the relationship between the soul and body. Alemanno was also deeply interested in al-Batalyawsi's *The Imaginary Circles*, as Kaufmann had demonstrated.[47] This interest was, however, by no means an exception in fifteenth-century Florence. Some decades earlier another Florentine author, R. Moses ben Yo'av, had been attracted to this book.[48] A third translation of this book is extant in Florence in a fifteenth-century Spanish hand.[49] Consequently, al-Batalyawsi's book was known in Florence long before Alemanno's arrival sometime in the 1480s. Presumably following the view of a late fourteenth-century Castilian author, R. Shmuel ibn Motot, who translated parts of al-Batalyawsi's book into Hebrew, Alemanno describes the nature of man as follows: "The body of man is composed from the powers that rule over the world. Behold, he is in the image of the constitution of the world in general, because all [those powers] operate on him and he is linked to the celestial host. And, behold, he is in the likeness of the *Merkavah*, to receive the divine power that is emanated on them and from them onto him when he actualizes his intellect, and he is holy like their holiness and pure like their purity."[50] This is indubitably a hermetic vision of man, whose body is construed as corresponding to the macrocosm, and the sympathy between the two structures ensures the reception of the macrocosmic influx onto the body. The absorption of this supernal influx is conditioned by human actions like intellection and purification. Again, a static sympathy invites a certain *regimen vitae* in order to actualize the structural affinity between the two.

Let me turn now to a remark found in the margin of one of the folios of

Alemanno's *Collectanea:* "The greatest proof in existence that man exercises free-will[51] is that all the creatures manifestly follow their aim,[52] determined for them by nature, and this is obvious in the case of vegetables and animals and the spheres, with the exception of man who does not have, by [his] nature, an aim to follow straightforwardly and constantly without changing [the path]. But every man has one aim, [chosen] by his free-will, and thereby the orders of man[53] are different from [these of] all the [other] creatures."[54] The assumption that nature regulates the behavior of all the other beings with the exception of man, who chooses his aim freely, seems to coincide with Pico's view that man does not have a determined nature but shapes himself. The human will is emphasized here as the *principium individuationis* of man in comparison to all the other creatures. However, this passage does not mention the transformation of man into a different being as the result of his free choice, as Pico maintained. Alemanno quotes this passage in the name of someone who told it to him, or more exactly, from his mouth (*mi-pi*). Thus we are indirectly told that the person was a contemporary of Alemanno with whom he had contact. Unfortunately, the name of the person does not appear; in its place there is the acronym *HQYDL*. Since these letters do not signify anything in Hebrew, they must be decoded. I propose to understand them as follows: Q, for the word *Conte*, spelled *Qonti* in Hebrew. Y stands for the name Yohanan, namely Giovanni. D and L are difficult and they may stand for a form of della Mirandola. Such a reading fits perfectly with the way Alemanno spelled Pico's name in the introduction to his Commentary on the Song of Songs. There he refers to Pico as *ha-'Adon, 'Adoni Qonti Yo'ani Delamirandola*.[55] The H of the acronym apparently stands for the first letter of the word *ha-'Adon*, Q stands for the first letter of *Conti*, and the continuous spelling of Delamirandola accounts for the use of the letters D and L. It should also be mentioned in this context that Alemanno and Pico discussed Alemanno's intention to compose a commentary on the Song of Songs. Interestingly enough, the observation that man exercises free will occurs in the margin of R. Abraham Abulafia's *Sitrei Torah*, an exposition of the alleged secrets of the *Guide of the Perplexed*, part 1, secrets 5–6. This book had been translated by Flavius Mithridates for Pico, and it had a considerable influence on his vision of Kabbalah as well as his understanding of Maimonides as a mystic.[56]

There are several passages in Alemanno's *Collectanea* that may refer to his association and collaboration with Pico. Alemanno writes:

The view of those who maintain that out of God [the soul has appeared] involves the views of those who assert that it is God who is to be worshipped and to Him that we should cleave, since it is possible that she [the soul] shall return to the source from whence she was extracted, as it is said "and the spirit shall return to the Lord who gave her" [Eccles. 12:7]. And the other opinion involves all the other false opinions and the variety of idolatry, because they think vain [things] that to Him she will not cleave but to one of the spiritual forces, to whom it is possible to cleave. Understand this because it is a wondrous [issue]. From the mouth of *Qidal* [this might also be read as *Qadosh*]."[57]

The same source, *Qidal* or *Qadosh*, is cited in another passage in Alemanno's *Collectanaea:* "The sages of Greece, [who were] the interpreters of the Torah, said that the custom of the ancients like Laban and Abimelekh was that when they wanted to dream a veridical dream and remove the non-veridical dreams, they put under their heads a leaf of *labro*, whose smell is very good, and they put on them *lazio castro*, and then they dreamed veridical dreams, in order to know what are their deeds. From the mouth of Qidal."[58] These passages where Alemanno may be describing his discussions with Pico are not the only instances of possible oral exchanges between him and the Christian thinker. Immediately after the last passage Alemanno writes, "More from his mouth: he found in one of the books that it is said that Pythagoras, the sage, found that the brain of the human spine is transformed into a serpent." Alemanno then compares this view to a similar rabbinic statement.[59] It should be emphasized that if the person referred to by the acronym *Qidal* is indeed Pico, the manner of referring to discussions with him, *mi-pi* ("from the mouth") evinces a certain amount of respect. In fact, it seems that Alemanno preserved in his *Collectanea* other testimonies of face-to-face discussions with Christian thinkers, but a discussion of these goes beyond the scope of this chapter.[60]

Alemanno's name is never mentioned expressly in Pico's writings. It is only from the passage in the introduction to Alemanno's book, quoted above, and from the testimony of Pico's nephew that we know a relationship between the two existed.[61] This omission is remarkable: Alemanno, a very learned author, much older than Pico, refers to the young count explicitly in quite eulogistic terms while Pico mentions neither Alemanno nor Flavius Mithridates, the translator to whose laborious activity he owed so much of his knowledge of Kabbalah. Although Pico clearly drew ideas from kabbalistic sources, he is silent about those who helped him gain access to this difficult literature. Apparently, it was easier to give credit to sources when they were ancient or dead, as we see from the opening to Pico's *Oratio*, than when they were alive. It was not simply a matter of Pico failing to mention his Jewish sources, but the same reticence appears in the work of his younger contemporary Leone Ebreo, who does not mention his Renaissance Florentine sources.[62] The most "glorious" epoch of the intellectual intercourse between Jewish and Christian thinkers is therefore less open than it could have been.

Conclusion

As mentioned at the beginning of this essay, I propose to read the ascent of the active mode as defining the peak of human activity as an alternative to the mentalistic attitude of Aristotelian-oriented philosophy. With the general critique of Aristotelianism that emerged in the early fifteenth century, the acceptance of a more theurgical and magical vision of human activity became increasingly widespread. This is obvious in the case of Jewish literature with the growing importance of R. Abraham ibn Ezra at the end of the fourteenth century that is indicated by the composition of ten supercommentaries on his commentary on the Pentateuch.[63] It is in the vein of ibn Ezra, with whom he was well acquainted, that Alemanno wrote a passage that pits the opinions of a philosopher against those of a Kabbalist:

> If you [namely, a philosopher] will say to me: What is this dream which you entertain about the preparations hidden from the eyes of the philosophers, who neither know nor understand what these [preparations] mean to you? For they [philosophers] say: "Let us come to wisdom and [intellectual] union only by the way of intellectual speculation or by sudden intuition, but not by magical actions, buildings, vessels, prayers, vain things and many dreams, things which are unfounded in the eyes of the philosophers, the men of intellect and reason." [But] all the things we said are the words of the ancients who knew the nature of the existing beings, the relations between them, the way in which they are linked with one another and how to prepare a receptacle for the reception of the influence of the superior bodies. This was conspicuous to them as a result of [their] wisdom and experience, just as the preparations of the plants and the seeds and the lands so that they will receive the propitious influx that is flowering there is conspicuous to the cultivators of the land. And just as it would be strange for someone who does not know the manner of cultivation and plowing and planting and grafting that produce things in such a manner, it will be strange in our eyes, if we did not see the light of those preparations of how the divine light and his goodness and mercy will be born in us by means of these preparations that the powers and *sefirot* will receive and emanate. And if you had studied or believed the preparations of the masters of the forms[64] and secondary natures and the contrivances[65] of nature, your spirit will not be confused by anything I told you because it is holy.[66]

It is probable that Maimonides is the implied target of this imaginary dispute between a mentalistically oriented philosopher and the hermetically oriented Alemanno.[67] In lieu of intellectual development as the main avenue for achieving perfection, a much more ritualistic and performative attitude is proposed as an alternative. This appears to be the most explicit example of a confrontation between the two religious approaches: Maimonides' intellectualism is criticized from a hermetic and kabbalistic point of view.

The above discussions may be understood as part of what has been designated as the revolt of certain Renaissance philosophers against their medieval predecessors. Since I consider medieval culture a variegated field, which continues to embrace much earlier philosophical views and opinions, it would be simplistic to reduce the above discussion to the enumeration of medieval antecedents for what are generally thought to be Renaissance conceptions. Phenomenologically speaking, I would argue that rabbinic texts dealing with the image of God and the ability of human beings to affect both divine and natural events by means of ritual performance precede the kabbalistic discussions described above. These discussions were, no doubt, expressed in much more sophisticated neoplatonic, Pythagorean and hermetic terms, some of which were extremely ancient, and these presentations served as important bridges to circles of intellectuals deeply immersed in neoplatonic and hermetic ways of thinking.

Let me summarize the above discussion: the emergence during the Italian Renaissance of an anthropology that emphasized the importance of activism and the flexibility of the status of man in the cosmos occurred in a milieu where Jewish thinkers were active and the Kabbalah gradually became influential in Christian circles. The reception of the Kabbalah was significantly indebted to the growing diffusion of Neoplatonism and Hermeticism. I suggest that the parallel between the ascent of the more dynamic concept of man on the one hand and the wider influence of Kabbalah on the other is not a matter of lines of thought that never met; on the contrary, they intersected in Florence, and one of the major figures who facilitated this encounter was Yohanan Alemanno. However, while Alemanno's thought remained in the shadows in both Jewish and Christian culture, Pico's dynamic view of man moved to the center of European culture, where it had a profound effect. The wide reception of Pico's view of man contributed to the idea that he originated this way of thinking. This last assumption, like others related to the notion that Pico was the first to "marry" Hermeticism to Kabbalah, a view expressed by Yates, is open to debate.[68] The separate dissemination of the activistic approaches derived from the blend of Neoplatonism and Hermeticism on the one hand, and the Kabbalah on the other, both having much earlier sources, prepared the ground for the wide reception of Pico's anthropology.

Notes

1. Frances A. Yates, *Giordano Bruno and the Hermetic Tradition* (London: Routledge and Kegan Paul, 1964), 155–56.

2. Ibid., 156.

3. See Brian Copenhaver, "Hermes Trismegistus, Proclus, and the Question of a Philosophy of Magic in the Renaissance," in *Hermeticism and the Renaissance*, ed. I. Merkel and A. G. Debus (Washington: Folger, 1988), 79–110; idem, "Hermes Theo-

logus: The Sienese Mercury and Ficino's Hermetic Discourse," in *Humanity and Divinity in Renaissance and Reformation: Essays in Honor of Charles Trinkaus*, ed. John W. O'Malley, Thomas M. Izbicki, and Gerald Christianson (Leiden, Neth.: E. J. Brill, 1993), 149–82; Ioan P. Couliano, *Eros and Magic in the Renaissance* (Chicago: University of Chicago Press, 1987), 236 n. 32.

4. On the supercommentaries on ibn Ezra, see below, note 63.

5. See Georges Vajda, "Un chapitre de l'histoire du conflit entre la Kabbale et la philosophie," *Archives d'histoire doctrinale et littéraire du moyen âge* 23 (1956): 127–30; idem, "Deux Chapitres du 'Guide des Égarés' Repensés par un Kabbaliste," in *Mélanges offerts à Étienne Gilson de l'Académie française* (Toronto: Pontifical Institute of Mediaeval Studies; Paris: J. Vrin, 1959), 51–59; Ephraim Gottlieb, "Clarifications Concerning the Writings of R. Joseph Gikatilla," in *Studies in the Literature of Kabbalah*, ed. J. Hacker (in Hebrew) (Tel Aviv: Tel Aviv University, 1976), 105–6, 110–17. On Gikatilla and the *Guide*, (Hal) see also Moshe Hayyim Weiler, "Inquiries into R. Joseph Gikatilla's Kabbalistic Terminology and His Relation to Maimonides," *Hebrew Union College Annual* 37 (1966): 13–44, and the numerous footnotes to parallels in the *Guide* enumerated in Asi Farber, "A New Fragment from R. Joseph Gikatilla's Preface to *Ginnat 'Egoz*," *Jerusalem Studies in Jewish Thought* (in Hebrew) 1 (1981): 158–76; See also Idel, "Maimonides and Kabbalah," in *Studies in Maimonides*, ed. I. Twersky (Cambridge: Harvard University Press, 1990), 31–82; idem, "Abulafia's Secrets of the *Guide*: A Linguistic Turn," in *Perspectives on Jewish Thought and Mysticism*, ed. A. Ivri, E. R. Wolfson, and A. Arkush (Amsterdam: Harwood Academic Publishers, 1998), 289–329; idem, "Mystical Interpretations of Maimonides' *Guide of the Perplexed*," forthcoming.

6. Allison P. Coudert, *Leibniz and the Kabbalah* (Dordrecht, Neth.: Kluwer Academic Publishers, 1995); eadem, *The Impact of the Kabbalah in the Seventeenth Century: The Life and Thought of Francis Mercury van Helmont, 1614–1698* (Leiden, Neth.: E. J. Brill, 1999).

7. See the examples in Idel, *Kabbalah: New Perspectives* (New Haven: Yale University Press, 1988), 175–78; Charles Mopsik, *Les Grands textes de la Cabale: Les rites qui font Dieu* (Lagrasse: Verdier, 1993), 338–455; Boaz Huss, *Sockets of Fine Gold: The Kabbalah of Rabbi Shim'on Ibn Lavi* (in Hebrew) (Jerusalem: Magnes Press, 2000), 192–211.

8. David Kaufmann, *Die Spuren al-Batalyawsis in der Juedischen Religionsgeschichte* (Leipzig, Ger., 1880). For the Arabic source (unknown to Kaufmann when he printed the two Hebrew translations of R. Moses ibn Tibbon and R. Shmuel ibn Motot in 1880), see Miguel Asin Palacios, "Ibn al-Sid de Badajoz y su 'Libro de los cercos' [Kitab al-Hida'iq]," *Al-Andalus* 5 (1940): 45–154. Georges Vajda identified a third, anonymous Hebrew translation, which he describes in "Une version hébraique inconnue des 'Cercles Imaginaires' de Batalyawsi," in *Semitic Studies in Memory of Immanuel Loew* (Budapest: J. Kertesz, 1947), 202–4. For the identity of this translator, see Benjamin Richler, "The Identification of the Anonymous Translator of the *Book of the Imaginary Circles*" (in Hebrew), *Qiriat Sefer* 53 (1978): 577. For the *floruit* of this thinker in the early twelfth century, see Hartwig Derenbourg, "Al-Batalyousi," *Revue des études juives* 7 (1883): 274–79.

9. *'Efsharut*. This term can be also translated as "possibility."

10. Kaufmann, *Die Spuren*, 27–28. It should be mentioned that the beginning of this passage is attributed in both the Arab original and the Hebrew translation to the "sons of Israel."

11. On the impact of this book in general, see the detailed introduction by Kauf-

mann, *Die Spuren*; Alexander Altmann, "The Ladder of Ascension," in *Studies in Mysticism and Religion Presented to Gershom G. Scholem*, ed. E. E. Urbach, R. J. Zwi Werblowsky, and Ch. Wirszubski (Jerusalem: Magnes Press, Hebrew University [ha-Mekhirah ha-rashit: Yavneh, Tel-Aviv], 1967), 6–17, 23–24; Idel, "The Ladder of Ascension: The Reverberations of a Medieval Motif in the Renaissance," in *Studies in Medieval Jewish History and Literature*, ed. I. Twersky (Cambridge: Harvard University Press, 1984), 83–88; Moshe Idel, "The Sources of the Circle Images in *Dialoghi d'Amore*" (in Hebrew), *Iyyun* 28 (1978): 162–66; Huss, *Sockets of Fine Gold*, 37, 96–97.

12. Moshe Idel, "The Anthropology of Yohanan Alemanno: Sources and Influences," *Annali di storia dell'esegesi* 7 (1990): 93–112.

13. *Derashot R. Nissim Gerondi*, ed. L. Feldman (Jerusalem: Makhon Shalem, 1977), 15. On this author, see Warren Zev Harvey, "Nissim of Gerona and William of Ockham on Prime Matter," *Jewish History* 6 (1992): 87–98.

14. See Moshe Idel, *Studies in Ecstatic Kabbalah* (Albany: State University of New York Press, 1989), 9, 25, n. 46. See also *Derashot R. Nissim*, 14.

15. See Kaufmann, *Die Spuren*, 6, n. 4.

16. On the influence of al-Batalyawsi on Bibago, see Kaufmann, *Die Spuren*, German part, notes to pages 55–56. Kaufmann dealt only with *Derekh 'Emunah*. On Bibago, see Menachem Kellner, *Dogma in Medieval Jewish Thought: From Maimonides to Abravanel* (Oxford: Littman Library, 1996), 165–78, 205–6.

17. *Zeh Yenahameni* (Constantinople, 1532), fol. 12b. It seems that the influence of Kabbalah in this small treatise of Bibago is greater than in his great opus, *Derekh 'Emunah*. See ibid., fols. 3a, 9b.

18. Ibid., fol. 12a, b.

19. *'Ehad ba-'enoshut*.

20. This means it is able to receive new forms.

21. R. Shem Tov ben Shem Tov, *Sefer ha-'Emunot* (Ferarra, 1556), fol. 108a. On this figure, see Ephraim Gottlieb, "R. Shem Tov ben Shem Tov's Way to Kabbalah," *Studies in the Literature of Kabbalah* (in Hebrew), 347–56; D. S. Ariel, "Shem Tob ibn Shem Tob's Kabbalistic Critique of Jewish Philosophy in the *Commentary on the Ten Sefirot*" (Ph.D. diss., Brandeis University, 1982).

22. On the relationship between the idea of man as the microcosm and the notion of human dignity in Pico, see Ernst Cassirer, "Giovanni Pico della Mirandola," *Journal of the History of Ideas* 3 (1942): 319–38.

23. I have discussed this matter in a separate study. See Moshe Idel, "The Magical and Theurgical Interpretation of Music in Jewish Texts: Renaissance to Hasidism" (in Hebrew), *Yuval* 4 (1982): 33–63.

24. Idel, *Kabbalah: New Perspectives*, 118–22.

25. Commentary on Ten Sefirot, MS. Milano-Ambrosiana 62, fol. 121a. This text is found also in MS. Oxford-Bodleiana 1565/9, which was probably written sometime in the mid-fourteenth century.

26. See, for example, *'Otzar 'Eden Ganuz*, MS. Oxford-Bodleiana 1580, fols. 96–97; *Hayyei ha-Nefesh*, MS. München 408, fol. 38b.

27. *Megillat ha-Megalleh* (Berlin: Mekize Nirdamin, 1924), 57.

28. MS. Mantua-Community 21, fol. 121b.

29. See Idel, *Studies in Ecstatic Kabbalah*, 9.

30. R. Menahem Recanati, *Commentary on the Torah* (Jerusalem: Mekize Nirdamin, 1961), fol. 51b. Recanati quotes from the anonymous *Sefer ha-Yihud* without

mentioning its source. This late thirteenth-century work emphasized the importance of theurgy; see MS. Milano-Ambrosiana 62, fol. 113a. See Idel, *Kabbalah: New Perspectives*, 184–91.

31. On man as microcosm in this book, see also *Sefer ha-'Emunot*, fols. 63b, 101b.

32. See Kaufmann, *Die Spuren*, 21–22, 24–25.

33. *Sefer Ha-Kuzari*, vol. 4, no. 3. R. Shem Tov is very fond of ha-Levi's book. See *Sefer ha-'Emunot*, fols. 13b, 26a, 27b, 49b, 52b.

34. Cf. *Sefer ha-'Emunot*, fols. 109a, 111a. For the origin of this view in Plotinus (*Enneads*, vol. 4, no. 8, 8), the so-called *Arabic Theology of Aristotle* (vol. 4, no. 41), and thirteenth-century Kabbalah, see Isaiah Tishby, *The Wisdom of the Zohar: An Anthology of Texts*, trans. D. Goldstein (London: Littman Library, 1991), 752.

35. For the cultural atmosphere among the Castilian Jews in the fifteenth century, see Joseph Hacker, "On the Intellectual Character and Self-Perception of Spanish Jewry in the Late Fifteenth Century" (in Hebrew), *Sefunot* n.s. 2 (1983): 21–95. A hitherto unknown fifteenth-century kabbalistic text composed in Castile in R. Shem Tov's time has been discovered by Boaz Huss, "*Sefer Pokeah 'Ivrim*—New Information on the History of Kabbalistic Literature" (in Hebrew), *Tarbiz* 61 (1992): 489–504.

36. See Harry A. Wolfson, *Crescas' Critique of Aristotle* (Cambridge: Harvard University Press, 1929). Interestingly enough, as pointed out by Warren Z. Harvey, Crescas had been influenced by some kabbalistic views. See his "Kabbalistic Elements in Crescas' *Light of the Lord*" (in Hebrew), *Jerusalem Studies in Jewish Thought* 2 (1983): 75–109. For more on this figure, see Aviezer Ravitzky, *Crescas' Sermon on the Passover and Studies in His Philosophy* (in Hebrew) (Jerusalem: Israeli Academy for Science and Humanities, 1988); Shalom Rosenberg, "The *Arba'ah Turim* of Rabbi Abraham bar Judah, Disciple of Don Hasdai Crescas" (in Hebrew), *Jerusalem Studies in Jewish Thought* 3 (1983–4): 525–621. Crescas influenced both Alemanno and Giovanni Francesco Pico della Mirandola, who studied with Alemanno's son, Isaac.

37. See Gershom Scholem, "On the Story of R. Joseph della Reina," in *Hokhma Bina veDaat. Studies in Jewish History and Thought Presented to Alexander Altmann on the Occasion of His Seventieth Birthday* (in Hebrew), ed. Siegfried Stein and Raphael Loewe (Published in association with the Institute of Jewish Studies, London, by the University of Alabama Press), 100–108; idem, "The Maggid of R. Joseph Taitachek and the Revelations Attributed to Him" (in Hebrew), *Sefunot* o.s. 11 (1971–78): 69–112; Georges Vajda, "Passages anti-chrétiens dans *Kaf Ha-Qetoret*," *Revue de l'histoire des religions* 117 (1980): 45–58; Moshe Idel, "Inquiries in the Doctrine of *Sefer Ha-Meshiv*," *Sefunot* 2 n.s., no. 2, ed. J. Hacker (Jerusalem: Makhon Ben Zvi, 1983), 185–266; idem, "Neglected Writings by the Author of *Sefer Kaf ha-Qetoret*" (in Hebrew), *Pe'amim* 53 (1993): 75–89; idem, "Magic and Kabbalah in *the Book of the Responding Entity*," in *The Solomon Goldman Lectures*, ed. M.I. Gruber (Chicago: Spertus College of Judaica Press, 1993), 125–38; idem, "The Attitude towards Christianity in *Sefer ha-Meshiv*" (in Hebrew), *Zion* 46 (1981): 77–91. An English version is printed in *Immanuel* 12 (1981): 77–95; idem, "The Origins of Alchemy According to Zosimos and a Hebrew Parallel," *Revue des études juives* 144 (1986): 117–24; idem, *Messianic Mystics* (New Haven: Yale University Press, 1998), 126–32.

38. The reasons for the marginality of this book in the fifteenth century are discussed by Meir Benayahu, "A Source about the Expellees from Spain in Portugal and Their Exit after the Decree of 1506 to Thessaloniki," *Sefunot* 11 (1971–78): 236–44 [Hebrew]. Neither were the more elaborated critiques of various sciences in the above-

mentioned *Sefer ha-Meshiv* available in Italy before the expulsion of the Jews from the Iberian Peninsula in 1492.

39. Compare, however, Abraham Melammed, "La 'dignitas Hominis' nelle opere dei pensatori ebrei in Spagna e in Italia nel tardo Medioevo e nel Rinascimento" (in Hebrew), *Italia* 3 (1982): 39–88, especially 68, 70, 72.

40. On this last topic of Kabbalah and Hasidism, see Moshe Idel, "Enoch the Shoemaker" (in Hebrew), *Kabbalah* 5 (2000): 265–86.

41. Idel, "The Anthropology of Yohanan Alemanno"; idem, "The Throne and the Seven-Branched Candlestick: Pico della Mirandola's Hebrew Source," *Journal of the Warburg and Courtauld Institutes* 40 (1977): 290–92; Arthur Lesley, "The 'Song of Solomon's Ascents': Love and Human Perfection According to a Jewish Associate of Giovanni Pico della Mirandola" (Ph.D. diss., University of California, Berkeley, 1976); Fabrizio Lelli, *Yohanan Alemanno, Hay Ha-'Olamim [L'Immortale]* (Firenze, It.: Leo S. Olschki, 1995); idem, "L'educazione ebraica nella seconda metà del '400, Poetica e scienze naturale nel '400, Poetica e scienze naturali nel Hay Ha-'Olamim di Yohanan Alemanno," *Rinascimento* 36 (1996): 75–136; B. C. Novak, "Giovanni Pico della Mirandola and Jochanan Alemanno," *Journal of the Warburg and Courtauld Institutes* 45 (1982): 125–47.

42. Moshe Idel, "The Study Program of Rabbi Yohanan Alemanno" (in Hebrew), *Tarbiz* 48 (1979): 310–12.

43. Alemanno appears to have held two different views in two different books though in both accounts magic is conceived of as very high.

44. The book mentioned here is different from the better-known printed *Sefer Raziel*, which François Secret has discussed at length. See his "Sur quelques traductions du *Sefer Raziel*," *Revue des études juives* 128 (1969): 223–45; Moshe Idel, "The Magical and Neoplatonic Interpretations of the Kabbalah in the Renaissance," in *Jewish Thought in the Sixteenth Century*, ed. B. D. Cooperman (Cambridge: Harvard University Press, 1983), 193–94.

45. *La-hafokh*.

46. MS. Oxford-Bodleiana 1535, fol. 95b.

47. Kaufmann, *Die Spuren*, German part, 56–60.

48. See the text printed by Umberto Cassuto, "Un Rabbino Fiorentino del Secolo XV," *Rivista Israelitica* 4 (1907): 229.

49. See MS. Firenze Medicea-Laurentiana 493, which has been described by Richler (see note 8 above). I found an additional manuscript of this translation in another Italian library, Vatican 270.

50. MS. Oxford-Bodleiana 2234, fol. 3a. On ibn Motot, see Georges Vajda, "Recherches sur la synthèse philosophico-Kabbalistique de Samuel ibn Motot," *Archives d'histoire doctrinale et littéraire du moyen âge* 27 (1960): 29–63.

51. *Ba'al behirah*.

52. *Takhlitam*.

53. *Sidrei ha-'Adam*.

54. MS. Oxford-Bodleiana 2234, fol. 17a.

55. *Shir ha-Ma'alot*, MS. Oxford-Bodleiana 1535, fol. 20a.

56. See Chaim Wirzubski, *Pico della Mirandola's Encounter with Jewish Mysticism* (Cambridge: Harvard University Press, 1989), 84–99.

57. *Collectanea*, MS. Oxford-Bodeliana 2234, fol. 10a.

58. Ibid., fol. 26a.

59. Ibid., fol. 17a.

60. For example, MS Oxford-Bodeliana 2234, fols. 22a, 132a.

61. See the studies mentioned in note 41 above.

62. See Shlomo Pines, "Medieval Doctrines in Renaissance Garb? Some Jewish and Arabic Sources of Leone Ebreo's Doctrines," in *Jewish Thought in the Sixteenth Century*, ed. Cooperman, 390–91.

63. There are several lists compiled by modern scholars that enumerate the numerous supercommentaries. See the studies of Moritz Steinschneider, "Supercommentare zu Ibn Ezra," *Juedische Zeitschrift* 6 (1868): 121–31; Naftali ben Menahem, "The Commentators on ibn Ezra's *Commentary on the Pentateuch*" (in Hebrew), *'Areshet* 5 (1961): 71–92; and the more conceptual analyses of Eleazar Gutwirth, "Fourteenth Century Supercommentaries on Abraham ibn Ezra," in *Abraham ibn Ezra and His Age*, ed. F. D. Esteban (Madrid: Asociación Española de Orientalistas, 1990), 147–54; Uriel Simon, "Interpreting the Interpreter: Supercommentaries on Ibn Ezra's Commentaries," in *Rabbi Abraham ibn Ezra: Studies in the Writings of a Twelfth-Century Jewish Polymath*, ed. I. Twersky and J. M. Harris (Cambridge: Harvard University Press, 1993), 86–128; Dov Schwartz, "The Philosophical Interpretation to Abraham ibn Ezra," *'Alei Sefer* 18 (1996): 71–114.

64. *Tzurot*, namely talismans. For this term see also Alemanno, *Collectanea*, fol. 26b in a text translated and analyzed in Moshe Idel, "Magic Temples and Cities in the Middle Ages and the Renaissance," *Jerusalem Studies in Arabic and Islam* 3 (1981–82): 186–87. I have identified R. Shmuel ibn Zarza as the intermediary text between the Arabic source of the astro-magical concept of temple in al-Mas'udi and Alemanno.

65. *Tahabbulot*. On the connection between this term and magic, see Alemanno's text printed and analyzed in Moshe Idel, "The Study Program," 311–12, 320 n. 73.

66. *Sha'ar ha-Hesheq* (Halberstadt, Ger., 1860), fol. 34b; MS. Oxford-Bodleiana 1535, fol. 106a, b. For more on this text, see Idel, "The Study Program," 326, and for a fuller context, Moshe Idel, "Astral Dreams in R. Yohanan Alemanno's Writings," *Accademia* 1 (1999): 123–24.

67. See the description of practices related to dreams and idolatry criticized in the *Guide of the Perplexed*, vol. 3, trans. Shlomo Pines (Chicago: Chicago University Press, 1963), 29, 516–17.

68. On the issue of the "marriage" of Hermeticism and Kabbalah, see Moshe Idel, "Kabbalah and Hermeticism in Dame Frances A. Yates's Renaissance," in *Esoterisme, gnoses & imaginaire symbolique: Mélanges offerts à Antoine Faivre*, ed. R. Caron, J. Godwin, W. J. Hanegraaf, and J.-L. Vieillard-Baron (Louvain, Belg.: Peeters, 2001): 71–90.

3
Jews, Humanists, and the Reappraisal of Pagan Wisdom Associated with the Ideal of *the* Dignitas Hominis

Fabrizio Lelli

De Dignitate Hominis

The reappraisal of the ideal of the *Dignitas hominis* induced most of the Italian Humanists from the end of the fourteenth century to reread accounts of historical figures of the past, putting an emphasis on their biographical characteristics. Caesar, Brutus, or Cato were no longer considered as *"figure,"* embodying allegorical values *sub specie aeternitatis*. On the contrary, these characters were restored to their pristine human condition though still representing the virtue that had been peculiar to them during their lifetime and that had been the main reason for their survival in history. Their high moral values were no longer separated from their historical personalities but dependent on them, as in the classical literary genre of the *vitae* of Greek and Latin biographies.

Thus those ancient heroes often became actual *exempla* of virtue to be followed by later generations. For instance, Cato was no longer, as he had been for Dante, an allegorical representation of the virtue of *Libertas*, separated from his actual political and historical role. In the *Purgatorio,* the Roman politician, although having lived historically before the advent of Christ, behaved and was portrayed statically as a medieval man of wisdom, acting as the guardian of the liberty of the Christian souls destined to salvation. During the fifteenth century, Cato, while still considered a paradigm of *Libertas*, became an example of man's struggle for liberty against tyrants, reacquiring his historical status as a pagan living in the age of Caesar who was inspired by stoicism.[1]

This trend of reevaluating historical biographies made it possible for Humanists to attribute historical significance also to legendary figures, hitherto renowned as very ancient prophets who had assembled *corpora* of writings in which they had disclosed secrets that could be interpreted, according to a medieval reading of sacred history, as pointing to the advent of Christ. Hermes Trismegistus, Zoroaster, and Orpheus, partly divested of their halos of holiness, could now be portrayed as men who had lived in a well-determined period of time.[2] Therefore it became possible to represent even their physical appearance in paintings and sculptures.

Contemporary with the relief in the Cathedral of Siena showing Hermes Trismegistus, dated 1488, which we will take into account later, is the relief attributed to Francesco di Giorgio Martini in the church of San Domenico representing Orpheus (Fig. 3.1). In his hands he is holding a mirror, instead of the lyre, the more frequent attribute of this *priscus philosophus:* this is not surprising if we compare this relief to a passage from Ficino's *Theologia Platonica* (Platonic Theology),[3] where the philosopher calls Orpheus "Apollo, the living eye of the heavens." Orpheus uses the power of the sun's rays (that is, Apollo) reflected by his mirror, here a magical instrument, to tame the wild beasts around him. The portrait of the ancient poet is closely linked to Orpheus's role of *priscus philosophus,* of a magician who knows the secrets of nature. However, according to a Christianized hermetic reading, in the image of the mirror reflecting sunrays, that is divine power, we can also perceive the symbol of wisdom, which Ficino himself associates with hermetic literature in the following passage of his early work *Di Dio et Anima* (About God and the Soul): "According to Mercury [Hermes], God's power is the reason for the creation

3.1. Francesco di Giorgio Martini [?], *Adam* (or *Orpheus*), Siena, San Domenico.

of every existing thing. Wisdom is like an immense mirror, where the images of all things shine."[4] Following such a reading, we could consider the engraving in Siena as a representation of Adam (or rather Adam's soul—in other words, man's soul) contemplating God's light through the mirror of hermetic knowledge in order to better perceive the nature of creation and especially his own nature, man having been created "in His image and likeness."[5] Whatever interpretation we may offer for the Siena relief, both Adam and Orpheus are portraits of ancient figures, of two *prisci philosophi*, endowed with very marked human characteristics while at the same time being the humanistic Hermetic or kabbalistic icon of the wise man, who is capable of resorting to divine magic to control the whole of creation.

The historical significance associated with legendary figures also appears in the superb decorations of the *Picture-Chronicle*, generally attributed to the fifteenth-century Florentine goldsmith and engraver Maso Finiguerra but more recently assigned to Baccio Baldini: this series of ninety-nine drawings "representing scenes and personages of ancient history sacred and profane" can be viewed as the best and most complete paradigm in art of the conceptions of the *prisca philosophia* animating Florentine cultural life around the middle of the fifteenth century.[6] Among the illustrations comprised within this half historical, half legendary chronicle we can find, for instance, the representation of the physical appearance of the ancient Persian magician Hostanes as well as those of Aristotle and Moses.[7]

Such an emphasis on sacred figures of the remote past in the context of prophetic history was partly due also to the humanistic reappraisal of the *Hebraica Veritas*.

In his *Apologeticus*, written between 1454 and 1459, the Florentine Giannozzo Manetti attempted to portray a sort of sacred history of mankind, embracing the period from the creation of Adam to the fifteenth century. This encyclopaedic work, which seems to inherit the tradition of the medieval *Summae*, is shaped after the patterns of classical rhetoric, and the title itself, apparently inspired by the literary traditions of medieval apologetics, was probably chosen to disguise the author's real interest in Jewish and pagan culture. Indeed, a closer analysis of the sections of the treatise where the role of Judaism in history is questioned allows us to consider Manetti's work as one of the first humanistic examples of a philological investigation of biblical history. In particular, Manetti emphasizes the role of the Hebrew Pentateuch, interpreted as a literary work. Its author, Moses, is depicted by Manetti resorting to biographic patterns derived from classical tradition, which constitute also the main scheme of Manetti's interpretation of other biblical figures.[8]

Unlike most of his Christian contemporaries, Manetti despised pagan sacrificial religion, contrasting it with the noble cult of the Jews, the only people in ancient times who honored their one God by immaculate worship.[9] The purity of Jewish rites allowed many Jews to attain such a level of perfection as to be in a position to obtain divine revelations. Therefore prophetic status should only have been achieved after a life conducted according to moral and intellectual criteria. Of the Jewish prophets, Moses was certainly the most significant in describing this process of human perfection leading to the knowledge of God. Manetti maintains that Moses already had great wisdom even before receiving God's revelation, arguing that the period of Moses' life, which is not described in the Bible, should be deeply investigated in order to bring out its value as an *exemplum* for man's behavior.[10]

Basing himself on his conversations with Neapolitan Jewish scholars, as well as on midrashic sources, Manetti reports the different stages of Moses' active and intellectual training, that led to him being, for instance, a brave commander of Pharaoh's army, which defeated the Ethiopians.[11] Moses' intellectual skill allowed him to be a distinguished orator who pleaded on behalf of his people before Pharaoh, as well as a good lawyer, capable of writing a praiseworthy code of laws.[12] Moses' rhetorical skill clearly emerges in the books he wrote: the description of the patriarchs in the book of Genesis highlights how talented he was in illustrating them as *exempla priscorum virorum*, examples of ancient heroes, destined to be held in high esteem by their descendants.

Manetti does not interpret Genesis in allegoric terms, and the patriarchs are not necessarily to be seen as Christ's predecessors. According to this Humanist, the biblical text is on the whole to be read according to literary and rhetorical rules. From this point of view Moses should be considered as a historiographer of his people's traditions who, following the classical model of historiography as an *opus rhetoricum maxime*, included the noble deeds of his ancestors in the narrative sections of his book dealing with the ancient patriarchs.

Such a literary approach to the biblical text does not differ greatly from the rhetorical investigation of the Scripture carried out by Manetti's younger contemporary Judah Messer Leon. His handbook *Sefer Nofet Zufim* (The Book of the Honeycomb's Flow) is based upon the assumption that Moses and the biblical prophets, when expressing the revelations they had received from God in written form, employed the same rhetorical rules that at a later stage Greek and Roman orators were to canonize in their production.[13] For both Manetti and Messer Leon, Moses is a perfect orator, capable of persuasion when addressing his people and of writing a moral history of the Jews. If for Ficino or Pico, Plato was an Attic Moses, for Manetti, and indeed for Messer Leon, Moses was certainly a Jewish Thucydides or Livy.[14] Here we have an example of the re-interpretation of a prophetic, as well as historical figure from the remote past, a *priscus philosophus*, according to classical philological patterns.

A similar process of the pagan rereading of biblical figures appears in contemporary art. From the first half of the fifteenth century, prophets and other main characters of the Scripture were portrayed according to patterns stressing their human personae rather than their prophetic connotations. We have one of the best examples of this artistic trend in Donatello's statue of the prophet Habakkuk, which once decorated Giotto's bell tower in Florence: the prophet is represented as an old bald man with a fierce and sad look, and wearing a sort of Roman toga, his general appearance turning this statue into a real portrait of a fifteenth-century man. If we compare this pattern with the more traditional representation of a prophet, such as, for instance, the fourteenth-century Giovanni da Milano's Daniel in the Cappella Rinuccini (Santa Croce, Florence), we clearly notice the less personal character of this painting.

If Manetti assumed that Moses, like the patriarchs, can be seen as a universal exemplum of moral virtue, Yohanan Alemanno, one of Messer Leon's students, who shared the same interest as his teacher in a rhetorical reading of Holy Writ, considered Moses as an exemplum for his own life. In his *Hay ha-ʻolamim* (The Immortal), Alemanno describes the stages of human life a man must live through and the disciplines he should learn in order to attain a rational knowledge of God.[15] When dealing with the adolescence of his ideal man, Alemanno suggests, following Moses' example, that he is to move from place to place in order to acquire the worthiest features of different cultures. If Moses was already wise before meeting the God of Israel, this was also due to his wanderings and to the different cultures he had encountered in his youth. Here are Alemanno's words:

> It is then necessary that the adolescent change the place of his residence, moving from house to house, from town to town, in order for his soul and his nature to become accustomed to any sort of food, to any meal time, to any clothing and habit, so that he will be well disposed to any human nature. Thus, he will not resemble an animal, that, being sedentary by nature, never changes its habits. We may observe that such was Moses' attitude, who lived two years in his home, then in Pharaoh's house, first in the land of Egypt, then in Midian and Nubia; likewise behaved Abraham, Isaac and Jacob, who never settled in only one place or followed only one system of thought, but accustomed their sensitive, imaginative and rational soul to observing the change of different things.[16]

The art of that period shows a special interest in Moses' biography: subjects representing Moses' childhood, especially the so-called *Trial of Moses*, were relatively popular. The main source for the few Christian medieval representations of this iconographic theme is the twelfth-century compilation of

Petrus Comestor's *Historia Scholastica*, where the legend seems to derive from Josephus's *Jewish Antiquities*. However, Giorgione's *Trial of Moses*, today in the Uffizi Gallery (Fig. 3.2), strikingly differs from the previous representations of the subject: Giorgione seems to emphasize some details that do not appear, for instance, in Benozzo Gozzoli's fresco, now destroyed but which once decorated the Camposanto in Pisa. We can observe that, in Giorgione's painting, the characters depicted near Pharaoh's throne cannot be explained without

3.2. Giorgione, *The Trial of Moses in Front of Pharaoh*, Florence, Uffizi Gallery. Alinari/Art Resource, N.Y.

resorting to midrashic literature: in fact, according to a recent study, they represent Pharaoh's three counselors mentioned in the midrashic compilation titled *Sefer ha-yashar* (The Book of the Righteous), in other words, Balaam, Jethro, who saved the child Moses by suggesting the trial, and Job. In the account given in *Sefer ha-yashar* it is also affirmed that "all princes of the realm" were present at the trial,[17] and this might well explain the large number of people in the painting. In addition, the three standing figures on the right can be interpreted as astrologers, the one in the middle being probably Johannes Regiomontanus. The latter, while lecturing at the University of Padua around 1460, associated the names of Abraham, Moses, and Prometheus with the founding fathers of astronomy.[18] Indeed, Prometheus is probably represented in the relief decorating Pharaoh's throne in Giorgione's painting. Classical and Hebrew sources are here clearly connected to the concept of the *prisca philosophia:* Prometheus, Moses, and the Egyptian astrologers manifestly represent the quest for a closer connection between man, the heavens, and God, shared by three of the major philosophic and religious cultures of the ancient world, in other words, Greek, Jewish, and Egyptian.[19]

Another passage concerning adolescence from Yohanan Alemanno's *Hay ha-'Olamim* can also be useful in understanding the penetration of these cultural connections in Italian Jewish milieus. Here Alemanno affirms, following Averroes, that a man should devote himself to art before proceeding to develop the ethical, rational, and intellectual parts of his soul. Alemanno attributes a more important role to the practical arts than his source, Averroes's *Commentary* on Plato's *Republic,* seemingly inspired by humanistic contemporary views. As Avraham Melamed has clearly pointed out, Alemanno considers the shift from the natural to the political stage of human life as an important and even necessary step along the path leading to the knowledge of God. Melamed observes the affinity of Alemanno's conception with the myth of Promethus,[20] explicitly connected to a peculiar concern for contemporary art, which may be compared to Manetti's and Ficino's conceptions of the distinction of man's nature from the other animals, also based on his creative power.[21]

Also on this basis, Giorgione's painting can be interpreted as a representation of the practical part of the human intellect (Prometheus's relief), the ethical political part (Pharaoh and his counselors), and the rational one (the astrologers); all this is certainly to be transcended by the divine intellect possessed by Moses from his childhood (Fig. 3.2).

This interpretation can be confirmed by a comparison with the above-mentioned *Picture-Chronicle,* where Prometheus is represented molding a *homunculus* on the same page and with the same dating as Pharaoh.[22] In the same *Chronicle* a further drawing represents Hermes Trismegistus practising necromantic rituals along with Hercules.[23]

56   *Fabrizio Lelli*

This image of Hermes was the source for the relief carved in 1488 on the floor of the Cathedral of Siena by Giovanni di Stefano. An inscription in its lower part reads: "Hermes Mercurius Trimegistus / Contemporaneus Moysi"[24] (Fig. 3.3).

To what extent was the Hermetic tradition accepted within Italian Jewish

3.3. Giovanni di Stefano da Siena, *Hermes Trismegistus*. Detail of the floor. Duomo, Siena, Cathedral. Alinari/Art Resource, N.Y.

milieus? Recent studies have clearly shown that Jewish scholars were in the habit of quoting the authorities associated with the esoteric chain of the *prisci philosophi,* mainly on the basis of the Arabic Hermetic texts, which had been diffused in Hebrew versions since the Middle Ages.[25] The actual influence of the Greek Hermetic corpus, translated by Marsilio Ficino, seems to have been limited to the reappraisal of this tradition by Jewish scholars during the fifteenth century. Nonetheless, Alemanno, who generally refers to Hermes adducing Arabic texts in a Hebrew version, seems to reevaluate the role of the human Hermes when he adds a marginal note to his *Liqqutim* (Collectanea), in which he appears very proud to reveal that he has read, in a non-Jewish book, of the place where the historical Hermes was buried. Alemanno affirms that "according to Mandavilla's book the tomb of Hermes is in Constantinople. His body was buried there 3500 years ago."[26]

A younger contemporary of Alemanno, who studied in Florence in the second half of the fifteenth century, Elijah Hayyim of Genazzano, also dealt with the role of the *prisca philosophia* in his treatise '*Iggeret Hamudot* (Epistle of Delights).[27] According to his views, the study of pagan wisdom can be useful when it contributes to the confirmation of the truth contained in the Hebrew Bible. His assumptions are based not only on the Arabic tradition but also on contemporary humanistic literature. If Humanists believe in the antiquity of the pagan wise men, and they think Moses was their contemporary, then Abraham and the patriarchs, being more ancient and closer to God, would have witnessed a more reliable form of knowledge. Although Genazzano refuses the neoplatonic interpretation of kabbalistic doctrines, which was common in Jewish Florentine milieus during the fifteenth century, he is ready to accept the role of the *prisci philosophi* as evidence of the greater antiquity of Abraham. Genazzano writes that in "an ancient book which has been attributed to Zoroaster I found some words on the subject of metempsychosis: this doctrine was revealed to the Indians by the Persians, to the Persians by the Egyptians, and to the latter by the Chaldeans, who had been taught by Abraham, whom they later expelled, being jealous of him because he assumed that the soul was the origin of every movement of the body."[28] I would like to emphasize, not so much the use made by Genazzano of the same sources employed by contemporary Humanists, but rather the fact that the author seems here to be concerned with the human Abraham more than the prophet. Genazzano later states that the Abraham he is dealing with is the patriarch who had not yet received the revelation of God. It is Abraham the Mesopotamian who is taken into account here, who was a wise man even "before obtaining [divine] revelations through the Shekhinah."[29] Can these words be thought of as a reference to Pico's words in his *Heptaplus* where, speaking about ancient philosophy, he deals with "Abraam sapientissimus"?[30] Unlike Maimonides, who condemns the reading of the magic Arabic work generally known as *Nabatean Agriculture*, Genazzano affirms that this book is worthy of being read since it was composed by Abraham himself before he reached his prophetic status. It therefore represents evidence of his wide human knowledge as well as of the importance he attributed to practical disciplines.[31] Moreover, the high value given to agriculture as a practical discipline is a peculiar feature of humanistic thought, which recurs in Ficino's and Pico's, as well as in Alemanno's works.[32]

Genazzano's teacher, Binyamin ben Yo'av of Montalcino, rabbi of the Florentine community around the middle of the fifteenth century, was a kabbalist, a talmudist, and an apologete, who used to debate with the Sienese erudite Pietro de' Rossi in the first half of the century. The latter interpreted the figure of King Solomon as that of an outstanding and prolific writer who could be compared to Aristotle.[33] Alemanno also praised Solomon's extraordinary wisdom in his commentary on the Song of Songs, *Hesheq Shelomoh* (Solomon's Desire), which was dedicated to Pico della Mirandola,[34] where the biography of the biblical monarch was based mainly on midrashic literature. The artistic representation of Solomon is not infrequent in fifteenth-century Christian art; indeed, Giorgione painted the biblical subject of the *Judgement of Solomon* (Fig. 3.4), complementary to the aforementioned *Trial of Moses*.[35] Both paintings represent the virtues of two biblical characters, endowed with very special knowledge; both figures are represented in a very individualistic way. Both subjects can be said to be based on the aggadic interpretation (in other words, a narrative explanation) of the Bible.

A further interpretation of Giorgione's two paintings could be a kabbalistic one: as Moshe Idel has clearly pointed out,[36] Isaac of Acco, in his *Sefer 'Ozar Hayyim* (Treasure of Life), had already dealt with a Hebrew version of the myth of Prometheus in the fourteenth century. Isaac affirms that he received a legend from a Christian source in which the role played by Prometheus had been attributed to King Solomon. Isaac himself may have associated the name of the biblical king with the name *MoSHeH*, in other words, Moses.[37] Although, according to a more recent interpretation, the three Hebrew consonants *mem, shin, heh* should be read as an acronym of *Metatron, Sar ha-panim*,[38] the reading of it as *Moses*, as had been suggested by Idel, could explain the connecting link between the characters of Moses, Solomon, and Prometheus in Giorgione's paintings: they could be seen as alluding to a prophetic history of mankind not dissimilar to the one contained, for instance, in the *Picture-Chronicle* although Giorgione seems to be more closely dependent upon the midrashic and kabbalistic tradition than his humanist contemporaries, mostly relying on Augustine and patristic authorities.

3.4. Giorgione, *Judgement of Solomon*, Florence, Uffizi Gallery. Alinari/Art Resource, N.Y.

De Dignitate Foeminei Sexus

In Alemanno's *Commentary on the Song of Songs* Solomon's political wisdom is compared to Lorenzo de Medici's.[39] It was apparently customary for Jewish communities to praise their rulers attributing to them the characteristics of the glorious biblical King; this can be ascertained by reading the chronicles of the ceremony organized in Pesaro in 1484 for the wedding of Costanzo Sforza and Camilla d'Aragona. On that occasion the local Jewish community took part in the ceremony wearing Oriental clothes and accompanying a pantomime elephant ridden by a lady of the community, playing the role of the Queen of Sheba. Arriving before Costanzo Sforza, she saluted him in Hebrew as the new King Solomon.[40] Here the Queen of Sheba can be viewed as evidence of the reappraisal of the dignity of women within the context of the revival of the virtues of the ancient ladies, who were to act as examples of noble behavior for fifteenth-century ladies. This tradition had been in fashion in Florence since the previous century when Giovanni Boccaccio, who dedicated his *Decameron* to the Florentine ladies, composed the short treatise *De claris mulieribus* (On Famous Women). In addition to Boccaccio's work, another compilation of the lives of famous women enjoyed widespread acclaim partly as a result of the beautiful woodcut illustrations appearing in the first edition of the work, printed in Ferrara, in 1497. I am referring to the late fifteenth-century *De plurimis claris selectisque mulieribus opus prope divinum, novissime congestum* (A Newly Compiled Almost Divine Work on Several Famous and Exemplary Women) by Friar Giacomo Filippo da Bergamo. The author, basing himself on Boccaccio, introduced examples of Jewish and Christian women in his treatise, something Boccaccio had intentionally discarded.

In Boccaccio's as well as in Giacomo da Bergamo's work the reappraisal of ancient heroines was partly based on the revival of women's classical biographies (Plutarch had devoted an important work to the *Virtues of Women*), partly on the medieval tradition of courtly love, in the context of which aristocratic ladies played an outstanding role. It is worthy of note that Giacomo da Bergamo also decided to introduce examples of significant biblical heroines, which were popular in the fifteenth century, a time when a clear political message was attributed to them; for instance, Judith generally represented the ideal of *Libertas* against monarchic forms of government whereas Queen Esther and the Queen of Sheba were frequently praised as symbols of strength and devotion within a monarchic context. Such reading of the biographies of biblical heroines was common in both Christian and Jewish milieus. A significant example is the late fifteenth-century poem by Avigdor of Fano in praise of women, titled '*Ozer nashim* (Women's Supporter). Avigdor wrote his work as a poetic response to a Tuscan Jewish literate, Avraham of Sarteano, who had expressed himself in misogynist terms, inspired by the Sienese poetry of the previous century which parodied the high praises addressed to women by the Dolce Stil Novo poets. Among the examples of biblical heroines, Avigdor emphasized those of Esther and Judith. These are his verses:[41]

Above all others, sweet fragrance,
delightful doe she has been created,

gifted with all beauty all her life long,
bewildering all young girls who saw her proceeding in the streets,
[I will praise] Esther, ruling by virtue of her beauty,
a stray lamb of the people of Israel.
Wearing linen and silk dresses,
she separated her inner qualities from her appearance,
and turned pain into joy stretching out her hand,
in order to convince the king to stretch out his golden sceptre and save her
people [. . .]
Behold too the powerful redemption
which was offered to us by a lady who is named after our people,
since she has seen their great affliction,
she has been frightened by the might of the army of her enemies,
but, with the sword drawn in her right hand, in her left hand
she has brought the king's head into the town walls.
Judith headed to an uncircumcised man
and, by holding this ruin [in other words, the sword] in her hands,
she has carried his [Holophernes'] head and let it hang down [from Betulia's walls].

The *laudatio* of Judith in Avigdor's poem is clearly reminiscent of the artistic representation of the biblical heroine in many celebrated works of late fifteenth-century Italian artists. Unlike the frequent iconographies based on the biblical text, which show Judith accompanied by her servant, holding a basket containing Holophernes' head (for example, Botticelli's painting in the Uffizi, Francesco di Giorgio's relief on the floor of Siena Cathedral), Avigdor seems to be influenced by a different iconography, probably based on contemporary woodcuts, and represented in painting, for instance, by Matteo di Giovanni, Sodoma, and Botticelli himself in a later painting.[42] In the latter iconography Judith herself carries Holophernes' head in her left hand, "the sword drawn in her right hand."

Similarly, the praise of Esther is reminiscent of another masterpiece of a major Florentine painter active in the first half of the century, Andrea del Castagno. The wealthy Florentine Carducci family had commissioned a fresco for their country residence, based on the praise of the Florentine virtues (another topic that was popular at the time and that had been dealt with by the humanist chancellors of the Florentine Republic as well as by Yohanan Alemanno).[43] Andrea del Castagno's fresco, which can rightly be considered the first secular wall painting of the Florentine Renaissance, represents a series of famous characters, arranged in three triads—Florentine warriors (*condottieri*), famous women, and Tuscan poets. They seem to be united by the idea of freedom. In the middle of the series, Queen Esther, a very rare subject in medieval and early Renaissance Christian art, appears in all her regal, though very human, beauty.[44] The inscription under her portrait is still legible: "Ester, la regina di

Persia, liberatrix" (Fig. 3.5). The lives of Esther and Judith also appear in Giacomo da Bergamo's *De claris selectisque mulieribus*. The woodcuts in the 1497 edition recall both the iconographies of the paintings just described and Avigdor of Fano's poetical representation of the two heroines (Figs. 3.6, 3.7, 3.8). Avigdor later introduces the exemplum of the queen of Naples, Isabella Chiaromonte, the first wife of Ferrante d'Aragona, whose life Giacomo da Bergamo describes with similar words.[45] Isabella's *laudatio* immediately follows Judith's exemplum. After recalling the reader's attention, by expressing the cruel though victorious image of Holophernes' head ("She has carried his head and let it hang down [from Betulia's walls]"), Avigdor continues:

From now on I will not necessarily seek [foreign] climates or regions,
since, by paying attention to my verses, you will realize
that in this fertile land,
when the Angevin came against us,
and the war minister, the count, rose with him
against our king and our father Ferrante,
his wife, the queen, decided to rise too;
she rose with her wisdom and took to her feet,
and her words produced portentous effects everywhere.
She is, among her people, like the queen of Sheba,

3.5. Andrea del Castagno, *Queen Esther*, Florence, Uffizi Gallery. Alinari/Art Resource, N.Y.

Jews, Humanists, and the Reappraisal of Pagan Wisdom

3.6. Anonymous, *Esther*, woodcut engravings from Iacopus Philippus Bergomensis, *De plurimis claris selectisque mulieribus opus prope divinum novissime congestum*, Ferrara 1497, f. xxxvir.

the words of her wisdom are delightful to the ear,
she came in the evening and returned in the morning,
to hear people cry for help and to rescue them.
A survivor and a fugitive left her on the throne,
until the third or the fourth generation,
and said to her: "Come along, arise!" Then she donned her armour,
rode her horse, as elegantly as any well-trained man, and
moved around her kingdom a second time.
Did she not meet the King of Portugal,
Did she not overcome her enemies,
by beating them in war,
by felling them down under her soles,
victorious also on their eighth generation?
I long to compare her with the power of my prayer,
since she judges her people by a justice worthy of a hero.[46]

3.7. Anonymous, *Judith*, woodcut engraving from Iacopus Philippus Bergamensis, *De plurimis claris selectisque mulieribus opus prope divinum novissime congestum*, Ferrara 1497, f. xxxiiv.

As was typical in midrashic literature, a biblical example could be used to represent an event that had occurred at a later period. The actualization of the images of Esther and Judith finds its best expression in the triumphant Isabella, who did not hesitate to save her husband's throne from the threatening power of the Angevins and Neapolitan nobles who wanted to put an end to the rule of Ferrante of Aragona. Avigdor probably drew Isabella's example from Bergamo's work though a further exemplum, concerning a Jewish lady, was certainly due to the author's own poetic skill. In order to conclude his poem, Avigdor adapts the genre of the humanistic *laudatio* to Anna, the daughter of the famous Tuscan banker Yehi'el of Pisa and the wife of the rich merchant Eli'ezer of Volterra:

From now on I will never more leave the borders of my home,
to seek the name of a lady whose deeds are blessed by God.

3.8. Anonymous, *Isabella Chiaromonte*, woodcut engraving from Iacopus Philippus Bergamensis, *De plurimis claris selectisque mulieribus opus prope divinum novissime congestum*, Ferrara 1497, f. cliv.

No such lady did ever exist, as far as I know:
am I not referring to the daughter of the noble Da Pisa,
her husband Da Volterra's crown?
Today I will praise her with my verses.
Her husband's great name is Eliʿezer.
Behold her wisdom and her grace,
praise and dignity helping her,
she is a gracious lady and her name is Grace [Hanna].
Blessed be her husband now and forever.[47]

From what we have previously affirmed it should be evident that in the humanistic environment the biographies of biblical personages, shaped on the basis of classical rhetorical patterns, were in many cases to become moral examples for contemporary life. Similar patterns were also adopted by contemporary Jewish poets and thinkers to reread their own sources in Renaissance garb, thus allowing them to display a peculiar interest in all the major cultural issues of the time.

On one hand we have observed Alemanno's reinterpretation of Moses' and Solomon's lives based on the Midrash and the use of the virtues of the biblical monarch to praise Lorenzo the Magnificent; on the other hand we have seen how Giorgione represented Moses' childhood, basing himself on the Midrash and adapting the lives of Moses and Solomon within a prophetic history of mankind. With Avigdor of Fano we witness a further adaptation: the humanistic *laudatio*, intertwined with biblical models and associated with the classical biographic genre and the Italian Stil Novo tradition, is adopted by a Jewish poet to celebrate a contemporary Jewish lady.[48]

The fifteenth-century Italian revival of classical culture, along with the humanistic reappraisal of the *Hebraica Veritas*, allowed Italian Jews to use the same motifs that inspired early Renaissance thought, literature, and art. This shows their deep concern with the various themes that animated Italian cultural life in the early Renaissance.

Notes

1. On the reinterpretation on a historical basis of Caesar, Brutus, and Cato, see, for example, Leonardo Bruni's *Dialogi ad Petrum Histrum*, where the humanist Niccolò Niccoli, during the first day of his debate with Bruni and Coluccio Salutati on the authorities of Dante, Petrarca, and Boccaccio, condemns the historical mistakes in Dante's *Comedy*. See Eugenio Garin, *Prosatori latini del Quattrocento* (Milano-Napoli: Riccardi, 1952); *Dialogi ad Petrum Paulum Histrum*, ed. S. U. Baldassarri (Florence: Olschki, 1994).

2. Chronological data associating the *prisci philosophi* of the so-called Hermetic chain and biblical figures could have been found by Humanists in Augustine, *De civitate Dei* 18, 39, where the author witnesses a theory that will be the basis of the contemporary Christian and Jewish fifteenth-century reappraisal of the ancient cultural tradition represented by the Bible in respect to the later Hermetic tradition. Augustine is among the first Christian authors to establish that Hermes lived later than Abraham and Isaac, even later than Moses since the latter was born in the same period as Prometheus, ancestor of Hermes Trismegistus.

3. Marsilio Ficino, *Theologia Platonica, Opera*, vol. 8, no. 2 (Basilea 1576), 295.

4. Cf. Paul O. Kristeller, *Supplementum Ficinianum* (Florence, 1937), 132: "La potentia di Dio è ragione secondo Mercurio efficiente di qualunque creatura. La sapientia è come un immenso specchio, nel quale le similitudini di tutte le cose risplendono." On this passage, see also Sebastiano Gentile, "In margine all'epistola 'De divino furore' di Marsilio Ficino," *Rinascimento*, 2d ser., 23 (1983): 33–77, where the Hermetic motif of God as the source and the supernal light is taken into account on the basis of the epistle *De divino furore*.

5. Andre Chastel, *Arte e umanesimo a Firenze al tempo di Lorenzo il Magnifico* (Torino: Einaudi, 1964), 277–78 prefers to see the image as a representation of Orpheus

whereas Gustav F. Hartlaub ("Ein unbekanntes Werk des Francesco di Giorgio," quoted by Chastel, 278, n. 1) had already tried to identify this personage as Adam though basing himself on Pico instead of Ficino. Martini's relief can be compared with a painting on copper (now in Galleria Borghese, Rome), executed by Jacopo Zucchi in the second half of the sixteenth century in the environment of Cardinal Ferdinando de' Medici, in which Adam is portrayed in the midst of God's Creation, holding an astrolabe in his right hand. The two works seem to have been influenced by Hermetic and Platonic trends of thought that deeply affected Renaissance scholarly milieus. See Philippe Morel, "Jacopo Zucchi, Allegoria della creazione," in *Villa Medici. Il sogno di un cardinale. Collezioni e artisti di Ferdinando de' Medici*, ed. M. Hochmann (Rome: De Lucca, 1999), 298–99. I wish to express my thanks for this reference to my colleague Massimiliano Rossi of the University of Lecce.

6. See Sidney Colvin, *A Florentine Picture-Chronicle, Being a Series of 99 Drawings Representing Scenes and Personages of Ancient History Sacred and Profane by Maso Finiguerra, Reproduced from the Originals in the British Museum with Many Minor Illustrations Drawn from Contemporary Sources and a Critical and Descriptive Text by Sidney Colvin* (London: B. Quaritch, 1898). On the attribution of the drawings to Maso Finiguerra, see also Chastel, *Arte e Umanesimo a Firenze al tempo di Lorenzo il Magnifico*. 191–92; Lucy Whitaker, "Maso Finiguerra, Baccio Baldini and the *Florentine Picture-Chronicle*," in *Florentine Drawings at the Time of Lorenzo the Magnificent*, ed. E. Cropper (Bologna: Nuova Alfa Editoriale, 1994), 181–96.

7. See *A Florentine Picture-Chronicle*, tabs. xx, xxi.

8. See Giannozzo Manetti, *Apologeticus*, ed. A. de Petris (Rome: Edizioni di storia e letteratura, 1981), 14 and passim. Ch. Dröge, *Giannozzo Manetti als Denker und Hebraist*, Judentum und Umwelt 20 (Frankfurt am Main: Verlag Peter Lang, 1987), 69–76.

9. Compared to previous authors who wrote works *adversus Iudaeos*, Manetti held the Talmud and other rabbinic writings in high esteem.

10. Cf. Dröge, *Giannozzo Manetti*, 74.

11. Ms. Vaticano, Urbinate Latino, 154, c. 17r. Compare the midrashic anecdotes on Moses' stay among the Ethiopians in L. Ginzberg, *The Legends of the Jews*, vol. 2 (Philadelphia: Jewish Publication Society, 1925), 283–89. Moses' youth is extensively dealt with in the midrashic collection known as *Sefer ha-yashar* (The Book of the Righteous), which might have been composed in Naples or elsewhere in southern Italy during the fifteenth century. Manetti, who debated on biblical exegesis with Neapolitan Jewish scholars, could have had access to the traditions contained in *Sefer ha-yashar*.

12. MS. Vaticano, Urbinate Latino, 154, c. 17r.

13. Cf. Abraham Melamed, "Rhetoric and Philosophy in Judah Messer Leon's *Nofet sufim*" (in Hebrew), *Italia* 1, 2 (1978): vii–lxxxviii. On the appraisal of rhetoric in fifteenth-century Jewish milieus in Italy, see also Alexander Altmann, "*Ars Rhetorica* as Reflected in Some Jewish Figures of the Italian Renaissance," in *Jewish Thought in the Sixteenth Century*, ed. Bernard D. Cooperman (Cambridge: Harvard University Press, 1983), 1–22.

14. Cf. Dröge, *Giannozzo Manetti*, 76.

15. See Alemanno, *Hay ha-ʿolamim (L'Immortale). Parte I: La Retorica*, ed. F. Lelli (Firenze: Olschki, 1995).

16. See Alemanno, *Hay ha-ʿolamim*, 151–52.

17. D. Haitovsky, "Giorgione's Trial of Moses: A New Look," *Jewish Art* 16–17

(1990–91): 27. For midrashic references, see *Midrash Shemot Rabba*, vol. 1, 26; Ginzberg, *The Legends of the Jews*, vol. 2, 272–75, as well as the contributions mentioned in note 18. It should be stressed that according to recent scholarly research, the midrashic collection titled *Sefer ha-yashar* could have been composed at the very end of the fifteenth century in Southern Italy, possibly in the Neapolitan environment; see *Sefer ha-yashar*, ed. J. Dan (Jerusalem: Mosad Byalik, 1986), 15–16; Jacqueline Genot-Bismuth, *Sefer ha-yashar*, vol. 1 (Paris: Université de la Sorbonne Nouvelle, 1986), 24, 51–52; see also *Sefer ha-yasar; First Ladino Translation . . . A Critical Edition* by M. Lazar (Los Angeles, 1998), xiii–xiv, 438–41.

18. See Rachel Wischnitzer, "The Three Philosophers by Giorgione," *Gazette des Beaux-Arts* 27 (1945): 203, 204; Haitovsky ("Giorgione's Trial of Moses: A New Look," 27) identifies the middle figure with Regiomontanus on the basis of a later Renaissance woodcut.

19. On the link of Prometheus, Moses, and Egyptian Hermetic culture, see also the reference to Augustine's *De civitate Dei* mentioned above, note 2.

20. A. Melamed, "The 'Dignitas Hominis' in the Works of Jewish Thinkers in Spain and Italy in the Late Middle Ages and the Renaissance" (in Hebrew), *Italia* 3 (1982): xxxix–lxxxvii.

21. *Hay ha-ʿolamim*, MS. Mantova, Biblioteca Comunale, Fondo Israelitico 21, c. 170r:

He will make sometimes use of clay, pitch, or wax in order to make a pot or an image of what exists above, in the heavens, or below, on the earth, or a portrait of a man or of a woman. He will sketch it using compasses, or will draw it using red colour (*sinopia*), thus reproducing a figure of flesh and blood, dressing it in white or black, so that when a man happens to pass by without knowing anything concerning his work, he will be persuaded within himself that what he sees is alive and will not believe what he will be told, that it is just a work made by human hands. He will work this way all his life long, also using wood, stones, silver, gold, and any durable material. And on the walls of his city he will engrave fortified towns, towers, large houses with windows and doorways, in vivid or opaque colors, fields, gardens, and orchards, vineyards and olive groves, as well as any sort of tree depicted according to various forms and styles in various colours, reproduced in the right proportions.

This passage should be compared to both Manetti's and Ficino's conceptions of man's dignity: see G. Manetti, *De dignitate et excellentia hominis* (Milano-Napoli: Ricciardi, 1950[?]), 68–69, where the author deals with Prometheus, and 86–87, where he discusses man's creative power on the basis of the evidence of Plato, Moses, David, etc.; see also Ficino's *Theologia Platonica*.

22. See *A Florentine Picture-Chronicle*, tab. xv.

23. See *A Florentine Picture-Chronicle*, tab. xvii.

24. The revival of the Greek Hermetic tradition allowed the Humanists to compare pagan and biblical figures, classical and Jewish cultures; from this point of view, Hermes could then be a contemporary of Moses. See also above, note 2.

25. See Moshe Idel, "Hermeticism and Judaism," in *Hermeticism and the Renaissance*, ed. I. Merkel and A. Debus (Washington, D.C.: Folger Shakespeare Library, 1988), 59–76; Fabrizio Lelli, "Ermetismo e pensiero ebraico," *Bulletin de Philosophie Médiévale* 35 (1993): 92–103.

26. *Liqqutim*, Ms. Oxford, Bodleian Library, Reggio 23 (= Neubauer 2234), c. 39v. See also Lelli, "Ermetismo," 103. Alemanno's quotation derives from the Italian

version of the *Voyage d'outre-mer* by Jean de Mandeville; see *I viaggi di Giovanni da Mandavilla, volgarizzamento antico toscano ora ridotto a buona lezione coll'aiuto di due testi a penna,* per cura di Francesco Zambrini (Bologna: Forni, 1968), 23–24. On the basis of earlier medieval travel books, Mandeville wrote that a golden plate had been found on an ancient tomb discovered by the emperor of Byzantium in Saint Sophia, with the following inscription: "Jesus Christ will be born from the Virgin Mary, and I believe this." The author himself affirmed that it was certainly the tomb of Hermes, the "wise philosopher," as he calls him. In Mandeville's work it is assumed, on the basis of the inscription already mentioned, that Hermes's body would have been buried two thousand years before Christ. Alemanno evidently wrote his note in the year 1500.

27. See Eliyyah Hayyim ben Binyamin da Genazzano, *La lettera preziosa (Iggeret hamudot),* ed. Fabrizio Lelli (Florence: Givntina, 2002).

28. Genazzano, *Iggeret hamudot,* 152. See also Moshe Idel, "Differing Conceptions of Kabbalah in the Early Seventeenth Century," in *Jewish Thought in the Seventeenth Century,* ed. Isadore Twersky and Bernard Septimus (Cambridge: Harvard University Press, 1987), 137–200, par. D.

29. Genazzano, *Iggeret hamudot,* 237.

30. See G. Pico della Mirandola, *Heptaplus,* in *Oratio de hominis dignitate, Heptaplus, De ente et uno e scritti vari,* ed. E. Garin (Firenze: Vallecchi, 1942), 172.

31. Genazzano, *Iggeret hamudot,* 237–38; Maimonides, *Guide of the Perplexed,* vol. 3, 29.

32. See Fabrizio Lelli, "L'educazione ebraica nella seconda metà del '400. Poetica e scienze naturali nel *Hay ha-'olamim* di Yohanan Alemanno," *Rinascimento,* 2d ser., 36 (1996): 75–136, especially notes 14, 27.

33. See G. Fioravanti, "Pietro de' Rossi (1403–1459). Bibbia e Aristotele nella Siena del '400," in *Università e città: cultura umanistica e cultura scolastica a Siena nel '400* (Firenze, It.: Olschki, 1981), 87–127; Fabrizio Lelli, "Umanesimo laurenziano nell'opera di Yohanan Alemanno," in *La cultura ebraica all'epoca di Lorenzo il Magnifico,* ed. Dora Liscia Bemporad and Ida Zatelli (Firenze, It., 1998), 49–67.

34. See Arthur M. Lesley, *The 'Song of Solomon's Ascents' by Yohanan Alemanno: Love and Human Perfection According to a Jewish Associate of Giovanni Pico della Mirandola* (Ph.D. diss., University of California, 1976), 51–67.

35. For the midrashic references to this episode, see Ginzberg, *Legends of the Jews,* vol. 4, 130–31.

36. Moshe Idel, "Prometheus in Hebrew Garb" (in Hebrew), *Eshkolot* 5–6 (1980–81): 119–20; idem, *Messianic Mystics* (New Haven: Yale University Press, 1998), 304–5.

37. Idel, *Messianic Mystics,* 304.

38. See again *Messianic Mystics,* 422, n. 64, where Idel refers to such an interpretation.

39. See A. Melamed, "The Hebrew 'Laudatio' of Yohanan Alemanno in Praise of Lorenzo il Magnifico and the Florentine Constitution," in *Jews in Italy: Studies Dedicated to the Memory of U. Cassuto,* ed. Haim Beinart (Jerusalem: Magnes Press, 1988), 1–34; Lelli, "Umanesimo laurenziano."

40. See Lelli, "Umanesimo laurenziano," 57. For a printed trascription of the Vatican manuscript, see T. De Marinis, *Le nozze di Costanzo Sforza e Camilla d'Aragona celebrate a Pesaro nel maggio 1475* (Firenze, It.: Vallecchi, 1946), 36–38, tab. 22.

41. See Avigdor of Fano's *'Ozer nashim,* vv. 70–128. My translation has been based on the Hebrew text presented by A. Neubauer, "Zum Frauenliteratur," *Israelitische Letterbode* 10 (1892): 97–105.

42. I am referring to the following paintings: Matteo di Giovanni, *Judith*, Bloomington, Indiana University, Study Collection; Sodoma, *Judith*, Siena, Pinacoteca Nazionale; Sandro Botticelli, *Judith*, Amsterdam, Rijksmuseum.

43. See Melamed, "The Hebrew 'Laudatio.'"

44. It is worthy of notice that Esther appears together with the Cumean Sibyl and Tomyris, the queen of the Massagetes, who beheaded King Cyrus. The three examples of famous women are flanked by three Florentine warriors on the left and three Florentine poets on the right.

45. Iacopus Philippus Bergamensis, *De plurimis claris selectisque mulieribus opus prope divinum novissime congestum*, Ferrara, 1497, cc. CLIv–CLIIv:

[Isabella Chiaromonte] Erat maxime eloquens maximeque oratoris suavitate praedita. Post Alfonsii autem regis mortem Ioannes Renati filius ex Gallia Transalpina cum exercitu in regnum venit ut id regnum paternum sibi recuperaret [...] Quo audito e vestigio Ferdinandus rex Neapolitane urbis custodiam huic sue uxori regnique omnis commendans ipse assumpto valido exercitu rebus omnibus ornato ut castra castris opponeret contra hostes profectus est. Que civitatis administratione suscepta sex prope annis eam magno consilio maximaque prudentia administravit atque in summa quiete et pace amoreque civium conservavit.

It is worth recalling that Bergamo's work was dedicated to Beatrix of Aragona, Isabella's daughter.

46. See Avigdor of Fano's '*Ozer nashim*, vv. 70–128. My translation has been based on the Hebrew text presented by Adolf Neubauer, "Zum Frauenliteratur," 103.

47. See Neubauer, "Zum Frauenliteratur," 103.

48. A similar melting of kabbalistic, Hermetic, and pagan tradition, connected to the major concept of the *Dignitas Hominis* and the *laudatio*-praise of women, can be found at the beginning of the sixteenth century in the Latin work *De nobilitate et praecellentia foeminei sexus*, composed by Heinrich Cornelius Agrippa of Nettesheim, where the author, better renowned for his Christian kabbalistic and magical encyclopaedia *De occulta philosophia* (Occult Philosophy), does not hesitate to refer to the kabbalistic tradition to exalt the dignity of woman, who, according to his own words, is more similar to God than man, since the Hebrew name of Eve is almost composed by the letters of the tetragrammaton. See H. C. Agrippa, *De Nobilitate et Praecellentia Foeminei Sexus*, ed. Ch. Béné (Geneva: Droz, 1990), 52.

4

The Mechanics of Christian-Jewish Intellectual Collaboration in Seventeenth-Century Provence: N.-C. Fabri de Peiresc and Salomon Azubi

Peter N. Miller

Nicolas-Claude Fabri de Peiresc (1580–1637) was one of the most famous Europeans of his generation. A polymath and an antiquary at a time when the former seemed possible and the latter admirable, he belonged to a circle of great men that included Galileo, Pope Urban VIII, Joseph Scaliger, Peter-Paul Rubens, and Tommaso Campanella, among many others.[1] With all these famous friends it is easy to forget that for Peiresc, as for all early modern scholars almost without exception, the closest and most common contacts were with the nearest, but not necessarily best-known, associates. These exchanges tended, for obvious reasons, to be spoken rather than written. This poses problems for the historian. Recapturing a quotidian intellectual life that was conducted face to face is extremely difficult at a distance of nearly four hundred years. But dependent as he is on written sources, even when some do survive, the inquirer faces a delicate challenge: how to bring an oral exchange to life using only its written traces.

What follows is an attempt to shed light on one of those local intellectual friendships that was conducted, in good measure, orally. Yet because of the chance survival of some of Peiresc's conversation notes, we are in a position to illuminate how in at least this one representative exchange scholarly talk functioned as a tool of discovery. Peiresc's interlocutor in the conversation was the rabbi of Carpentras. And so, this tale can be viewed, simultaneously, as a contribution to our understanding, still relatively primitive, of an entirely different problem: how a Christian and a Jew in early modern Europe collaborated to advance learning.[2]

Salomon (he signed his name Selomo) Azubi's relationship with Peiresc was noted by Pierre Gassendi in his extraordinary *Life of Peiresc* for the year 1633. Having, in the previous paragraph, mentioned the arrival in Avignon of

Athanasius Kircher, and of his visits to Peiresc in Aix, Gassendi continued: "He invited also, at the same time, *Solomon Azubius*, not inferiour to the ancient Rabbins in learning. He brought with him certain Astronomical Tables, which he had by him."[3] Azubi's name comes up occasionally in letters exchanged by Peiresc and Gassendi concerning astronomy and a couple of times in those to Claude Saumaise dealing with Coptic questions but is otherwise absent from the almost gazettelike letters Peiresc sent to the Dupuy brothers in Paris and to Cassiano dal Pozzo and Lucas Holstenius in Rome. In short, Peiresc's relationship with Azubi was not so important to him, just another one of those many contacts with local figures whose names dot Peiresc's correspondence—often the only traces these men have left behind them. But this very ordinariness explains, for us, the importance of this story in any future *Alltagsgeschichte* of the Republic of Letters. Its matter-of-fact nature only amplifies the fact that this was a collaboration between a Christian scholar (who happened also to be an *abbé commendataire*) and a rabbi.

What is known of Salomon Azubi is summarized in an article appended to Tamizey de Larroque's publication, early in the last century, of five of Azubi's letters to Peiresc. Three others, located in a dossier of astronomical papers, remain unpublished.[4] Azubi was born in Sophia, probably in the 1580s, and is first reported in France in 1619 at the head of the rabbinical court in Carpentras. The letters were spared the fate of most of early modern Jewish ephemera because his friend, Peiresc, was one of learned Europe's most devout letter writers and letter preservers. Even so, testimony to the perils of loose paper, Peiresc's own copies of the letters to Azubi have disappeared. The surviving correspondence dates from the years 1632 to 1635. By 1636 Azubi had already left Provence for Turin, and the next year he is found in Livorno. He was still there in 1647.

Peiresc probably met Azubi in print long before they met face to face. The first document found in Peiresc's file on Near Eastern languages is a poetic broadside praising Cosimo de' Bardi, the bishop of Carpentras and Papal vice legate at Avignon, that was written by Azubi. The encomium is titled "Canticum Canticorum Salomonis," in reference to the first four words of the Song of Songs and a pun on the name of its author, who is described as a "natif du Levant, Docteur en la Loy Hebraique, habitant de Carpentras" (Fig. 4.1).[5] What is extraordinary about this piece is, first, that it exists at all: that the leading printer in Avignon (Sanctissimi Domini nostri, Urbis & Universitatis Typographi) was willing to print a panegyric by the rabbi of a nearby town and that the final product received the requisite permission from the clerical authorities. Second, the form of the document, a columnar array of Hebrew, French, and Latin texts, echoes, visually, the layout of the great Polyglot Bibles of Alcalá and Antwerp, as well as classical Jewish printed books, such as Bom-

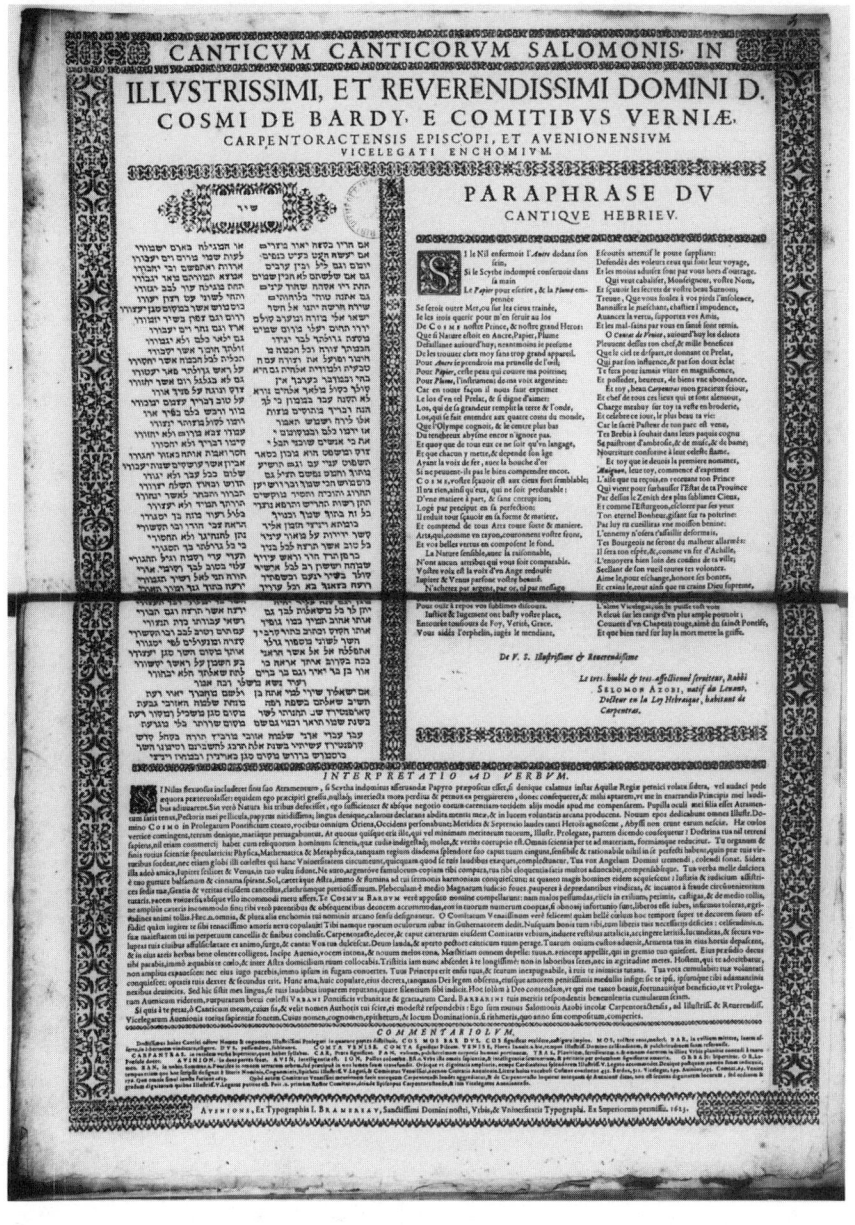

4.1. "Canticum Canticorum Salomonis," a poetic broadside praising Cosimo de' Bardi, the bishop of Carpentras and papal vice-legate at Avignon, written by Azubi. Paris, BN MS. Lat. 9340, fol. 4. Cliché Bibliothèque Nationale de France.

berg's rabbinical Bible. The work is dated by the printer to 1623, long before the name of its author appears in Peiresc's correspondence.

It was not until 1630 that Peiresc, perhaps remembering this document, sought to make contact with Azubi. In a memorandum titled "on desireroit de scavoir"—but which was clearly written with a specific person in mind—Peiresc began by wondering if "Rabby Salomon" still lived at Carpentras or had been carried off by the Plague (Fig. 4.2).[6] This is the first clue to dating, since we know of a major outbreak in Provence in 1630. As far as Peiresc was concerned, his chief interest in opening up this channel was books; for filing purposes he characterized Azubi's reply as "Memoire pour les livres Hebraiques de Carpentras."[7] But the questions that follow reflect a curiosity about much more than literature, taking in the history of the local Jewish community, its book collections, archives, and the method of calculating the new year.[8] These are the same sorts of questions that he addressed to Théophile Minuti about Syria, Thomas d'Arcos about Tunisia and Cassien de Nantes about West Africa, and that he daily asked of the mute survivors of the shipwreck of antiquity in his study.[9] Peiresc's interest in the Jewish community of Provence was part of a wider Christian fascination with the Jews in their midst; it was at just this time that Leon Modena sought to answer some of these queries with his *Historia de gli riti hebraici*.[10] That Peiresc also asked if Azubi possessed any Samaritan material suggests a date after 1628 and the beginning of Peiresc's intense focus on Samaritana.[11] But the clearest indication of timing can be found on Azubi's autograph reply to the questionnaire, which is dated, in Peiresc's hand, Tuesday 3 September 1630 (Fig. 4.3).[12]

The memoir would have reached Peiresc just before the revolt of the *Cascaveux* at Aix drove him and other officials out of the city. Between this upheaval and the outbreak of the Plague, Peiresc's correspondence was disrupted for the good part of a year, cutting off even this most well-connected of men from the rest of the world. It was, indeed, not until 1632 that this interest in the Jews of Carpentras and their rabbi could be followed up.

In fact, it is this same questionnaire that provides us with an important piece of evidence for the date of any resumption. For on his secretary's copy, kept, like so many similar documents, for research purposes, Peiresc scribbled in his own hand additional information about the structure of the Jewish community with its three "Berurim" (he likened them to the "consuls" of towns like Marseille), three financial auditors, six counselors, two judges, and three in charge of poor relief. He also jotted down information about the beginning of the Jewish New Year in 5393/1632 that would seem to indicate that all the new material had been added some time after the turn of that year. And, since this information about the structure of the Jewish community could only have

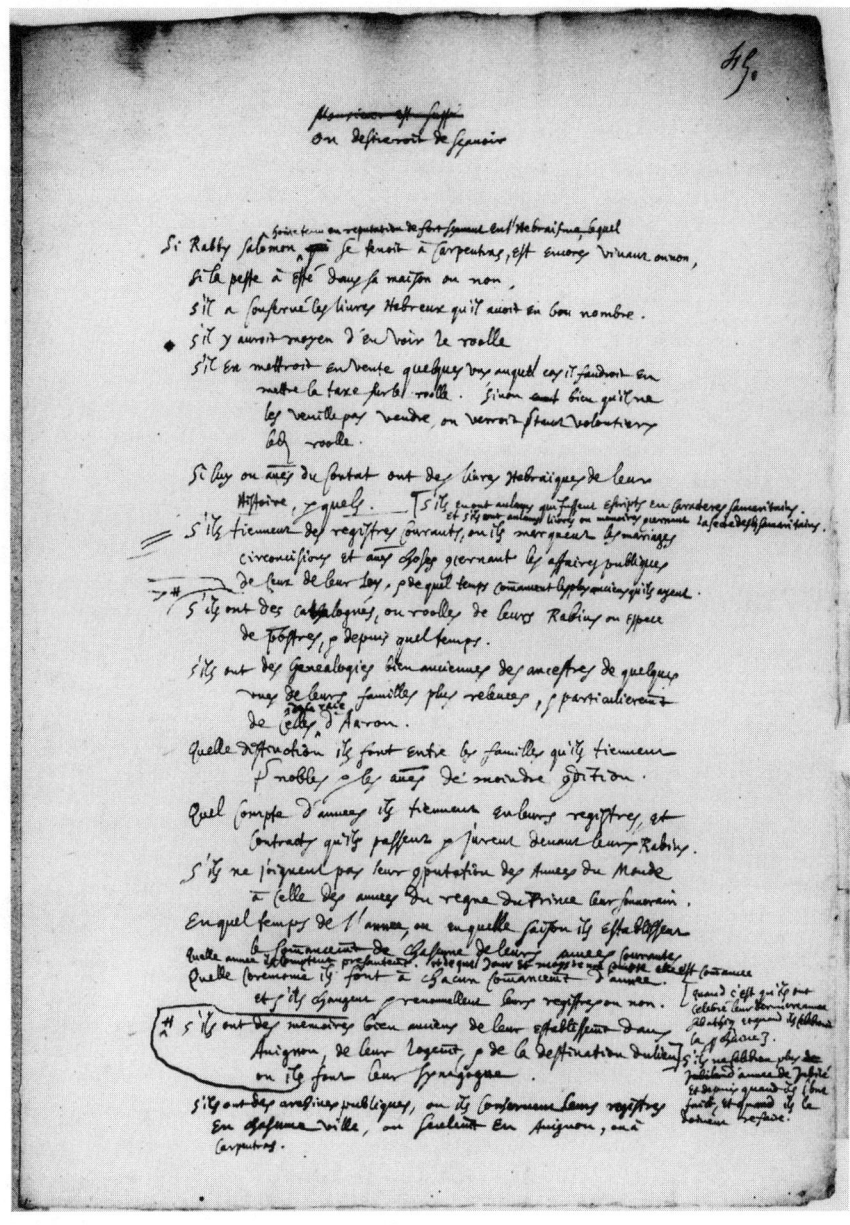

4.2. Memorandum titled "On desireroit de scavoir." In it Peiresc wondered if "Rabby Salomon" still lived at Carpentras or whether he had been carried off by the Plague. Paris, BN MS. Lat. 9340, fol. 45. Cliché Bibliothèque Nationale de France.

on il font leur sinagogue, bien est vray quil rend que leur Religion
est Saluterre en ce pais depuis 5 ou 6 ans ou ...

11. Il n'ont point de Catalogue ny rolle de leurs rabins

12. Il n'ont point en ce pais aulcune genealogie enrieures de leurs familles
de plus illustre, soy de la race d'Aaron, que pource que ceux
de la race ont quelques privileges parmy eux est cause quilz se
maintiennent de la race auquel pais (s) a escrit. Il ne vray (se) n'est ce
de constantible. Ce du levant Il y a quelques races ç maison illustres qui
tiennent qhe descendent de la Maison de David.

13. Il n'ont point de distinction de Nobles ou de moindre condition ou gloire
de personne dorly de leur religion qui font preferes à tour
come aussi ceux de la race d'aaron sont preferes aux autres rabbins

14. Il tiennent leur registre e contient par le compte d'annes de la
creation du Monde qui tiennent de cest année 5390 finissant
... pro Sain ... September 1630° que l'on compte
5391 an ... lequel premier jour de la lune ordinairement
... jour de la lune de Septembre, appelle
solum le Mois de Taffri.

15. Il ne tiennent point leur computation des annees du monde d'icelles
depannes des leur Rogne do leur prince parceque n'en on point, Il est vray
qu'en temps passe quand ils avoient Il comptoien du Regne d'un &c en
maintenant du monde.

16.17 pour le sixiesme article est inclus dans le 14.? ensemble
le 17.?

18. par le passé de 6 ans en 6 ans l'annee, ont semoient ... kompetty
... convoy pour ... le temple qui devoit ...
maintenant il n'en tienssent aucun du temple de courd de
Marbres. Et quicun soy après cost fiste, quant la fort de
... est continuer d'Lazirothy de ... ls
offri ... aux mays avant les stples
des convoys.

19. ne tienneut aulcuns articles publiques ... aux ...
anyons

Fait à ... le lundy 3° Sept ... de l'Incarnation N.S. ...

4.3. Azubi's autograph reply to Pereisc's questionnaire on Samaritan material, dated, in Peiresc's hand, Tuesday 3 September 1630. Paris, BN MS. Lat. 9340, fol. 286v. Cliché Bibliothèque Nationale de France.

come from a member of it, and the only such person in Peiresc's circle was Azubi, circumstantial evidence would point to some new contact.¹³

Surviving correspondence with Azubi puts us on still surer footing. In the first of his letters to Peiresc, dated 17 December 1632, Azubi began by acknowledging the great hospitality shown him in Aix. Mention of a meeting between them in the past tense in a letter from Peiresc to Gassendi of 7 December establishes a terminus ad quem.¹⁴ In a later letter Azubi himself ruled out travel in the month of Jewish holidays that followed the New Year; from Peiresc's own hand we know that the New Year 5393/1632 occurred on the last day of September. So the earliest possible terminus a quo for Azubi's visit would be the end of October.¹⁵

They met, then, some time in November 1632. A memorandum in Peiresc's hand with the filing label "R. Salomon Azuby. *1632. Nov*" offers documentary proof. Given the range of things they talked about, it is possible that Azubi remained *chez* Peiresc for several weeks. As astonishing as this might seem—and there probably is no other early modern example of a Christian scholar playing host to a fellow scholar-rabbi for such an extended stay—we know from Peiresc's correspondence with Gassendi that it was not a one-time event: Azubi also spent July of 1633 visiting with Peiresc at Aix.¹⁶

What did Peiresc and Azubi talk about in November 1632? We can answer this because Peiresc kept records of important conversations. In this he followed the example of one of his role models, the Genoese-Paduan Gian Vincenzo Pinelli.¹⁷ Some of those notes from his talks with Azubi have survived, and these enable us, within certain limits, to reconstruct their exchanges.¹⁸

The memoire labeled "R.SALOMON AZUBY. *1632* Nov.," and beneath it, in ancient Hebrew script, "She'nat Sh'tayim," documents one strand in their discussions.¹⁹ The page is divided, roughly, into three columns listing types of coins, their inscriptions in the old Hebrew script, and their Latin translation. All these are in the same hand, Peiresc's. It seems likely that he sought Azubi's help with the inscriptions. In his first letter Azubi mentioned that he was replying separately to Peiresc's questions concerning "des monoyes anciennes que les Juifs servoient d'un cicle [*shekel*] en bas."²⁰ Perhaps this memoir reflects that conversation.

That Peiresc's discussions with Azubi about the Samaritans began with coins and their inscriptions is an example of learned ontogeny repeating phylogeny: Peiresc's wider interest in oriental studies also began with the desire to read the inscriptions on ancient Jewish coins. These were written in the old Hebrew script that was adopted by the Samaritans but dropped by the Jews returning from captivity in Babylonia. In Padua in 1600 to study law (his father's plan) Peiresc worked with a rabbi on deciphering these inscriptions.[21] Documents from this early engagement also survive.[22]

Peiresc's lifelong fascination with weights, measures, and coins ensured a continuing interest in the ancient Hebrew script.[23] But it was only in the years after 1628, triggered by the news from Paris of a plan to publish the Samaritan Pentateuch as part of the Polyglot Bible, that the Samaritans, and not merely the alphabet they shared with pre-exilic Jews, became a major focus of his intellectual life. Peiresc organized and subsidized expeditions to the Levant seeking Samaritan materials, activated his network of merchant friends in Marseille and Toulon to look out for Samaritana, and applied his considerable charms to the location and acquisition of Samaritan materials elsewhere in Europe.[24] Indeed, at the very time that Azubi was visiting, in November 1632, Peiresc was setting out his view on the importance of Samaritan studies in a long letter to Jean Morin, the Parisian translator of the Pentateuch, that was accompanied by some of Peiresc's prized Samaritan artifacts, including the long-lost letters written by the high priest in Gaza in response to queries from Joseph Scaliger.[25]

But if Peiresc sent the autographs of Scaliger's letters to Morin, how then are we to account for the copies in Samaritan, Hebrew, and Latin that are found in his dossier?[26] We know for a fact that Peiresc's Hebrew hand was not the Sephardic cursive of the letters. Nor do the occasional Samaritan words found in Peiresc's papers match the fluent script of the letters. In Peiresc's circle those capable of reading and writing Samaritan were François de Gallaup-Chasteuil, Morin, and Azubi. The former left Aix in 1631 along with the French ambassador to Constantinople M. le Marcheville. He then proceeded to Lebanon where he earned some fame as the "solitaire du Mont Liban." In Peiresc's dossier is a comparison made by Gallaup-Chasteuil of the Samaritan Pentateuch with the Masoretic text and also a letter to Peiresc of 28 October 1630 that tries to untangle the Samaritan calendar. It also explicitly mentions, in passing, "vostre lettre samaritaine."[27]

These were, presumably, the letters to Scaliger. And they had, in fact, passed through Gallaup-Chasteuil's hands to Peiresc after their rediscovery in 1629.[28] Was he, then, the one who copied them for Peiresc? We know that only three weeks after sending the letters to Morin, Peiresc had received back from him a copy. Peiresc commented to Pierre Dupuy that there were only some slight differences between this and "another version of them that had been made at Beaugentier [sic]."[29] Indeed, a contemporary life of Gallaup-Chasteuil suggests that he visited Peiresc at Belgentier during the outbreak of Plague and there prepared "his observations on the Samaritan Pentateuch"—probably the comparison of the two Pentateuchs preserved in Peiresc's dossier.[30] And yet neither his Hebrew nor his Samaritan hands resemble those in any of the

Samaritan documents found in Peiresc's papers, including those celebrated letters to Scaliger. Indeed, the only person in Peiresc's circle able to write in the Sephardic hand used for the Hebrew and who knew Samaritan was Azubi.[31] Moreover, in the Hebrew transcriptions the tetragrammaton is consistently abbreviated—something that only a Jew would do. No certain examples of Azubi's Samaritan hand survive though we do find the same use of long descenders in his Hebrew documents and in the Samaritan script found amidst Peiresc's papers. The only person in Peiresc's circle who knew Hebrew, Samaritan, Arabic, French, and possibly Latin was Azubi. Comparison of the Hebrew hand with an astronomical manuscript, in Hebrew, bearing Azubi's name in the colophon offers conclusive proof that the Hebrew copy of the Samaritan letters, at the least, was executed by Azubi.[32]

What else was on the agenda in November 1632? Here we can rely on a three-page memo labeled by Peiresc: "*1632 / Librorum Hebraicorum / Index R. Salomon Azoby. / alia quaesita / de CORTINA / ARCAE &c.*," but which goes far beyond books[33] (Fig. 4.4) The first part of the titulus no doubt refers to the fourth of Peiresc's queries of 1630, answered by Azubi, "Il en a donné le roolle."[34] The inventory itself survives in Peiresc's dossier, labeled "Roole des libvres de sig' Rabby Salomo Azobi juif de Carpentras."[35]

But the title of the document is somewhat misleading. For even the books it mentions were actually locating guides to follow up on points that came up in conversation. These included "Quenaphaim, Les Ailes. / Les Tables Astronomiques du Rabi IACOB de Tarascon d'environ 200. ans," upon which Peiresc and Azubi would work over the next two years, the *Me'or 'Eynaim* of Azariah de Rossi—Peiresc made specific reference to the section titled "Imrei Binah," which dealt with chronology and the priestly vestments (at page 109)—, the *Alichot 'Olam*, or "camin del mondo," which is a history of the rabbis of the Mishnah and Talmud, and a book titled *Ihius Assadikin* [sic], which was an itinerary of tombs in the Holy Land. These scientific and historical topics all touched on matters of interest to Peiresc. Other subjects and authors mentioned here include books of history, such as the *Seder 'Olam*, "La Chronologie des Talmudistes" and the book of Joseph Bengurion (*Sefer Yosippon*), travel, specifically, the *Massahot* of Benjamin of Tudela, ritual, the *She'erit Joseph* on calendars, and grammar, the dictionary of talmudic Hebrew titled *Sefer Aruch*. There is also a brief note on Maimonides' intellectual accomplishments as the summarizer of "tout le Talmud, le More Philosophie, la declaration du Misnaioth, & de Medicine." On the book of Job, Azubi apparently recommended the commentary of Rabbi Meir Arama, "Meiri Job," as the best. Peiresc also noted simply "Le Cosry," presumably reflecting a newly stimulated interest in Yehuda Ha-Levi's *The Kuzari*.

From books that stand in for ideas, the memorandum turns to books

4.4. First page of a three-page memo labeled by Peiresc "1632 / Librorum Hebraicorum / Index R.Salomon Azoby. / alia quaesita / de CORTINA / ARCAE &c." Paris, BN MS. Lat. 9340, fol. 290. Cliché Bibliothèque Nationale de France.

dealing with weights, measures, and monies. It then shifts to particular points disconnected from particular books. So, for example, after noting, "Those [books] which treat receptacles for sacrifices," Peiresc jumped to a very specific issue, one that reflected his particular interests alone: "And particularly of those that do *not have feet*. To make sure the priest attends to stirring it for fear that the blood either congeal or harden, so that it remain liquid in order to be able to be poured on the altar."[36]

Following the same pattern, the next set of headings seems to signal not so much general topics of discussion as specific facts learned. The first deals with Rashi's interpretation of the Deuteronomic command to explain the Torah "well" as meaning in seventy different languages. Peiresc, himself deeply committed to comparative scholarship, as well as a prime mover on behalf of the Polyglot Bible, would have immediately seen in this a theological support for sacred philology. "It is," he wrote, "similarly, necessary to look into what they say, that each word in the Bible can be understood in 70 or 72 different ways."[37] The next topic was the Ark of the Covenant, supposedly hidden by King Josiah before the Babylonian Captivity, and where on it the high priest placed the incense. Both of these referred to biblical passages or objects; the third discussed the laws concerning the etrog ("citron")—when it was used and what made it kosher. The following two headings are, again, terse lapidary: concerning the first fruits brought to the temple in the autumn and the tent poles of the tabernacle. For the latter, Peiresc used the word "cortine," evoking the tripods used by ancient pagans (a subject of particular importance for him after the discovery of a tripod near Fréjus in 1630).[38] The memoir concludes, simply, "For the passages concerning the movement of the earth."

This is a fascinating document. It provides us with a concrete, and extremely rare, agenda of a learned conversation and offers an example of how the needs of a Christian scholar and the knowledge of a Jewish one fit together. But as an outline it would seem to presuppose the existence of other, more detailed treatments of these same topics. This material survives.

The most interesting of these notes have a Hebrew text at the top of the page, in Azubi's Sephardic semicursive hand, and usually contain a topical incipit, the appropriate biblical citation, sometimes prefaced by "as it is said" (*she-ne'mar*), and often include Rashi's interpretation of the passage. On rare occasions Azubi also gives the locus for the talmudic discussion. Peiresc tended to scrawl his own comments, explanations, and amplifications in French at the bottom of the page, sometimes including information not found in the Hebrew and therefore certainly reflecting Azubi's oral contribution. This enables us to see both what it was that they were talking about—what Peiresc thought particularly memorable—and also how they worked: with a pen and paper in front of them.[39]

In all, we possess six documents drawn up by Azubi that refer to a subject indicated on the summary memorandum: the ark, citron, sukkah, measures, versions of the text, and mobility of the earth. There are three additional notes on matters not mentioned elsewhere: construction of the tabernacle, drinking cups, and the Constantinople Hebrew Polyglot Bibles. These reflect specific concerns of Peiresc at that time. The page on drinking vessels ("POCULA"), for example, might reflect an inquiry that Gassendi dated to 1632 when Peiresc sought to establish a connection between the later form of ritual cups and their origins in hollowed-out human skulls.[40] The discussion of the Constantinople Polyglot surely echoes Peiresc's involvement with the publication of the Paris Polyglot.

The content of the page labeled "TETRAPLES de Constantinople / TETRAPLES de / HELIEZER du Constantinople" (Fig. 4.5) had to have been provided by Azubi, as it did not concern a passage from the Bible but rather contemporary Jewish history. Azubi, a native of Sofia, and hence the cultural sphere of Constantinople, noted for Peiresc the languages of this version—Aramaic, Hebrew, Arabic, and Persian versions, along with the commentary of Rashi—as well as its publication history—in Constantinople in the house of Eliezer son of Gershom from Soncino in the year 5306. Peiresc identified the commentator, "Rabby Salomon Iarki qui est ce qu'ils appellent par abbregé" Rashi, and then noted to himself that this was an acronym, another indication of Peiresc's rather limited Jewish learning. Peiresc, or more likely Azubi, added that this printing house produced very few other Hebrew books. Below, in a finer hand, Peiresc commented extensively on the way in which the different versions were prepared by the printer: the paraphrase of Onkelos was in Aramaic only while the Arabic and Persian versions had the first word of each "article" (verse?) printed in ancient Hebrew, as if to provide a guide to those unfamiliar with the language. Peiresc compared this to the layout of his Arabic language Samaritan Pentateuch in which the *incipit*s were also in the original language but the body of the text in Arabic characters.[41] Why was Peiresc interested in this information? Because he had just received a copy come from Constantinople. In a letter to the brothers Dupuy of 15 November 1632, he notes its receipt and then proceeds to describe its contents and publication history using exactly the information found on this note and prepared with the assistance of Azubi—whose name is not mentioned in the letter to Peiresc's closest collaborators.[42]

The issues raised by the practice of Polyglot scholarship, more relevant for Christians than for Jews, were the subject of another discussion. "Traductions du Texte / Versiones Pentateuchae" contained a lemma provided by Azubi, the verse at Deut. 27:8 on the duty to explain the Torah, along with Rashi's interpretation that "explain well" meant "in seventy languages." After

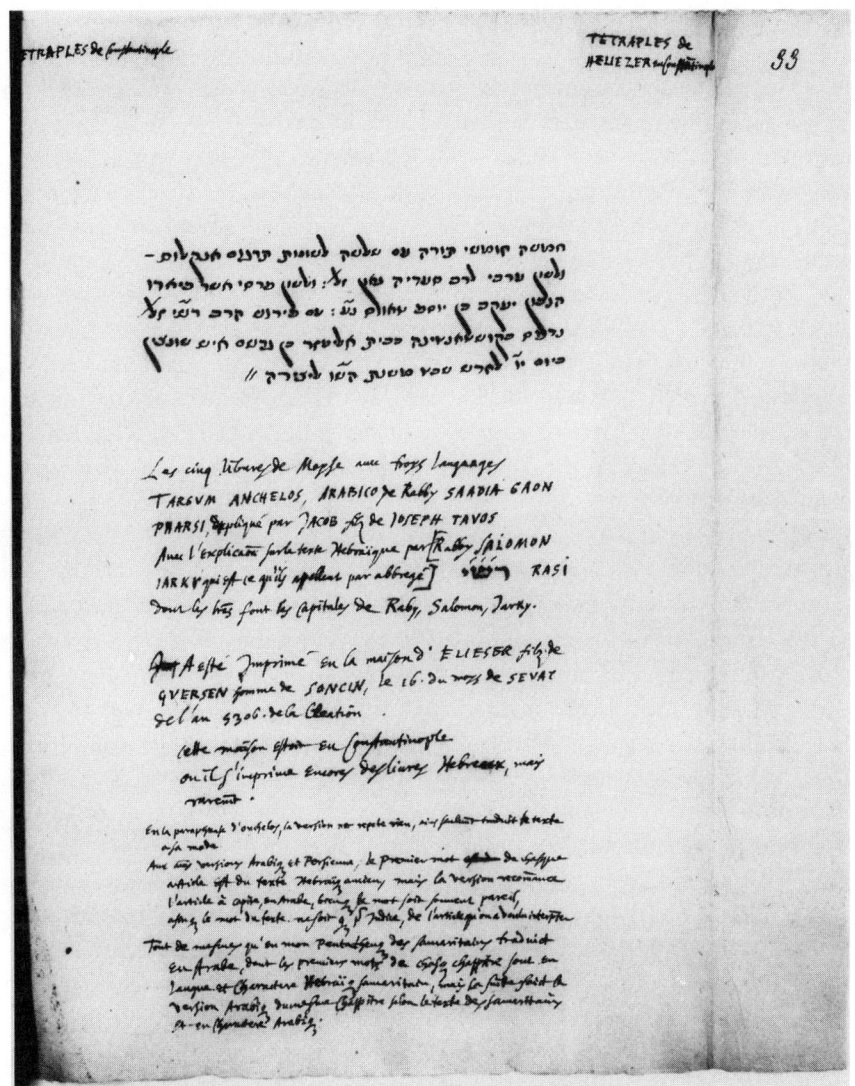

4.5. "TETRAPLES de Constantinople / TETRAPLES de / HELIEZER du Constantinople." Paris, BN MS. Lat. 9340, fol. 33. Cliché Bibliothèque Nationale de France.

translating these texts, Peiresc, presumably taking direction from Azubi, went on to note that "the anonymous Tradition sees the number of 70 in the word *heitev*" and supported this with a convoluted *gematria*. Peiresc added, "The Talmud says that there are 70 faces or interpretations that one can give to the Torah."[43] This is the classical Jewish justification for the multiplication of textual interpretations. It offers the best defense of the kind of comparative philological approach to sacred literature embodied in the Polyglot Bibles—but which was not invoked by the Christian scholars who worked on them.

Finally, the concluding cryptic reference to "the passages on the mobility of the earth" helps identify a memoir now in one of Peiresc's dossiers on astronomy. It cites several verses from Job chapter 28, God's speech "out of the whirlwind." Peiresc put a Galilean gloss on the divine reference to the fundaments of the earth: "presupposes that it has a circular movement around its axes, or poles, or bases, or columns, or mortars."[44]

In the first letter Azubi wrote to Peiresc after returning home to Carpentras, he offered a prayer that God never let him forget the honor, courtesy, and unmerited favors Peiresc had showered upon him in Aix.[45] Azubi referred to a series of queries by Peiresc that he was answering "in the enclosed memoir"—now lost—ranging from the ancient *shekel* to the place where the high priest left the censer in the Temples to the times and the fruits that were brought as sacred to the vases in which sacrificial blood was received and the flags and blazons of the twelve tribes. We have already seen that some of these themes were discussed at Aix a month earlier. But what is clear from this, as from the conversation notes, is that Peiresc was interested in those antiquities of the Jews that exactly corresponded to the antiquities of the pagans that already intrigued him.

The other major topic of the letter, announcing its paramount importance in their relationship, was astronomy. Azubi explained that he had undertaken to have a copy made of the "Astronomical Tables" of Rabbi Manuel of Tarascon—one of the books listed by Peiresc in the overview of their conversation and flagged for further investigation.[46] The *Shesh-Kenafayim*, or "six wings" of Isaiah 6:2, was composed by Immanuel b. Jacob Bonfils around 1365 and contained tables for determining both new moons and eclipses, adapted to the Jewish calendar and the latitude of Tarascon from the calculations of the ninth-century astronomer al-Battani.[47] The project of transcription and translation occupies much of their later collaboration and drew in those of Peiresc's friends who were also interested in the history of astronomy and its medieval Jewish practitioners, among them Samuel Petit of Nîmes and Wilhelm Schickard of Tübingen, both Protestant, as well as Gassendi, the canon of Digne.[48] Azubi brought the letter to a close by extending his warmest greetings *Je baiseray, avec tout humble respect, les mains* to Peiresc's brother Vallavez and his wife and son.[49]

Many of the subjects mentioned in this first letter were revisited in subsequent ones. Peiresc must have replied immediately because two weeks later Azubi wrote for a second time and referred to the indescribable honor and contentment that he received from Peiresc's letter. It had been carried by one of Peiresc's lackeys along with several Samaritan books on which his comments were desired. Azubi explained that he had sent his previous letter via Avignon along with a response to Peiresc's memoirs. The lackey would be sent back with a letter and several additional books that had been mentioned by Azubi in his previous missive.[50] Azubi also included his notes (*cartes*) on the Samaritan volumes as well as a rough-and-ready concordance to Peiresc's Samaritan-Arabic Pentateuch. Like so many of Peiresc's collaborators, especially the less famous ones, Azubi was overwhelmed by a willingness to serve. "All my desires," he wrote, "are only to seek out for you some new book or rare and curious thing and to work for you and employ my study to give you some contentment." He cherished Peiresc's commands "more than anything in the world." Again, he ended by kissing the hands of Peiresc's brother, nephew, and sister-in-law.[51]

Azubi's third letter begins with old business—the project to translate a medieval Hebrew astronomical table. Azubi moved on to report that a friend of his in L'Isle sur la Sorgue possessed a medal that depicts a figure he thought might be Moses on the obverse with the text of the second commandment on the reverse. Knowing Peiresc's style of thought, Azubi asked the friend to make a copy that, even though not to his complete satisfaction, he was now sending to Peiresc. He added, "There is in this town one of my friends who, being informed of your curious desires, did some investigating in this place for similar little curiosities." L'Isle sur la Sorgue was one of those Provençal towns that once contained a sizeable enough Jewish population to warrant the existence of a *Juiverie* whose location is preserved to this day. Peiresc's correspondence reveals the extent of his reliance on a network of local people for many of his finds; Azubi seems to suggest that it even extended into the Juiveries of Provence.[52]

In the summer of 1633, barely six months after his first stay *chez* Peiresc, Azubi visited again. The subject of their discussions, so far as we can tell, was astronomy. Peiresc wrote to Gassendi that Azubi had brought his copy of the "Tables Astronomiques in order to work on its translation." He had also brought observations on the last two eclipses "that he made according to the rules of those Tables."[53]

These materials all survive. Peiresc's copy of *Quenapha'im/Les Ailes*, the astronomical tables of Rabbi Manuel, bears Azubi's marginal notes in Hebrew and Peiresc's corrections of the translation. Atop the first page Peiresc identifies it as "a translation dictated" by Azubi in 1633.[54] Peiresc also retained a copy of Azubi's "Ampliation des expositions" of Rabbi Manuel and his application of its calculations to the eclipses of 1632 and 1633—one of the rare examples of Jewish astronomy in early modern Europe not to come from Rudolph II's Prague. In the margins of Azubi's discussion of the solar eclipse of 8 April 1633, Peiresc scribbled in, for comparison's sake, the observations made by Kepler and Gassendi.⁵⁵ The point of Azubi's effort was made clear at the end of this discourse: "These two comparisons and examples of the eclipses of the moon and sun suffice for anyone to be able to use the Tables, *des Aisles*, for finding all the lunar and solar eclipses in whatever the year."⁵⁶ This collaborative project coincided with the peak of Peiresc's effort to coordinate a simultaneous eclipse observation around the Mediterranean with the hope of improving the accuracy of sailing charts.⁵⁷

Peiresc reported the results of Azubi's calculation of the eclipse of October 1632 to Gassendi in a letter from the end of July 1633.⁵⁸ Gassendi complained that Azubi had modernized his tables to accommodate changed times, destroying their historical value and making it more difficult to evaluate their author's achievement.⁵⁹ Peiresc—who elsewhere had directed the same complaint at others—replied that he had brought this to the attention of Azubi who declared that whatever changes he had made followed those of "all our printers of breviaries" and such like, but that he, nevertheless, also preserved the unaltered original from which the kind of information Gassendi desired could be had.⁶⁰ By the end of December, Peiresc had received Azubi's translation of Rabbi Manuel's tables "à demy françoise et à demy provençale" and transcribed a copy for Gassendi to send on, if he thought it worthwhile, to Schickard in Tübingen.⁶¹

Azubi entered Peiresc's circle in 1632. So did Athanasius Kircher. And the story of Azubi's relationship with Peiresc loses an important dimension if the story of Azubi's relationship with Kircher is omitted.⁶² The German Jesuit and the Sephardic rabbi could have found each other through their common location or common interests—only fourteen kilometers separated the polyglot in Avignon from the polyglot in Carpentras—but it is most likely that they were brought together by their mutual friend in Aix.

Three letters from Azubi to Kircher, in Hebrew, survive. The longest one is undated and addressed to Kircher at Carpentras. It has been suggested that Kircher might have visited there in 1632, but given its proximity to Avignon, it is possible that he visited there at any time and any number of times.⁶³ The letter takes up a query for information about the calculation of the Jewish calendar. Azubi answered, rhetorically, by identifying himself with the ancient Hillel who was asked (by a Gentile) to summarize the entire Torah while standing on one foot. He then went on, with an equal flourish, by referring Kircher to the Babylonian Talmud, tractate *Rosh Ha-Shanah*, "already known to His Excellency." After protesting that everything he was going to say was found in the Talmud, Azubi proceeded to lay down the major rules for establishing the calendar, calculating the leap years, and fixing the new moons. He concluded by suggesting to Kircher that if he remained uncertain about some of the explanations, they should meet in person: "Tell me if you wish to come to my house of study, or if I should go to yours"—though observing that it might be easier if Kircher came to him because he possessed the books whose arguments they would needs be studying.⁶⁴

A second letter bears the date of 23 Nisan 5393 (3 April 1633) and responds to a request for an interpretation of the high priest's breastplate and phylacteries. Azubi answered Kircher's question with another question, explaining that since no more specific theme was requested, he did not know if Kircher was interested in the mystical interpretation which, he wrote, "would demand a great deal of time because I will have to prepare for you almost a small treatise," or whether Kircher wanted only concrete information. This, he noted, was very easy to come by, and he referred Kircher to the appropriate verses in the Pentateuch. The letter's postscript asked if he could borrow for a short time "that little book" on "science and astronomy" (*chochmah limudit*).⁶⁵

These are arresting images, of Kircher sitting in the *Bet Midrash* in Carpentras, or of Azubi thumbing through Kircher's library, and they suggest a reality of learned exchange taking place beyond the testimony of the existing correspondence. But the reality of this relationship, unlike the one between Peiresc and Azubi, was somewhat different: the engagement with the "native informant" was part of a strategy that aimed at conversion.

A letter from Peiresc to Kircher of 3 August notes in passing that he ought to have received "the response of poor Rabbi Salomon Azuby to your paper. He is very much your servant."⁶⁶ What was this "paper," and what was this "response"? The answer to these questions is found in a letter from Azubi to Kircher, written on 21 July 1633 while at Peiresc's home in Aix. Azubi began: "The Lord and Senator, the councillor de Peiresh [sic] showed me the arguments that you sent him to show me the true difference between Christians and Jews." Since the letter had not been addressed to him, he would not have replied except "to please the will of the Lord of Peiresh." However, because it was forbidden for Jews, "as we are oppressed under the hand of the gentiles," to debate Christians in matters of theology, Azubi requested that Kircher obtain permission from the lord of the place, or from the Inquisitor, for him to respond point by point. And then, he promised, Kircher would hear "things that you have never heard in your life."⁶⁷

So now we know. Kircher was proselytizing his Jewish collaborator and was told off. There is no immediate reply to Azubi's request for an intellectual "safe passage." But in a letter to Peiresc that must have been written almost immediately after receipt of Peiresc's, the same one that included Father Scheiner's account of the trial, condemnation, and abjuration of Galileo, Kircher launched into a tirade against Azubi. He condemned his "inhumanity, insubordination and manifest haughtiness—in one word, the sign of a Jewish spirit and stiff-neckedness." This was manifested in translations from the Hebrew that he had made which threatened "to pervert our sacred law," and which Kircher was transmitting so that Peiresc could "see the perverse heart of the Jewish genius."[68]

Not only did Kircher's attack not damage Peiresc's close relations with Azubi, it actually compelled Peiresc to defend him. In his reply of 17 August, Peiresc tried to explain away the disagreement between his two friends as a consequence of a stylistic "rudeness" that testified to the "barbarousness and rusticity of his birthplace." Azubi's flowery Hebrew sounded exalted, but it did not take into consideration the nature of the recipient and possible misinterpretation—presumably accentuated by the gap between the high rhetoric of the Hebrew and the more basic knowledge of the interlocutor. "Since I have found him of such good nature in every other thing and so modest," Peiresc concluded, "I would have a hard time believing that he had the slightest bad intention."

Peiresc nowhere conceded Kircher's main claim. Instead he very delicately suggested that it was simply a question of an unsophisticated sense of practical judgment on Azubi's part. His solution to this quarrel was elegant, if a bit disingenuous. He had asked Azubi for Kircher's letter and would now ask Kircher for Azubi's. As if once the material evidence were eliminated, the animosity would disappear too.[69] But the exchange is also astonishing for the further light it sheds on the easy relationship of the two men. Azubi trusted Peiresc to share with him banned controversial material and Peiresc took Azubi's part against Kircher.

In fact, this relationship seems to have deepened in the aftermath of this attack. Later that summer Peiresc asked Azubi to go to Mazan, near Carpentras, on his behalf and investigate a strange story that was making the rounds about a thunderclap that sounded during celebration of the Mass. This was just the sort of tale that Gassendi bears in his *Life* of Peiresc in order to arraign the credulousness of the masses and signal the importance of careful method.[70] In his reply Azubi explained that he "made diligence" to inquire from the vicar of Mazan himself, who was present at the event and who sent him a discourse that he was in turn sending on to Peiresc. Mazan was only about seven kilometers east of Carpentras, and so Peiresc may have turned to Azubi purely for the sake of convenience. Nevertheless, what is so striking here is the *abbé commendataire*, Peiresc, employing the rabbi, Azubi, to make inquiries of the local parish priest—and the priest informing the rabbi who in turn told all to the abbé.

In the second part of the letter Azubi introduces us to an equally revealing, if more obscure, story. He thanks Peiresc for intervening on his behalf in the "affair of St Canat"—otherwise unidentified—and asks for copies of the *arrets* of the Parlement. He explains that he would send Peiresc "the money" as soon as possible and apologizes for his inability to come and thank Peiresc in person in the coming weeks: the "feste des trompettes" (Rosh Ha-Shanah) would begin in two days, which was followed a few days later by the "feste de l'expiation" (Yom Kippur), and a few days later still by the "feste des Tabernacles." These were solemn holidays in which "we are obliged to gather together" for almost a month, at the end of which he would again be at Peiresc's service.[71] The letter seems to refer to some favor of a legal nature either performed by Peiresc, or by another at Peiresc's request.

The three unpublished letters from Azubi to Peiresc all date from the summer of 1634. They do not add substantially to our knowledge of the content of their intellectual collaboration, but they do document additional contacts between them and further suggest the extent to which Azubi was integrated into Peiresc's local network of support services. The first of these, dated 5 May 1634, begins with Azubi reporting that immediately upon his return to Carpentras he had resumed work on "la declaration ou ample explication" of the Tables of Rabbi Jacob, which Peiresc had set him on "when I was at Aix." Had Azubi just then returned from Aix, or does this refer to an earlier visit? His next comment is equally revealing, not only of his relationship with Peiresc but of how Peiresc operated. Azubi noted that he had not yet had the opportunity to go to Avignon and pick up the books that Peiresc had charged the bookseller, a "M^r. Rey," to have ready for him but that M^r. Rey had promised that they would be waiting for him the following weekend.[72] Behind every great learned figure, like Peiresc, there lay a host of almost always nameless drones, like this Mr Rey. Recent scholarship has called attention to the importance of the printing trade in the learned economy, and to the role of household servants who assisted in the work of their masters; Peiresc himself acknowledged his gardeners and bookbinders as assistants in his astronomical observations.[73]

The second and longest of the unpublished letters opens another window into the mechanics of local learned life—and demonstrates, again, how little religion seemed to isolate Azubi or affect his participation in Peiresc's Provençal circle. He acknowledged receiving a letter from Peiresc dated 24 June to which he responded on 10 July. This letter, along with some interpretations of Hebrew inscriptions, was handed to someone heading to Marseille who promised to detour to Aix and drop the letters. But the carrier never made it to Aix, and the package was returned to Azubi. Only in the last week, while at Cavaillon, had he found someone else, a "Mr du Samarans" of Aix, "who promised to return it to your own hands." The rest of the letter was responding to a later note from Peiresc, dated 1 July, that had arrived in the meantime. Azubi apologized for failing to properly carry out Peiresc's wish, "which was to take the book." Does this refer to some book that he was to get from Mr Rey in Avignon? There was apparently some disagreement between Azubi and the bookseller over the book's physical condition.[74]

In his letter of 20 August, Azubi replied to an undated letter of the previous week that contained the usual discussion of the vicissitudes of the post and the route taken by Peiresc's most recent letter. He answered what must have been another request to go to Avignon and do some favor for him: "To serve you, I cannot fail to depart for Avignon next Monday to work." Further discussion of Rabbi Manuel's Tables followed. In what seems to be a postscript, Azubi explained that he had detained Peiresc's lackey until that morning "a cause du Sabath."[75] Does this mean that the messenger was put up for the day in the rabbi's home? Or was he lodged somewhere else in the town on Azubi's credit? We simply cannot know.

Azubi's role within Peiresc's circle of local helpers is the subject of another letter, written in June of 1635. Azubi describes a visit to the town of Velleron, twelve kilometers south of Carpentras, where he was sent by Peiresc to look for an ancient tomb. In this instance, yet again, Peiresc used Azubi to investigate a matter in which no specifically Jewish knowledge was necessary. If Azubi's expertise in Hebraica had initially caught Peiresc's attention, their years of working together seem to have encouraged him to look upon Azubi as simply another reliable collaborator.

Having located the tomb, Azubi proceeded to provide Peiresc with a detailed description that included its measurements—all this mirroring the master's practice. Azubi then interrogated the peasants for news of what might have been in the tomb. His narrative of the moment brings it back to life: "And while I was looking at the tomb, many local people gathered in order to find out what I was interested in," among whom was a woman whose husband had been with the group that had discovered it. She explained that the excavators had come upon a terra cotta urn that they carelessly broke, revealing its contents: ash, some small bones, and seven or eight little glass vials while around the urn were found a plate and some terra cotta spoons. All of these, save two, had been broken by their children after being in use for some time. The woman responded affirmatively to Azubi's request to see them. After his offer to purchase one was rebuffed, the rabbi invoked the authority of an otherwise unidentified "Madame de Breuil" who prevailed upon the peasant woman to give them as a gift to Azubi. He was not sending them with the bearer of the letter in order to ensure their safe handling; since he and his family were leaving Provence via Marseille, he would deliver them personally to Peiresc. Especially worthy of note is that the rabbi was able to call upon a local noblewoman for assistance with a recalcitrant peasant. The last paragraph of the letter contains Azubi's request that Peiresc help him obtain a safe conduct for his passage out of Provence.[76]

Azubi's departure from the region has been dated, largely on the basis of this letter, to 1635. But a leaf in Peiresc's file containing a Hebrew transcription was labeled by Peiresc "names of the ancient patriarchs wherein is established the genealogy of Mohammed in the Arabo-Samaritan MS. book in 4°, excerpts of Samaritan interspersed in the Arabic text of the volume, by Rabbi Salomon Azubi the 13th February 1636 at Aix."[77] While it would seem that this refers directly to material mentioned by Azubi in his letter of 3 January 1633, the dating is unequivocal. Indeed, we know from Peiresc's correspondence with the circle of Saumaise that he expected to see Azubi at least one *additional* time, in late summer 1636.[78]

What is the wider importance of this collaboration between a famous man and a forgotten one? First of all it suggests something of the place that Hebrew was to occupy in modern scholarship. No longer privileged as the sacred language of the Bible, it now took its place among a group of languages, each of which was in the process of gaining a history in the first half of the seventeenth century: Samaritan, Syriac, Coptic, Arabic, and Persian.[79] Arias Montano, in his volume of apparatus to the Antwerp Polyglot (1572; reprinted separately 1593), began the exploration of the Hebrew language and Jewish rituals as the "antiquities of the Jews," akin to the Roman antiquities that were being studied in such exquisite detail at that time. Peiresc's questions of Azubi follow in this line of approach. He asked for help with understanding precisely those aspects of ancient and modern Jewish society that had pagan parallels: weights and measures, religion, calendars, coins. In the generations after Peiresc, this fascination with the Bible as a history of ancient Near Eastern culture preempted, for more and more people, the identity of the Bible as a sacred document. The rise of oriental studies and the crisis of *historia sacra* are consequences of this shift.

Second, the materials preserved in the Peiresc papers offer unique insight into the mechanics of early modern Jewish-Christian collaboration. We know that Christian scholars who wanted to learn Hebrew tended to begin their studies with Jews or Jews already converted to Christianity. The examples of Scaliger's *chevruta* with Philippus Ferdinandus and G. J. Vossius's talks with R. Menasseh ben Israel immediately come to mind. But in neither these nor any other known example do we have any record of what, *exactly*, they talked about nor how, *exactly*, they studied together. The preservation of Peiresc's conversation notes and memoranda allow us to reconstruct his studies with Azubi in their concreteness. In many cases we see that Azubi provided the raw information—the text—which they then discussed, Peiresc jotting down what he wanted to know on the same page as Azubi's Hebrew contribution. Learned talk remained anchored to the text. Their joint astronomical observations have left no trace, except for the translations produced by Azubi and the tantalizing reality of the two men spending summer nights in Peiresc's observatory scanning the skies of Provence and talking about, what—life in the Ottoman Empire? Peiresc's unruly nephew? Mediterranean flora and fauna? the history of Judaism? All questions we cannot answer.

What we can say for sure is that this was a collaboration between two very unusual figures. The third, and last, observation that ought to be made concerns the personal dimension of intellectual life that is exposed in these documents. Whether or not Azubi composed the Latin as well as the French and Hebrew versions of his welcoming poem for the arrival of the new vice legate, we cannot but be astonished at his desire to produce a literary greeting for the new bishop. He entered into his relationship with Peiresc with equal enthusiasm, visiting the great scholar, writing to him, expressing a willingness to serve as his agent, sending his warmest greetings to Peiresc's family. The letters to Kircher, too, are full of willingness to discuss and debate with the learned Jesuit. But they also show that Azubi was not afraid or ashamed to stand up to him and point out his errors.

Azubi's relationship with Peiresc seems extremely close. Are there other early modern examples of rabbis who visited, repeatedly, for up to a month in the home of a Christian scholar? (As for the question of whether the rabbi ate off Peiresc's plates—otherwise unanswerable—we can say that Peiresc himself often consumed only spring water and melons, a limited, if not perhaps kosher diet. Or was Azubi like Jacob Bernays, who spent three months at the Prussian embassy in London in 1851 and consumed nothing but tea?) And yet, with all this interest in the Christian Republic of Letters, we have no indication that Azubi ever neglected his duties as rabbi of the community of Carpentras or that he ever thought of renouncing membership in the Jewish world for the Christian. From Provence, after all, he moved on to serve the communities of Turin and Livorno. He is a Jew fascinated with a world of learning that extended beyond the four cubits of the law.

Finally, what do we learn about the other principal from this episode? First, that Peiresc did not know a great deal of Hebrew. What he got from Azubi was, on the whole, quite elementary: textual loci and the occasional Rashi but otherwise none of the great legal and homiletic sources. During these same years, in Peiresc's own extended circle, Jean Morin in Paris and John Selden in London were making long marches through the midrashic, talmudic, and medieval commentaries that would transform sacred philology and create a postbiblical Jewish history. Peiresc's polymathy, in this case, appears more as an inclination, or even a life-style, than an already acquired expertise. What Peiresc knew was enough to make connections between intellectual discourses that tended to be kept separate but not enough to establish secure arguments.

But the way Peiresc related to Azubi also reflected on him. It is proof that he lived his declared antipathy to dogmatism. He often emphasized the need to take the bad with the good and to tolerate the idiosyncrasies of his friends for the good they did him, recognizing all the while that he might possess characteristics that they had to work equally diligently to accommodate.[80] In his relationship with the rabbi of Carpentras we do not once catch a whiff of polemic. Absent is the drumbeat of proselytizing that resonates through even his extremely close friendships with Protestant scholars such as Hugo Grotius, Giulio Pace, Claude Saumaise, and Samuel Petit. Indeed, in Peiresc's vast correspondence we do not come across the sort of casually anti-Jewish comment that one expects from even the best disposed of Christian scholars. Instead we encounter an unusual sympathy for him and for the state of the Jews. Peiresc made excuses for Azubi with his closest friend, Gassendi, and defended him outright against a potential protegé, Kircher. As for the Jewish people, when writing about the miserable condition of Christians living under Ottoman rule, Peiresc explained that they "are accommodated, as Jews are accommodated among us, in those places where they are suffered at all."[81]

From what we can deduce of Peiresc's feelings about Azubi the evidence is again unequivocally warm. While Azubi was staying with him in Aix in July of 1633, Peiresc encouraged him to visit Gassendi in Digne and work together on astronomy. Azubi apparently demurred, saying his "sickness" made this impossible "even though," Peiresc added, "I offered him one of our horses and a guide and to pay for it all."[82] In a second letter Peiresc observed that "the poor man wants so much to see you that I afterwards resolved to send him to your home, and to loan him one of our horses so that he could stay two or three days with you and learn something about this matter."[83] A week later, in the postscript to his next letter to Gassendi, Peiresc ended simply "Old Rabbi Salomon Azubi has gone home, without having had the courage to go see you."[84] One is struck both by the rabbi's desire to meet with the other great scholar and by Peiresc's real empathy for a friend's feelings—a compassion and insight into the complexity of human emotions that we tend not to associate with the great early modern polymaths.

Notes

1. See my *Peiresc's Europe: Learning and Virtue in the Seventeenth Century* (New Haven: Yale University Press, 2000). The fullest biography remains Pierre Gassendi, *Viri Illustris Nicolai Claudii Fabricii de Peiresc Senatoris Aquisextiensis Vita* (Paris, 1641),

translated as *The Mirrour of True Nobility and Gentility* (London, 1657). Modern lives have been written by Pierre Humbert and Georges Cahen-Salvador though neither contain any references. Much better is Henri Leclerq, "Peiresc," in Fernand Cabrol and Leclerq, vol. 14 of *Dictionnaire d'archéologie chrétienne et de liturgie* (Paris: Letouzey et Ané, 1939), 1–39. Substantial biographical information can be gleaned from the detailed work of Cecilia Rizza, *Peiresc e l'Italia* (Turin, It.: Giappichelli Editore, 1965); Sydney Aufrère, *La Momie et la tempête. N.-C. F. de Peiresc et la "curiosité egyptienne" en Provence au début du XVIIe siècle* (Avignon, Fr.: A. Barthélemy, 1990); *Peiresc. Lettres à Claude Saumaise et à son entourage*, ed. Agnès Bresson (Florence: Leo Olschki, 1992); and David Jaffé, "Peiresc—Wissenschaftlicher Betrieb in einem Raritäten-Kabinett," in *Macrocosmos in microcosmo*, ed. Andreas Grote (Opladen, Ger.: Leske and Budrich, 1994), 301–22.

2. For the importance now attached to working papers like these, see William H. Sherman, *John Dee: The Politics of Reading and Writing in the English Renaissance* (Amherst: University of Massachusetts Press, 1995), and Lisa Jardine and Anthony Grafton's classic "'Studied for Action': How Gabriel Harvey Read His Livy," *Past and Present* 129 (1990): 30–78. The subject of collaboration between Christians and Jews is too vast for summary. For the early modern period alone one might begin with the essays collected in *Jewish Thought in the Sixteenth Century*, ed. Bernard Dov Cooperman (Cambridge: Harvard University Press, 1983); *Jewish Thought in the Seventeenth Century*, ed. Isadore Twersky and Bernard Septimus (Cambridge: Harvard University Press, 1987); and *The Autobiography of a Seventeenth-Century Venetian Rabbi: Leon Modena's "Life of Judah,"* trans. and ed. Mark R. Cohen (Princeton: Princeton University Press, 1988). Several recent monographs study this phenomenon; for example, Aaron Katchen, *Christian Hebraists and Dutch Rabbis: Seventeenth Century Apologetics and the Study of Maimonides' Mishneh Torah* (Cambridge: Harvard University Press, 1988); Peter T. Van Rooden, *Theology, Biblical Scholarship, and Rabbinical Studies in the Seventeenth Century* (Leiden: Brill, 1989); Stephen Burnett, *From Christian Hebraism to Jewish Studies: Johannes Buxtorf (1564–1629) and Hebrew Learning in the Seventeenth Century* (Leiden, Netherlands: Brill, 1996). But our knowledge of how this collaboration actually worked remains external, circumstantial, or ex post facto. Missing in every case that I know of are the notes taken during conversation which served as the basis for the scholarship that made manifest its existence. This is "ground zero" for anyone interested in the mechanics of how Christians learned from Jews.

3. Gassendi, *Mirrour of True Nobility*, year 1633, 85–86.

4. Jules Dukas's "Notice Complémentaire," in Tamizey de Larroqué, "Lettres Inédites écrites a Peiresc par Salomon Azubi," *Revue des études juives* 11 (1885): 5–37, reprinted in *Les Correspondants de Peiresc* (Geneva: Slatkine Reprints, 1972), vol. 1, 609–41.

5. Paris, Bibliothèque Nationale (henceforth BN) MS. Lat. 9340, fols. 3, 4.

6. That Peiresc intended this for Azubi is reflected in the initial title, crossed out but still legible: "Monsieur est suppl[iqué?]." The autograph of the memoire is found in BN, MS. Lat. 9340, fol. 45; the secretary's copy, with some additions by Peiresc in his own hand, is at folio 108. A selection of Peiresc's questions and Azubi's answers has been published by Jean-Pierre Rothschild in the appendix to "Deux Bibliothèques Juives Comtadines vers 1630," *Revue des études juives* 145 (1986): 100–102.

7. BN, MS. Lat. 9340, fol. 286v. Peiresc titled the secretary's copy of his questionnaire "Memoire des livres de Rabby Salomon Azubi" (BN, MS. Lat. 9340, fol. 108v).

8. Peiresc's pattern of underlining always offers insight into how he read his documents. In Azubi's memorial Peiresc underscores references to circumcision (no. 8), communal books, and, in particular, chronicles (no. 9), the age of the community (no. 10), its social stratification (no. 13), and its method of computing the calendar (no. 14). BN, MS. Lat. 9340, fol. 286.

9. For the convergence between ethnography and archaeology, see the author's "Taking Paganism Seriously: Anthropology and Antiquarianism in Early Seventeenth-Century Histories of Religion," *Archiv für Religionsgeschichte* 3 (2001): 183–209.

10. Modena's text was first published in Venice in 1614 with the title *Vita, riti e costumi de gl'Hebrei*. The second edition under the more familiar title was published in Paris in 1637 from a manuscript brought back from Venice by Peiresc's friend and correspondent Jacques Gaffarel.

11. For this, see my "An Antiquary between Philology and History: Peiresc and the Samaritans," in *History and the Disciplines*, ed. Donald Kelley (Rochester: University Press of Rochester, 1997), 163–84.

12. MS. Lat. 9340, fol. 286v.

13. In a finer hand elsewhere on that same sheet Peiresc also revealed his extreme ignorance of the Jewish calendar: not knowing that the day began with the previous nightfall. "Et de leur computation d'annees depuis la Creation du monde dont la 5391me commence le sammedy sept. Septembre. *1630* que se recontroit le premier jour de la Lune a leur conte. Et toutefois la lune avoit faict dez le vendredy precedent 6. Sept [next four lines are crossed out]. La Lune fit le vendredy 6 ^{me} Sept. a [gap in original] heures qui estoit le vray commencement de leur feste du sabath qui anticipe dez le jour precedant du sammedy aprez le crespuscule, qui est appeller entr'eux inter duas vesperas" (BN, MS. Lat. 9340, fol. 108v; this passage was omitted by Rothschild in "Deux Bibliothèques juives comtadines"). Azubi discussed the dating of the year 5390 in point 14 of his response to Peiresc's questionnaire (BN, MS. Lat. 9340, fol. 286v).

14. Peiresc to Gassendi, 7 December 1632, *Lettres de Peiresc*, vol. 4, 268.

15. Azubi to Peiresc, 2 September 1633, *Les Correspondents de Peiresc*, 649–50. At the bottom of his secretary's copy of the questionnaire Peiresc wrote: "Le 1 jour de la lune de Septembre dernier *1632* / Ils ont commencé de compter leur an 5393" (BN, MS. Lat. 9340, fol. 108v).

16. On 10 July 1633 Peiresc wrote to Gassendi: "Nous avons icy depuis sept ou huict jours le bonhomme R. Salomon Azuby" (*Lettres de Peiresc*, vol. 4, 324). On the thirty-first of that same month he wrote again: "Le bon R. Salomon Azubi s'est retiré chez luy" (*Lettres de Peiresc*, vol. 4, 335). Toward the end of the month, but perhaps while Azubi remained his guest, Peiresc also received visits from the Capucin monks Gilles de Loches and Caesar de Roscoff on their way from Egypt back to Brittany.

17. For Pinelli's practice, see Paolo Gualdo, *Vita* . . . *Pinelli* (Augsburg, 1607); for Pinelli's influence on Peiresc, see Marc Fumaroli, "Nicolas-Claude Fabri de Peiresc. Prince de la République des Lettres," in *IVe Centenaire de la Naissance de Gassendi. Conférence organisée par l'Association Pro-Peyresq dans la Maison d'Erasme à Anderlecht le mercredi 3 juin 1992* (Brussels, 1993, privately printed), 22–26; for Peiresc's practice of conversation, see Gassendi, *Mirrour of True Nobility*, bk. 6, 176. For the importance of conversation for one of Europe's great letter writers, see Peiresc to Holstenius, 29 January 1629, *Lettres de Peiresc*, vol. 5, 303: "Mais il est malaisé de bien exprimer ses conceptions par la seule escritture; il y fault la veue et communication de preseance."

18. These include a long document that seems to provide an overview of books and ideas they discussed (BN, MS. Lat. 9340, fols. 290–91), and another that refers only to Samaritan coins (fol. 106). In addition to these, there are eight other documents, some of which contain only a sentence and others an entire page of text, that seem to be more detailed (fols. 22, 23, 26, 27, 28, 29, 31, 32). These have writing by Azubi in Hebrew and Peiresc in French and seem to have been produced as working papers in the course of conversation.

19. BN, MS. Lat. 9340, fol. 106. The coins mentioned here are illustrated by one "Bonard" in "Hebraeorum Numismata Argentea et Aerea Antiqua. A Nic. Fabricio D. De Petrisco Passim Observata et Coquista" (BN, MS. Dupuy 667, fols. 133–34).

20. Azubi to Peiresc, 17 December 1632, *Les Correspondants de Peiresc*, vol. 1, 643.

21. Gassendi noted that he studied Hebrew and Samaritan with a rabbi in Padua in 1601 in order "to interpret the inscriptions of shekels, and other such like pieces." Gassendi, *Mirrour of True Nobility*, year 1601, 42.

22. See BN, MS. Lat. 9340 fols. 13, 16, 17, 18, 19. The latter pages actually reproduce the inscriptions in Peiresc's hand along with his drawings of the reverse. Is this the same "Juif de Padoue" whose object "escripte en l[et]tres hieroglifiques" Peiresc copied out? BN, MS. F. Fr. 9530, fol. 259.

23. So did his desire to serve Scaliger, especially in regard to the recovery of the Samaritans' letters to him that had gone astray in 1590. The Samaritans remained linked to Scaliger even after his death in 1609. See the fascinating document discussed by J. G. Fraser and dated to 1613–16 ("A Prelude to the Samaritan Pentateuch Texts of the Paris Polyglot Bible," in *A Word in Season: Essays in Honour of William MacKane*, ed. James D. Martin and Philip R. Davies [Sheffield, Eng.: JSOT, 1986], 223–47).

24. On Peiresc's oriental studies, see the author's "A philologist, a traveler and an antiquary rediscover the Samaritans in seventeenth-century Paris, Rome, and Aix: Jean Morin, Pietro della Valle, and N.-C. Fabri de Peiresc," in *Gelehrsamkeit als Praxis: Arbeitsweisen, Funktionen, Grenzbereiche*, ed. Helmut Zedelmaier (Tübingen, Ger.: Max Niemeyer Verlag, 2001); "The antiquary's art of comparison: Peiresc and *Abraxas*," in *Zu Begriff und problem der philologie (ca. 1580 bis ca. 1730)*, ed. Ralph Häfner (Tübingen, Ger.: Max Niemeyer Verlag, 2001); and more generally, Aufrère, *La Momie et la Tempête*.

25. Peiresc to Morin, 8 November 1632, *Antiquitates Ecclesiae Orientalis*, [ed. R. Simon] (London, 1682), 179–92.

26. The original is BN, Sam. 11; Peiresc's copies in the three languages are in MS. Lat. 9340, fols. 95–103 and, in a secretary's hand in Latin only, in Car Bibl. Inguimbertine, MS. 1831, fols.151–55. According to Jean-Pierre Rothschild, *Catalogue des manuscrits Samaritains* (Paris: Bibliothèque nationale, Départment des manuscrits, 1985), 12. Of the two Latin letters in MS. Lat. 9340, the first is in the hand of the annotator of Peiresc's Samaritan manuscript and the second in Peiresc's own.

27. The comparison is at BN, MS. Lat. 9340, fols. 70–75, and the letter follows at fol. 76.

28. Their itinerary, from the time of their recovery in Marseilles until they reached Peiresc, was recorded by him on a piece of scrap paper: BN MS. Lat. 9340, fols. 93r–v, reproduced in *Peiresc's Europe*, figs. 9a, b.

29. "J'ay veu la version que le Morin a faicte des Epistres des Samaritains à feu Mr della Scala et y ay trouvé quelque difference d'une aultre version qui en avoit esté faicte à Beaugentier, mais ce n'est pas en chose de bien grande importance et qui ne

soit aussy bonne à prendre d'une façon que d'aultre, le remerciant bien humblement de la communication de la sienne, et par mesme moyen vous, Monsieur, qui avez daigné prendre la peine de la transcripre, done je vous suis bien redevable." Peiresc to Dupuy, 28 November 1632, *Lettres de Peiresc*, vol. 2, 382. Morin's version might have reached Peiresc on 19 November with the letter of Dupuy's to which this is a response.

30. "Pendant cet exercise laborieux, la peste affligeait la Provence: ce qui obligea Monsieur de Chasteuil de se retirer à Baugency, chez le célèbre Monssieur de Peiresc, son bon ami. C'est dans ce temps là qu'il fit ses Observations sur le Pentateuque Samaritain, nouvellement apporté du Levant, et présenté à Monsieur de Peiresc, par le père Théophile Minuti, religieux minime. Ces Observations furent depuis envoyées, avec le texte Samaritain, à Gabriel Sionite, savant maronite, professeur en arabe au Collège Royal, pour être insérées dans la Grande Bible Polyglotte, que l'on imprimait alors à Paris." Marchety, *Abregé de la vie de Monsieur de Chasteuil, Solitaire du Mont Liban*, in Jean de la Roque, *Voyage de Syrie et du Mont-Liban* (Beirut: Dar Lahad Khater, 1981), 164.

31. The handwriting of the Hebrew version of the Samaritan letters (BN MS. Lat. 9340, fols. 95–97) exactly matches that of Azubi in Fr. 9531 fols. 48–51. As for circumstantial evidence, the memorandum labeled "R. SALOMON AZUBY. Nov. 1632" is inserted by Peiresc immediately following the Samaritan letters at folio 106.

32. There remains the difficulty of place: Azubi visited Peiresc in Aix, where he lived during sessions of the Parlement, but Peiresc referred to a translation made at Belgentier, where he spent the holidays and summer recess.

33. BN, MS. Lat. 9340, fols. 290–91.

34. BN, MS. Lat. 9340, fol. 286r, no. 4

35. BN, MS. Lat. 9340, fols. 281–83 and 284–85. Both were published by Rothschild in "Deux Bibliothèques juives comtadins vers 1630."

36. "Et particulierement de ceux qui n'avoient *pas de pieds*. Pour tenir le prebstre en soing de le remuer de peur que le sang ne se figeast ou gelast, afin qu'il se maintinast [chec] liquide pur le pouvoir verser sur l'autel." BN, MS. Lat. 9340, fol. 290r.

37. "Il fault voir, ce qu'ils disent pareillement que chascune parole de la bible se peult entendre en 70 ou 72 façons differantes." BN, MS. Lat. 9340, fol. 290v.

38. For discussion, see Ingo Herklotz, *Cassiano dal Pozzo und die Archäologie des 17. Jahrhunderts* (Munich: Hirmer, 1999), 52–53.

39. It is not likely that they were sent after the fact by Azubi and then annotated by Peiresc because there is no mention in Azubi's letters of sending these sorts of documents.

40. Gassendi, *Mirrour of True Nobility*, year 1632, 75–76. On this, see Miller, "Peiresc in Africa: Arm-Chair Anthropology in the Early Seventeenth Century," in *Les premiers siècles de la république européenne des lettres, 1368–1638*, ed. M. Fumaroli (Paris, forthcoming).

41. BN, MS. Lat. 9340, fol. 32v. The first part of this note, describing the content, layout, date, and place of publication of the Constantinople Hebrew Polyglot reappears almost verbatim, in the postscript of Peiresc's letter to Pierre and Jacques Dupuy of 15 November 1632, suggesting a firm terminus ad quem for at least this particular discussion with Azubi, whose visit goes unmentioned in Peiresc's letter to the Dupuy brothers (*Lettres de Peiresc*, vol. 2, 370–71). For more on the Constantinople Polyglots, see Lorenzo Amigo Espada, "Una aproximación al Pentateuco de Constantinopla (1547)," *Estudios biblico* 48 (1990): 81–111; Joseph Hacker, "Printing at Constantinople in the Sixteenth Century" (Hebrew), *Areshet* 5 (1972): 457–93.

42. "J'oublois de vous dire que j'ay receu de Constantinoble le livre en hebreu dont on m'avoit accusé l'expedition, et avons trouvé que ce n'estoit qu'un Pentateuque des Juifs en forme de Tetraple, contenant le texte hebraïque assemblé par colonnes avec la paraphrase caldaïque de Onkelos et la version en langue persienne faicte par Rabi Jacob Tanos, ensemble la version arabique de Rabi Saadia Gueon mise en teste de la page et l'explication du texte hebraïque par Rabi Salomon Jarki mis au fondz de la page, le tout imprimé l'an 5306 en la maison de Eliezer de Soncin qui estoit en Constantinoble bien que ceste ville n'y soit pas nommé." Peiresc to Dupuy, 15 November 1632, *Lettres de Peiresc*, vol. 2, 370.

43. "La traditive sans autheur cherche le nombre de Septante dans le mot *heitev*. Le Talmud dit que la Loy a Septante faces ou interpretations differantes que s'en peuvent faire." BN, MS. Lat. 9340, fol. 31v.

44. "Presuppose qu'elle aye un mouvement circulaire a l'entour de ses axes, ou poles, ou bases, ou colomnes, ou mortiers." BN, MS. F.Fr. 9531, fol. 91r.

45. "A Dieu ne plaise que l'oubly aye ce pouvoir sur moy de me faire passer de la memoyre l'honneur et les faveurs que sans mérite mien, vostre courtoisie a prodigué en moy, dans vostre maison à Aix," Azubi to Peiresc, 17 December 1632, *Les Correspondants de Peiresc*, 643. A document that has the appearance of homework, rather than face-to-face collaboration, is a digest, in Azubi's Hebrew hand, of citations from the Bible in the thirteenth-century Catalan *Breviari d'Amor*, by Matfredi Ermengaudi (BN, MS. Lat. 9340, fol. 5).

46. BN, MS. F.Fr. 9531 fols. 48–51 is translated at folios 32–42. Peiresc identifies the text as follows: "Des expositions de Raby Emanuel filz de Jacob sur les Aisles ou Talbes Astronomiques concernant les Ecclypses solaires et Lunaires. Par Raby Salomon Azuby (de Sophia en ~~Alban~~Romanie) en y appliquant la supputation des Ecclypses tant lunaire que Solaire arrivez touts deux en l'an 393 du sixiesme millesme de la Creation" (Peiresc adds: "Qui est de Christ 1633").

47. For basic facts, see "Bonfils, Immanuel ben Jacob," vol. 4 of *Encyclopedia Judaica* (Jerusalem: Keter Publishing House, 1972), 1207.

48. Peiresc to Gassendi, 24 July 1633, *Lettres de Peiresc*, vol. 4, 330–31.

49. Azubi to Peiresc, 17 December 1632, *Les Correspondants de Peiresc*, 645.

50. The *Shalshelet Ha-Kabbalah*, mistakenly attributed to Rabbi Abraham Bar-David (in fact, written by Gedaliah b. Yosef Iahia), the *She'rit Yosef* of R. Josef b. Verga, and the *Sodot kol Ot ve'Ot* (Azubi refers to the *Otiot Rabbi Akiva*).

51. "Toutz mes desirs, ne sont qu'a rechercher quelque nouveau libvre ou chose rare et curieuse pour vous en faire part et employer mon estude pour vous donner quelque contentment." Azubi to Peiresc, 3 January 1633, *Les Correspondants de Peiresc*, 645–47.

52. "Il y a en ceste ville un de mes amis qui estant informe de vostre curieux desir a faict recherches en ce pais pour semblables galanteries." Azubi to Peiresc, 9 March 1633, *Les Correspondants de Peiresc*, 647–49.

53. Peiresc to Gassendi, 10 July 1633, *Lettres de Peiresc*, vol. 4, 324.

54. BN, MS. F.Fr. 9531, fol. 2r.

55. BN, MS. F.Fr. 9531, fols. 32–41; the Hebrew original follows at folios 48–51.

56. "Ces deux comparaisons & exemples d'Eclipse de lune & de soleil suffiront pour se pouvoir chascun servir des *Tables, des Aisles* [underscoring Peiresc's], pour trouver toutes Eclipses luneres & soleres en quelle année que ce soit." BN, MS. F.Fr. 9531, fol. 41v.

57. Gassendi, *Mirrour of True Nobility*, year 1600, 146; year 1612, 156; year 1628, 26; year 1635, 132.

58. Peiresc to Gassendi, 24 July 1633, *Lettres de Peiresc*, vol. 4, 330–31.

59. "Il a alteré la première page des dites tables, pour les rapporter à nostre temps, plus tost que de la laisser comme l'autheur l'avoit escrite en la rapportant à son temps." Gassendi to Peiresc, 28 December 1633, *Lettres de Peiresc*, vol. 4, 403.

60. "Pour les tables de R. Manuel, j'avoys desjà faict les reproches dont vous vous plaignez au bon R. Salomon Azuby, lequel m'advoua qu'en la transcription premiere qu'il fit faire, il avoit faict de bonne foy cette alteration comme font toutz noz imprimeurs de breviaires quand ils raffraichissent les Tables que se mettent en teste pour regler le kalendrier, mais j'ay l'original sur lequel il n'y a point d'alteration, qui monstre d'estre escrit depuis quelques centaines d'années." Peiresc to Gassendi, 5 January 1634, *Lettres de Peiresc*, vol. 4, 411. A month or so later Peiresc forwarded to Gassendi Azubi's original text (Peiresc to Gassendi, 22 February 1634, vol. 4, 462). For Peiresc's own argument against "modernization," see Peiresc to Alvares, 28 November 1633, *Lettres de Peiresc*, vol. 7, 33.

61. Peiresc to Gassendi, 20 December 1633, *Lettres de Peiresc*, vol. 4, 395.

62. I discuss the relationship between Peiresc and Kircher in "Kircher, Peiresc, and the Foundation of Coptic Studies; Or, the Quest for Barachias Nephi," in *Athanasius Kircher*, ed. Paula Findlen (London: Routledge, 2003).

63. Dukas, "Notice Complementaire," 19.

64. Azubi to Kircher, undated, Rome, Pontifical Gregorian University, APUG 568 fols. 277r–v, 276av. The letters from Azubi to Kircher and from Peiresc to Kircher are cited from "The Correspondence of Athanasius Kircher: The World of a Seventeenth-Century Jesuit," *http://150.217.52.68/kircher/index.html*.

65. Azubi to Kircher, 3 April 1633, Rome, Pontifical Gregorian University, APUG 568 fol. 279r.

66. "Cependain vous recevrez la responce du pavure R. Salomon Azuby à vostre papier, Il est fort vostre serviteur, et s'eu retourné chez luy à Carpentras." Peiresc to Kircher, 3 August 1633, Rome, Pontifical Gregorian University, APUG 568 fol. 371v.

67. Azubi to Kircher, Rome, Pontifical Gregorian University, APUG 568 fol. 298r:

[To] the precious spirit and man of wisdom. Learning and science is his portion. The wise and learned Father Athanasius: The Lord and Senator, the councillor de Peiresh, showed me the arguments that you sent to him to show to me on the true difference that is between the Christians and the Jews. And since you did not write to me it was not expected that I should write you, except to satisfy the will of the Lord de Peiresh and to fulfill his commandment have I written to you this letter. In short: and I say that you know already that we are oppressed beneath the hand of the Christians and we do not have the right to speak on the matter of faith what is in our hearts, and that our words are built on the foundation of truth and justice. Therefore, my Lord, this I ask of you, that you ask permission for me from the Lord of the place, the vice-legate, or from the Lord inquirer, that is, the Inquisitor, that we be given the permission to answer your words. And then you will see that you were not right. I will answer you and show you the many errors in your words in what you relate to us and our faith. And I have already shown some of them to the Lord de Peiresh. And without this permission I cannot answer you in writing on your arguments even if all or most of them are far from the truth. Therefore, try to obtain the permission mentioned above, and you will hear a thorough answer to your words—things that you never heard in your life. Things good and sweet. And with this I will bring my words to an end with a prayer to God to raise you up on the wings of heavenly victories as you desire and as desire those who love you. Solomon Azubi the Sepharadi. Written in Aix, the day 21 Juillet in the year 1633 to their way of counting.

68. "*Ad literas* porro *Rabbi Salomonis* quod attinet, nescio quid in iis inhumanitatis, contumaciae, & manifestae superbiae, uno verbo *Signa Judaici ingenii, & durae Cervicis* deprehenderim. Verum omittere non potui quin eas ex hebraeo in Latinum translatas vobis transmitterem, ut D.V. aspiciat coram perversitatem ingenii Judaici, ut dum ad eorum bonum laboramus, ut convertantur et vivant. Uti magis, ex insita quadam virulentia, in sanctam legem nostram pervertantur. plura non scribo. D.V. facile ex literis eius superbiam deprehendet." Kircher to Peiresc, 9 August 1633, BN, MS. F.Fr. 9531, fol. 214v). Underlining is Peiresc's. This letter was for filing purposes labeled by Peiresc "de GALILEI ABIURATIONE" and, below, "de SALMONE AZUBIO." Note that the original of Kircher's letter (BN, MS. F.Fr. 9538 fol. 228) omits any mention of Azubi in its filing titles, nor are these passages underlined.

69.

Pour le regard du S.r Salomon Azuby, j'avoys bien decrivé q[ue] la rudesse de son style p[ro]cedoit aultant et plus de la Barberie et rusticite du lieux de sa naissance, et de la difficulte d'exprimer ses conceptions, et de traduire v[ost]re langage au sien, q[ue] d'autre chose. Et de faict, com[m]e je luy evay faict reproche, il en est desplaisant à la mort, n'ayant jamais pensé à vous tenir aucune p[ro]pos qui vous peusse fascher. À ce qu'il m'eu escript, et voudroit avoir baille de son sang, p[our] d'achepter l'original de sa l[ett]re, p[our] fascher d'en adouscir le style, et le moderer le plus qu'il luy seroit possible. Ayant affecté certaines locutions tenües p[our] plus elegantes, en sa langue sans considerer, qu'elles pouvoient estre prises en mauvaise part, estant dictes trop crüent, com[m]'il a faict. Car je l'ay esprouvé de si bon naturel en toute au[ltr]e chose et si modeste, q[ue] j'ay bien de la peine à croire qu'il ayt eu de mauvaise intention. C'est la vente qu'avant q[ue] vous escrire il me dict les difficultezs qu'il avoit trouvees en v[ost]re escripte. Sur ce q[ue] les Chrestiens se p[er]suadent, disoit il, qu'ils tiennent et broyent des choses fort absurdes, qu'ils ne tiennent nullem[en]t, de sorte qu'en vain on se mettoit en peine, de les desmouvoir de telle croyance, puis q[ue] c'estoit chose bien elognee d'icelle. Et q[ue] en plusieurs articles on faisoit equivoque, et qu'on interp[re]toit leur advis, tant au q[uon]traire du seux qu'ils luy donnoient. C'est p[our]quoy il demandoit p[er]mission, p[our] vous pouvoir, rendre article par article les responces de leurs autheurs. Or com[m]e les termes, d'absurdité et d'imposture, des articles de croyance, qu'ils ne sont pas d'accord de croire, peuvent estre relatifs, non seulem[en]t à ceux qui en sont les premiers autheurs, mais aussy à ceux qui leur en sont encores aujourd huy la guerre com[m]e vous faisiez, je crains q[ue] n'ayant person bien distinguer com[me] il devuoit v[ost]re p[er]sone, de celle des autheurs, de telles choses qu'on leur impute com[m]'absurdes, et qu'ils tiennent eux mesmes tres absurdes. C'aura esté ce qui vous aura faict prendre en mauvaise part son discours, mais p[our] v[ost]re satisfaction, ie l'envoyeray guere quand vous seray icy, et m'asseure q[ue] vous demeurerez mieux edifié de son p[ro]cede q[ue] vous ne croyez. Et p[er] cet affect je vous suppliè d'apporter quant et vous l'original de sa l[ett]re, et je luy manderay qu'il apporte l'original de v[ost]re escripte.

Peiresc to Kircher, 17 August 1633, Rome, Pontifical Gregorian University, APUG 568, fol. 198v–199r. I am grateful to Nick Wilding for making available to me his transcriptions of Peiresc's letters to Kircher.

70. For example, Gassendi, *Mirrour of True Nobility*, year 1599, 21; year 1601, 38; year 1602, 67, 73; year 1618, 187; year 1621, 205.

71. Azubi to Peiresc, 2 September 1633, *Les Correspondants de Peiresc*, 649–50.

72. "Je ne suis pas estre encore en Avignon pour prendre les libvres que m'avez donné charger attendant le libraire Sr Roy qui m'a promis de venir sabmedy ou diman-

che prochain, et j'iray avec luy." Azubi to Peiresc, 5 May 1634, BN, MS. F.Fr. 9531, fol. 46r.

73. Adrian Johns, *The Nature of the Book: Print and Knowledge in the Making* (Chicago: University of Chicago Press, 1998). On the role of servants, see Steven Shapin, *The Social History of Truth: Civility and Science in Seventeenth-Century England* (Chicago: University of Chicago Press, 1994), ch. 8. Peiresc to Thomas d'Arcos, 30 May 1636, *Lettres de Peiresc*, vol. 7, 180.

74. Azubi to Peiresc, 7 August 1634, BN, MS. F.Fr. 9531, fol. 42r–42v. The bulk of the letter contained a detailed discussion of the preface of Rabbi Manuel; in conclusion Azuby sought Peiresc's help in acquiring a book of Joseph del Medigo's recently published in Amsterdam, perhaps referring to the astronomical work *Sefer Elim* (1629).

75. "Je ne faudray pour vous servir aller depart en Avignon lundy prochain pour servir." Azubi to Peiresc, 20 August 1634, BN, MS. F.Fr. 9531, fol. 44r–v.

76. "Et cependant que je regardois ce tombeau, plusieurs paisans s'assemblèrent pour s'informer de ma curiosité." Azubi to Peiresc, 5 June 1635, *Les Correspondants de Peiresc*, 651–53.

77. "Noms des p[at]riarches anciens d'ou est fix la genealogie de Mohamet dans le livre Arabe-Samaritain in 4.º M.S. extraicts du Samaritain entrelassé dans le texte Arab dudit volume par le Raby Salomon Azubi le 13.Februar.1636, à Aix." BN, MS. Lat. 9340, fol. 170r. The verso contains the Hebrew translation in Azubi's Sephardic hand.

78. Peiresc to Saumaise, 22 July 1636, *Lettres à Claude Saumaise:* "J'attends de jour à autre le passage de Raby Salomon Azubi, qui alla dernierement de Carpentras en Piemont et me promit de repasser par icy." Peiresc to Paul Du May, 20 August 1636, *Lettres à Claude Saumaise*, 311: "J'attans tousjours le Rabby Salomon Azui pour vostre service."

79. Daniel Droixhe, "La Crise de l'Hebreu langue-mère au XVIIᵉ siècle," in *La République des lettres et l'histoire du Judaïsme antique XVIᵉ–XVIIᵉ siècles*, ed. Chantal Grell and François Laplanche (Paris: Presses de l'Université de Paris-Sorbonne, 1992), 66–99; and this author's "The 'Antiquarianization' of Biblical Scholarship and the London Polyglot Bible, 1653–57," *Journal of the History of Ideas* 63 (2001): 463–82. See also U. Eco, *The Search for the Perfect Language*, trans. J. Fentress (London: Blackwell, 1995); and M. Olender, *Les langues du paradis: Aryens et sémites, un couple providentiel* (Paris: Gallimard, 1989).

80. See my *Peiresc's Europe*, 143–46.

81. "À cause que les Chrestiens n'y sont tenus en guiere de respect, et casez comme les Juifs sont casez parmy nous aux lieux, où l'on les souffre." Peiresc to Mersenne, 1 May 1634, *Mersenne Correspondance*, vol. 4, 108.

82. "Je luy offrisse un de noz chevaulx et un guide et de le desfrayer." Peiresc to Gassendi, 10 July 1633, *Lettres de Peiresc*, vol. 4, 324.

83. "Ce pauvre bon homme a tant d'envie de vous voir que je suis aprez à le faire resoudre d'aller en voz quartiers [in Digne], et luy bailleray un de noz chevaux, affin qu'il aille demeurer deux ou trois jours avec vous pour apprendre quelque chose en cette matiere." Peiresc to Gassendi, 24 July 1633, *Lettres de Peiresc*, vol. 4, 330–31.

84. "Le bon R. Salomon Azubi s'est retiré chez luy, sans avoir courage de vous aller voir." Peiresc to Gassendi, 31 July 1633, *Lettres de Peiresc*, vol. 4, 335. Perhaps courage was, indeed, the appropriate word.

5

John Selden's De Jure Naturali . . . Juxta Disciplinam Ebraeorum *and Religious Toleration*

Jason P. Rosenblatt

Selden and Rabbinic Scholarship

In 1753, during the most intense phase of the controversy surrounding the Jewish Naturalization Act, or Jew Bill, the English printer William Bowyer responded with measured remarks to a speech made in Common Council against the bill. The adversary's principal argument had been that to "collect the Jews together" would both falsify Christian prophecy, which requires that they be "dispersed and scattered," and verify Jewish prophecies of restoration.[1] Bowyer's argument in favor of the bill is consistently humane. Where his adversary repeated the accusation that divine providence requires permanent Jewish exile, Bowyer argues instead that only providence can account for Jewish survival: "Their *preservation* through so many ages, notwithstanding their various changes and unsettled state, is what discovers the particular guidance of Heaven":

Without a singular Providence, a people disunited, and divided into an infinite number of distinct families, banished into countries whose language and customs were different from theirs, must have been mingled and confounded with other nations, and all traces of them must, these many ages, have entirely disappeared. In spite of the general aversion conceived against them, in spite of the efforts of all those nations who hate them, and who have them in their power, in spite of every human obstacle, they are preserved by a supernatural protection, which has not in like manner preserved any other nation of the earth.[2]

Bowyer ridicules his opponent's fears that Christian prophecy will be disconfirmed: "What! to collect them all into England, and then to transplant them to Jerusalem! Not a hundred probably will be naturalized in ten years; and before we shall make a nation of them, we may trust that the 'Times of the

Gentiles may be fulfilled.'"³ In fact, Bowyer insists on the harmony of the Jewish and Christian prophecies: "Now I always apprehended the Jewish Prophecies are the very same in which the Christians believe; and if the latter have any which the former reject, I hope they are in no particular inconsistent."[4] As if to demonstrate this harmony, Bowyer cites in the same breath "Origen, Chrysostom, and Seder Olam," who share the same opinion regarding the restoration of the Jews.[5] Bowyer's perplexingly casual use of an obscure, midrashic, chronological work of the second century as if it were as well known as the writings of the church fathers resembles the similar and frequent use of the same work by John Selden, particularly in his study of rabbinic methods of chronological calculation, *De Anno Civili et Calendario Veteris Ecclesiae seu Reipublicae Judaicae* (1644). It turns out that Bowyer, the most learned English printer of his age, was very familiar with the writings of Selden (1584–1654), the most learned Englishman of his age. He wrote an epitome of Selden's study of the Sanhedrin, *De Synedriis Veterum Hebraeorum*, and that as well as "other memoranda from that learned Writer, were the result of his superintendence of the complete edition of Selden's works in his press, 1722–1726."[6]

Being aware of Bowyer's role as printer of the still-definitive *Joannis Seldeni Opera Omnia* (1726), edited by David Wilkins, helps explain certain characteristics of the little tract: investing with equal authority ancient Christian and postbiblical, rabbinic Hebrew sources; according respect to historical documents in a style identical to Selden's (as in a reference to the hospital founded in London for such Jews as should convert: "Temp. Henry II. which is now the Office of the Rolls"); even concluding, as Selden often does, with the very same signature figure of passing over with a deprecating ring that the rhetoricians call *praeteritio*: "I meddle not with the political reasons for or against this Bill: my design was only to shew, that Christianity is no ways affected by it."[7] Bowyer, like Selden, displays liberal worldly wisdom.

Acting on the belief that the stories we tell about others reveal even more about ourselves, recent and justly well-regarded studies of England and the Jews, during a period that includes Selden's lifetime, have demonstrated that a culture's representation of "otherness" has important consequences for its own self-imagining.[8] The often vile racist stereotypes unearthed by James Shapiro in *Shakespeare and the Jews* can only have meaning if our fantasies about others reveal our deepest fears about ourselves. The fear and loathing of Jews as child abductors, murderers, and cannibals can help explain the confused struggles among the English in the early modern era to develop a religious and national identity in a turbulent time. Judaism as a race, nation, and religion is defined as different in every way from the English Protestantism that it threatens to contaminate.

Inevitably, Shapiro's exhaustive and valuable attempt to reconstruct a

Renaissance audience's experience of *The Merchant of Venice* in the light of its preconceptions about Jews involves recourse to the most destructive myths and stereotypes. He acknowledges but understandably does not concentrate on an exception such as John Selden, whose rabbinic researches, unlike those of his other great contemporary, English talmudic scholar John Lightfoot, are free of Judeophobia.[9] One might argue that Selden is precious precisely because he is uncommon, like the courageous few who throughout history have refused to be swallowed up by the mob. Generally skeptical toward harmful myths, Selden has a humanist's respect for historical investigation and an antiquarian's interest in the documents of the past simply because they exist.[10] A polymath, he wrote a half dozen rabbinic works, some of them immense, which respect, to an extent remarkable for the times, the self-understanding of Judaic exegesis. *De Diis Syris* (1617), an analysis of the pagan gods of the Hebrew Bible, is a pioneering study of cultural anthropology and comparative religion. Its literary influence extends to the work of Ben Jonson and to the list of pagan gods in John Milton's *Ode on the Morning of Christ's Nativity* and book 1 of *Paradise Lost*.[11] *De Successionibus ad Leges Ebraeorum in Bona Defunctorum* (1631) addresses the question of intestate succession according to Jewish law. *De Successione in Pontificatum Ebraeorum* (1638) explores the laws relating to the ancient Jewish priesthood. *Uxor Ebraica* (1646) analyzes the theory and practice of the Jewish laws of marriage and divorce, which Selden admired. On the very last page he suggests parenthetically (because it was a point of honor for him to bury the dead) that the canon law of divorce still in force in England be reformed and brought more closely into conformity with Jewish law. Selden's motto was *peri pantos ten eleutherian* [liberty above all things], and *De Synedriis et Praefecturis Juridicis Veterum Ebraeorum* (1650–55), a study of the Sanhedrin written shortly after the execution of Charles I, contains a remarkable Maimonidean discussion of whether that court could try kings not only for crimes like murder that anyone could commit but also for those that only kings could commit. Occupying 1,132 huge folio columns in the *Opera*, *De Synedriis* deals primarily with the constitution of Jewish courts, including the Sanhedrin, which, as Selden notes pointedly, was not priestly in composition. Its understated argument is thoroughly Erastian, demonstrating that matters at present under the jurisdiction of ecclesiastical courts in England were in ancient times decided by Jewish courts that could well be called secular.[12] The implicit argument is that the Sanhedrin might serve as a positive model for Parliament. Taken together, these rabbinic works constitute a notable exception to those products of the English Renaissance that emphasize otherness and difference.

Selden's important contribution to political theory and international law, *De Jure Naturali et Gentium juxta Disciplinam Ebraeorum* (1640), 847 folio pages, is surely one of the most genuinely philosemitic works produced by a Christian Hebraist in early modern Europe. Selden accepts the universal validity of the nonbiblical, rabbinic *praecepta Noachidarum*, the seven Noachide laws, which serve for him as the law of nature. Selden bases his theory on the Talmud, which he believes records a set of doctrines far older than classical antiquity.[13] Natural law consists not of innate rational principles that are intuitively obvious but rather of specific divine pronouncements uttered by God at a point in historical time. Selden discusses the rabbinic identification of natural law with the divinely pronounced Adamic and Noachide laws, considered by rabbinic tradition as the minimal moral duties enjoined upon all of humankind. He quotes from the *locus classicus* in tractate Sanhedrin (56a–b), which includes the traditional enumeration of the laws: prohibitions of idolatry and blasphemy; injunction to establish a legal system; commandments against bloodshed, sexual sins, and theft; and a seventh law, not applicable to vegetarian Adam but added after the flood and based on Genesis 9:4, forbidding anyone to eat flesh cut from a living animal. Selden devotes an entire book of *De Jure* to each of the seven commandments, and he follows the order set by Maimonides, which emphasizes their decalogic nature. The first two, like the first table of the law, deal with the relations between human beings and God while the rest govern relations among human beings.[14] While Selden accepts the authority of this postbiblical, rabbinic, universal law, he rejects the absolute authority of the biblical ten commandments on the grounds that they were given only to the Jews.

In *De Jure* Selden sets down ideas regarding the nature of Judaism and its attitude toward gentiles that are far more charitable than those circulating in other contemporary works addressed to Christian audiences. Selden did not live to see Cromwell's Whitehall Conference, and one can never be certain that his reverence for ancient Jewish learning and toleration of contemporary Jews would have extended so far as activity on behalf of readmission. Since Menasseh Ben Israel first set foot in England in 1655, a year after Selden's death, one can assert that during Selden's lifetime no exponent of Judaism in England with a body of published scholarship equaled him in talmudic learning. Indeed, theology rather than rabbinic law was Menasseh's forte, so Selden, had he lived, might not have yielded to one whose writings he knew well and cited frequently. That would make Selden the supreme *parshan*, or interpreter, by default. England, after all, unlike some other European countries its size, never produced a great medieval or early modern rabbinic sage, a fact related to the expulsion of the Jews under Edward I in 1290.

The double vision explicit in the term *Christian Hebraism* signals the topic's profound ambivalence and inevitably raises questions of displacement and appropriation. The royalist poet John Cleveland epitomizes the problem in

The Mixt Assembly. The chief satirist of the parliamentary cause portrays the mixed membership of the Westminster Assembly, clergy and lay, as a grotesque mismatch:

Like Jewes and Christians in a ship together,
With an old Neck-verse to distinguish either. (45–46)[15]

The beginning of Psalm 51 that could save the neck of a condemned person claiming benefit of clergy was in black-letter Latin. For Cleveland, the biblical text distinguishes the Christian, who can save himself by his identity and his proficiency, from the Jew. The irony that *Sefer Tehillim* was written in Hebrew by a Jew is lost on him.

The central figure of the poem is the Westminster Assembly itself, portrayed as a giddy "Antick dance" (67), forcing enemies to be partners so that "every *Gibelline* hath got his *Guelph*" (87):

But *Selden*, hee's a Galliard by himself,
And well may be; there's more divines in him
Then in all this their Jewish *Sanhedrim*. (88–90)

Selden, the only person who escapes unequivocal censure in this angry poem, is a galliard, "a man of courage and spirit" (OED, which quotes line 88). Because of his unmatchable greatness, no partner can be found for him, especially from an assembly such as this one. He is his own man, one who includes dancer, dance, and music: galliard is also "a quick and lively dance in triple time" as well as "the air to which the galliard is danced" (OED). A lay member of the assembly, Selden is worth more than all the Anglican and Presbyterian divines who compose the clerical membership put together. Cleveland praises Selden's authentic scholarship, which, during the years that the assembly convened, consisted almost entirely of rabbinica, and alludes perhaps to the forthcoming magisterial *De Synedriis*, a study of the *Synedrium Magnum* whose seventy-one members make up a civil court that Selden holds up as a model for Parliament. Admiring the scholarship but deploring its subject, Cleveland sneeringly brands as Jewish the assembly that he hates almost as much as he does the Parliament whose ordinance created it. Cleveland's praise of Selden as one who contains many—and as one whose authentic Jewish learning exposes the folly of a body reviled for its resemblance to a Jewish institution—underscores the conflicting tonalities of Christian Hebraism.

If Christians in early modern England are at best ambivalent toward Jews, it should be noted that the Talmud is neither monolithic nor consistent in its attitude toward non-Jews—not surprising when one considers that the category is large enough to include the universal progenitors Adam and Noah and the Roman oppressors who destroyed the second temple. Selden's talmudic scholarship reflects the profound ambivalence of its sources. In *De Jure Naturali* he asserts that the righteous among the gentiles enjoy a share or portion of the world to come (*"Piis ex Gentibus Mundi pars seu sors est in futuro seculo"*), and the range of authorities he cites in support of this view includes the Talmud itself, which is the primary source, as well as his favorite commentary on the Talmud, Maimonides, and his own contemporary, Menasseh Ben Israel.[16] His learning is so wide ranging that he can find two places in Maimonides that define the crucial term in the talmudic passage, "the righteous among the gentiles—lit., 'the nations of the world'":

Whoever accepts upon himself the fulfillment of these seven precepts and is precise in their observance is called one of the righteous among the gentiles and will merit a share in the world to come. This applies only when one accepts them and fulfills them because the holy one, blessed be he, commanded them and informed us through Moses our teacher that they were commanded from of old to the children of Noah. But if one decides to perform them as a result of personal preference rather than because God commanded them, then such a person is not a proselyte of the dwelling-place [i.e., a partial proselyte, who renounces idolatry for the sake of acquiring limited citizenship], nor of the righteous among the gentiles, nor of their wise persons.[17]

Omitted are most of Selden's gap fillings, definitions, paraphrases, synonyms, pronominal identifications, and other clarifications that are present in virtually all of his translations of ancient texts. He can discriminate legally between the partial proselyte, or *ger toshav*, who makes a formal commitment in the presence of a court, and the righteous gentile who accepts the Noachide precepts with the proper intent but without formalizing the acceptance. He knows that when the Talmud deprives the corrupt generation living at the time of Noah's flood from either sharing in eternal life or standing in judgment (*"judicio"*), the reference is to the day of great judgment (*"diem Judicii Magnum"*).[18]

Selden is fully aware of talmudic dialogue and of opinions that either qualify or contradict one another. He knows the judgment of R. Meir that "even a pagan who conscientiously observes the law is considered to be equal to the high priest" (*"etiam Paganum qui diligenter legem observaverit veluti Pontificem maximum habendum"*) and the equally extreme reaction of R. Yohanan that "a non-Jew who engages in the study of Torah is liable for execution."[19] But Selden embeds the latter view only within tractate Sanhedrin's resolution of the contradiction in its chapter on the four methods of execution: the Talmud explains that R. Meir is referring to a non-Jew who studies the seven Noachide laws that non-Jews are obligated to observe. (He indeed is worthy of praise.) But a non-Jew who keeps the rest of the laws (as an Israelite, and with the authority of an Israelite, Selden adds) is condemned to death.[20]

In a prefatory statement in *De Jure* Selden appeals to biblical and talmudic precedent for publishing opposed points of view as a means of distinguishing more readily between truth and falsehood, with Proverbs 11:14 and 24:6 ("for in the multitude of counselors there is safety") as his central text: "*Et erit salus ubi multa consilia sunt,* seu ut in Ebraeo *u-t'shu'ah b'rov yo'etz & salus in plurimis consiliariis.*"[21] The talmudic penchant for including all opinions provides the subtext of Milton's praise of Selden and his *De Jure Naturali et Gentium* ("natural and national laws") in the *Areopagitica*. Addressing Parliament, Milton also employs this firmly established usage and points to Selden, M.P. for the University of Oxford, to authorize it: "Whereof what better witnes can ye expect I should produce, then one of your own now sitting in Parliament, the chief of learned men reputed in this Land, Mr. *Selden,* whose volume of naturall & national laws proves, not only by great autorities brought together, but by exquisite reasons and theorems almost mathematically demonstrative, that all opinions, yea errors, known, read, and collated, are of main service & assistance toward the speedy attainment of what is truest."[22] In conversation at table, during the last year of his life, Selden recalled how his own *History of Tithes* (1617), which aroused so much clerical vehemence by treating tithes as a matter of civil right rather than as due *jure divino,* was years later consulted by clerics looking to justify the institution: "a book so much cried down by them formerly (in which, I dare boldly say, there are more arguments for them than are extant together anywhere): upon this, one [Gerard Langbaine, Provost of Queen's College, Oxford] writ me word [in a letter dated 22 August 1653] that my history of tithes was now become like *Pelias hasta,* to wound and to heal."[23]

Selden may present opposing points of view, but it is usually not too difficult to deduce his own opinion. Regarding the Talmud's position on eternal life for righteous non-Jews, we are lucky to have a clear expression of Selden's opinion late in life as well as evidence regarding the one talmudic text, out of many on the subject, that he considered to be definitive. The *Dictionary of National Biography,* acknowledging Selden's enormous erudition and his genius for "direct, simple, and effective" conversation, describes his prose style in both Latin and English as digressive, prolix, and "embarrassed." To read Selden's scholarly prose is to recall Bizet's celebrated comment on Berlioz that he "had genius without talent."[24] Fortunately, his secretary, Richard Milward, transcribed his *Table Talk,* which, besides revealing an extraordinary talent for lucidly expressed analogy, presents his most characteristic opinions, mostly from the 1640s until the end of his life, including many of the ideas that are expressed more laboriously in *De Jure Naturali et Gentium.* The rabbinic foundation of many of those dinner-table conversations has never been recognized.

His simple comment on salvation is uncommon, perhaps unique in mid-seventeenth-century England, for its religious sympathy:

We may best understand the meaning of *t'shu'ah, salvation,* from the Jews, to whom the Saviour was promised. They held that themselves should have the chief place of happiness in the other world; but the gentiles that were good men, should likewise have their portion of bliss there too. Now by Christ the partition-wall is broken down, and the gentiles that believe in him, are admitted to the same place of bliss with the Jews. And why then should not that portion of happiness still remain to them who do not believe in Christ, so they be morally good. This is a charitable opinion.[25]

The source of this view is "Gemara Babylon. Ad tit. *Aboda Zara* cap. 1. Fol. 3a," which Selden cites numerous times.[26] In the relevant passage,

R. Meir used to say, "From where do we know that even a gentile who busies himself with Torah is equal to the high priest? It teaches, [*You shall keep my laws and rules*], *which if a man do, he shall live in them* [Leviticus 18:5]. It does not say 'Priests, Levites and Israelites' but rather 'man.' This teaches that even a gentile who busies himself with Torah is like a high priest." Rather [the Gemara answers], they do not receive a reward equal to one who is commanded and fulfills, but equal to one who is not commanded and fulfills. For R. Hanina said, "Greater is one who is commanded and fulfills than one who is not commanded and fulfills."

Clearly, Selden knows this text, with its counterintuitive distribution of greater rewards to one who is obliged over one who does good voluntarily. The idea underlying the passage is the contrast between the authority of the human will and the law of God. When a person acts in obedience to a Torah commandment, the merit is considered greater.

At least in *Table Talk*, as in *De Jure*, Selden views soteriology not through the lens of the prooftexts of Christian apologetics, in which Christ was given and sacrificed from the beginning of the world, but according to the Jews, whose rabbinic hermeneutic applied to Leviticus 18:5 promises eternal life ("*shall live*") to the ethical person who performs the Torah's "*laws and rules.*" The talmudic passage addresses the question of who inherits eternal life, and the answer applies not to the Israelite priest or Levite and not even to the Israelite layperson but rather to any human being (*ha' adam*). These are also the main elements of the Good Samaritan parable, perhaps the most beautiful in the entire New Testament, which, in the history of its interpretation, and despite its message of inclusiveness, raises disturbing questions about religious exclusivity, as does the complete text of *Avodah Zarah 3a*. The lawyer (*nomikos*) in Luke asks the question, "What shall I do to inherit eternal life?" (10:25). When Jesus responds with another question, "What is written in the law? How do you read?" (10:26), the lawyer answers with two commandments from the

Hebrew Bible: "You shall love the Lord your God" (Deut. 6:5) and "You shall love your neighbor as yourself" (Lev. 19:18). This time Jesus's response echoes Leviticus 18:5, the central text of the talmudic passage: "You have answered right; do this and live" (Luke 10:28). The lawyer provides the occasion for the parable by asking further, "And who is my neighbor?" (Luke 10:29), and Jesus answers with the story of the man who fell among thieves, was beaten, and left for dead. The audience, hearing that a priest and Levite pass by on the other side, expects the parable to be anticlerical and the third person to be an Israelite, but instead it is an outsider, a Samaritan, who binds the wounds, treats them with oil and wine, carries the half-dead man to the inn, leaves money with the innkeeper for further care, and promises to return.[27] The neighbor is no longer only an Israelite but includes anyone who shows mercy by loving another as himself.

Frank Kermode provides arcane and divergent readings of the parable from the church fathers as examples of "the interminability of interpretation." Certainly one of the interpretive constants in this parable of radical inclusiveness is a rejection of Judaism: "The priest and Levite represent the inefficacious old dispensation"; "the basic pattern—Christianity going on beyond the failure of Judaism."[28] To this very day, and not only among Christian sects that would consign Jews to hell, the parable is cited as an example of Jewish xenophobia and ethnocentrism. These interpreters point out that the neighbor one is commanded to love in Leviticus 19:18 is a fellow Jew while Jesus broadens the definition to include everyone. Of course the same chapter in Leviticus contains the command "Thou shalt love [the stranger] as thyself, for ye were strangers in the land of Egypt" (19:34).

Selden's attitude toward contemporary Jews is wittily tolerant, falling somewhat short of love: "Talk what you will of the Jews, that they are Cursed, they thrive where'er they come; they are able to oblige the Prince of their Country by lending him money; none of them beg; they keep together; and for their being hated, my life for yours, the Christians hate one another as much."[29] Selden has a highly developed sense of irony, and this ingenious defense relies for its effectiveness on a hostile attitude toward an imaginary opponent of the Jews. That opponent represents the vast majority of his countrymen, who portray contemporary Jews as cursed and hated. As was noted, the main intent of one of Selden's immense scholarly books may be deliberately tucked away in a parenthesis, and the key phrase in this brief monologue is the casually brutal "my life for yours." Selden's treatise *The Duello* (1610) traces the history and set forms of single combat between appellant and defendant, who swear oaths before betting their lives. In this instance Selden makes his point that "Christians hate each other as much" as soon as his opponent accepts his challenge of "my life for yours." Both the challenge and its acceptance expose the bloody-mindedness of one Christian Englishman willing to take the life of another in order to prove that Christians hate Jews even more than they hate each other.

The Early Reception of *De Jure*

In the rest of this chapter I want to provide a sampling of responses to the specifically rabbinical scholarship in Selden's *De Jure Naturali et Gentium*. Selden's admiration of rabbinic thought and his toleration of contemporary Jews should be measured against the legacy in seventeenth-century England of medieval patterns of diabolization based ultimately on John 8:44. Catholics could always convert, but, as David S. Katz has noted, "the demonological, supernatural element in the early modern attitude to the Jews . . . renders it quite different from other forms of opposition to religious minorities and outcasts."[30] In such a context, what would it mean to find in a magisterial work by the most learned person in the country a chapter title near the end (and in Selden important matters are always addressed near the end) on the promise of eternal life, heavenly or divine *(Coelestis, seu Divini)*, held out to the entire human race *(Noachidas seu Universum genus humanum)*, according to the opinion of the Hebrews *(ex Ebraeorum sententia)*?[31] More important, what would it mean to read a work that explicitly and consistently insists on the divine nature of the nonbiblical, exclusively rabbinic *praecepta Noachidarum*? It should become clear that Selden's younger contemporaries, who used the scholarship contained in *De Jure Naturali* in the service of liberalism and inclusiveness in politics and religion, would not have been able to read the work without finding striking examples of Jewish charity toward those outside.

Selden is not the first scholar in the early modern period to treat the Noachide laws. His intellectual hero Hugo Grotius discusses them at some length in his pioneering work *De Jure Belli et Pacis* (Paris, 1625), and Richard Hooker, in *The Lawes of Ecclesiasticall Politie* (London, 1593), believes that the Apostolic Decree in Acts 15:28–29 contains a remnant of them. Hooker, whose remarks about Jews are contradictory and sometimes shockingly hostile, nevertheless believes in the continuity of rabbinic and Mosaic laws and the gospel. The Noachide laws are designed for all of humankind. When Christianity was in its infancy, gentile Christians kept the Apostolic Decree, which reduces the seven Noachide laws to three; and Jewish Christians were bound to observe even the ceremonial Mosaic law, such as circumcision.[32] Selden develops hints about the Noachide laws that he would have found in Grotius. These ideas bear upon questions of the development of international law and the problem of establishing minimal conditions that enable otherwise differing persons and groups to live in peace. They also build bridges between cultures, as, for example, in the commonalities between the *praeceptum Noachidarum* and the *jus gentium* of Roman law, which regard the resident alien as possessed of certain inalienable human rights.

Discussions of Noachide law in the seventeenth century that refer to Selden respectfully and often reverentially appear in the work of Isaac Newton, Henry Burton, John Lightfoot, Henry Stubbe, Henry Hammond, Jeremy Taylor, James Harrington, Edward Stillingfleet, John Toland, Samuel Pufendorf, Lancelot Addison (father of Joseph), and Sir John Vaughan, among many others. It is also clear that Selden's Hebrew scholarship influences Ben Jonson, John Milton, and Thomas Hobbes. Even so, it is not difficult to demonstrate that Selden's rabbinic influence has been neglected. The OED defines "Noachic" only as "of or pertaining to Noah" and "Noachian" only as "of or relating to the patriarch Noah or his time, esp. *Noachian deluge*, the Flood." Its illustrative quotes mingle, apparently without recognizing the difference, references to Noah and the flood and those that speak of the connection between the Apostolic Decree and the *praeceptum:* "The Noachick precepts are reduced to abstinence from blood and unclean meats" (1773); "four restrictions, which belonged to what was called the Noachian dispensation" (1879); and "the Gentile world . . . under the Noachic covenant" (1863). John Milton, writing on divorce in one of the non-Pauline chapters of his "De doctrina Christiana," follows "Selden, [who] demonstrated particularly well in his *Uxor Hebraea*, with the help of numerous Rabbinical texts [or testimonies], [that] the word *fornication*, if it is considered in the light of the idiom of oriental languages, does not mean only adultery." In the still-definitive Columbia University Press edition of *The Complete Prose Works of John Milton*, Bishop Charles Sumner, translating "*multis Rabbinorum testimoniis*," elides the phrase's central term so that it becomes only "numerous testimonies."[33] Since the OED began with James Murray and the Columbia Milton editors rely on the first translation of *De doctrina Christiana* by the bishop of Winchester (1790–1874), the elision could serve as a synecdoche of the twentieth century's continuing an effacement of early modern rabbinical scholarship begun in the nineteenth.

Despite Selden's ability to be friends with people of very different political and religious beliefs—it is said that the commons came to him to learn of their rights and the lords to learn of their privileges—it is still surprising to see how different his readers can be from one another. They include William Laud, archbishop of Canterbury, and Jeremy Taylor, chaplain in ordinary to Charles I. Taylor gave his longest, most ambitious, and most neglected work the Maimonidean title *Ductor Dubitantium* (1660) and dedicated it to Charles II.[34] The first two chapters of book 2 contain endless passages translated from *De Jure*, some of them acknowledged. Laud and Selden became friendly in 1635, and, according to Peter Heylyn, Selden became "both a frequent and a welcome guest at Lambeth House, where he was grown into such esteem with the archbishop that he might have chose his own preferment in the court (as it was then generally believed), had he not undervalued all other employments in respect of his studies."³⁵ The preacher Henry Burton, like the lawyer William Prynne and the physician John Bastwick, attacked the pompous sumptuosity of Lambeth as well as other abuses of clerical privilege. In retaliation Laud charged them with sedition, and in 1637—the year that Milton wrote *Lycidas*, that "foretells the ruin of our corrupted clergy then in their height"—ordered that their ears be cut off. It is said that 100,000 people, most of them sympathetic to the martyrs, crowded around the scaffold to see this gruesome punishment carried out.

Where the ceremonialists of the Laudian church accepted and converted in a transformed but recognizable state the pagan, Jewish, and Catholic past, the puritans rejected it in favor of scriptural sufficiency.³⁶ They compared Anglican ritual with both the "old cast rudiments" of the Jewish ceremonial law and "the new-vomited Paganisme of sensuall Idolatry."³⁷ It is surprising, then, to find a positive reference to rabbinic scholarship derived from Selden's *De Jure* in an open letter from Burton to his fellow sufferer Prynne, published as *A Vindication of Churches Commonly Called Independent* (1644).³⁸ Burton, a radical Independent, rejects Prynne's idea of a national church, which he proposed on the grounds that it would resemble the national church of the Jews. Burton's attitude toward the Jews changes in the course of the treatise. He explains why the Independents cannot accept Presbyterianism:

You require absolute obedience to the generall consent of Assembly and Parliament. Nor we dare not pin our faith upon the generalitie of mens opinions. The generalitie of the votes of the *Jewes* State carried it away, to crucifie their King. If the whole world might vote this day, the generalitie would be against Christ, as he is indeed the onely Anoynted King, Priest, and Prophet. What if the generalitie vote amisse, while yet they may *conceive* all to be right, because *consonant* to what they most affect? No. . . . ³⁹

And yet Burton bases his rejection of the proposed analogy between the national church and the nation of the Jews on the inimitable superiority of the latter:

For bring us any one Nationall, that is one intire Church, or congregation, as that of the Jewes was: or, that is of one family, as that was: or, that is a type of Christs spirituall Kingdome, as that was: or, that is the universall Church of God visible on earth, as that was: or, that is governed by the like lawes, that that was: when your selfe doe confesse, that the government of your Nationall Churches is to be regulated by humane lawes, customes, manners, and not by Gods word alone; whereas that of the Jewes was wholly governed by Gods own Law, and not at all by the Lawes of men. . . . In a word, your

Nationall Churches are a mixed multitude, consisting for the greatest part of prophane persons, being as a confused lump, whereof there are nine parts of leaven to one of pure flowre, so as the whole is miserably soured, and the flowre made altogether unsavoury: But that of the Jewes, in its naturall and externall constitution, was all holy, an holy Nation, a royall Priesthood, a peculiar people, all the congregation holy, every one of them: So as in no one particular, doe your Nationall Churches hold parallell with that of the Jewes, no not in the least resemblance.[40]

The rabbinic reference comes at a crucial moment in the argument, when Burton asserts that no human law may bind the conscience. Regarding anyone's conscience, "be it never so erroneous, as that of the Papists," one may go no further than "to instruct and admonish, and labour to enforme and rectifie: enforce it you may not": "And brother let me put it to your *Conscience*, Doe you thinke it equall, that either your conscience should be a rule of mine, or mine of yours? And if no one mans conscience may be the rule of anothers; certainly neither may all the mens consciences in the world be the Judge of any one mans. How ever we finde neither rule, example, nor reason from Scripture, to force men to religion originally; yet the Rabbins say, if man kept the seven precepts of *Noah*, he might not be forced further."[41] The entire paragraph shows clear signs of the influence of *De Jure*, in which Selden postulates a hypothetical state of total natural freedom, upon which the laws of nature supervened. The laws were not innate but had to be learned so that the only condition truly natural to human beings was freedom. Selden identified natural, or universal, law as the *praecepta Noachidarum*, uttered by God at a specific moment in historical time, when he made plain to humankind what he would punish them for.[42] There is no other universal law apart from this divine revelation. Moreover, regarding Burton's point that there is no rule, example, or reason "to force men to religion originally, it is . . . remarkable, that the law of *Noah* regarding Idolatry was *Negative*, and onely told them they were not to worship *Idols, Angels, Sun* and *Moon,* and such Gods as were not the Lord *Jehovah*, but as to the positive part we find nothing expressed that they were to do necessarily."[43] It is important to remember that when Selden speaks of the negative laws against stealing and adultery, he is thinking not of the biblical prohibitions in the ten commandments, which are binding only on the Jews, but rather of the *praecepta*, which originate in the Talmud:

I cannot fancy to myself what the law of nature means, but the law of God. How should I know I ought not to steal, I ought not to commit adultery, unless somebody had told me so. 'Tis not because I think I ought not to do them, nor because you think I ought not; if so, our minds might change: whence then comes the restraint? From a higher power; nothing else can bind. I cannot bind myself, for I may untie myself again; nor an equal cannot bind me, for we may untie one another. It must be a superior, even God Almighty.[44]

Burton continues by answering Prynne's objection that sects and divisions will multiply "*under pretence of Christian liberty*" and subvert "*all setled maintenance for the Ministery by tythes*": "As for Tithes: what Tithes, I pray you, had the Apostles? Such as be faithfull and painfull Ministers of Christ, he will certainly provide for them: as when hee sent forth his Disciples without any *purse*, or provision, he asked them, *Lacked you any thing*? They said, *Nothing*. Surely, *the labourer is worthy of his hire*. And as for Ministers maintenance by Tithes, I referre you to the judgment of your learned brother Mr. *Selden*."[45] Burton's sufferings of torture and imprisonment taught him toleration though his fellow martyr remained unmoved. Prynne's remarkable treatise opposing the readmission of the Jews not only repeats vicious slanders against them but tells horrific stories in which they are both brutally persecuted and blamed for their own victimization: "although they were miserable, yet they were pittied by none," he notes approvingly.[46] Burton refers to Selden as Prynne's "learned brother"only because both were lawyers and members of the Inns of Court, Prynne of Lincoln's Inn and Selden of the Inner Temple. Certainly relations between them would not have been cordial. In 1633 Selden was one of the "grandees" representing the Inner Temple, one of the sponsors of a "splendid royal mask" mounted by the four Inns of Court. The purpose of presenting the mask was to "manifest the difference of their opinion from Mr. Prynne's new learning, and serve to confute his *Histrio Mastix* against interludes."[47]

An imprisoned voice far more in tune with Burton than with Prynne was that of William Penn, whose remarks on toleration echo *De Jure*. In a letter from the Tower dated 1 May 1669 to the Lord Arlington, principal secretary of state, "by whose Warrant I was committed," Penn asks:

What if I differ from some Religious Apprehensions? Am I therefore incompatible with the being of Human Societies? Shall it not be remembered with what success kingdoms and common-wealths have lived under the ballance of diverse parties? And if the politicks of the most judicious and acute inquisitors after these affairs are of any worth, they are not at a stand in delivering their sense with great sharpness, "That it is the securest prop of all Monarchical Governments." Let it not be forgotten, that under the Jewish Constitution, the utmost they required from Strangers, to entitle them to Freedom, was an Acknowledgment to the Noachical Precepts, (never denied by me); nor was it better with them in latter days, than whilst the Pharisees, Scribes, Esseans, Sadducees, & c. had the free exercise of their consciences, all differing among themselves.[48]

John Milton's *Samson Agonistes*, like Shakespeare's *Merchant of Venice*, taps into the roots of early modern England's powerful and contradictory social, psychological, and religious problems, but with sympathy for Judaic self-understanding. Samson actually names Selden's *De Jure Naturali et Gentium* when he reminds Dalila that when the Philistines asked her to betray him, they violated "the law of nature, law of nations" (891), as she did by complying. A number of critics have seen Samson's entering the temple of Dagon as a violation of the law and as an example of zeal, which is a sort of puritan code word for antinomianism. But Selden in *De Jure* reads Christ's driving the money changers from the temple as an act in accordance with the talmudic law that sanctions zealous acts when done by the religiously dutiful (*Homines pii*). This talmudic law from tractate Sanhedrin would not have been lost on the revolutionary and defender of the regicides, John Milton.

The idea of universal law, and its relation to international relations, is of capital importance in *Samson* because it allows for conversation between Israelite Samson, whose ethical sense is informed by law, and Philistine tempters such as Dalila and Harapha. Samson depends on the law for both self-justification and self-condemnation. What is remarkable in the text of *Samson Agonistes* (there is nothing like it in the text of Judges) is that Samson agonizes over what seems to be a venial offense (revealing the source of his strength, which is not a sin traceable to scripture) but he easily shrugs off the far more serious charges that he is "a Murderer, a Revolter, and a Robber" (1180) and that he twice married a Philistine or Canaanite enemy. Selden's complex discussion of law in *De Jure* helps make sense of the arguments that Samson uses in justifying his actions. There is more to be said about the topics of *De Jure*'s influence on toleration and on *Samson Agonistes* than can be contained within the limits of this chapter.

Tempering Scriptural Severity

I should like to conclude by emphasizing two influential rabbinic ideas in Selden's *De Jure*. The first, less surprising, limits Jewish enmity against outsiders to the seven idolatrous nations inhabiting Canaan. The radical Independent Henry Stubbe, whose ideas about civil religion derive largely from *De Jure*, summarizes Selden's argument on this point:

The *Israelites* were not . . . obliged to destroy all their Neighbours that were Idolaters, they never practised such a thing, nor is the omission thereof laid to their charge. . . . The Law in its letter, and as farr as man had power to execute it, was limited to the seven Nations, which God had given to the Children of Israell for a possession: Deut 12. 1. *These are the statutes, and the judgments which the Lord thy God giveth thee* (so *Exod.* 34.13). They should destroy all monuments of Idolatry in those dominions: and this is the judgment of the *Jewish* Doctors, as Mr. *Selden* reports them *de jur. natur.* l.2.c.2. It is commanded us that we destroy all foreign worship out of our land; but beyond our precincts it is not commanded us that we should persecute and destroy it. In case they made any additional conquest, that law did not reach them; yet did they by an intervenient right (as Mr. *Selden* phraseth it) abolish and extripate [*sic*] Idolatry in such places, *viz.* least it should become a snare unto them. Amongst the *Jews* there lived sundry other people called under the generall name of *Strangers*, which as to matters of common equity, had one and the same law or justice which an *Israelite* had: such were the *Gibeonites* and the reliques of the *Canaanites* that were undestroyed: such were those which joyned with them when they came out of *Egypt*, such were the *Proselytes* or *Strangers in the gate* who were not *Jewes*, but were all bound up (say the *Jewes*) to the seven precepts of *Noah*.[49]

Stubbe copies out many pages from *De Jure* on the seven nations and on Judaic tolerance of those who fall outside of that category. One of Stubbe's correspondents was John Locke, whose library included, among other titles by the same author, "Selden, *De Jure Naturali juxta Disciplinam Ebraeorum*, 4to, 1665. . . . Bought in Holland."[50] In his *Letter Concerning Toleration*, Locke's discussion of the seven nations in the context of the civil government of the Hebrews bears clear signs of the influence of Selden, a thoroughgoing Erastian:

Foreigners, and such as were strangers to the commonwealth of Israel, were not compelled by force to observe the rites of the Mosaical law: but, on the contrary, in the very same place where it is ordered that an Israelite that was an idolater should be put to death, there it is provided that strangers should not be "vexed nor oppressed," Exod. xxii.21. I confess that the seven nations that possessed the land which was promised to the Israelites were utterly to be cut off. But this was not singly because they were idolaters; for if that had been the reason, why were the Moabites and other nations to be spared? No; the reason is this: God being in a peculiar manner the King of the Jews, he could not suffer the adoration of any other deity, which was properly an act of high treason against himself, in the land of Canaan, which was his kingdom; for such a manifest revolt could no ways consist with his dominion, which was perfectly political, in that country. All idolatry was therefore to be rooted out of the bounds of his kingdom; because it was an acknowledgment of another God, that is to say, another king, against the laws of empire.[51]

The second idea, the final one of this essay, pervades Selden's most important rabbinical writings and comes closest to touching the contradictions of early modern England. It corrects the puritan distinction between the purity, clarity, and humanity of "the Law of *Moses*" and the contamination, obscurity, and cruelty of "the Pharisaical tradition falsely grounded upon that law."[52] Such a distinction allows Milton at once to overthrow the statements of Christ and Paul against divorce in the New Testament while claiming to honor them. He can control the damage by explaining the statements as Christ's attempt "to lay a bridle upon the bold abuses of those over-weening *Rabbies;* which he could not more effectually doe, then by a countersway of restraint, curbing their wild exorbitance almost into the other extreme."[53] At the same time Milton can rely on rabbinic exegesis supporting divorce in both *De Jure* and *Uxor*

Ebraica in order to reach a juridical position identical to that of the most extreme among the overweening rabbis, the Pharisees: "this law [of divorce] bounded no man; he might put away whatever found not favour in his eyes."⁵⁴

Most Christians of the early modern period contrast the "Hebrew truth" (*Hebraica veritas*) of the Bible with the rabbinical fables of the Talmud. Selden, throughout his writings, contrasts the severity of the literal text of the Hebrew Bible with the humaneness of rabbinic interpretations of the text and of rabbinic law. His letter to Ben Jonson on 28 February 1616 is the earliest dated example of his entry into the field of Jewish studies. Answering a query about "the literall sense and historicall of the holy text usually brought against the counterfeiting of sexes by apparell," namely Deuteronomy 22:5, Selden provides an elegant loophole for his friend Jonson, who is writing for a transvestite English stage in which men take the parts of women. Following Maimonides in both his "*More Nebochim*" and "*Misnah Thorah*," he refers to Hebrew proscriptions about clothing as being in opposition to ancient practices of worshiping Mars and Venus: men invoking Venus in women's clothing and women honoring Mars in men's armor. This would prohibit cross-dressing only as part of an idolatrous rite.⁵⁵

In *De Jure* Selden examines the halakhic restrictions that make it very difficult for a court to sentence a blasphemer to death—this despite numerous biblical verses (for example, Exodus 22:20, Leviticus 24:15–16, Deuteronomy 17:2ff.) insisting on that punishment. Selden cites the rabbis, who limit blasphemy to profaning the name of God. And it must be in public. Not only that, but a court neither sentences an offender to be whipped nor to be put to death unless the act has been performed with deliberate intent and in front of witnesses, and after warning has been given.⁵⁶

In *Table Talk* Selden, like the great medieval rabbinic commentator Rashi, interprets the *lex talionis* of an eye for an eye (Exodus 21:24) by the light of the talmudic tractate Baba Kamma 84a: "*An eye for an eye, and a tooth for a tooth. That does not mean, that if I put out another man's eye, therefore I must lose one of my own, (for what is he the better for that?) though this be commonly received; but it means, that I shall give him what satisfaction an eye shall be judged to be worth.*"⁵⁷ Selden's recognition of the humaneness of rabbinic law helps account for his acceptance of the Noachide precepts and his rejection of the biblical ten commandments as an alternative dispensation intended only for the Jews. The contemporary relevance of his remarks on the Sabbath in *Table Talk* has been recognized. The right way of keeping the Sabbath was among the most bitter points of dispute between the Anglicans and the puritans, and the controversy over *The Book of Sports* has been well documented. Supporting his apparently casual pronouncement against Sabbath observance is the vast body of scholarship in *De Jure:* "Why should I think all the fourth commandment belongs to me, when all the fifth does not? What land will the Lord give me for honouring my father? It was spoken to the Jews with reference to the land of Canaan; but the meaning is, if I honour my parents, God will also bless me. We read the commandments in the church-service, as we do David's Psalms; not that all there concerns us, but a great deal of them does."[58] Selden does not feel bound by either the ceremonial law or the conditional moral law contained in the decalogue. To conclude where we began, with the learned printer William Bowyer, the editor of his remarks on the Jew Bill notes that "this little tract was well received by those who were superior to narrow prejudices,"[59] and the same might be said of most of the readers of Selden's half dozen rabbinical works, erudite Christians willing to cope with Selden's difficult Latin in order to learn about Jewish laws and institutions. Of course the number of Englishmen not in thrall to narrow prejudice was considerably smaller in Selden's lifetime than in Bowyer's or in our own. It is at least worth remembering that in the first half of the seventeenth century the most learned person in England rejected the biblical decalogue as intended only for the Jews and accepted the rabbinic Noachide laws as binding upon all of humankind. On the basis of those laws and the talmudic discussions occasioned by them, he expressed hope in eternal life for those outside his own confession, rejected the myth of Jewish xenophobia, and emphasized the humaneness of rabbinic exegesis.

Notes

1. "REMARKS on a SPEECH made in COMMON COUNCIL, on the Bill for permitting Persons professing the JEWISH Religion to be Naturalized, so far as Prophecies are supposed to be affected by it" (1753), collected in *William Bowyer: Miscellaneous Tracts*, ed. John Nichols (London, 1785), 453–55. Bowyer was a leading member of the London book trade in the eighteenth century, and major works by Defoe, Pope, Swift, and many others bear his imprint. See Keith Maslen, *An Early London Printing House at Work: Studies in the Bowyer Ledgers* (New York: Bibliographical Society of America, 1993).
2. Bowyer, *Miscellaneous Tracts*, 457.
3. Ibid., 455. For the "Times of the Gentiles," see Luke 21:24.
4. Ibid., 453.
5. Ibid., 454.
6. John Nichols, preface to *Miscellaneous Tracts*, vii–viii. A letter from Dr. Wotton, sent to Bowyer in 1726, regarding the three volumes in six of Selden's monumental *Opera Omnia*, attests to the delicate handling it received from two learned readers. Dr. Wotton thanks Bowyer "for the trust you have reposed in me, in lending me the new *Selden*. Assure yourself it shall be particularly taken care of." To which Mr. Clarke subjoins, "I can only add my thanks to the Doctor's, for the great treasure you have sent us. They came down safe; and I will take as much care as possible that they receive no

damage. I have already put new coats upon them, that change of air and other like accidents might not affect them. I shall not think of returning them till the roads are fair again; nor shall I forget your directions about hay" (39).

7. Bowyer, *Miscellaneous Tracts*, 458. See, for comparison, the conclusion of "John Selden's Letter to Ben Jonson on Cross-Dressing and Bisexual Gods," ed. Jason P. Rosenblatt and Winfried Schleiner, *English Literary Renaissance* 29 (1999): 74: "With what ancient fathers as Cyprian & Tertullian specially have of this text, or others dealing on it as it tends to morality, I abstain to meddle." See also Selden's Apology in *Titles of Honour* (1614), sig. c4v: "There are, which have in part handled some of my Titles, and as their Purpose. I abstain from comparison"; and *The Historie of Tithes* (1617), 486: "But I abstain from censure."

8. See especially Michael Ragussis, *Figures of Conversion: "The Jewish Question" and English National Identity* (Durham: Duke University Press, 1995); and James Shapiro, *Shakespeare and the Jews* (New York: Columbia University Press, 1996).

9. Shapiro (*Shakespeare and the Jews*) makes the important point that in his scholarship Selden draws upon examples from the Bible, the Talmud, and medieval Anglo-Jewish history, thus "collapsing any simple distinction between the ancient Israelite and the modern Jewish nation" (174).

10. A serious and unfortunate example of antiquarian devotion to documents overcoming skepticism would seem to be the records of Jewish ritual murder in his brief *Treatise on the Jews in England* (1617). Gerald J. Toomer, who generously read an earlier draft of this essay, argues that Selden's position on the matter cannot be so easily determined. His history of the Jews appears in the third edition of Samuel Purchas's *Pilgrimage* (1617), and parts of it—such as a reference to "one cruell and (to speake the properest phrase) Jewish crime . . . usuall amongst them"—sound like Purchas rather than Selden. More important, in a transcript provided by Professor Toomer of the relevant sections of William Prynne's *Short Demurrer to the Jewes Long Discontinued Remitter into England* (1656), Prynne asserts that Purchas did not print unaltered what Selden submitted to him, and Selden was angry with Purchas "for abusing him in such a manner, and his Readers likewise" (1). Selden took the stories of ritual murder from Matthew Paris, who had a virulent hatred of the Jews. A number of questions complicate the matter, including the relation of Selden's original *Treatise* to what Prynne calls "such a poor maimed account given of [the Jews] . . . so different from that delivered (to Purchas)" (1). Professor Toomer believes that Selden, reproducing his sources in a mostly straightforward narrative, "was already too much of a skeptic to endorse the stories of Matthew Paris as is done in Purchas's rendering." The one example in the *Treatise* that seems to derive directly from an archival source and is accompanied by one of Selden's characteristic learned notes is not of an accusation of ritual murder but rather of forced circumcision in Norwich. But "the Jewes after procured the boy to be seene, and his member was found covered." Selden then refers to an ancient Hellenistic technique of "Chirurgery, [whereby] the skinne may be drawne forth to an uncircumcision" (173 of Purchas; Selden, *Opera Omnia*, 3:1461). Does Selden believe that the Jews of medieval Norwich practiced this surgical technique? There are more questions than answers. What can be asserted is that no Christian can be found in early modern England who unequivocally rejected the blood libel.

11. I am indebted to Prof. Yosef Kaplan of the Hebrew University, Jerusalem, for a copy of one of the earliest sale catalogs known in Hebrew bibliography, the *Catalogus Librorum* (Amsterdam, 1693) of the Dutch Sephardic rabbi Isaac Aboab da Fonseca

(1605–93), which lists on signature A3, "Iohan: Seldeni de dys syris Syntagmata edition, Tertia Lipsiae, 1662." This entry suggests that not only did Selden read the rabbis, but the rabbis also read Selden. In 1641, following the Dutch conquests in Brazil, Aboab became the *hakham* of the community at Recife (Pernambuco), thus becoming the first American rabbi.

12. See on this point Jonathan R. Ziskind's introduction to his edition, *John Selden on Jewish Marriage Law: The Uxor Hebraica* (Leiden, Neth.: E. J. Brill, 1991), 18.

13. See Richard Tuck, *Philosophy and Government, 1572–1651* (Cambridge: Cambridge University Press, 1993), 214. I am greatly indebted to all of Professor Tuck's writings on Selden, especially *Natural Rights Theories: Their Origin and Development* (Cambridge: Cambridge University Press, 1979).

14. Selden, *De Jure Naturali et Gentium juxta Disciplinam Ebraeorum* (London, 1640), 118–19. He lists the ordinances as *"de Cultu extraneo,"* *"de Maledictione Nominis sanctissimi* seu *Numinis,"* *"de Effusione Sanguinis* seu *Homicidio,"* *"de Revelatione Turpitudinum* seu *Turpitudine ex concubitu,"* *"de Furto ac Rapina,"* *"de Judiciis* seu *Regimine forensi ac Obedientia Civili,"* and *"de Membro animalis viventis* non comedendo." His list is based on Maimonides' distinction between those commandments that are *"inter Hominem & Numen sanctissimum"* and those that are *"inter Hominem & proximum suum."*

15. *The Poems of John Cleveland*, ed. Brian Morris and Eleanor Withington (Oxford: Clarendon Press, 1967), 27.

16. Selden, *De Jure Naturali et Gentium*, 832. His sources include tractate Sanhedrin, "Maimonidis tractatu *de Poenitentia*, cap. 3" and "Manasseh Ben Israel . . . *de Resurrectione*, Amstelodami, 1636, lib. 2. cap. 8 & 9" and "ad Deut. quaest. 163. Hispanice 2. Latine."

17. Selden, *De Jure*, 833: "Quicunque susceperit in se septem Praecepta, atque monitus ea cautius observaverit . . . ipse est ex eis qui vocantur Pii ex Gentibus Mundi, atque ei sors est in seculo futuro. Eum vero intelligimus qui ea observaverit ideo quod praeceperit Deus O. M. ut legislator. Nam & per Mosem Magistrum nostrum nobis notum fecit, imperatam fuisse antiquitus Noachidis eorum observationem. Ceterum si sponte solum, seu ex suo potius arbitratu (non habita imperantis Numinis sanctissimi ratione) ea observaverit, nec pro Proselyto Domicilii, nec pro aliquo ex Piis ex Gentilibus Mundi habetur, neque in numero Sapientum eorum censendus est." The two cited Maimonidean texts are "Halach. Melakim c. 8. Adde eundem Halach. *Isuri Bia* cap. 14."

18. Selden, *De Jure*, 832.

19. Ibid., 833.

20. Ibid., 833, referring to Sanhedrin 59a: "Intelligendum est de septem praeceptis Paganis propriis. Nam quod ad caetera attinet; docetur in Titulo Sanhedrin capite de quatuor Poenarum capitalium generibus Paganum qui observaverit legem (qua Israeliticam, atque in ditione Israelitica) mortis esse reum."

21. Ibid., 8.

22. *Complete Prose Works of John Milton*, vol. 2, gen. ed. Don M. Wolfe (New Haven: Yale University Press, 1953–82), 513.

23. *The Table Talk of John Selden*, ed. Samuel Harvey Reynolds (Oxford: Clarendon, 1892), 179–80. The letter is preserved in the Bodleian, MS. Selden supra 109 fol. 463. The allusion is to Ovid, *Remedium Amoris*, 47, which describes the spear of Achilles, made of wood from Mount Pelion. Telephus could be cured only by the spear that inflicted the wound.

24. Undated letter (June 1871) to Leonie Halevy, in *Lettres de Georges Bizet: Impressions de Rome; La Commune (1871)* (Paris, 1907), 322; cited by Isaiah Berlin in *Three Critics of the Enlightenment: Vico, Hamann, Herder*, ed. Henry Hardy (Princeton: Princeton University Press, 2000), 104. See also Edward Gibbon's note on Selden's *De Diis Syris* in *The History of the Decline and Fall of the Roman Empire*, chap. 15, n. 9; cited by Anthony Grafton in *The Footnote* (Cambridge: Harvard University Press, 1997), 3: "For the enumeration of the Syrian and Arabian deities, it may be observed, that Milton has comprised, in one hundred and thirty very beautiful lines, the two large and learned syntagmas, which Selden had composed on that abstruse subject."

25. *Table Talk*, 170–71. In the Georgetown University library's copy of the 1892 edition there is a check beside the penultimate sentence and, in the margin, "!?!"

26. See, for example, Selden, *De Jure*, 117, 833.

27. For an elegant and comprehensive reading of the parable, see Frank Kermode, *The Genesis of Secrecy* (Cambridge: Harvard University Press, 1979), 34–39; see also John Drury, *The Parables in the Gospels* (New York: Crossroad, 1985), 132–36. Drury finds in 2 Chronicles 28:14ff. a source in the Hebrew Bible for good Samaritans who similarly clothe the naked, anoint, provide food and drink, and carry.

28. Kermode, *Genesis of Secrecy*, 36; Drury, *Parables*, 134.

29. *Table Talk*, 79.

30. David S. Katz, *Philo-Semitism and the Readmission of the Jews to England* (Oxford: Clarendon Press, 1982), 3.

31. Selden, *De Jure*, 833.

32. Richard Hooker, *Of the Lawes of Ecclesiasticall Politie* [1593], *The Folger Library Edition of the Works of Richard Hooker*, gen. ed. W. Speed Hill (Cambridge: Harvard University Press, 1977), vol. 1, bk. 4, chapter 11, 308–19.

33. John Milton, *De doctrina Christiana*, vol. 15 of *The Works of John Milton*, gen. ed. Frank Allen Patterson (New York: Columbia University Press, 1931–38), 15:171.

34. Taylor's *Ductor Dubitantium* embraces two encyclopedic volumes of cases of conscience. In his mature scholarship Selden relies on the Buxtorf edition of *The Guide of the Perplexed*, *More Nebuchim: Doctor Perplexorum, conversus a Johanne Buxdorfio, fil.* (Basel, 1629). He also uses and quotes the Hebrew version of Samuel Ibn Tibbon (Sabbioneta, 1553). In late works he sometimes quotes the Arabic original from a manuscript owned by Edward Pococke. As a young scholar in *De Diis Syris* (1617) he cites an earlier edition of Maimonides, by the Italian orientalist and Hebraist Agostino Giustiniani, *Rabi Mossei Aegyptii Dux seu Director dubitantium aut perplexorum* (Paris, 1520).

35. Peter Heylyn, *Life of William Laud* (London, 1671), 303. Heylyn, an apologist for Laud, may be overstating the warmth of their relationship. In correspondence G. J. Toomer points out that Selden's first book entirely devoted to a Jewish topic, *De Successionibus*, was written in prison, "where the government with which Laud was already associated had put him." And the only extant letter from Laud to Selden, dated 29 November 1640, when Laud was already in deep trouble with the Long Parliament, "hardly suggests any intimacy between them . . . but only a desperate attempt by Laud, address[ing] an influential member [of Parliament], to display, too late, a spirit of compromise."

36. For an excellent discussion of the warring ideologies of the Laudian church and puritan Calvinism, see Achsah Guibbory, *Ceremony and Community from Herbert to Milton: Literature, Religion, and Cultural Conflict in Seventeenth-Century England* (Cambridge: Cambridge University Press, 1998).

37. John Milton, *Of Reformation*, in *Complete Prose Works of John Milton*, vol. 1, gen. ed. Don M. Wolfe (New Haven: Yale University Press, 1953–82), 520.

38. Milton's second edition of *The Doctrine and Discipline of Divorce* was also published in 1644. Where the first edition of 1643 bears no trace of Selden's influence, the second reveals it everywhere: in its arguments, in its final chapter (vol. 2, 22), whose proof is "*referr'd to Mr.* Seldens *Book* De jure naturali et gentium," and even in its division into books and chapters with italicized headnotes summarizing each chapter, an homage to Selden found in no other prose work by Milton.

39. Henry Burton, *A Vindication of Churches Commonly Called Independent* (London, 1644), 38.

40. Ibid., 31.

41. Ibid., 39–40.

42. See the lucid and concise discussion of Selden's theory of natural law in Richard Tuck's "The Ancient Law of Freedom: John Selden and the Civil War," in *Reactions to the English Civil War, 1642–1649*, ed. John Morrill (London: Macmillan, 1982), esp. 139–45.

43. Henry Stubbe paraphrasing Selden's *De Jure* in *An Essay in Defence of the Good Old Cause; or A Discourse Concerning the Rise and Extent of the Power of the Civil Magistrate in Reference to Spiritual Affairs* (London, 1659), 108.

44. *Table Talk*, 101.

45. Burton, *Vindication*, 56–57.

46. William Prynne, *A Short Demurrer to the Jewes Long Discontinued Remitter into England* . . . (London, 1656). In one of many stories of small-scale persecution (he also recounts large-scale examples, such as the massacre of the Jews of York) Prynne tells of a Jew who refuses to satisfy King John's exorbitant demands for cash. The king commands his tormentors that they should pull out one of his teeth every day until he pays a fine of ten thousand marks of silver: "And when at last for 7 dayes space they had pulled out 7 of his teeth, with intollerable torment, and now on the 8 day the Tormentors had begun the like work again; this Jew, an over-slow provider for his profit, gave them the aforesaid money, that he might save the 8 tooth to himself, the other 7 being pulled out: who, with much more wisdom, and less pain, might have done so before, and have saved his 7 teeth, having but 8 in all" (16). Prynne laughs at the Jew, the way Renaissance Jews would have laughed at Shylock, for his stubbornness, stupidity, and lack of self-interest.

47. Bulstrode Whitelock, *Memorials of the English Affairs*, vol. 1 (1682; Oxford, 1853), 1:53.

48. "The Author's Life," in *Select Works of William Penn: To Which is Prefixed a Journal of His Life* (London, 1771), vi.

49. Stubbe, *An Essay in Defence of the Good Old Cause*, 106.

50. John Locke, *Two Treatises of Government*, ed. Peter Laslett (Cambridge: Cambridge University Press, 1967), app. B, "Sources of 'Two Treatises' in Locke's Reading," item #74, p. 144. See also Locke's letter to Stubbe in *The Correspondence of John Locke*, ed. E. S. DeBeer, 8 vols. (Oxford: Clarendon Press, 1976–89), 1:109–12.

51. Locke, *A Letter Concerning Toleration*, tr. William Popple [1689], ed. John Horton and Susan Mendus (London and New York: Routledge, 1991), p. 40.

52. Milton, "The Doctrine and Discipline of Divorce," in *Complete Prose Works*, 2:307.

53. Milton, *Complete Prose Works*, 2:283.

54. Ibid., 2:656–57.
55. Introduction, "John Selden's Letter to Ben Jonson," 46, 54.
56. *De Jure*, 248–50: "*profanare Nomen Divinum dicebatur* . . . . Et *b'rabim* seu publice atque *b'farhesia*, quod ex Graeco desumtum *palam ac aperte* significat, id profanere dicebatur si in Ebraeorum decem praesentia commiserat. . . . *Nimirum nullum peccatum flagra aut mors sequebatur, nisi id sponte commissum esset, adessentque testes & praecessisset admonitio legitima.*"
57. *Table Talk*, 168.
58. Ibid., 169–70.
59. Nichols, *Miscellaneous Tracts*, 453.

6

Censorship, Editing, and the Reshaping of Jewish Identity: The Catholic Church and Hebrew Literature in the Sixteenth Century

Amnon Raz-Krakotzkin

In September 1553, by a decree of the Roman Inquisition all copies of the Talmud that were found in Rome were gathered, and on the ninth of that month (Rosh Hashanah) they were set on fire in the Campo dei Fiori, the square that during the sixteenth and seventeenth centuries witnessed many burnings, both of books and of human beings. On the twelfth of September a bull signed by Pope Julius III was sent throughout the Catholic world, demanding the confiscation and burning of all copies of the Talmud.[1] The detailed decree explained that the Talmud provides clear evidence that the Jews have abandoned the Bible of Moses and that it contains passages contrary to the laws of morality and nature, along with blasphemous vituperations against Christianity. It emphasized that the prohibition against using the Talmud was applied to Christians as well, with the threat to excommunicate all who disobeyed. The initiative, which Cardinal Carafa (later Paul IV) supported, led, in subsequent years, to a wave of burnings in different cities, the last of which took place in Cremona in 1559.[2]

Such extreme actions were to be gradually replaced with (or at least accompanied by) a complex and systematic mechanism of censorship established by both the church and secular authorities in order to guarantee constant control of written culture, including Hebrew books. Besides the publication of *Indices Librorum Prohibitorum*, which determined the list of books that were absolutely prohibited, the practice of discussing the contents of many works in detail was developed in order to determine which contents should be removed from books in order to permit their publication and reading. Hebrew literature was also subject to the constant control of censors, who checked printed books as well as books prior to their publication.

Church policy toward Hebrew literature, as expressed in these measures, is commonly examined on two complementary levels: on one level, it is seen as a link in the continuous struggle of the Church against rabbinic literature, which began with the burning of the Talmud in the thirteenth century; on another level they have been examined alongside the various restrictive orders promulgated during the same period against Italian Jewry, which reflect ever-increasing attempts to restrict Jewish freedom and to exclude Jews from the larger Christian society. These steps are most clearly expressed in the papal bull *Cum nimis absurdum*, published by Pope Paul IV, which was designed to diminish contact between Jews and Christians by prohibiting Jews from owning real estate and blocking Jewish entry into various professions. This policy was enacted alongside other economic restrictions, expulsions, and ghettoization in different Italian cities during the second half of the sixteenth century.

Both of these perspectives are essential for understanding certain fundamental aspects of church policy and the contradictions in that policy. It is not my intention to dispute or to denigrate the value of either. Both are supported by declarations of the initiators and executors of this policy. A different and illuminating analysis of these events has been provided by Kenneth Stow in his extensive work on church policy. Stow argues that the measures taken by the church against the Jews and their books must be understood within the framework of Paul IV's messianism and that they were intended to induce the Jews to convert.[3] This framework is, however, not sufficient for a comprehensive evaluation of the historical role of censorship. In this essay, I would like to present a different perspective on the issue and briefly develop several arguments. These arguments do not contradict the aforementioned perspectives but place them within a larger and more nuanced context.

First it is important to recognize that one can speak of the censorship of Hebrew literature only as part of the general framework of censorship established by the Catholic Church in this period against the background of the transition to print on the one hand and the spread of heresy on the other.[4] Moreover, rather than a measure directed against the Jews alone, censorship was initiated precisely because Christians were reading Jewish literature, and thus it should be examined in the framework of the rise of Christian Hebraism. As such, censorship must be seen as a means of incorporating Jewish literature into Christian discourse and into the category of permitted knowledge. Censorship therefore embodies two contradictory but at the same time complementary dimensions of Christian Hebraist discourse: separation and integration—separation of the Jews from Christians and the integration of Jewish literature in Christian culture.

Second, censorship should not be seen only as an agent that denies knowledge; it must also be seen as one of the factors that had a constitutive role in the reshaping of literacy during the critical stage of the transition to print. Censorship is undoubtedly a controlling agent with a definite role, the intention of which (in the case of church measures) is to define the boundaries of orthodoxy. Yet it is necessary to examine it in relation to other agents who took part in the cultural process that accompanied the invention of print, such as the publishers and editors, who are commonly described as playing a "positive" role in opposition to the censors. The practice of censorship entailed a careful reading of various texts and the authorization of what the church considered permissible knowledge. Censorship should also be examined as part of the birth of modern structures of control and the rise of the modern centralized state.

The approach that is satisfied in presenting Catholic censorship as an oppressive agent directed against the Jews follows a positivistic historical approach, which describes the history of culture as the struggle of "the free and creative spirit" against the oppressive power that prevents its realization and progress. This evaluation of the role of censorship is also based on the image of the Counter-Reformation as a reactionary movement that struggled against any expression of rationalism and science. Recent discussions in various fields have challenged this attitude and led to a much more complex understanding of the role of censorship in the formation of new modes of writing and reading.[5]

The focus on reading and the consumption of texts forces us to pose the question of censorship differently. Underlying the view of censorship as an agent that denies knowledge is the assumption that a text has one and only one meaning. According to this perception, each act of censorship is by definition an erasure of knowledge. Reception theories emphasize that the text receives its meaning through the reader and through the dynamic interaction in which the text is actualized in different ways.[6] Therefore, in order to measure the actual impact of censorship it is insufficient to note only what has been erased; one must also compare the spectrum of readings of a censored text with the potential readings of an uncensored one.

The focus on reading stands at the core of the study of the history of books and has proved to be particularly fruitful for the study of the transition to print.[7] It enables us to examine the relationship between the invention of print, the rise of new modes of control and authority, and contemporaneous cultural and social developments. The emphasis on reading is associated with the examination of the various agents who participated in the preparation of the printed book.[8] We should ask what the relation is between the censor's demands and the demands of other agents such as the publisher, printer, and editor, particularly at a stage when professional distinctions were not so clear. At the same time we should also bear in mind the resistance of the reader and remember that he or she is not a passive consumer but an active participant whose cultural background determines the possibilities of reading.⁹ The dialectic of censorship is based on the interaction between different readers and different agents. In the words of Roger Chartier:

> On the one hand, every reader has to deal with an entire set of constraints and obligations. The author, the bookseller-publisher, the commentator and the censor all have an interest in keeping close control over the production of meaning and in making sure that the text that they have written, published, glossed or authorized will be understood with no possible deviation from their prescriptive will. On the other hand, reading, by definition, is rebellious and vagabond. Readers use infinite numbers of subterfuges to procure prohibited books, to read between the lines, and to subvert the lessons imposed on them.[10]

This approach toward censorship is also associated with recent reevaluations of the Counter Reformation church. The image of the church as nothing but an extreme manifestation of reaction and oppression has been replaced by a much more complex approach, which presents Catholic policies and attitudes as a serious attempt to approach the crisis of knowledge and authority.[11] Earlier origins of this reform have been emphasized as well as its role in shaping modern attitudes and institutions. This also involved a reevaluation of the role of the Roman Inquisition in general and of the practice of censorship in particular.[12] Several scholars have examined the role of the Inquisitor as a "mediator" between both orthodoxy and heterodoxy and elite and popular culture. Of great relevance to our discussion here is Rivka Feldhay's reading of Galileo's trial where she interprets the trial as a dialogical process in which the different perceptions of knowledge within the Christian world (of Dominicans and Jesuits) were discussed.[13]

On these grounds I shall argue that the actual intervention of the censors did not simply and necessarily prevent readings and that it was to a large extent compatible with principles that Jews employed when they themselves edited Hebrew literature. As such it had a constitutive role but one that did not necessarily impede or come into conflict with major trends in Jewish thought during the period. It is not that censorship had no impact on Hebrew literature and on Jewish consciousness; rather that from the historical point of view it participated in the global process of modernization. Censorship had a role in shaping modern Jewish literacy and in the constitution of new patterns of Jewish self-definition. Following Annabel Patterson in her illuminating study of censorship and literature in early modern England, we can say that to a certain extent we owe to the censors our notion of Hebrew literature and also the emergence of a new kind of Jewish discourse.[14] They had an important role in the formation of what came to be defined as Jewish literature, as we know it to this day, and they contributed to the rise of new modes of reading and collective identities.

It should be emphasized that this does not mean neglecting the oppressor/oppressed relations embodied in the phenomenon of censorship. It is not my intention to "defend" the Inquisition and the act of censorship or to underestimate the violence embedded in the erasures left in books and manuscripts. My intention is to analyze the role of censorship in relation to other agents and through the interrelations of Jews, Christian Hebraists, and converts engaged in the process of printing Hebrew books. The case of the Hebrew canon provides us with the opportunity to reveal the dialectics of censorship since we can examine it on two different levels and in terms of two different discourses, the first associated with print production and the second with Jewish-Christian theological polemics. These analyses may enlighten both fields of scholarship. Accordingly, it is possible to analyze the dialogue between the editors, censors, authors, and readers inherent in this process while tracking the resistance of Jewish readers.

The burning of the Talmud must be seen as part of a much wider policy directed by Cardinal Carafa (later Paul IV) during which many books were defined as heretical and set on fire.[15] Carafa expressed the extreme and most severe position in regard to the struggle against heresy in this period. Already in 1542 he was in charge of the reorganization (and, in fact, the establishment) of the Roman Inquisition, and he later initiated the growing control over the printing industry. The messianic attitude attributed to him was thus expressed in his desire to purify Christian belief and his jealous struggle against the wide spectrum of opinions that were now defined as heterodox.[16]

In the *Index Librorum Prohibitorum*, initiated by Paul IV and published after his death in 1559, the Talmud and its interpretations were included along with the works of approximately 550 authors, some of which were permitted only decades before, including the works of both Protestants and humanists.[17] Among those who were totally forbidden in the Index were authors like Rabelais, Marsilius of Padua, and Erasmus.[18] What should be emphasized is that the Talmud was included in an Index that was explicitly directed at the Christian world (*Universis Christi fidelibus*). The Talmud was cataloged under the category of "unrecognized authors" (*Incertorum Auctorum libri prohibiti*), and its place in the Index is similar to the category held by biblical translations in vernacular languages and magical works. Like those other compositions, it was considered both blasphemous and a threat to the authority of the church. Defining the Talmud as "heretical" (a definition whose origins go back to the thirteenth century) signified in this context its integration into the European Christian context.

The banning and confiscation of the Talmud were evidently also acts of restriction that attempted to prevent Jews from engaging with the basic text of their tradition. As a result many Jews began to read and study the text clandestinely, in a way that was similar to other groups in early modern Europe in Catholic and Protestant countries alike. Evidence as to the impact of the prohibition can be found in complaints of Jews during the second half of the sixteenth century, concerning the difficulties they addressed in their studies.[19] What should be emphasized here is that the motivation of the church was not solely to injure the Jews but to control the reading of the Talmud by Christians as well. Censoring the Talmud was therefore part of the entire struggle against heresy in this period, particularly in the context in which different beliefs were cataloged as "Judaization."[20] In Venice, for example, the law that prevented the owning of Hebrew literature was associated with laws against "Judaization" and was directed at Christians.[21] The fear of the Talmud that first arose in the thirteenth century came together with the growth of interest in Jewish literature by Christian scholars, which received a new significance in the age of the Reformation and within the context of humanist culture and the transition to print. It is obvious that the initiators of the policy of burning the Talmud (as well as its opponents) aspired to bring about the conversion of the Jews, but even more important was their wish to prevent the spread of heresy into the Christian world.[22] It is true that the church devoted great effort to converting Jews at this time; however, church policy remained ambivalent, and, following the experience of the Spanish Marranos, the converts themselves became the source of fear and suspicion as a potential fifth column within the Catholic Church. Some of the measures were directed against the converts themselves. Accordingly, in various cases (including the Iberian Peninsula, even after the expulsion of the Jews), Latin translations of Jewish biblical exegeses were prohibited, but they were not prohibited in the original Hebrew version. The first reference to Hebrew literature in papal instructions controlling the print industry referred to translations from Hebrew and Arabic, not to texts in the original Hebrew. This shows that the church's prohibitions were directed at Christians rather than Jews.[23] Hebrew books were included only in later similar instructions as part of the widening of control over literature.

Book burning, at least in the massive and concentrated form characteristic of the mid-sixteenth century, was a temporary policy with regard to the Talmud although the prohibition against the Talmud itself remained. It expressed an apocalyptic, even hysterical, desire to reverse reality, which arose when the Catholic hierarchy became increasingly aware of the implications of print and of the irreversibility of the Reformation. It was one aspect of the severe policy of Paul IV, one that was linked to other aspects of the watershed in the history of the Catholic reform in these years. Book burning was instigated by the church in an attempt to establish the limits of orthodoxy and to define clear boundaries between Catholicism and Protestantism. It was a manifestation of the crisis of authority within the church as it faced the reality of the Reformation, the invention of print, and the spread of heresy. Lacking effective tools to counter the new reality of print culture, the church resorted to methods successfully employed in the previous age. The burnings (including those of human beings) were a ritual occurrence in a public place often in the center of the print industry, directed at a largely Christian audience and making real the fear of the very same demonic element going up in flames. The burning was supposed to be a cleansing ritual ridding Christian society of the baneful influence of the Talmud. It was a ritual that gathered both Jews and Christians and can be seen as a manifestation of the interest in the Jewish corpus on the part of Christians. The burning of the Talmud was a consequence of the satanic and magical status that was attributed to it, the same criteria that applied to many other books that were seized and destroyed. The Hebrew letters in Hebrew books were perceived as a clear manifestation of the conjunction between the sacred and the demonic and, at the same time, of orality and literacy. The sacred Hebrew letters, the letters of *matrix linguarum*, are "released" from the demonic composition (the "Oral Torah") in which they were "captured."[24]

The extreme policy of book burning changed gradually as its limitations were revealed. The burnings, including the burning of the Talmud, and the mass prohibitions aroused open criticism, which in turn raised severe theological problems.[25] The extreme measures proved to be insufficient and were replaced by a serious discussion of various beliefs and bodies of knowledge. This is not to say that massive prohibition disappeared, but that it was now associated with a continuous discussion of contents that should be permitted and with attempts to establish a permanent mechanism of control over the production of books. The discussion of Hebrew literatures in the second half of the sixteenth century was part of this general process.

The total rejection of rabbinical literature, as well as the ritual burnings, raised serious theological problems, which the church was forced to deal with in the context of the challenge of the Reformation. The Protestant denial of the sacred authority of patristic tradition forced the church to emphasize its sacrality. This in turn obliged the church to reexamine its attitude toward postbiblical Jewish traditions. A total ban and invalidation of later Jewish literature would have strengthened (by analogy) the Protestant rejection of patristic sources, and the church was well aware of this. It was, of course, inconceivable for a Catholic to expect Jews to convert on the basis of the principle of *sola scriptura*. This constellation of circumstances resulted in the tension in the church's attitude toward rabbinical literature.

The question of censorship was a leading theme during the Council of Trent (in the sessions that preceded the burnings and particularly the third session, 1562–63, that followed it) and was associated with many doctrinal and administrative issues.[26]

Due to the resolutions accepted at Trent, a new Index was published in 1564 by Pius V where the number of prohibited books was significantly smaller. The Talmud was included in the Index, but it was declared that "if it will be presented without the title Talmud and without attacks and slanderous words against Christianity, it will be tolerated."[27] The implication of this decision was, at least theoretically, the permission to print and read the Talmud after the removal of specific sections. Under these conditions the composition could be authorized in principle and included within the boundaries of permitted literature that were decided at Trent. At least temporarily, the Talmud was no longer perceived as a dangerous composition but rather as a composition that contains blasphemous declarations that should be removed. The insistence on the prohibition of the title "Talmud" was explained in a memorandum of the secretary to the council's committee of the Index, the Portuguese Dominican Francisco Forieru, recently published by Parente: "Let them expurgate them themselves, but let them not dare to do so under the name of Talmud, whose errors have been so often rebuked and condemned by the Holy Roman See."[28] This declaration demonstrates the ambiguous attitude associated with the conditional permission. It also explains that the removal of the name "Talmud" was motivated by the church's intention to reject the Talmud's claim to authority as well as its demonic image without prohibiting access to its contexts by both Christian and Jewish readers.

This conditional permission was never realized. In the words of Fausto Parente, "in the following three decades, that *si tamen* would engender fervid hope and bitter disappointment among the Jews."[29] During the following decades the issue was raised many times, and on several occasions (in the late seventies and in the time of Sixtus V) serious attempts were made to come to an agreement that would enable the publication of the Talmud. In 1578 the printing of the Talmud in Basel was undertaken under the supervision of the Hebraist Marco Marino.[30] This was a Christian initiative that followed the instructions of the Index. The version was based on the Bomberg and Justinian editions, although many sections were omitted. But although the regulations for expurgation were rigid and were perceived by Jews as restrictive and as damaging to the text, even this edition was not authorized by the church. An initiative of Sixtus V in 1589 to issue principles that would enable the republication of the composition also failed, and in the new *Index Librorum Prohibitorum* that was published in 1596, the prohibition against the Talmud was renewed. It was argued that it was impossible to correct it and to remove all the errors and blasphemous paragraphs. And it was clarified that the prohibition was also directed against Christians.[31]

This policy, however, should be seen in the larger context of the discussion over the boundaries of permitted knowledge. First, the censorial debate over the Talmud, including its final prohibition, was based on the same principles that were employed toward other bodies of knowledge such as vernacular translations of the Bible, and astrological and scientific literature. It followed similar principles that were employed in the discussion of authors like Erasmus and Bodin.[32] As was indicated by Fragnito, the debate over the publication of the Talmud was a framework in which some of the general principles of censorship were shaped.[33] It is therefore misleading to examine it as an isolated case. The continuous debate also reflected the differences between Jesuit and Dominican perceptions of knowledge and mission, in a way similar to that demonstrated by Rivka Feldhay in relation to the Galileo affair.[34] Accordingly, it was the Jesuit cardinal Robert Bellarmine who argued that it was more probable that the Jews would convert as a result of their knowledge of Hebrew literature and not as a result of its prohibition.[35] It should be emphasized that the question of the Jews was hardly discussed at Trent, and the attitude toward the Talmud was determined by the same principles that directed the general discussion about written culture and the control of print.[36]

Moreover, what must be emphasized is that acts of prohibition and destruction against the Talmud *were explicitly associated with the authorization of the rest of Hebrew literature.* This included the Mishna, prayer books, and halakhic literature based on the Talmud. In other words, the burning was not intended to prevent the Jews from their religious practice even though it condemned and confiscated the composition that provided the authority for their practice.[37] Jews had access to talmudic literature through various commentaries and summaries, such as the interpretation of the Rif (R. Alfasi). More important, the Jews were permitted to possess books of codification, such as Maimonides's *Mishne Torah*, Yaakov b. Asher's *Turim*, and, later, the contemporary *Shulhan Aruch* of R. Yoseph Karo, a book that became, within a few years, the canonical source of Jewish law and the study of halakha. These were among the most popular books at the time among Jews, many of whom could not afford to buy the expensive multivolume Talmud and were, in any case, unfamiliar with its difficult text and complex annotations. The availability of such works, and their explicit permission, does not diminish the impact of the burning of the Talmud on the Jewish community, but it does put it in a broader context. These works were the main source for the constitution of Jewish life and religious praxis. Although all these books were now to be revised by censors, this revision was usually minor.

The important principle established at the Council of Trent concerned the implementation and institutionalization of expurgation as a permanent method of control. The expurgation of texts—that is, the erasing of sections from books as a prerequisite to authorized reading and printing—symbolizes the creation of new power/knowledge relations: once again, power was not manifested in a massive and public fashion but rather in a detailed and precise manner. Control became an inseparable part of the production of books, whether directly by censors or indirectly by the internalization of its rules by authors and publishers. Expurgation is by its very nature a complex action that demands discussion and reference to the contents and meaning of each paragraph in the text being censored. In order to expurgate, censors were obliged to determine which elements of the text were anti-Christian or heterodox but also which were permissible. Expurgation was therefore not simply a negative activity; it was also an important factor in defining orthodoxy and determining the boundaries of Catholic consensus. In many cases it served as a substitute for the total condemnation of books. The implementation of the policy of expurgation began together with the mass burnings: Julius III's bull prohibiting the Talmud also demanded that other Hebrew texts be reviewed and censored, an action that was partially initiated by the Jesuits, following an appeal of the Jews.[38] In 1557 a Jesuit initiative led to a temporary confiscation of Jewish books for careful examination, but they were later returned.[39] However, in these stages its implementation was sporadic and nonsystematic. It was partially institutionalized at the end of the century as part of the censorial project in the period of Clement VIII.[40]

The institutionalization of the censorship of Hebrew books followed the same stages that marked the general institutionalization of censorship. Later this practice was performed on two levels: censorship of books before publication and the expurgation of manuscripts and exemplars of printed books. Censorship was integrated into the practice of preparing books for publication, in order to be authorized. At the same time, a body of censors was established by the Inquisition (and by other agents of the church and secular authorities). The institutionalization of censorship of Hebrew books was discussed separately, but according to similar principles, and by the same figures that shaped the policy of the church, particularly after the establishment of the Congregation of the Index in 1571. In 1578 a commission was established whose purpose was to prepare a complete list of those sections in Hebrew literature that were to be expunged. The commission concentrated particularly on the rabbinic commentaries of the Bible, a corpus that interested many Hebraists. The commission produced an "index" that marked different passages in the compositions they examined, but its activity was far from being satisfactory and did not provide the tools for systematic and permanent control. Its conclusions (titled "Censura in Pentateuch") looks more like a Hebraist collection or polemical treatise.⁴¹ As follows from the analysis of Piet van Boxel, it marks a stage in the transition from polemics to later indexes that contained a long list of short passages to be removed from most Hebrew books.⁴² During the nineties, comprehensive and detailed indexes were produced; the most influential of them was *Sefer Ha-Ziquq (Index Expurgatorius)*, that was composed by Domenico Gerosolimitano, one of the most influential censors. It was composed at the same period as the church's production of the first general *Index expurgatorius*.⁴³ The genre of the *Index Expurgatorius*, the Index that contained all the terms and passages that should be removed from various compositions, reflects a serious attitude toward postbiblical Hebrew literature, demanding meticulous readings of Jewish texts. As such it became part of the Christian Hebraist discourse that developed at the same time and followed similar rules.

Meanwhile a body of inquisitorial censors was established, the majority of whom were Jewish converts. In later stages Christian Hebraist scholars joined the converts in the activity of editing and censorship. A good example for this link between Christian Hebraism and censorship can be found in the work of Johannes Buxtorf, as discussed by Stephen Burnett.⁴⁴

An examination of the expurgation policy and practice of the Catholic Church in this period demonstrates great inconsistency: not only were there differences between individual censors, but censors in different regions approached Jewish texts differently. There were also inconsistencies among decisions of the same censor in different copies. This inconsistency was not simply arbitrary but reflected the ambivalence embodied in the entire process of censorship. The practice of censorship reveals different and conflicting approaches, different readings and rereadings. The actual censorship was the conclusion of dialogue and debate between representatives of different attitudes and different institutions within the Catholic establishment as well as of dialogue and debate between the censors and the Jews.

The concrete role of the censor vis-à-vis other agents can be examined in the framework of the Hebrew printing shops, in which Jews, Christians, converts, editors, and censors worked together. Hebrew printing started in the fifteenth century, and its first formative stage was represented by the project directed by Gershom Soncino, where, following manuscript traditions, the methods of the humanists were employed to prepare critical editions of major Jewish texts.⁴⁵ Following Soncino, the critical stage in the establishment of Hebrew culture occurred in print shops owned by Christians, particularly Daniel Bomberg, who had a monopoly on Hebrew print in Venice from 1516 until the 1540s, when additional Christian printers entered the market for Hebrew books in Venice as well as other cities.⁴⁶ In fact, the majority of the Hebrew book industry in Italy was concentrated in print shops that were owned by Christians.⁴⁷ It therefore turns out that at this critical stage it was not the Jews who had the exclusive say in determining the final version of the books of which they were the main consumers. The formative stage of the Hebrew book, the point at which both the content and the form of "Hebrew literature" were defined for generations, occurred within a Christian Hebraist context. Printing was a Christian Hebraist praxis intended to produce texts not only for Jews (who were, naturally, its wider audience) but also for Christians. This fact is crucial for an evaluation of the role Catholic censorship played in shaping the category and contents of Hebrew literature.

Print shops in Venice and other Italian cities employed editors and proofreaders, some of them Jews—including some of the more prominent personalities of Italian Jewry—as well as some converts.[48] The Hebrew print shop was therefore a fascinating meeting place between people holding different religious identities, who worked according to similar regulations and principles.[49] The final versions should be seen as the conclusion of the dialogue between those participating in the process. We may assume that the joint work involved disagreements on religious grounds. We may also assume that the Christian publishers hoped for the conversion of the Jews who worked with them.[50] However, they all shared the same humanistic methods and a similar attitude with regard to the text.[51]

There were great differences between converts in their reactions toward Hebrew literature. Some of them played an active role in the burning of Hebrew books and were among those who demanded the prohibition of the Talmud. Others, however, reflected a much more complicated attitude and shared the assumptions of the Hebraists.[52] The converts' function in the print shops was based on similar criteria to those employed by Jews and Christian Hebraists, even after their conversion. They saw themselves as bearers of the Hebrew tradition and aspired to preserve it. Converts who were employed as editors emphasized their Jewish origins in the colophons added to the printed books.[53] The converts continued to read the same corpus they had studied as Jews, but they read it differently, intending to integrate it into their new context and even to base their new identity on this reading. For a long period they therefore played the role of mediators between the Jewish public and the Christian Hebraists, demonstrating the dual consciousness shared also by the other participants in the process. The work of the converts in the printing process, both as editors and censors, reflects a dialogue between the two sides of their identity. This "internal dialogue" also represents the dialogue that was associated with the entire process. Obviously, their interpretation of this literature was meant to match the text with their new identities as Christians, but their primary intention was to preserve the texts. It is difficult to indicate essential differences between editing done by Jews and by converts. A number of them converted during their work as editors, and it is difficult to find a change in the nature of their work before and after this decision. The debate between scholars as to whether certain editors were converts or not proves how difficult it is to clearly distinguish between Jews and converts in terms of their editorial work.[54]

The censors, most of whom were converts, fit into this framework. The religious identity that was shared by many of the editors and the censors demonstrates how blurred the professional roles were. The principal starting point for most censors was similar and involved determining the text and preparing it for publication according to their new belief. Occasionally the same person was both editor and censor, combining the responsibility of two roles.[55] The actual role of the censor was the erasing of texts that did not fit the regulations of the church, especially in regard to sections that were considered anti-Christian. But it is important to remember that the censor also had an interest in preserving the text, and that is how contemporary Jews saw his activity. Hence the very distinction between editing and censoring is problematic. Differences between these functions can be traced through the omissions of passages in editions that were prepared (and expurgated) by convert editors in earlier stages. Yet these differences also demonstrate the common principles that directed editors and censors.

In order to substantiate this claim it is necessary to look closely at the principles and textual practices of censorship and the way in which they were implemented in regard to Hebrew texts. These regulations were elaborated in detail in the *Index Expurgatorius (Sefer Ha-Ziquq)*, composed during the 1590s, by the most influential censor, Domenico Gerosolimitano, who gave his imprimatur to hundreds of censored volumes.[56] The index is composed of a preface that contains ten basic principles, followed by a complete description of what is to be erased in hundreds of Hebrew printed books.[57] The regulations may be divided into three groups: 1) blasphemy and attacks on Christianity, 2) things that contradict the Bible, and 3) elements labeled as superstitious beliefs. These categories reflect the traditional polemics against rabbinic literature, but now they were integrated into the text itself.[58]

Although the actual intervention of censors in most Hebrew books was minimal,[59] it still played an important role in the definition of the boundaries of Jewish existence. The main mission of the censors was to expunge polemical aspects, and remove anti-Christian readings. Most of Gerosolimitano's instructions (and the praxis of the censors) dealt with expressions and passages that were correctly interpreted as attacks against Christianity. Indeed, obviously offensive anti-Christian paragraphs and whole sections denigrating Catholic practice and beliefs were removed from Hebrew books. Special attention was devoted to descriptions of the Church as idolatrous since similar accusations came also from Protestants. Accordingly, whole sections that were perceived as blasphemous and offensive to the Catholic Church were eradicated. Thus, for example, the words "the nations of the world are not called human" were inconsistently removed. There are many such examples, but there is no evidence that contemporary Jews understood these passages as essential or that their removal was perceived as a form of oppression.

A central place was given to the erasing of words such as "goy," "convert," "Edom," "zurot" (icons), and "idol," when they carried obvious anti-Christian connotations or had become anti-Christian. These terms had a constitutive role in the shaping of Jewish discourse as markers of the boundaries between Jews and non-Jews. The "goy," the gentile, is essential for the self-definition of the Jew. These are terms that organized the dialogic/polemic dimension of the texts and consequently the boundaries of identity and of community. However, the censors were well aware of this fact: in many cases they were concerned with finding replacements for these terms so that while any anti-Christian understanding would be avoided, a notion of the "other" would remain. These changes were intended to replace the actual Christian other with a distant and abstract other, which was used to organize the text in a way that prevented an anti-Christian reading. Accordingly the term *Gentile* ("goy") was replaced by *babel* so that the "other" through which the boundaries of Jewish identity were defined dissociated the goy, the Gentile, from the Christians of the present. Similarly, in Radak's (R. David Kimchi's) commentary on Psalms, certain words were changed to make the text less offensive to Christians.[60] For example, the phrases "And Nevel is King of the nations" (14/1) was changed to "King of Babel," and "at this time the gentiles' worship is idolatry" was changed to "there are some idolatrous nations" (86/2). The concern manifested here is that Catholicism must not be considered as idolatry. A similar attempt to dissociate the text from Christianity is expressed in changing an expression like "*anyone* who disobeys the Rabbis" (*Makor Hayim*, Venice and Sabbioneta) into "any *Jew* who disobeys the Rabbis." This change is meaningful because it implies that no one who reads the text is obliged to accept its religious demands except "Israel the Reader."

In all these cases the censor changed the parameters of the argument so that it was not explicitly understood as anti-Christian, but left the content intact. The concern of the censor to find replacements testifies to his intention to preserve the texts and their essential meaning rather than damage them. The censor did not intend to limit the possibilities of reading; he even wanted to enlarge it so that it would include Christian readers. Moreover, Gerosolimitano's *Sefer Ha-Ziquq* explicitly states that in case these terms are essential for the description of ritual and if their replacement or deletion will distort the intention of the phrase, they should not be removed. Article 3 specifically affirms that "if it refers to Jewish Law—it should be confirmed." Article 2 says that "if it is obvious that the phrase refers to idolatry that existed previous to our Lord—it should be confirmed."

In fact these changes form the lion's share of the changes demanded by the censors. In many cases the changes and omissions were left in later editions and were accepted by the Jewish public. It is important to emphasize that the central topics of the Jewish-Christian religious debate—the Messiah or the eternity of the Torah—were outside the authority of the censor and remained in the texts. Even paragraphs on the uniqueness of the people of Israel were not taken out unless they expressed anti-Christian sentiments, such as the desire for the destruction of kingdoms. Moreover, the level of interference by censors in the halakhic legislative corpus was minimal. In other words, both Jewish practice and Jewish belief were not affected in any substantial way by the Christian censorship of Hebrew texts. Hence, one might claim that the act of censorship was an official recognition of Jewish autonomous religious praxis.

It is important to realize that even before the inquisitorial regulations were promulgated and the mechanism of censorship established, Jewish printers and publishers adopted similar principles. Already in editions published by Soncino, who followed previous manuscript traditions, many paragraphs were omitted, whose removal was later made mandatory by the censors. Several historians have tried to explain this as a result of the fear of censorship, but there is no evidence to support this. There is no reason to assume that the Jews did not remove these texts voluntarily and that the obliteration of anti-Christian paragraphs did not fit their own values. It is more probable to assume that this was an editorial decision whose intention was to avoid defining Judaism in anti-Christian terms. It is interesting that Soncino describes his work as "expurgation" in the same manner as Reuchlin in his defense of the Talmud during the Pfefferkorn affair. Their understanding of the term was quite similar and referred to the same contents. Bomberg continued in the same line, and although in his print the level of "expurgation" of anti-Christian texts was improved, it is interesting that in the editions published by the Christian printer, many obviously anti-Christian passages remained untouched.

These omissions did not satisfy the censors. Books that were printed during the fifties and sixties already contained a much higher level of censorship, that is to say that such paragraphs were removed in a more systematic way. *Sefer Ha-Ziquq* demanded the removal of many more paragraphs, even though it still left many anti-Gentile phrases in Hebrew books. However, the main line remained the same. In any case, it is problematic to claim that the anti-Christian sentiments were decisive in defining Jewish identity in the period. Either Jews did indeed hold anti-Christian views but did not need them in written books, or else they rejected them. In many cases, the omissions evidently damaged texts, and Jews could resist them in many ways. Among the passages omitted were polemical interpretations of the Bible, that were expunged from Midrashic literature and medieval commentaries. However, generally speaking, it is hard to identify what the Jews saw as restrictive about these measures. On many occasions, their complaints were directed more against the requirement that they pay the salaries of the censors, thus making censorship another form of taxation. This is not to deny the oppression embodied in the inquisitorial control or the intention of its executors to advance the conversion of the Jews. But it does clarify the boundaries of this activity and the dialogical dimension embodied within the censor's act of reading. It is not that censorship had no impact, but that its impact was not necessarily oppositional or negative for the main trends in Jewish culture at the time.

In this respect, censorial intervention contributed to the construction of what may be called an autonomous Jewish self-definition, that is to say, to the establishment of an identity that was separated from the Christian-Jewish polemics through which it had previously been defined. Thus, censorship claimed to define the attributes of Judaism disconnected from the actual "goy" and without using the Christian as the "other" against whom the self is defined. The erasure of *goy* from the Hebrew text should not be seen as the erasure of the identity "Jew," but rather as the initiation of a different definition. The change or omission of these words therefore marks both the creation of a common Jewish-Christian context and of a common text (though of course not a common canon or a common reading)—but a text that provides the conditions for autonomous Jewish existence.

An obvious example of Jews adopting an autonomous sense of identity can be found in the Italian prayer books of the period. The prayer "Blessed be He who hath not made me a goy" was changed to "Blessed be He who hath made me Israel," with a shift from negative to positive terms. And although this change was episodic and was eventually rejected, it points to a different notion of identity and reflects a significant aspect of Jewish culture in Counter-Reformation Italy. In response to the inquisitorial accusations, Jewish writers insisted that the terms to which Christians objected do not refer to Christians.[61] Although these statements were written under pressure of the confiscation and destruction of books, it is wrong to interpret them only as apologetic. Polemics and an anti-Christian attitude evidently remained essential for self-definition, but they were no longer a central element in the construction of identity. Although this change was not caused by censorship, it does clarify the way that censorship, whose immediate impact was minimal, integrated within the global process.

These principles also stand out in the Jews' involvement in the process of censorship, a fact revealed long ago by Sonne in a significant and controversial article.⁶² Later, and after the establishment of the mechanism of censorship, Jews actually participated in the censorship commissions established by the church, and they were involved in the discussions during the Council of Trent and later.⁶³ After the burning of the Talmud, the Jews nominated five rabbis to take charge of expurgating Hebrew texts according to the instructions of the Church.⁶⁴ Evidently, this involvement was forced upon them, but there is no reason to assume that they saw their work as being in contradiction to their beliefs or principles. They even took part in the formation of Church regulations and in advising the censors. Many of the regulations were the outcome of these negotiations, and the representatives could minimize the intervention, or come to agreements about the principles for editing the new editions. As was emphasized by Sonne, an earlier index composed by Avraham Provenzali later served many inquisitorial censors and provided the basis for the index prepared by the convert Hypolitus thirty years later.⁶⁵ The expurgation of passages by Jewish editors who were employed in the publishing industry followed similar patterns as those of the inquisitorial censors, both before and after the establishment of official censorship. In a contract between the publisher Conti of Cremona and Yosef Ottolenghi, it was determined that the Jewish publisher would be responsible for both editing and censorship.⁶⁶ Both functions were undertaken in this case by the convert Vittorio Eliano, but in other instances they were done by Jews. It is interesting that in many instances editions now considered superior are those in which the level of censorship was higher and that were censored under the supervision of Jewish scholars.⁶⁷ In fact the Hebrew word *ziquq* (literally: distillation) referred both to editing and expurgation.⁶⁸ In several places, the Jews were ordered to remove prohibited sections from their books.⁶⁹ In other cases, Jews initiated such examinations, and prepared the books for the examination of the censor, in order to facilitate the procedure that finally provided official permission to keep these books.

On certain occasions, Jews resisted what seemed to be too severe a policy. Such was the obliteration of the line in the prayer '*Aleynu le-Shabe'ach* "that Thou did not make us as the goyim of the land, for they pray to Hevel and Riq (idols), to a God who will not redeem them." Following the censor's orders, in many editions a blank remained in this place, so that the reader could add the missing lines. Later, the line was restored in some of the editions, although it was totally removed from many others.⁷⁰ Another obvious example was the attitude of the Jews towards the Basel edition of the Talmud, where many sections were removed. But it is interesting that the Jews' main resentment was directed, not towards the omissions but towards the additions the censors made to the text, which were directed at the Christian reader and emphasized the difference between the teachings of the rabbis and the Christian authors, and the superiority of Christian morality.[71] In any case, this edition was prohibited by the authorities of the Church.

However, in most cases the censored sections have remained out of editions until the present.[72] There are many cases in which a blank remained for a while until it completely disappeared in later editions. Robert Bonfil demonstrated the process in a paragraph from Avraham Sava's *Zror ha-Mor* (*The Bundle of Myrrh*). Following the instructions of the Index, this passage was removed, and a blank remained. However, in later editions, the blank itself was removed.[73] This example is typical, though in other incidents noncensored editions were printed.

The most extensive censorship can be found in Ashkenazi prayer books, where the anti-Christian attitude was much more significant than in Sephardi or Italian Jewish traditions. Many of these anti-Christian expressions were already removed from the editions of Soncino.[74] Indeed, some anti-Christian paragraphs were restored in later editions in Poland, but many other prayers and *piyutim* (hymns) have disappeared. They reveal the revengeful perception of redemption characteristic of early Ashkenazi culture, as has been recently revealed and examined by Israel Jacob Yuval.[75] Ashkenazi culture, as it was shaped in Eastern Europe in this period, continued to reveal an anti-Christian sentiment, censorship notwithstanding. Thus, censorship had an obvious constitutive role in what may be seen as the process of the sublimation of identity.

Censorship goes hand in hand with other main aspects of Jewish culture at the time, influenced only partially by the restrictions of the Church.[76] The evaluation of Jewish culture in this period has seen a remarkable revision during the last decades. The older attitude that saw censorship as nothing but oppression was based on the perception of the Counter-Reformation as a period marking the decline and stagnation of Italian Jewry, which allegedly followed the ideal and harmonious period of the Renaissance. This perception has been challenged lately by several scholars.[77] As Robert Bonfil has demonstrated, not only was the idealistic image of Renaissance Jewry exaggerated and distorted, it is in the period of the Counter-Reformation and Baroque, the period of segregation and ghettoization, that Jewish culture had more intimate relations with the Christian world than before.[78] Although Bonfil emphasizes the restrictions that were imposed on Jews, he has also analyzes the internal development of Jewish culture, which, while remaining distinct from Christian culture, at the same time followed similar directions and responded to similar issues and questions. According to Benjamin Ravid's observations, the ghetto provided the Jews with a defined place within Christian society, allowing Jews to become an organic, though marginal, part of the larger Christian world.[79]

The same thing can be said for censorship. While censorship did limit what Jews could read and in this sense had a negative impact, it also allowed for the creation of an autonomous Jewish sphere and identity that was not predicated on the polemics against Christianity. Furthermore, censorship was not just better than expulsion, it resulted in the validation of Jewish literature as a legitimate part of both Jewish and Christian culture. The dialectics of censorship thus contribute another dimension to the discussion of the shaping of Jewish culture in early modernity. They clarify the ambivalent attitude of the Church, an ambivalence embodied within Hebraist discourse. The minimal censorship employed upon halakhic legislative literature demonstrates the autonomous sphere defined by the censors. In this case, the lack of significant expurgation is a statement that ensures Jewish autonomy.

Censorship thus participated in the larger process of the transition of Jewish identity to modernity: from a discourse based on theological terms and embodied within the theological debate to a definition of Judaism in terms of "ethnicity" and "culture," the concepts that were to dominate the modern discourse. This was a long, multifaceted and complicated process, in which Catholic censorship played only a limited role. But the printing press in general, and censorial discourse in particular, provides a unique opportunity to analyze the transition to modernity. As I tried to demonstrate elsewhere, the entire Hebraist discourse embodies this transition.[80]

Thus, both in the act of conversion and in the act of censorship, the censors reveal aspects of modern Jewish discourse. The dialectics of censorship is part of the process of re-definition of Jewish existence and Jewish identity in Europe. The censor participated in the definition of Judaism as a "religion," that is to say, as a set of rituals and beliefs that he himself rejected, and as an important textual tradition. While abandoning obedience to the Law, these figures continued to read the same corpus. Interestingly, through this, he dialectically prepares the foundation for the modern perception of Judaism and history.[81] Dominant trends in modern Jewish thought were founded on the attempt to distinguish Judaism from polemics, and to locate Judaism as part of a "Judeo-Christian" culture. Jewish historians (including those who described censorship as an act of oppression) in fact shared his ideas, and rejected the same passages he omitted. They tried to describe Jewish history as autonomous, yet compatible with dominant "Western" values. However they transferred these values, while adopting the Protestant perception of the Catholic Church as an expression of reaction and arbitrary oppression.

A good example of the relations between censorship and contemporary Jewish perceptions can be found in the famous seventh chapter of Ibn Verga's *Shevet Yehudah* (The Tribe of Judah), as well as in other parts of this book. The entire book tries to describe and explain persecutions against the Jews and their expulsions and distinguish between different Christian attitudes. The seventh chapter allegedly records a conversation between the King and a Christian scholar, "Thomas," who defends Judaism and debunks the superstitions attributed to it. Just like the censor, Thomas defines Jewish identity apart from the theological debates, as a noble ethnicity, the predecessor of Ancient Israel who carries wisdom important for the Christian faith and represents an autonomous culture that fits the values of Christian society and thought. Thomas rejects the libels against the Jews and refutes them as popular prejudices that should be condemned. He argues (through the Christian moderator) that anti-Christian sentiments do not accurately represent Judaism and the Jews. The book, which is dedicated to the analysis of historical persecutions against the Jews, distinguishes between different Christian attitudes towards the Jews and consciously identifies with an ideal image of the Hebraist.

It is striking that the Jewish author presented his own beliefs through the eyes of a Christian as the perspective through which Jewish identity is to be defined. Ibn Verga's work was intended for Jewish readers, and the Christian scholar serves as a literary mediator, through which Jewish self-consciousness is shaped. This is the same point of view from which the convert censor is working, and the chapter demonstrates a desire to accommodate Jewish self-definition to Christian Hebraist discourse while at the same time emphasizing the autonomous nature of Judaism as both a religion and an ethnicity. Ibn Verga's text reflects the perspective and attitudes of the censor in several respects. First, he chooses a learned Christian to argue for the validity and value of Judaism, and this in a composition that is clearly addressed to Jews. The Christian perspective cannot thus be simply presented as "external"—it is part of a Jewish text, part of an internal discussion of Jewish identity. Second, the elements that he points to are very similar to the categories of the censor, and like the censor he rejects anti-Christian sentiments. In other words, the image of Judaism presented by Ibn Verga through the perspective of the Christian scholar is identical to the image of Judaism dictated by the censor. The author consciously tries to present Judaism as a religion compatible with the values of European elites. He does not blur the theological differences or hide the oppression of the Jews. His own image of Judaism, however, is not very different from that of the censor. He thus enables us to clarify the concrete, unintentional, implications of censorship. Ibn Verga voluntarily accepts the principles of the censors (with the exception of the prohibition of the Talmud). Polemics against Christianity continued to be significant among Jews, but they were not published and were not essential for questions of interpretation and historical perceptions.

The censor's demand to remove anti-Christian readings can thus be seen as dialectically contributing to the development of modern Jewish consciousness: he continues to read the same corpus but without commitment to the halakhic law. Later, conversion was no longer necessary for the rejection of

Halakha by Jews. To a certain extent, therefore, the figure of the censor is a precursor of the modern secular Jewish scholar, who reads from a similar perspective.

I do not intend to ignore the repressive aspects of censorship but rather to point to its presence in later Jewish discourse and especially in the perspective from which Jewish history, including the history of censorship, was written. Interestingly, Jewish historiography traditionally accepted the Protestant perception of the Catholic Church during this period. However, scholars who claim that censorship had a negative impact on Jewish culture have accepted the same values and principles that directed the censors in their attempt to write Jewish history as autonomous and to isolate the discussion of the Jews from polemics against Christianity. The focus on censorship is therefore relevant to major aspects of modern Jewish discourse. We should realize that the perception of Judaism that directed later Jewish developments was based on this same perspective. What should be emphasized is that later generations and the modern Jewish discourse established since the eighteenth century follow in the footsteps of the early modern censors by defining Jewish identity as an autonomous culture that developed apart from Jewish-Christian polemics but shared the same cultural and moral values as the dominant Christian culture. This does not mean that anti-Christian sentiments did not arise; they continued to serve as a tool of resistance in different contexts. But at least partially, the censor participated unconsciously in the reshaping of Jewish identity. A close reading of censorship and an awareness of the dialogic nature of this praxis in the sixteenth and seventeenth centuries can therefore lead to an awareness of our own perceptions and modes of reading.

The insights of Carlo Ginzburg in "The Anthropologist and the Historian" acquire dimension in this context.[82] In his essay Ginzburg emphasizes the fact that the historian reads "behind the ears of the inquisitor." Unlike the approach to medieval popular culture, and to a certain extent, converts, we do have a direct access to the Jews and their culture and are not dependent on the files of the Inquisitors. Their approaches, as well as their resistance, are documented. In spite of these essential differences, however (or perhaps because of them), it is important to note that our own perception of "Judaism" and our methods of reading are based on similar values and similar categories to those elaborated within early modern Hebraist discourse. In summary, modern Jewish historiography, which condemned the Inquisition, in fact followed the values it dictated.

Notes

1. Moritz Stern, *Urkundliche Beiträge ueber die Stellung der Päpste zu den Juden* (Kiel, Ger.: H. Fiencke, 1893–95), 98–102.

2. William Popper, *The Censorship of Hebrew Books* (New York: Knickerbocker, 1899; reprint: New York: Ktav Press, 1969); Kenneth Stow, "The Burning of the Talmud in 1553 in the Light of Sixteenth Century Catholic Attitudes towards the Talmud," *Bibliothèque d'humanisme et renaissance* 34 (1972): 435–59 (reprinted in *Essential Papers on Judaism and Christianity in Conflict, From Late Antiquity to the Reformation*, ed. J. Cohen [New York: New York University Press, 1991]); Avraham Berliner, "Censur und Confiscation hebräischer Bücher im Kirchenstaate," *Jahres-Bericht* (Berlin: Rabbiner Seminar zu Berlin, 1889–1992), 29–53; Meir Benayahu, *Haskama Ve-Reshut Bi-dfusei Vinizea* (Copyright, Authorship and Imprimatur for Hebrew Books Printed in Venice) (Jerusalem, 1971); Avraham Yaari, *Srifat Ha-Talmud Be-Italia* (The Burning of the Talmud in Italy) (Jerusalem, 1958); Marvin J. Heller, *Printing the Talmud: A History of the Earliest Printed Editions of the Talmud* (Brooklyn: Im Hasefer, 1992); Mauro Perani, "Confisca e censura dei libri ebraici a Modena fra cinque e seicento," in *L'inquisizione egli ebrei in Italia*, ed. Michele Luzzati, Biblioteca di Cultura Moderna 1066 (Roma e Bari: Laterza, 1994), 287–320; Fausto Parente, "La Chiesa e il *Talmud*," in *Storia d'Italia*, vol. 11 of *Gli ebrei in Italia*, ed. Corrado Vivanti (Torino, It.: Giulio Einaudi editore, 1996), 521–643; P.C. Ioly Zorattini, "Censura e controllo della stampa ebraica a Venezia nel cinquecento," in *Manoscritti, frammenti e libri ebraici nell'Italia dei secoli XV-XVI*, ed. Giuliano Tamani and Angelo Vivian (Rome: Carucci, 1991); Fausto Parente, "The Index, the Holy Office, the Condemnation of the Talmud, and Publication of Clement VIII's Index," in *Church, Censorship, and Culture in Early Modern Italy*, ed. Gigliola Fragnito, trans. Adrian Belton (Cambridge: Cambridge University Press, 2000), 163–93. On censorship in Germany, see Stephen G. Burnett, "Hebrew Censorship in Hanau: A Mirror of Jewish-Christian Coexistence in Seventeenth-Century Germany," in *The Expulsion of the Jews, 1492 and After*, ed. Raymond B. Waddington and Arthur H. Williamson (New York: Garland, 1994), 199–222.

3. Kenneth Stow, *Catholic Thought and Papal Jewish Policy, 1555–1593* (New York: Jewish Theological Seminary of America, 1977).

4. For general surveys of censorship, see Antonio Rotondo, "La Censura Ecclesiastica e la cultura," *Storia d'Italia*, I documenti 5 (2) (Turin: Giulio Einaudi editore, 1973), 1397–1492; Paul Grendler, "Printing and Censorship," in *Cambridge History of Renaissance Philosophy*, ed. Charles B. Schmitt (Cambridge: Cambridge University Press, 1988); Paolo Simoncelli, "Documenti interni alla congregazione dell'indice, 1571–1590: Logica e ideologica dell'intervento censorio," *Annuario dell'istituto storico italiano per l'età moderna e contemporanea* 33–34 (1983–84): 189–215. Over the last decades we have witnessed the publication of many new and illuminating studies dedicated to the study of ecclesiastical censorship. Among these studies one should mention the vast project of the Roman Indices directed by Bujanda (Jesus M. De Bujanda, *Index des livres interdits*. Editions de l'Université de Sherbrooke, 10 vols. [Paris: Librairie Droz, 1990]) and Gigliola Fragnito's study of the condemnation of biblical translations (Gigliola Fragnito, *La Bibbia al rogo: La censura ecclesiastica e i volgarizzamenti della scrittura, (1471–1605)* (Bologna: il Mulino, 1997). This interest has increased following the opening of the general archive of the Congregation of the Doctrine of the Faith in Rome in 1998. This event has already yielded the publication of new and insightful studies: Peter Godman, *The Saint as Censor: Robert Bellarmine between Inquisition and Index*, Studies in Medieval and Reformation Thought 80 (Leiden: Brill, 2000); *Censura ecclesiastica e cultura politica tra cinquecento e seicento*, ed. Cristina Stango (Firenze, It.: Leo S. Olschki, 2001); *Church, Censorship, and Culture in Early Modern Italy*, ed. Gigli-

ola Fragnito, trans. Adrian Belton (Cambridge: Cambridge University Press, 2000); *L'Inquisizione e gli storici: Un cantiere aperto,* ed. G. Berardi (Rome: Accademia nazionale dei Lincei, 2000).

    5. On the general level, Foucault's approach to power/knowledge relations is especially relevant for the discussion of censorship. Foucault rejected the approach that maintained that knowledge can develop only outside the limits of power and focused instead on the way power is manifested within different discursive frameworks and in the production of knowledge. See Michel Foucault, *Power/Knowledge: Selected Interviews and Other Writings,* ed. Colin Gordon (New York: Pantheon, 1977); idem, *Discipline and Punish: The Birth of the Prison,* trans. Alan Sheridan (London: Allen Lane, 1977), 25–30; idem, *The History of Sexuality,* trans. Robert Hurley (New York: Vintage, 1980), 92–96. For a Foucaldian approach to the analysis of censorship, see Sue Curry Jansen, *Censorship: The Knot that Binds Power and Knowledge* (New York: Oxford University Press, 1988).

    6. For the extensive literature and various approaches that have developed in this direction, see Roland Barthes, "The Death of the Author," in Barthes, *Image, Music, Text,* trans. Stephen Heath (London: Fontana, 1977); Umberto Eco, *The Role of the Reader* (Bloomington: Indiana University Press, 1979); Wolfgang Iser, *The Implied Reader: Patterns of Communication in Prose Fiction from Bunyan to Beckett* (Baltimore: Johns Hopkins University Press, 1978); Jane F. Tomkins, ed., *Reader-Response Criticism: From Formalism to Post-Structuralism* (Baltimore: Johns Hopkins University Press, 1980); Susan R. Suleiman and Inge Crosman, eds., *The Reader in the Text: Essays on Audience and Interpretation* (Princeton: Princeton University Press, 1980); Paul Ricoeur, *Time and Narrative* (Chicago: University of Chicago Press, 1984–85).

    7. See for example: Natalie Z. Davis, *Society and Culture in Early Modern France* (Stanford, Calif.: Stanford University Press, 1975); Carlo Ginzburg, *The Cheese and the Worms: The Cosmos of a Sixteenth-Century Miller,* trans. John and Anne Tedeschi (Baltimore: Johns Hopkins University Press, 1980); Anthony Grafton, *Defenders of the Text: The Traditions of Scholarship in an Age of Science, 1450–1800* (Cambridge: Harvard University Press, 1991); Robert Darnton and Roger Chartier, "Texts, Printing, Readings," in *The New Cultural History,* ed. Lynn Hunt (Berkeley and Los Angeles: The University of California Press, 1989), 154–75. See particularly the volume *A History of Reading in the West,* ed. Roger Chartier and Guglielmo Cavallo, trans. Lydia G. Cochrane (Amherst: University of Massachusetts Press, 1998).

    8. On the print revolution and its impacts, see Elizabeth Eisenstein, *The Printing Press as an Agent of Change,* 2 vols. (Cambridge: Cambridge University Press, 1979). For an examination of the different factors that participated in the process, see, among others: Brian Richardson, *Print Culture in Renaissance Italy: The Editor and the Vernacular Text* (Cambridge: Cambridge University Press, 1994); idem, *Printing, Writers, and Readers in Renaissance Italy* (Cambridge: Cambridge University Press, 1999).

    9. Ginzburg, *The Cheese and the Worms.* Ginzburg examines the way the miller Menoccio read several texts and the interpretation of the miller's discourse by the Inquisitors.

    10. Roger Chartier, *The Order of Books: Readers, Authors, and Libraries in Europe between the Fourteenth and Eighteenth Centuries,* trans. Lydia G. Cochrane (Stanford, Calif.: Stanford University Press, 1994), viii.

    11. On the various aspects of the Counter Reformation, see the bibliographical essay by William V. Hudon, "Religion and Society in Early Modern Italy: Old Ques-

tions, New Insights," *American Historical Review* 101 (1996): 783–804; R. Po-Chia Hsia, *The World of Catholic Renewal, 1540–1770: New Approaches to European History* (Cambridge: Cambridge University Press, 1998); Robert Bireley, *The Refashioning of Catholicism, 1450–1700: A Reassessment of the Counter Reformation* (Washington, D.C.: Catholic University of America Press, 1999); David M. Luebke, ed., *The Counter Reformation: The Essential Readings* (Oxford: Blackwell Publishers, 1999); John W. O'Malley, ed., *Catholicism in Early Modern History* (St. Louis, 1988); Eric Cochrane, "Counter Reformation or Tridentine Reformation," in *San Carlo Borromeo: Catholic Reform and Ecclesiastical Politics in the Second Half of the Sixteenth Century*, ed. John M. Headley and John B. Tamaro (Washington, D.C.: Folger, 1988), 31–46.

12. See John Tedeschi, "Preliminary Observations on Writing a History of the Roman Inquisition," in Tedeschi, *The Prosecution of Heresy: Collected Studies on the Inquisition in Early Modern Italy* (Binghamton, N.Y.: Medieval and Renaissance Texts and Studies, 1991), 3–21; Silvana Seidel-Menchi, "Inquisizione come repressione o inquisizione come mediazione? Una proposta di periodizzazione," *Annuario dell'Istituto storico italiano per l'età moderna e contemporana* 35–36 (1983–84): 53–77.

13. Rivka Feldhay, *Galileo and the Church: Political Inquisition or Critical Dialogue* (Cambridge: Cambridge University Press, 1995).

14. In her illuminating discussion on censorship and literature in England, Patterson demonstrated that "it is to censorship that we in part owe our very concept of 'literature' as a kind of discourse with rules of its own." Annabel Patterson, *Censorship and Interpretation: The Conditions of Writing and Reading in Early Modern England* (Madison: University of Wisconsin Press, 1984), 4. See also Cyndia Susan Clegg, *Press Censorship in Elizabethan England* (Oxford: Oxford University Press, 1997); Richard Dutton, *Licensing, Censorship and Authorship in Early Modern England* (Houndmills, Eng.: Palgrave, 2000); Kevin Sharpe, *Reading Revolutions: The Politics of Reading in Early Modern Europe* (New Haven: Yale University Press, 2000).

15. On the burning of books in this period, see Frede, "Roghi di libri ereticali nell'Italia del Cinquecento," in *Ricerche storiche ed economiche in memoria di C. Barbagallo*, vol. 2, ed. L. de Rosa (Naples, 1970): 315–28; Fragnito, *La Bibbia al rogo*,

16. The messianic impulse is emphasized by Stow, *Catholic Thought*.

17. "Thalmud Hebraeorum ejusque glossae, annotationes, expositiones omnes." Franz H. Reusch, *Die Indices Librorum Prohibitorum des 16. Jahrhunderts* (Tübingen, Ger.: Stuttgart Literarischer Verein Bibliotek, 1886), 176–208. This collection includes also earlier indices that were published by both secular authorities and by the church. The index is now republished by J. M. De Bujanda, *Index de Rome, 1557, 1559, 1564* (*Index des livres interdits*, J. M. Bujanda), 869–70. See Grendler, *Inquisition*, 79–85. Giulio Pesenti, "Libri censurati a Venezia nei secoli xvi–xvii," *La Bibliofilia* 58 (1956): 15–30. On the burning of the books by Erasmus, see Paul Grendler and Marcella Grendler, "The Survival of Erasmus in Italy," in Paul Grendler, *Culture and Censorship in Late Renaissance Italy and France* (Aldershot, Eng.: Ashgate, 1981).

18. On the discussion that preceded the publication of the index, see Bujanda, *Index de Rome*, 27–49.

19. See the documents collected by Avraham Ya'ari, *Srifat Ha-Talmud be-Italia* (The Burning of the Talmud in Italy) (Tel Aviv: Avraham Zioni, 1954); see also Heller, *Printing the Talmud*, 238–40.

20. Brian Pullan, *The Jews of Europe and the Inquisition of Venice, 1550–1670* (Totowa, N.J.: Barnes and Noble, 1983). A letter to the Inquisition in Florence clarified

that the prohibition includes Christian readers. It also associated the prohibition of the Talmud to the writings of Jean Bodin. The letter, dated 27 April 1596, was published by John A. Tedeschi, "Florentine Documents for a History of the Index of Prohibited Books," in *Renaissance Studies in Honor of Hans Baron*, ed. Tedeschi and A. Molho (Florence, 1971), 579–605, (republished in Tedeschi, *The Prosecution of Heresy: Collected Studies on the Inquisition in Early Modern Italy* [Binghamton, N.Y.: Medieval and Renaissance Texts and Studies, 1991], 273–319).

21. P. C. Ioly Zoratini, "The Inquisition and the Jews in Sixteenth-Century Venice," in *Proceedings of the Seventh World Congress of Jewish Studies* (Jerusalem: World Union of Jewish Studies, 1981), 83–92.

22. One of the contemporaneous explanations given to the burning was a story of a proselyte monk who incited against Christianity. Yoseph Ha-Cohen, *Emek Ha-Bacha*, 111.

23. Already in the decree *Inter sollicitudines* (published by Leo X in 1516), which demanded control over the printing press, the danger of translations from Greek, Hebrew, and Arabic was mentioned. See Mansi, *Sacrorum Conciliorum Collectio*, vol. 32 (Paris, 1907–27), cols. 912–13. Hirsch argues that the background of the announcement of the decree was the Reuchlin affair (*Printing*, 90).

24. On the use of Hebrew letters for magic by Christians, see Ruth Martin, *Witchcraft and the Inquisition in Venice, 1550–1650* (Oxford: Basil Blackwell, 1989), 90–98. On the perception of Hebrew as the "mother of all languages," see David Ruderman, *The Valley of Vision: The Heavenly Journey of Avraham Ben Hananiah Yagel*, translated from the Hebrew with an introduction by idem (Philadelphia: University of Pennsylvania Press, 1989), 56–59.

25. Grendler, *Inquisition*, 93–102. Godman, *The Saint as Censor*, 5ff. Grendler describes the appeal of the printers in Venice against the mass prohibition (ibid., 301–6). On the objection of the representatives of the universities, see Michele Jacoviello, "Proteste di editorie librai veneziani conto l'introduzione della censura sulla stampa a Venezia, 1443–1555," *Archivo Storico Italiano* 151 (1993): 27–56. The prominent critic was the Hebraist Andreas Masius. See his letter to Cardinal Piginus in Stow, "The Burning of the Talmud," 448–49.

26. For discussions of the questions and particularly the debates over the boundaries of knowledge, see Feldhay, *Galileo*, 71–92, and Eric Cochrane, *Italy, 1530–1630* (London, 1988). On the discussion of the index, see Bujanda, *Index de Rome*, 51–73.

27. "Si tamen prodierint sine nomine Thalmud et sine injuriis et calumniis in religionem christianem, tolerabuntur." Reusch, *Die Indices Librorum Prohibitorum des 16. Jahrhunderts*, 279; Bujanda, *Index de Rome*, 869–70.

28. Cited by Parente, "The Index," 168.

29. Ibid., 169. Parente's reconstruction of papal policy is based on the documents from the archives of the Holy Office opened recently.

30. B. Rekers, *Benito Arias Montano* (London: Warburg Insitute, University of London, 1972). Earlier, Montano was responsible for the controversial polyglot of Plantin in Antwerp that included references from rabbinic literature.

31. John Tedeschi, "Florentine Documents for a History of the Index of Prohibited Books," in Tedeschi, *The Prosecution of Heresy: Collected Studies on the Inquisition in Early Modern Italy* (Binghamton, N.Y.: Medieval and Renaissance Texts and Studies, 1991), 282–85.

32. See the detailed discussions in Godman, *The Saint as Censor*, and the volume

edited by Fragnito (*Church, Censorship, and Culture*). On several occasions the Talmud was mentioned together with the writings of Bodin, as in the document published by Tedeschi (see previous note).

33. Fragnito, *Church, Censorship, and Culture*, follows the findings of Parente. On several occasions the discussion of the Talmud was associated with the discussion of the writings of Jean Bodin and was formulated in similar terms.

34. Feldhay, *Galileo*.

35. Stow, "The Burning of the Talmud," 451–52. On Bellarmine's activity as censor, see Godman, *The Saint as Censor*. On his perception of knowledge as demonstrated during the Galileo affair, see Feldhay, *Galileo*, passim. It is interesting that Bellarmine, who supported the toleration of an expurgated version of the Talmud, was one of those who condemned the writings of Bodin.

36. Salo W. Baron, "The Council of Trent and Rabbinic Literature," in idem, *Ancient and Medieval Jewish History*, edited and with a foreword by Leon A. Feldman (New Brunswick, N.J.: Rutgers University Press, 1972), 355. On the discussion of the Jews, see Baron, *Social and Religious History of the Jews*, vol. 14 (New York: Columbia University Press, 1969), 17–25.

37. Hakohen, *Emeq Habacha*, 113. See also Ya'ari, *Srifat Ha-Talmud*, 204.

38. Popper, *The Censorship of Hebrew Books*, 37–38; Grendler, *Inquisition*, 93.

39. Berliner argued that it was a permanent confiscation. However, Sonne (*MiPaulus Harevi'i*, 123) proved that it was only for examination. This obviously comes out of several letters of the period. See Schwartz, "Michtavim al Dvar Gzirat ha-Talmud bishnat 1554," *Alim le-bibliographia u-lekorot Israel* 2 (1936): 49–52; Ephraim Kopffer, "Teudot Hadashot be-inian hadpasat Sepher Ha-Zohar," *Michael* 1 (1973): 308.

40. On the policy of expurgation since Paul IV, see Bujanda, *Index*, vol. 8, 100–108; 138–42. In Trent, see ibid., 813–21. On its institutionalization following the index of 1596: see ibid, vol. 9, 926–27. See also Vittorio Frajese, "Le licenze di lettura e la politica dell sant'uffizio dopo l'indice Clementino," in *L'Inquisizione e gli storici*, ed. Berardi, 179–220; G. Fragnito, "Aspetti e problemi della censura espurgatoria," *L'Inquisizione e gli storici*, 161–78.

41. On that index, see Gustave Sacerdote, "Deux Index expurgatoires de livres Hébreux," *REJ* 30 (1986): 262–71. And see the illuminating discussion of Piet van Boxel, "Cardinal Santoro and the Expurgation of Hebrew Literature," in *The Roman Inquisition, the Index, and the Jews: New Perspectives for Research*, ed. Stephan Wendehorst, Studies in European Judaism 8 (Leiden, Netherlands: Brill Academic Publishers, forthcoming).

42. Van Boxel, "Santoro." Van Boxel, who follows Gregory Martin's *Roma Sancta* (1581), suggests that the composition was intended not only for the revision of books but also for the sermons, which the Jews had to attend in the "Church of the Company of the Holy Trinity." And held by Santoro? This likely assumption shows the link between revision of Hebrew literature and missionary efforts, but it also demonstrates how this desire led to the definition of the boundaries of permitted Jewish knowledge and Jewish existence.

43. The first index was published by the church in 1599–1601 and was complemented in 1607: *Indicis Librorum expurgatorum in studiosorum gratiam confecti* (Romae: Ex Typographia R. Cam. Apost., 1607).

44. Stephen Burnett, *From Christian Hebraism to Jewish Studies: Johannes Buxtorf (1564–1629) and Hebrew Learning in the Seventeenth Century* (Leiden, Netherlands: E. J. Brill, 1996).

45. Among the studies dedicated to these stages, see David W. Amram, *The Makers of Hebrew Books in Italy, Being Chapters in the History of the Hebrew Printing-Press* (Philadelphia: Edward Stern and Co., 1909); C. D. Friedberg, *Toldot Ha-dfus Ha-ivri Be-Italia, Sfarad-Portuga ve-Turkia* (Tel Aviv: Bar-Yuda, 1956); A. M. Habermann, *Hasepher ha-Ivri behitpatchuto* (Jerusalem: Reuven Mass); A. Freiman and M. Marx, *Otzar Lemlechet Ha-dfus harishona bamea ha-15* (Berlin, 1924–31; reprint Jerusalem: Jewish National and University Library, 1968); Moses Marx, "On the Date of the Appearance of the First Printed Hebrew Books," in *Alexander Marx Jubilee Volume* (New York: Jewish Theological Seminary of America, 1950), 481–501; Peretz Tishbi, "Dfusei-eres (Incunabulim) Ivriim," *Kiriat Sepher* 58 (1983): 808–57; Malachi Beit-Arieh, "The Relationship between Early Hebrew Printing and Handwritten Books; Attachment or Detachment," *Scripta Hierosolymitana* 29 (1989): 1–26; Shifra Baruchson, *Sfarim Ve-Korim: Tarbut ha-kriah shel yehudei Italia bitkufat ha-renaissance* (Ramat Gan, Israel: Bar-Ilan University Press), 27–37. On the omitting of anti-Christian paragraphs, see Rabinowitz, *Ma'amar*, 28; Benayahu, *Ha-dfus ha-Ivri be-Cremona* (Jerusalem: Machon Ben-Zvi and Mosad Harav Kook), 53. Both explain this policy as a result of church control; however, they admit that such a mechanism did not exist. In fact, the obliteration of anti-Christian sections was part of the expurgation—the term used for editing!

46. On Bomberg, see, among others, Amram, *Makers*, 191–224; Habermann, *Hamadpis Daniel Bomberg v-reshimat sifrei beit dfuso* (Zefat, Israel: Museum of the Art of Print, 1978); Joshua Bloch, "Venetian Printers of Hebrew Books," *Bulletin of the New York Public Library* 36 (1932): 71–92; Benayahu, *Haskama Vereshut*, 17–24, 156–69; Avraham Rosenthal, "Daniel Bomberg and His Talmud Editions," in *Gli Ebrei e Venezia: Secoli xiv–xviii*, ed. Gaetano Cozzi (Milano: Edizioni communità, 1987), 375–416. Baruchson, *Sfarim*, 30–35.

47. Following the establishment of the guild of printing workers, Jews were not allowed to take part in this industry. See Benjamin Ravid, "The Prohibition against Jewish Printing and Publishing in Venice and the Difficulties of Leone Modena," in *Studies in Medieval Jewish History and Literature*, ed. I. Twersky (Cambridge: Harvard University Press, 1979), 135–53.

48. Some of the more prominent personalities of Italian Jewry took part in the process: Elia Levita, Bakhur, the Maharam of Padua, his son Rabbi Shmuel Katzenellenbogen, Avraham and David Provenzali, R. Avraham de Balmes, Chaim b"r Moshe Alton. In Cremona, Yosef Ottolenghi was the chief editor in Vincenzo Conti's printing press, according to the needs of his yeshiva.

49. On the print shop as a place of meeting and of new forms of collaboration between different groups, see Eisenstein, *Printing Press as an Agent of Change*, 136ff.

50. The charge of "missionary motives" was directed against Bomberg by several modern scholars. See, for example, Israel Mehlman, "Daniel Bomberg, the Printer of Venice," *Areshet* 3 (1963): 96–98; Benayahu, *Haskama VeReshut*, 17. However, there is no evidence of any pressure of this kind. In any case the production was directed toward the Jews, who remained the main customers of Hebrew books.

51. The most obvious representative of a humanistic approach in the first stage was R. Elia Levita, who had close relations with many Hebraists and who served as an editor of many volumes. Levita's converted grandsons were employed as editors and censors. The adoption of humanistic methods was taken for granted in the print industry. I use the term *humanistic methods* in the most elementary sense, as a set of principles with regard to texts, criticial reading and editing, determined in the print shops.

For a survey on the role of humanism in Italian Jewish culture, see David Ruderman, "The Italian Renaissance and Jewish Thought," in *Renaissance and Humanism: Foundations, Forms, and Legacy*, vol. 1, ed. Albert Rabil, Jr. (Philadelphia: University of Pensylvania Press, 1988), 382–433; Hava Tirosh-Rothschild, "In Defense of Jewish Humanism," *Jewish History* 3 (1988): 31–58.

52. On converts and their various attitudes, see S. Simonsohn, "Some Well Known Jewish Converts during the Renaissance," *REJ* 148 (1989): 17–52; Kenneth R. Stow, "A Tale of Uncertainties: Converts in the Roman Ghetto," in *Shlomo Simonsohn Jubilee Volume: Studies on the History of the Jews in the Middle Ages and Renaissance Period*, ed. D. Carpi et al. (Tel Aviv: Chaim Rosenberg School of Jewish Studies, Tel Aviv University), 257–81; "Conversion, Christian Hebraism, and Hebrew Prayer in the Sixteenth Century," *HUCA* 47 (1976): 217–36; Robert Bonfil, "Dubious Crimes in Sixteenth-Century Italy; Rethinking the Relations between Jews, Christians, and 'Conversos' in Pre-Modern Europe," in *The Jews of Spain and the Expulsion of 1492*, ed. Moshe Lazar and Stephen Haliczer (Lancaster, Calif.: Labyrinthos, 1997), 299–310.

53. For instance, Cornelius Adelkind in the colophon to the Responsa of Yosef Colon and to "Pardes Rimonim" of R. Shem-Tov Ibn Shaprut, when he calls himself Cornelius Adelkind of the house of HaLevy. The grandsons of R. Elia Levita used to mention their origin: "Me, Vittorio Eliano, the grandson of the head of grammarians" (Oxford, Bodleian Library, MS 1547, M 108).

54. For example, the debate whether Israel Cornelius Edelkind, who was employed as an editor in Venice, was baptized. See a survey of the various opinions in Heller, *Printing the Talmud*, 159–61. An example of this is found in the work of Giacomo Geraldino, who has been presented until recently as someone who injured Hebrew literature. Recently it became known that Geraldino is the Christian name of Rabbi Yosef Arles, one of the outstanding personalities of Italian Jewry, after his conversion. In a letter related to the issue of the confiscation of the Talmud, the author says, "I heard from the house of my uncle that there is good hope from the Talmud matter because Rabbi Yoseph Arli was authorized by the Pope to do all that he wants in the aforementioned matter." It is almost certain that the letter was written after Arles's conversion, and, if so, it is interesting that the Jews continue to refer to him by his Jewish name and with respect. In addition it turns out that the Jews considered his work as helpful rather than damaging. Buksenboim, *Igrot Melamdim* (Tel Aviv: Chaim Rosenberg School of Jewish Studies, Tel Aviv University, 1985), 10–15.

55. For example, in Cremona, Vittorio Eliano worked under the supervision of R. Yosef Ottolenghi. See the contrast between the publisher and the Jews in S. Simonsohn, "Choze le–hotza'at sfarim ivriim be-Cremona," in *Scritti in Memoria di Umberto Nahon*, ed. R. Bonfil et al. (Jerusalem: Fondazioni Sally Mayer, Raffaele Cantoni, 1978), 143–50.

56. On Domenico, see Pier Cesare Ioly Zorattini, "Domenico Gerosolimitano a Venezia," *Sefarad* 58 (1998): 107–15. Some of his autobiographical notes were published by G. G. Sacerdote, "I Codici Ebraici della Pia Casa dei Neofity in Roma," *Atti della Reale Accademio dei Lincei*, ser. 4, 10, 188.

57. The most complete manuscript of this composition is MS Vat. 273. The preface was first published by Nathan Porges, "Der hebraische Index Expurgatorius," in *Festschrift A. Berliner;* Parente, "La Chiesa e il *Talmud*," 605; S. Simonsohn, *The Jews in the Duchy of Mantua* (Jerusalem, 1977), 690–91; Popper, *The Censorship of Hebrew Books*, 93ff.

58. On a similar categorization, see Chen Merchavia, "A Treatise against the Talmud in the Days of the Talmud Burning in Italy," *Tarbiz* 37 (1968): 78–96.

59. See, for instance, Baruchson, *Sfarim Ve-Korim;* Robert Bonfil, "Reading in the Jewish Communities of Western Europe in the Middle Ages," in *A History of Reading in the West*, ed. Chartier and Cavallo, 158–59. Heller (*Printing*, 6) correctly poses the question: "If the present text [of the Talmud] is corrupted, why hasn't a corrected text, based on manuscripts and the first uncensored printed editions, been established?" In his examination of the activity of the censor Keuchen in Hanau Burnett concludes that "his definition of offensive or blasphemous material was fairly narrow" (Burnett, *Censorship*, 205).

60. R. David Kimchi, "A Commentary on Psalms" (Cremona, It.: Vincenzo Conti, 1561). On this, see E. Z. Melamed, "Perush Radak Le-Tehilim," *Areshet* 2 (1960): 35–69. This commentary is by its nature a polemic against Christianity.

61. An example is an apologetic treatise of Salomon of Modena, written in response to the charges of the convert Alessandro Franceschi, published and analyzed by David Ruderman in "A Jewish Apologetic Treatise from Sixteenth-Century Bologna," *HUCA* 50 (1979): 253–75. Modena's major concern was to dissociate any reference to "goy" in rabbinic literature from contemporary Christianity and to argue that the rabbis consistently had in mind pagan idolaters. Though it is clear that this treatise was written in response to an accusation of a convert censor, Ruderman emphasizes its Jewish origins and describes it as similar to Hameiri's approach.

62. I. Sonne, "Expurgation of Hebrew Books—the Work of Jewish Scholars," *Bulletin of the New York Public Library* 46 (1942): 975–1014.

63. Baron, "Trent," 365–66. On the negotiations of Jewish delegates concerning the publication of the Talmud, see Parente, "The Condemnation." Avraham David, "Heter le-hadpasat ha-Talmud be-Italia eser shanim le-achar sreifato," in *Ginzei ha-machon le-tazlumei yad ivriim* (Jerusalem: Jewish National and University Library, 1996), 21–22. On their involvement in the commission, see van Boxel, "Santoro."

64. Kenneth Stow, *The Jews in Rome*, vol. 2 (Leiden, Neth.: E. J. Brill, 1995), document 1607.

65. Sonne, "Expurgation of Hebrew Books," 979–82. The title of this index is *Purgatio aliquorum librorum hebraicorum incohata juxta breve Apostolicum Julii Tertii per Rabbinum Abraham Provincialem*. See Sacerdote, "Deux Index expurgatoires de livres Hébreux," 263.

66. "Item che il detto messer Vincentio sia tenuto et obligato far che il suo corettore non permetta che passi alchuno erore qual sia contra la fede christiana et relligione et sia obligato egli et ogni danno qual essi hebrei potessero patire per causa di questo perche detti hebrei nonse intendono ne voleno che sia stampato cosa alchuna contro." Simonsohn, *The Jews in the Duchy of Mantua*, 148.

67. Sonne, "Expurgation of Hebrew Books," 1004–10. Sonne's examples are from the Conti printing press in Cremona. Among the examples he gives is "Amudei Golah" from *Sefer Mitzvot Hagadol*, in contrast to R. Yaakov Segal's response that was not satisfactorily censored but also contained many errors. See also Simonsohn, "Choze," who in fact confirms these observations.

68. Sonne, "Expurgation of Hebrew Books," 994. Sonne argues that the first to use the term was Avraham Provinzali. It is interesting that Soncino described his work as "expurgation" in the same manner used by Reuchlin in his defense of the Talmud during the Pfefferkorn affair. But in many examples the term *zikuk* did not refer to

church censorship. Compare Benayahu, who argues that the Jews used the word as referring to editing (*Haskama ve-reshut*). However, the very distinction seems to be problematic.

69. Stern, *Urkundliche Beiträge*, 173–74, d.14, 16. In Venice the existence of a Jewish internal mechanism of censorship led the authorities to prefer such an arrangement (Parente, "The Index"; Benayahu, *Haskama ve-reshut*, 93–96).

70. On the versions of this prayer, see Naftali Wieder, *Hitgabshut Nosach Ha-tfila Bamizrach U-bama'arav* (Jerusalem: Machon Ben-Zvi, 1998), 453–68.

71. For example, Talmud Bavli, Baba Metzya, 24,1. However, the Christian faith obliges them to declare each and every loss. On the Basel edition, see Raphael Nathan Neta Rabinowitz, *Ma'amar al hadpasat ha-Talmud*, ed. A. M. Habermann (Jerusalem: Mosad Ha-Rav Kook), 74–76; Popper, *Censorship*, 56–61; Joseph Prijs, *Die Basler Hebraischen Drucke, 1492–1866* (Olten, Swit.: V. Graf, 1964), 175–91; Heller, *Printing the Talmud*, 241–53.

72. There were a few attempts to publish the censored paragraphs separately. We know about pamphlets or small books, which contained anti-Christian prayers. However, it seems that these publications did not have any significant impact. There are also several editions of censored passages from the Talmud, which contain anti-Christian paragraphs. These books are very short, and their impact was negligible.

73. Roberto Bonfil, "Le Biblioteche degli ebrei d'Italia nel rinascimento," in *Manoscritti, frammenti e libri ebraici*, ed. Tamani and Vivian, 137–50.

74. Daniel Goldschmidt, "Hashlama le-machzor yom ha-kippurim," *Kiryat Sepher* 31 (1955): 146–51.

75. Israel Yuval, *Shnei Goyim be-bitnech* (Tel Aviv: Alma and Am-Oved, 2000). Yuval pointed to the differences between the Ashkenazi revengeful perception of redemption and the Sephardic model of "proselytizing conversion." He emphasized those perceptions and beliefs that were condemned in the sixteenth century as part of the campaign against magic and popular practices. These passages proved to be of crucial importance for the reconstruction of early Ashkenazi culture.

76. Bonfil, "Reading in the Jewish Communities."

77. See the evaluations of the shift by Robert Bonfil, David Ruderman, and Hava Tirosh-Rothschild: David Ruderman, introduction in *Essential Papers on Jewish Culture in Renaissance and Baroque Italy*, ed. idem (New York: New York University Press, 1992), 1–32; Hava Tirosh-Rothschild, "Jewish Culture in Renaissance Italy: A Methodological Survey," *Italia*, 63–96.

78. Robert Bonfil, "The Historian's Perception of the Jews in the Italian Renaissance Period—Towards a Reappraisal," *REJ* 14 (1984): 59–82; idem, "Change in Cultural Patterns of Jewish Society in Crisis: The Case of Italian Jewry at the Close of the Sixteenth Century," *Jewish History* 3 (1988): 11–30; idem, *Jewish Life in Renaissance Italy* (Berkeley and Los Angeles: University of California Press, 1994); idem, "Changing Mentalities of Italian Jews between the Periods of the Renaissance and the Baroque," *Italia* 11 (1994): 61–79.

79. Benjamin Ravid, "The Religious, Economic, and Social Background and Context of the Establishment of the Ghetti in Venice," in *Gli Ebrei e Venezia*, ed. Cozzi, 211–59; idem, "From Geographical Realia to Historiographical Symbol: The Odyssey of the Word Ghetto," in *Essential Papers*, ed. Ruderman, 373–85.

80. Amnon Raz-Krakotzkin, "The Return to the History of Redemption (Or, What is the 'History' to Which the 'Return' in the Phrase 'The Jewish Return to His-

tory' Refers)," in S. N. Eisenstadt and M. Lissak, eds., *Zionism and the Return to History: A Reappraisal* (Jerusalem: Yad Ben-Zvi Press, 1998), 249–79 (Hebrew).

81. On this, see also Robert Bonfil, "Dubious Crimes in Sixteenth-Century Italy: Rethinking the Relations between Jews, Christians, and Converts in Pre-Modern Europe," in *The Jews of Spain and the Expulsion of 1492,* 299–310; Stow, "A Tale of Uncertainties."

82. Carlo Ginzburg, "The Inqusitor and the Anthropologist," in Ginzburg, *Clues.*

PART II

Imagining Differences

7
Skepticism and Conversion: Jews, Christians, and Doubters in Sefer ha-Nizzahon

Ora Limor and Israel Jacob Yuval

The Christian polemical literature against the Jews in the Middle Ages can be seen as the direct precursor of early modern Hebraism. Intellectually curious and religiously zealous, the Christian polemicist wished to become acquainted with his Jewish rival, to parley with him, to know his beliefs from within, and to convince him of the truth of Christianity. He might use peaceful means to achieve these goals or he might prefer harsh polemics, but in either case he had to attain a certain fundamental level of knowledge about the rival faith. From this point of view, the polemicist and the Hebraist did not differ significantly. However, the polemicist in the Middle Ages expressed his intellectual curiosity about his adversary's world within the cultural and religious context in which he had lived—that is, within the framework of the religious dispute—while the Hebraist lived in a world already imbued with empirical scientific curiosity.

The Christian-Jewish polemic can be divided into three stages. The earliest stage, which dates back to the very beginnings of Christianity until the twelfth century, focuses on the correct interpretation of the Holy Scriptures. The second stage, beginning in the twelfth century and reaching its peak in the thirteenth, involves the placing of the Talmud and philosophy in the arena of confrontation.[1] Placing the Talmud at the core of the Christian debate against Judaism also signifies the onset of Christian criticism of postbiblical Judaism, presenting it as a distortion of biblical Judaism. This new Judaism was perceived as being essentially anti-Christian, a hostile entity seeking to undermine the very existence of the church. This is one of the reasons for the deterioration of the status of the Jews in Christian society toward the end of the Middle Ages.[2] In the third stage Christian scholars of the early modern era seek to become acquainted with the entirety of Jewish religious, intellectual, and cultural life; they are no longer satisfied with limiting themselves solely to a discussion of what they perceive to be the anti-Christian aspects of Judaism.[3] Their course of study reflects a wider ethnographical and intellectual curiosity and does not limit itself exclusively to Jewish religious customs. Nonetheless the anti-Jewish motive nourishing the polemicists of the Middle Ages was still potent among the Hebraists, and among them too were those who wished to affirm the truth of Christianity by demonstrating the wretched nature of Jewish ritual and ceremonial practice.

The initiators of the change both in the second and third stages were the converts.[4] Their unique point of view placed them in a bridging position, allowing them to compare both religions, their old faith with their new one. The resultant criticism of their former religion, however, also had the effect of allowing their new coreligionists to become more closely acquainted with their former faith. This aspect of their work allows us to view their historical role in a more positive light than has been customary, especially among their contemporaries. Conversion was indeed perceived as treachery and as a desertion of religious and social loyalties, but it also functioned as a means of communication, which eventually allowed the rival religions to take their first steps on the long journey toward knowledge of each other. Hebraism was the climax of this process, but it is impossible to understand the Hebraism of the sixteenth and seventeenth centuries without understanding the world of interreligious polemic of the Middle Ages or the role played by converts.

The three aforementioned stages, which describe the religious polemic from the Christian point of view, are also reflected in the Jewish counterpolemic. Reacting to the missionary assault of the Christians, the Jews were forced to follow the agenda dictated by the rival party. Throughout the history of the polemic between the two religions the Christians have been the initiators while the Jews have felt themselves obliged to respond. *Sefer ha-Nizzahon* (Book of Contention or Book of Victory) by Rabbi Yom-Tov Lipmann Mühlhausen demonstrates some of these points in a very clear way.[5] This book was also written as a response to external challenges and thus illuminates some of the issues at the core of Jewish-Christian relations in the Middle Ages. For example: what were the topics of polemical debate, and what was the nature of this polemic? How well acquainted were Jewish scholars with Christianity as compared to the Christian knowledge of Judaism? What was the convert's role in the exposure of the Jewish way of life and its denunciation? Lipmann's book is the most widely known polemical work among Jews and Christians in the late Middle Ages and early modern period, and a milestone in the history of Judeo-Christian polemic. The answers the book offers to the questions raised above are illustrative not only of the cultural scope of its author but also of the atmosphere of the entire period. Lipmann wrote his book specifically to address the problem of conversion, which was indeed acute for fifteenth-century German Jews.⁶ The importance attributed to the book by the Jews as a weapon in the battle against conversion explains the wide extent of Christian response to it.

In his important introduction to Lipmann's *Sefer ha-Nizzahon* Ephraim Talmage writes that for the "People of the Book," bibliography counts much more than biography.⁷ This holds true also in the case of Rabbi Lipmann. We lack conclusive evidence concerning many of the details of his biography. Even the year of his birth is unknown, and the date of his death is a matter of dispute. According to the *Encyclopaedia Judaica*, he died after 1450, whereas the correct year of his death is thirty-seven years earlier, in 1421!⁸ Lipmann was a native of the small town of Mühlhausen in Thüringen, where a small Jewish community is recorded already in the thirteenth century.⁹ In the years 1407 and 1413 he is attested as a resident in Prague, but he traveled to other places in Bohemia and Poland as well.¹⁰ On several occasions he was involved in religious disputations, defending his faith and his community against Christian attacks. It is impossible to tell how successful this defense was. Lipmann was one of the leading Jewish intellectuals of his times and one of the first in the Holy Roman Empire who studied philosophy and Kabbalah along with rabbinic literature. He was the author of many treatises—halachic, liturgical, and hermeneutical—but he is known to posterity mainly for his polemical work *Sefer ha-Nizzahon*.¹¹

Sefer ha-Nizzahon was probably written shortly after 1400,¹² and it is renowned for its anti-Christian polemics. Yet the book is much more than this. Lipmann refutes opponents of normative Judaism, both outside the Jewish camp (Christians) and within it. For example, he criticizes the Sadduccees, identical for him with the Karaites, and another group, whom he calls "doubters" (*meharherim*), probably a group of Jewish skeptics who criticized the Bible, and still other groups that have yet to be identified. The result is kind of a *summa* of Jewish faith, a work that contributes not only to our knowledge of medieval religion but also to our general understanding of medieval culture, for the book's broad scope includes topics such as cosmology, the natural world, and the place of women in society, to mention just a few.

The general framework of the book is hermeneutical. The author comments on different verses of the Bible, starting from the book of Genesis and ending with the books of Chronicles. The book is divided into 354 paragraphs, corresponding to the number of days in the lunar year. As a result of this structure, topics are scattered in different places since Lipmann deals with them in the context of the biblical verse he interprets. The book is full of cross-references, and the reader is sent from one place to the other according to the subject under discussion. In order to help the reader find his way, Lipmann added a thematic table of contents organized in seven chapters according to the seven days of the week, each one of which deals with a general theme and refers the reader to a great many different chapters. For example, the first day of the week (Sunday) offers answers to Christian claims and demonstrates contradictions in the Christian faith. It tells the reader to find these arguments in 65 different sections. In spite of this complex structure, the book is didactic in contents and style. The author wants to instruct his reader. He has a lesson to teach.

Lipmann discusses practically every biblical reference that received a christological interpretation. He thus deals with, or, at least, touches upon, all the themes of the interreligious controversy: the question of God's unity, the incarnation, the messiah, the virgin birth, and the contrast constantly drawn by Christian apologists between Christian hegemony and Jewish exile. Although the book criticizes certain positions within Judaism, anti-Christian polemics pervade and color the whole of its Jewish theology. A special anti-Christian interpretive effort is devoted to the books of Isaiah and Psalms, presumably because of their special position in christological exegesis.

The circumstances under which the book was written are made clear in the appendix. Here, Lipmann digresses from the exegetic framework of the book and describes an event that took place in 1399 without, however, giving a clear idea of the surrounding circumstances. Lipmann's account is brief and somewhat vague, and he does not even state where the event occurred. According to his account, on the fourteenth of the month of Elul, 1399, a group of Jews were imprisoned after a convert named Peter leveled a series of accusations against them. The common denominator of these accusations was the claim that certain Jewish rituals and prayers were derogatory toward Christianity and even contained a request that God bring about its ruin. The Jews apparently languished in jail for an entire year and on the first of Elul, 1400, seventy-seven of them were executed. Three weeks later three more Jews were burnt at the stake. It appears that Peter himself died around the same time. The circumstances of his death, though possibly of natural causes, are unclear, but Lipmann apparently saw it as a punishment for Peter's deeds. It would seem that Lipmann was required to respond to Peter's accusations and that his answers were presented in the appendix to the book. The introduction of the account creates the impression that the execution of the Jews provoked Lipmann to write his book both as a defense of Judaism and as an answer to Peter's accusations.

Peter's criticisms of Judaism may be divided into two categories: criticism of the Jewish Scriptures and criticism of Jewish rituals. He attacks the prayer ʿAleynu on the grounds that it includes the verse "*Shehem mishtachavim laHevel vaRiq*" (for they worship emptiness and void). He claims that the word *vaRiq* refers to Jesus, as its numerical value is equal to that of Jesus.[13] Peter also interprets the verse "*Umitpallelim le'el lo yoshia*" (in Hebrew the word *yoshia* can be understood as an allusion to Jesus) as an insinuation against the Christian faith. Naturally, Peter did not miss the curse against the *Minnim* (heretics, or Christians) in the 'Amida.¹⁴ He understood that the phrase "*VeChol haMinnim keRega yo'vedu*" (may all the *Minnim* be destroyed at once) refers to the Christians, and he interpreted the words "*Umalchut zadon mehera te'aqer*" (uproot the wicked kingdom with haste) as a prayer for the destruction of Christian states. Likewise, on Yom Kippur the Jews express their hatred of the Christians in the *piyyut* (a religious poem) *Ha-Goyyim eymim*, which includes curses on the gentiles and a request to God to destroy them.¹⁵

According to Lipmann's account, in order to support his accusations, Peter forged letters containing blasphemous passages about Christian beliefs and claimed they were written by the Jews. He alleged that the Jews gave Jesus the derogatory title *tolé* (the hanged one) while the host was named *Lechem tamé* (impure bread) or *Lechem MeGo'al* (soiled bread) and the church was called *Zevel tamé* (impure dung).¹⁶ Peter also found fault with certain Jewish customs. He perceived the setting aside of *Challah* (a portion of dough) and the burning of *Chametz* (leavened bread) as having an anti-Christian intent. The burning of *Chametz* is done by the Jews on Pesach eve, which falls during Lent and shortly before or after Good Friday. This custom, in particular its timing, was seen by Peter as a deliberate scorn of the host, which is considered to be the body of Christ. He interpreted the burning of the *Chametz* in a similar fashion, as a disrespectful allusion to the crucifixion.

Lipmann's answers to these claims are artificial and unconvincing. They appear to be the tactics of a constrained responder, who must evade the criticism he is under. For example, Lipmann claims that the *Minnim*, for whose destruction the Jews pray, are not Christians but heretic Jews who waver between Judaism and Christianity. He describes them with the German term *zweifelte Ketzer* (doubtful heretics), thus claiming that the prayer refers to a specific contemporary social and religious group. *Zevel Tamé* (*Zevel* = dirt, dung) is explained as a church being impure (*Zevel* = *Zvul*, a house). *Lechem meGo'al* (*meGo'al* = soiled) he interprets as the bread of salvation (*meGo'al* = *nig'al*, redeemed). He reads the *piyyut* demanding the destruction of the nations conversely as a complaint against the gentile nations who wish to destroy Israel. In regard to other *piyyutim*, including one that requests the destruction of the Gentiles, Lipmann seems merely to be making excuses.

What was the accusation that led to the execution of eighty Jews? It seems improbable that such a mass execution was caused by the Jewish version of the prayer *'Aleynu* or the prayer of the *Minnim*, which had been common among Jews for many generations. The size of the executed group indicates that it was a collective accusation, such as a desecration of the host or a blood libel leveled against an entire community. The fact that Peter connects the burning of the *Challah* with Jewish scorn for the host suggests that the accusation was one of host desecration.[17] It is possible that in order to strengthen the claims against the Jews in this case other accusations were raised regarding the anti-Christian nature of Jewish liturgy and customs. But it is also possible that the accusation was of a more fundamental nature. Lipmann writes in the introduction, "We were caught by heresy" *(nitpasnu le-minnut)*. This sentence may be explained in two different ways. The first is that the Jews were imprisoned by what they call *Minnut*, in other words, the Christian authorities. The second is that they were imprisoned under the accusation of heresy (*Minnut*). The second explanation seems more likely, as the phrase "we were caught by heresy" is used with the same meaning in the talmudic story of Rabbi Eliezer ben Horqenos who was suspected of an inclination toward Christianity.[18] If this is the correct interpretation, it means that in this instance Judaism was regarded as a heresy that must be investigated by the Inquisition and expunged, contrary to the official teaching of the church since the time of Augustine, which stipulated that the Jewish religion must be allowed to exist within the world as a witness to the truth of revelation.[19] Another indication that the Jews were accused of being heretics may be found in Lipmann's answer to the claim regarding the curse of the *Minnim*. As mentioned above, the term he used for *Minnim* was *zweifelte Ketzer*, claiming that only this group was deserving of elimination, not the Christians, because they were neither Christians nor Jews. Thus although Lipmann agrees with his persecutors that heresy must be obliterated, he rejects the idea that Judaism is a heresy. Courts of the Inquisition were indeed active in Germany toward the end of the fourteenth century in order to combat the Waldensian heresy.[20] Their activity ranged from Erfurt to Prague, in the vicinity of Lipmann's places of residence. It does seem possible, therefore, that Lipmann's motive for writing his book was to cleanse Judaism of any form of heresy and present it to Christians in a legitimate orthodox form. That would explain why Lipmann directed his book not only against Christianity but also against Jewish heretics (such as the Karaites) and other groups (such as the "doubters").

When it comes to evaluating the importance of Lipmann's book, it is important to consider the extent of its dissemination. The degree of success that a work achieved in its own time is something that historians normally do not take sufficiently into account. But it is important for us to be concerned with questions such as: what polemical works did people actually read? Which, among the many works on the subject, did they consider worth including in their libraries? Which of these works were known also to their religious opponents? A simple way to evaluate the success of a work is to take into account the number of its extant manuscripts. Of course, we must use this criterion with caution since on the one hand many manuscripts have not survived and on the other new manuscripts are continually discovered. Nevertheless the quantitative criterion does at least give us some indications of tastes and tendencies. Even if the number of manuscripts that have reached us is not equal to the number copied, it still gives us some idea of the degree of interest the work aroused in its time and in later generations.

According to the scheme devised by Bernard Guenée,[21] six manuscripts indicate a small degree of success, fifteen a limited success, thirty a considerable success, and seventy a great success. If we wish to apply this scheme to polemical literature, one could say that the *Pugio fidei* (ten manuscripts) had a limited success, Gilbert Crispin's *Disputatio Iudaei et Christiani* (thirty-two manuscripts) had a considerable success, and Petrus Alfonsi's *Dialogus Moysis Iudaei et Petri Christiani* (seventy-two manuscripts) had a great success.[22] When applying Guenée's criteria to the Jewish world, we deal with a much smaller audience with its own particular literary preferences and traditions and with a smaller scale of dissemination. We also have to take into consideration the impact of pogroms, expulsions, and Christian censorship. Given the fact that *Sefer ha-Nizzahon* was a target for Christian attacks and criticism, its forty-four known manuscripts are a very impressive number indeed. This is the greatest number of manuscripts of any Jewish Ashkenazi work (not only polemical) known to us. Thirty of these are good and important manuscripts while the other fourteen are either very late or fragmentary. Since we know of cases in which the book was condemned and destroyed, and since it is probable that the book was included in Pope Benedict XIII's Index, it is reasonable to assume that the dissemination of *Sefer ha-Nizzahon* was much wider than the manuscript evidence suggests.[23] At the beginning of the sixteenth century, when the convert Johann Pfefferkorn made a great effort to confiscate and burn private and public Jewish libraries, *Sefer ha-Nizzahon* was one of his main targets, as he considered it to be the ultimate anti-Christian text, a dangerous text, an arsenal for Jewish anti-Christian arguments, and a major obstacle to the conversion of the Jews. The manuscripts of *Sefer ha-Nizzahon* had to be hidden and occasionally moved from one place to another. In the list of confiscated books in Frankfurt preserved in the city's archive the municipal notary wrote down a declaration the Jews had made concerning *Sefer ha-Nizzahon*: "Kein haben wir davon" (We don't have any copies).[24]

In the world of religious polemics, a successful work in one camp may cause retaliations in the other.[25] Some Christians tried to destroy *Sefer ha-Nizzahon*. However, others tried hard to study and even publish it in order to refute it. They dealt with it in one manner or another for about three hundred years, until the beginning of the eighteenth century, when the polemical storm finally calmed down.

Christians began to respond to *Sefer ha-Nizzahon* soon after it was written. The first reaction came from the bishop of Brandenburg, Stefan Bodeker (1384–1459), a few years after Lipmann's death.[26] Bodeker did not know Hebrew and probably had been told about the book's anti-Christian arguments by local converts. More responses followed. Some tried to condemn the book altogether; others tried to counter its arguments. Who were these Christians? Needless to say, first among them were the famous converts of the sixteenth century: Victor von Carben (in 1504), Johann Pfefferkorn (already mentioned) in 1507–28, and Anthonius Margarita in 1530. Polemicists and Hebraists were also among those who responded to the book: Reuchlin, who defended Jewish literature vehemently, condemned *Sefer ha-Nizzahon* in 1505, together with *Sefer Toledoth Yeshu* and Nahmanides' disputation. He believed them to be books of mockery, even in the eyes of the Jews, who did not take them seriously. Luther also knew of *Sefer ha-Nizzahon*. Sebastian Münster and Paul Fagius addressed the issues raised in the book in 1542, Iohann Buxdorf the elder in 1603, Wilhelm Schickard in 1623, Constantin l'Empereur in 1641, Theodor Hackspan in 1644, Johann Christoph Wagenseil and Stefan Girlovius toward the end of the century, and Eisenmenger in 1700.[27]

For many years Christian scholars tried to print the book but could not obtain a manuscript. In 1644 Theodor Hackspan, a professor of Hebrew at the University of Altdorf, succeeded in laying his hand on a copy. Hackspan looked for the book for a long time until he received word that a certain rabbi in the neighboring small city of Schnattach had a copy but would not show it to anyone. Hackspan then took some of his friends and paid an unwelcome visit to the rabbi, as if to dispute with him. When in the heat of the debate the rabbi took out the hidden manuscript in order to consult it, Hackspan immediately snatched the book out of his hands, ran off with it to his carriage, and took it back to Altdorf. He immediately sat down a few of his Hebrew students to copy the book, and soon the *editio princeps* came into being.[28] Although two Jewish editions were printed in the eighteenth and nineteenth centuries, Hackspan's edition is the best to date.[29]

Hackspan printed Lipmann's text with care and did not make any deliberate changes or alterations. However, the knowledge of his Hebrew scribes was far from perfect, and the standard of proofreading was very poor, so the book is full of mistakes, especially minor errors. Soon after becoming available, sections of the book were translated into Latin, and a full translation appeared in 1645. In 1674 Johann Christoph Wagenseil succeeded Hackspan as professor of languages in Altdorf, and during the same year he published his *Correctiones Lipmannianae* according to two other manuscripts he managed to obtain. In his famous collection of Jewish polemical literature, *Tela Ignea Satanae*, Wagenseil included answers to *Sefer Ha-Nizzahon*.[30]

7.1. Front page of Yom-Tov Lipmann Mühlhausen, *Sefer ha-Nizzahon,* ed. Theodor Hackspan (Nuremberg, 1644). Photo courtesy of the Center for Advanced Judaic Studies Library, University of Pennsylvania.

Lipmann's knowledge of Christianity and the reaction his book later aroused among Christian Hebraists can be illustrated by a comment he makes: "Rejoice greatly, Fair Zion; raise a shout, Fair Jerusalem! Lo, your king is coming to you. He is victorious, triumphant, yet humble, riding on an ass, on a donkey foaled by a she-ass (Zech. 9:9): The Christians interpret this as referring to Christ, basing their interpretation on the fact that there is a cross-like design on the ass's shoulders."[31] Did the Christians really suggest that God created asses with a cross on their backs in order to prove that the ass in Zechariah's prophecy was that same ass on which Jesus came down from the Mount of Olives? This claim of Lipmann was vigorously denied in the seventeenth century by Johann Schudt.[32] He wrote that "the asinine Rabbi Lipmann [*der eselhafte Rabbiner Lipman*] should have known that such a proof never occurred to any Christian," but in the same breath Schudt went on to recount popular Christian beliefs, according to which some animals bear the sign of the holy cross on their bodies. He cited reports by travelers in Italy about the cult of a holy she-ass in Verona. After the she-ass had completed her mission to carry Jesus, she was released, wandered for a while in Palestine, and then decided to travel to other lands. Without a ship she walked to Cyprus on the waves, which became flat and hard like crystal, and from there proceeded to Rhodes, Candia, Malta, Sicily, and finally to Venice. Disliking the air and the grass there, she went on to Verona, where she finally settled down. Her remains, buried in Verona, were regularly carried through the streets in a procession two or three times a year.

Jews also believed in the singular qualities of the ass. The fifteenth-century rabbi Seligmann Bing, in a massive volume of rather meager content, told a story of a Jew in Bingen who, anxious to cure his illness, tried to procure a piece of an ass's back with a crosslike shape. His chance came one day when he met a Christian boy leading an ass. The Jew pounced upon the ass, tore off a good-sized piece of skin from its back, and fled. As a result, the local Jews found themselves in considerable danger, for the Christians thought the Jew had intended to dishonor the cross. But they were wrong; simple Jews indeed believed that there was a cross on the ass's back and that it had remedial powers.[33] Observations of this kind, which are unfortunately quite rare in Lipmann's book, afford us a glimpse of popular beliefs that sometimes cross religious barriers. Naturally, when a book by a scholar of Lipmann's caliber made a statement of this kind, Christians reacted with considerable ridicule. The Jewish-Christian disputation in *Sefer ha-Nizzahon* reflects the discourse of the elite, not of simple people.

The general impression Lipmann's book makes is of prudence and respect for Christians. Lipmann was a philosopher and halakhist, a cultured, respectable person, and the humorous ass episode is not typical of his book. As against *Vetus Nizzahon*, written probably in the late thirteenth century, which contains fulminations against Christianity and repeated expressions of derision for the Virgin Mary—a convenient target for Jewish attacks—Lipmann stands out for the serious, respectful tone of his writing. Was this Lipmann's authentic attitude to Christianity? Or was it perhaps the attitude of a prudent polemicist, aware that mutual trust was the basis for dialogue and a prerequisite for persuasion? Alternatively, was he perhaps taking the pragmatic stand of a Jew familiar with the world around him, conscious that a more hostile book might cost him and his coreligionists dearly? It is not easy to determine which of these three alternatives applied; in any case, even if the reason was pragmatic or utilitarian, we may assume that the author would have internalized the attitude to some extent and made it his own.

Lipmann's responses to Christian arguments are generally sincere though sometimes he dismisses them out of hand (a practice he freely admits in the introduction to the book). Most, but not all, of his answers reflect conventional positions. Although he does not mention by name any of the earlier polemical literature, not even the earlier *Nizzahon Vetus*, written in Germany a few generations before his time, most of his knowledge of Christianity is derived from secondary Jewish sources. Very often he refutes arguments that were attributed to Christians in earlier Jewish polemics, such as *Sefer Joseph ha-Mekaneh* and *Nizzahon Vetus*. His method is to cite the verse, present the Christian interpretation, and refute it. It seems that he generally deals with the most common Christian interpretation, which he probably came to know either from internal Jewish sources or through conversations with Christians, and not by his own reading of Christian books. He constantly uses such expressions as "concerning this the Christians have said," "and now, the Christians have said," "and here, too, the Christians say," and so on. Sometimes his wording betrays actual conversations in which he took part, as we can see from the following comment: "and thereby I proved to them that they are behaving improperly when they threaten a Jew with death if he should refuse to convert."[34] Such statements along with others testify to daily contacts and to disputation as a constant mode of existence. No wonder one occasionally finds that Lipmann has internalized Christian positions or criticism. Among the arguments disputed in the book are the Pauline claim that the Christians are the "true Israel" (*verus Israel*); the Augustinian claim that Christians must protect the Jews' existence because they bear witness to the truth of Scripture;[35] and less weighty ones, such as Christian criticism of Jewish rituals or the argument that the ugly appearance of the Jews is proof of their rejection by God. Lipmann does not dispute the Christians' aesthetic sense but comforts his "ugly" brethren with the words, "for in the messianic age we will all be better looking than anybody else."[36]

Lipmann is particularly troubled by the contrast between the exiled and degraded state of the Jews and the success of the Christians. This subject was indeed a central one in the religious disputations between Jews and Christians toward the end of the Middle Ages. When Lipmann was writing, the Jews had long been expelled from England and France, and their position in other European countries was gradually deteriorating. For the Christians the great length of the exile was conclusive proof that Judaism had been absolutely rejected, and Lipmann could not but return again and again to this painful subject and deal with it, promising his readers that they would witness the fulfillment of prophecies of consolation. He even tried his hand at predicting the date of the redemption.[37] In his introduction Lipmann divides his disputants into groups according to the "Four Sons" of the Passover Haggadah, classifying the Christians as the son who does not know how to ask. This indicates his attitude to them: the Christians are not wicked, but they err and mislead others. As to the group of the "Wicked Son," however, Lipmann includes a group of people that he calls *meharherim*, those who doubt the truth of divine revelation and the authority of the Bible.

While internal evidence suggests that *Sefer ha-Nizzahon* may have been written in response to the execution of a community of Jews on the charge of host desecration, it is more difficult to identify the place and date of its composition. Conventional scholarly opinion suggests the work was written in Prague, where Lipmann is known to have lived and written no later than 1407. From the mid-fourteenth century to the early fifteenth century, Prague was the foremost political and cultural center in the Holy Roman Empire. Charles IV made Prague the dynastic capital. In 1348 the first university north of the Alps was founded in Prague, and the city became fertile ground for religious reforms and the absorption of new ideas, such as those of Wycliff and later Hus. As the place of composition, Prague is, however, problematic since there is no evidence that a public trial and execution of Jews took place there. The whole story is not mentioned by any other source. Is it possible that eighty Jews could have been put to death in the capital of the empire without the event leaving any trace in contemporary documents? Although still puzzled by the silence of the sources, we would like to present new circumstantial evidence that connects the book and the episode it describes, if not to Prague itself, at least to a place in close proximity.

The clearest indication that the book was written in Prague may be found at the end of the Hamburg manuscript of the work, which will be the basis for our forthcoming edition. R. Avigdor Kara of Prague added a poem in which he celebrated the book's completion. In the opening lines the two men are described as being close friends, in terms that imply that they were practically neighbors. A further, more indirect, proof that the book belongs to the Prague area can better explain the political circumstances in which it was written. Among Peter's many accusations, he cites from the *'Amidah* (Eighteen Benedictions) prayer the plea for the destruction of "the kingdom of evil" (*malkhut ha-zadon*), which he claims expresses the hope of the Jews for the destruction of Christian kingdoms. In his response Lipmann denies this interpretation. One might expect him to argue that the phrase refers to some kingdom characterized by evil, immoral behavior, where the basic precepts of religion are constantly violated. Instead, Lipmann offers the following definition: "They are those who are not of the royal seed, but crown themselves and in their wickedness seek to dethrone honest [legitimate] kings, debasing kingdoms and states; and for that reason they are called 'kingdom of evil.' And one should pray for their destruction."[38] According to this interpretation, a kingdom ruled by an illegitimate king, not of royal descent, is a "kingdom of evil," and it is for the destruction of such kingdom alone that the Jews pray. This unusual definition would probably not have attracted our attention had we not been aware that in 1400—that is, the same year the eighty Jews were burned as a result of Peter's accusations—King Wenceslas was deposed by the elector princes and replaced by Ruprecht of Pfalz, a noble "not of the royal seed." The deposed Wenceslas was the son of Charles IV, founder of the Luxemburg dynasty. Even after forfeiting the throne of the Reich, Wenceslas remained king of Bohemia until his death in 1419. In 1410 Ruprecht died, to be succeeded by Wenceslas's brother Sigismund. Thus from 1400 to 1410 Germany was ruled by a king who was not a member of the previous dynasty while Bohemia was ruled at the time by a deposed king. The possibility that Lipmann's explanation refers to this political situation is attractive. If this is indeed the case, one should read the text in its concrete political context: Lipmann is declaring the Jews' loyalty to Wenceslas, presumably in Bohemia. Lipmann specifies the exact date on which the Jews were executed, 22 August 1400. The execution took place on the same day that Wenceslas was deposed.[39] Is this just a mere coincidence?

Wenceslas, a pale shadow of his father, ruled over a divided kingdom, riven by dissension. His own kingdom, Bohemia, was also the scene of stark cultural and political contrasts. Particularly worthy of mention is the tension between Germans and Czechs, which was ultimately to come to the surface in Hus's sermons, which began in 1405, in his burning at Constanz in 1414, and in the Hussite Rebellion, which broke out in 1419. The princes who had elected Wenceslas had good reasons to depose him. The king was described as a habitual drunkard, a wastrel, and a good-for-nothing. In addition his enemies believed him to be a "Jew-lover."[40] A Jewish chronicle of the mid-fifteenth century, in fact, refers to Wenceslas as a personal friend of R. Avigdor Kara, who had, it is claimed, learned the true monotheistic faith from the latter,[41] and a work from the early sixteenth century refers to Wenceslas as a kind of crypto-Jew.[42] It seems that Jewish public opinion embraced the picture drawn by Wenceslas's opponents.

Wenceslas did indeed protect his Jewish subjects, not because of any sympathy for them but for purely utilitarian political reasons. As frequently happened in Germany, the royal protection granted to the Jews was at odds with the political ambitions of local rulers. In an attempt to fit the Peter story into this frame we may suppose that the trial and its outcome reflect the position of the anti-Wenceslas camp, who may have been found in church circles. If this was the case, the latter may have tried to vilify the king's Jewish protégés, accusing them of being a hostile element within the kingdom and warning the king against them. The details of Peter's accusations raise the possibility that the Jews may have been imprisoned on the charge of desecrating the host, but the trial was extended to include more comprehensive allegations, namely that the Jews were disloyal and endangered Christian society. The burning of a large number of Jews on the very day Wenceslas was dethroned makes it plausible to assume that this was no coincidence. The accused Jews were imprisoned for a whole year, and only when the king was deemed to be in a particularly weak situation did his opponents dare to execute them. This formula constantly repeated itself all over Germany: opposition circles would try to harm a ruler by attacking "his" Jews.

Knowledge of the supposed political circumstances of the affair may explain its importance in Lipmann's eyes and his decision to write a book defending Judaism from Christian attacks. Probably for the first time in the history of German Jewry a political element hostile to the Jews had taken advantage of a convert's testimony. On past occasions voluntary conversion had usually been a result of fascination with Christianity, its symbols, and its ceremonies.[43] Peter belongs to a new breed of converts whose primary motive for conversion was their dissatisfaction with Jewish religious practices and the traditional interpretations of Scripture. Such converts continued to scrutinize Judaism critically even after converting. Not only does *Sefer ha-Nizzahon* tell us of Peter's role in the accusations against the Jews, it also helps us reconstruct the cultural character of these converts before their conversion. They were the "doubters." Lipmann's criticisms of these individuals reveal their identity and the doubts they harbored against Jewish tradition: they were troubled by anthropomorphic expressions in the Bible and the Talmud, and pointed out contradictions and irrationalities. As described in *Sefer ha-Nizzahon*, such individuals were natural candidates for conversion. The affair of Peter and the burning of the Jews in 1400 convinced Lipmann that these persons were not only lost to Judaism, but that they also presented a grave threat even after their conversion. His book was an effort to use his persuasive powers to convince Jews not to convert. Jews who converted to Christianity in the unique cultural atmosphere of Bohemia at the end of the fourteenth century did so out of conviction and after they had scrutinized the Ashkenazi world and found it inadequate and narrow-minded, and its religious teachings incapable of coping with the intellectual challenges presented by the larger Christian environment. External evidence of the spiritual crisis experienced by German Jews at this time comes from a book titled 'Alilot Devarim (Made-up Charges), written by a Spanish Jew living in Italy in the fourteenth century, where he came into contact with Ashkenazi Jews.[44] In unusually impassioned language he deplores the failure of the Ashkenazim to master the skills of logic and rhetoric. They prefer the study of Talmud and its hairsplitting casuistry instead of logic, and this, the author claims, is the reason that the exile is being prolonged.

A similar picture is implied by Sefer ha-Nizzahon. The world of the "doubters" reflects the crisis of Ashkenazi Jewry in the late Middle Ages. The entire exegetical approach of German Jewry, as crystallized in the Middle Ages by the Tosafists and Hasidei 'Ashkenaz, avoided philosophy like the plague. Ashkenazi Jewry surrounded itself with a tangled web of religious rituals, a defensive barrier to preserve its unique identity and prevent any infiltration of Christian influence. At the end of the fourteenth century, however, this traditional structure collapsed, particularly in such places as Prague and Vienna, where universities were founded one after another and became vibrant cultural centers. What intellectual tools did a rabbi, however well versed in and Talmud and Jewish law and custom, have to contend with a theologian of the caliber of Heinrich Langenstein who had studied theology in Paris, moved to Vienna in the 1380s, and whose appointment to the new university of Vienna symbolized the *translatio studii* to the German Empire?[45] Lipmann's "doubters" were, we believe, members of the younger generation, who sensed the weakness of halakhic Judaism in the face of the new challenges presented by the rise of the new universities in the German Empire. These were people who first opened their windows a crack and then threw them wide open; they found themselves attracted by Christian culture not for utilitarian reasons but because they realized the cultural superiority of Christianity over the closed technical Judaism with which they were familiar. The encounter with Peter apprised Lipmann of the danger presented by the "doubters." They were liable not only to become Christians but subsequently to continue their struggle against Judaism and reveal its weaknesses in public.

Thus *Sefer ha-Nizzahon* is an attempt to grapple not only with Christianity but also with these "doubters." This attempt was born in the Prague circle, which, besides Lipmann, also included Avigdor Kara and Menahem Shalem. These scholars realized that it was vital to admit philosophy into their religious world. *Sefer ha-Nizzahon* is the first Ashkenazi polemical work to appeal to philosophical arguments. Unlike *Nizzahon Vetus*, which had confined itself to biblical exegesis, Lipmann's book was an "argument of the new type"—to quote Amos Funkenstein's famous definition—because it also argued on a rational plane.[46] Philosophy was a novel phenomenon on the Ashkenazi scene, and immediately, from its very first appearance there, it was mobilized for the struggle against Christianity. It was this struggle that forced Jewish scholars in Germany to make room for philosophy on their bookshelves.[47] Lipmann's book was designed to offer a more rational religious doctrine and an intelligent rejoinder to the challenge of the Christian disputant; accordingly, while being receptive to innovation in the very use of philosophy, the author took care to dress his writing up in traditional clothes, preserving the ancient literary genre of biblical commentary.

There is a remarkable similarity between Heinrich Langenstein, the theologian of Vienna University, and the circle of Jews in Prague.[48] A common subject among the Jewish scholars was the alphabet, whether in regard to the technique of writing or the inner mystical significance of the letters. Lipmann himself wrote a work titled '*Alfa Beta*.[49] Around that very time, Heinrich von Langenstein, too, wrote a book titled *De idiomate hebraico*,[50] devoted to the mystical meaning of the Hebrew alphabet. This similarity may indicate some concrete relationship or acquaintance, perhaps even an exchange of knowledge between the two parties; but the subject deserves further study. Cultural and literary connections also reflect personal contact. Lipmann does indeed mention having met senior clergymen from the southern German town of Lindau.[51] We believe that his knowledge of Christianity is based on the kind of encounters between Jews and Christians he himself mentions. Lipmann was not a Latinist although he quotes Latin excerpts from the New Testament here and there (which he cites in Hebrew transliteration). In one case he even suggests a supposed etymological derivation of the word *virgo* from *vir*,[52] but this is simply a popular etymology and one he most probably heard somewhere but did not invent. At one point he cites a sentence and attributes it to "Gregory."[53] However, it is almost impossible to imagine that Gregory the Great, or any other Christian, could have uttered the sentence as he reports it: *Qui non est circumcisus sicut Abraham Isaac et Iacob non potest introire in regnum caelorum* (Whoever was not circumcised like Abraham, Isaac, and Jacob cannot enter the kingdom of heaven). The Christian interpretations that Lipmann cites are, as far as we have been able to ascertain so far, classical interpretations of patristic exegesis, rendered in the *Glossa Ordinaria* and commonly known.

Lipmann knew some Christian liturgy and had some knowledge of Christian theological concepts. Probably most of his Christian knowledge came from conversations that he held at home, in the street, in the market, perhaps at the entrance to the church or synagogue. These were the venues of Christian-Jewish contact, where the everyday disputation between Christianity and Judaism took place. But it is precisely here that Lipmann disappoints—even annoys—the modern reader. Despite the broad scope of his book, he gives us absolutely no information concerning himself, his place, and his time, not even concerning the places where he had studied. The work lacks "scenery." It is thus particularly important to identify the one Christian mentioned in the book as conversing at length with Lipmann—he too is not named.

This person is mentioned several times in *Sefer ha-Nizzahon* and called variously "head of the clergy in Lindau," "priest in Lindau," and "leader of the priests."[54] He was clearly a churchman with a fairly high position in the local church hierarchy; he was not a bishop, for otherwise Lipmann would surely have referred to him not as *komer* or *kohen* but as *hegmon*, the equivalent Hebrew term for bishop. These designations might fit Marquard von Lindau, the *provinzial* of Lindau district from 1389 to 1392.[55] Marquard was a prominent intellectual and a prolific author, who left seventeen works in Latin and eleven in German. His works deal with scholastic philosophy and mystical lore, but he was also interested in biblical exegesis and wrote on the Ten Commandments. If our identification is correct, the character of this opponent, proficient in exegesis as well as scholastic arguments, is yet another indication of Lipmann's motives in enlisting philosophy for the defense of Judaism.

Lipmann did not read Latin literature, which would surely have been out of bounds for an Ashkenazi rabbi. He found it sufficient to glean various pieces of information about the other party's arguments, perhaps also to leaf through Christian books, which were just beginning to be written in German at that time. The transition to writing in the German vernacular in the second half of the fourteenth century lowered the Latin barrier previously separating Jews and Christians.

In conclusion one can claim that Lipmann's *Sefer ha-Nizzahon* reflects the particular circumstances facing German Jews in the fourteenth century. In this world it was a move of great novelty to answer the Christian challenge with a response based partly on the albeit limited admission of philosophy to the traditional scriptural and rabbinic canon. Thus the need to combat Christianity dictated a redefinition of the identity of Ashkenazi culture. Lipmann felt the urgent need to equip Jews—particularly those of them who had become "doubters"—with the resources necessary to hold their own in the face of the increasingly sophisticated polemical tools of the rival faith. *Sefer ha-Nizzahon* reflects the feeling of Jewish scholars that the old war of interpretation of verses and rabbinic maxims risked becoming a losing one, and that is why the book digresses into lengthy philosophical discussions that might be thought out of place in a polemical work. According to Lipmann's own table of contents, only one-third of the book is devoted to anti-Christian disputation. However, this figure is misleading. Not only does the book contain many more anti-Christian sections, but one can in fact claim that Christianity is the organizational principle of the entire book. The Christian challenge became an internal challenge. The traditional reaction of immersing oneself in the world of Halakhah and study of the Torah no longer provided an adequate defense against doubters of all kinds.

Before concluding, we return once again to the ass. Lipmann adopts a biblical wordplay, calling Peter *peter hamor*—Hebrew for a "firstling ass" (Exod. 13:13)—clearly treating Peter with much less respect than he does Christians in general. However, Lipmann's view of Peter should not mislead us in the attempt to sketch a cultural profile of the convert. He was the end product of those "doubters" who gave Lipmann such cause for concern and for whom he was writing. In that respect, Peter may be considered a forerunner of the converts in the coming centuries. He was perhaps the first in Germany to use his conversion as an opportunity to reexamine his former religion, with understandably unflattering results. Peter can be seen as a forerunner of the ethnographic study of Judaism, whose roots first emerged, therefore, at the turn of the fourteenth century. However, unlike other converts, such as Victor von Carben and Anton Margarita, Peter did not study Judaism in order to convince other Jews to convert, but only to find them guilty of defaming Christianity and consequently worthy of destruction.

Notes

1. Amos Funkenstein, "Changes in the Patterns of Christian Anti-Jewish Polemics in the Twelfth Century" (in Hebrew), *Zion* 33 (1968): 125–44 (reprinted as "Changes in Christian Anti-Jewish Polemics in the Twelfth Century," in *Perceptions of Jewish History* [Berkeley and Los Angeles: University of California Press, 1993], 172–201); idem, "Basic Types of Christian Anti-Jewish Polemics in the Later Middle Ages," *Viator* 2 (1971): 373–82; Jeremy Cohen, "Towards a Functional Classification of Jewish Anti-Christian Polemic in the High Middle Ages," in *Religionsgespräche im Mittelalter*, ed. Bernard Lewis and Friedrich Niewöhner, Wolfenbütteler Mittelalter-Studien 4 (Wiesbaden, Ger.: Herzog August Bibliothek, 1992), 93–114.

2. Jeremy Cohen, *The Friars and the Jews: The Evolution of Medieval Anti-Judaism* (Ithaca, N.Y.: Cornell University Press, 1982); idem, *Living Letters of the Law: Ideas of the Jew in Medieval Christianity* (Berkeley and Los Angeles: University of California Press, 1999).

3. Frank E. Manuel, *The Broken Staff: Judaism through Christian Eyes* (Cambridge: Harvard University Press, 1992); Hans-Martin Kirn, *Das Bild vom Juden in Deutschland des frühen 16. Jahrhunderts* (Tübingen, Ger.: J.C.B. Mohr, 1989).

4. Elisheva Carlebach, *Divided Souls: Converts from Judaism in Germany, 1500–1750* (New Haven: Yale University Press, 2001); Jeremy Cohen, "The Mentality of the

Medieval Jewish Apostate: Peter Alfonsi, Hermann of Cologne, and Pablo Christiani," in *Jewish Apostasy in the Modern World*, ed. Todd M. Endelman (New York: Holmes and Meier, 1987), 20–47.

5. Judah Kaufmann, *Rabbi Yom-Tov Lipmann Mühlhausen: The Author of "Nizzahon," the Scholar, and the Kabbalist* (in Hebrew) (New York: Trio Printing, 1927); Efraim Kupfer, "Concerning the Cultural Image of German Jewry and Its Rabbis in the Fourteenth and Fifteenth Centuries" (in Hebrew), *Tarbiz* 42 (1973): 113–47; Frank Talmage, ed., Introduction, *Sefer Hanizzahon* (Jerusalem: Dinur Center, 1983–84), ix–xxxvii; *Germania Judaica*, vol. 2, ed. Arye Maimon, Mordechai Breuer, and Yacov Guggenheim (Tübingen, Ger.: J.C.B. Mohr, 1995), 1129–31; Israel J. Yuval, *Scholars in Their Time: The Religious Leadership of German Jewry in the Late Middle Ages* (in Hebrew) (Jerusalem: Magnes Press, 1988), 105–7, 152–57; idem, "Magie und Kabbala unter den Juden im Deutschland des ausgehenden Mittelalters," in *Judentum im deutschen Sprachraum*, ed. Karl E. Grözinger (Frankfurt: Suhrkamp, 1991), 173–91; idem, "Kabbalisten, Ketzer, und Polemiker. Das kulturelle Umfeld des Sefer ha-Nizachon von Lipman Mühlhausen," in *Mysticism, Magic, and Kabbalah in Ashkenazi Judaism*, ed. Karl E. Grözinger and Joseph Dan (Berlin: Walter de Gruyter, 1995), 155–71; Daniel Lasker, "The Transubstantiation, Elijas's Chair, Plato, and the Jewish-Christian Debate," *Revue des Études Juives* 143 (1984): 32–39; idem, "Jewish Philosophical Polemics in Ashkenaz," in *Contra Iudaeos: Ancient and Medieval Polemics between Christians and Jews*, ed. Ora Limor and Guy G. Stroumsa (Tübingen, Ger.: Mohr, 1996), 195–213.

6. *Sefer Hammiknah*, ed. Hava Fraenkel Goldschmidt (Jerusalem: Mekize Nirdamim, 1970).

7. Talmage, Introduction, xii.

8. *Encyclopaedia Judaica*, 12, 499–502; Yuval, *Scholars in Their Time*, 106.

9. *Germania Judaica*, vol. 3, ed. Zvi Avneri (Tübingen, Ger.: J. C. B. Mohr, 1968), 550–53.

10. *Germania Judaica*, vol. 2 (n. 5 above).

11. An earlier book named *Sefer ha-Nizzahon* was written in Germany in the late thirteenth century. The Christian Hebraist Wagenseil called it *Nizzahon Vetus* in order to make a distinction between it and Lipmann's book, which was considered to be the *Sefer ha-Nizzahon* par excellence. See David Berger, *The Jewish-Christian Debate in the High Middle Ages: A Critical Edition of the Nizzahon Vetus* (Philadelphia: Jewish Publication Society of America, 1979), 33, 233 n. 2. The name *Nizzahon* is not only a title given to several polemical books, but also a generic definition of Jewish polemical, anti-Christian literature. On other *Nizzahon* books, see Judah Rosenthal, ed., *Sefer Joseph Hamekane* (Jerusalem: Mekize Nirdamim, 1970), xiii.

12. The *terminus ante quem* is 1409 because of a messianic calculation for the year 1410 included in the book (*Sefer ha-Nizzahon*, par. 335). However, as will be explained below, there are good reasons to suggest an earlier date for its composition.

13. The prayer ʿ*Alenu* was introduced to the daily Jewish prayerbook in the twelfth century, first in France and England and later on in Germany. On its anti-Christian interpretation see Naftali Wieder, "Because of an Anti-Christian and an Anti-Moslem *Gematriya*" (in Hebrew), *Sinai* 76 (1975): 1–14; Moshe Hallamish, "An Early Version of *Alenu Le-Shabeah*" (in Hebrew), *Sinai* 110 (1992): 262–65; Israel Ta-Shma, "The Origin and Status of *Alenu Le-Shabeah* in the Prayerbook," in *The Frank Talmage Memorial Volume*, vol. 1 (Haifa, Isr.: Haifa University Press, 1993), 85–95 (Hebrew section); Israel J. Yuval, *Two Nations in Your Womb: Perceptions of Jews and Christians* (in Hebrew) (Tel Aviv: Am Oved Publishers, 2000), 206–9, 212–16.

14. On the curse against the *minim* in Late Antiquity, see Peter Schäfer, "Die sogennante Synode von Jabne. Zur Trennung von Juden und Christen im 1./2. Jh. n. Chr.," *Judaica* 31 (1975): 54–64; Reuven Kimelman, "Birkat Ha-Minim and the Lack of Evidence for an Anti-Christian Jewish Prayer in Late Antiquity," in *Jewish and Christian Self-Definition*, vol. 2, ed. E. P. Sanders et al. (London: SCM Press, 1981), 226–44, 391–403; William Horbury, "The Benediction of Minim and the Early Jewish-Christian Controversy," *Journal of Theological Studies* 33 (1982): 19–61. On the Christian reaction to the Jewish curse in the Middle Ages, see Isidore Loeb, "La controverse de 1240 sur le Talmud," *Revue des Études Juives* 3 (1881): 51; Chen Merchavia, *The Church versus Talmudic and Midrashic Literature* (in Hebrew) *[500–1248]* (Jerusalem: Bialik Institute, 1970), 278–80; Yosef H. Yerushalmi, "The Inquisition and the Jews of France in the Time of Bernard Gui," *Harvard Theological Review* 63 (1970): 354–63; Hans-Martin Kirn, *Das Bild vom Juden im Deutschland*, 114–118.

15. Aharon Freimann, "*Titnem Le-Herpa*" (in Hebrew), *Tarbiz* 12 (1940): 70–74; H. Merhavia, "The Casuistic Poetic 'Rebuke' (*Shamta*) of Abraham B. Jacob" (in Hebrew), *Tarbiz* 39 (1970): 277–84; idem, "The Casuistic Poetic 'Rebuke' (*Shamta*) in Medieval Christian Polemic Literature" (in Hebrew), *Tarbiz* 41 (1971): 95–115; Yuval, *Two Nations in Your Womb*, 135–50.

16. On the Jewish anti-Christian language of hatred and despite, see Anna Sapir-Abulafia, "Invectives against Christianity in the Hebrew Chronicles of the First Crusade," in *Crusade and Settlement*, ed. Peter W. Edbury (Cardiff: University of Cardiff Press, 1985), 66–72; Elliott Horowitz, "Medieval Jews Face the Cross" (in Hebrew), in *Facing the Cross: The Persecutions of 1096 in History and Historiography*, ed. Yom Tov Assis et al. (Jerusalem: Magnes Press, 2000), 118–40.

17. On the host desecration accusations, see Friedrich Lotter, "Hostienfrevelvorwurf und Blutwunderfälschung bei den Judenverfolgungen von 1298 ('Rintfleisch') und 1336–1338 ('Armleder')," in *Fälschungen im Mittelalter (=Monumenta Germaniae Historica: Schriften*, vol. 33), V (Hannover: Hannsche Buchhandlung, 1988), 533–60; Miri Rubin, *Gentile Tales: The Narrative Assault on Late Medieval Jews* (New Haven: Yale University Press, 1999); eadem, "Desecration of the Host: The Birth of an Accusation," in *Christianity and Judaism*, ed. Diana Wood, Studies in Church History 29 (Oxford: Blackwell, 1992), 169–85.

18. B. Avoda Zara, 16b.

19. Joseph Shatzmiller, "The Albigensian Heresy as Reflected in the Eyes of Contemporary Jewry" (in Hebrew), in *Culture and Society in Medieval Jewry: Studies Dedicated to the Memory of Haim Hillel Ben-Sasson*, ed. Menahem Ben-Sasson et al. (Jerusalem: Zalman Shazar Center, 1989), 333–52; David Berger, "Christian Heresy and Jewish Polemic in the Twelfth and Thirteenth Centuries," *Harvard Theological Review* 68 (1975): 287–303; Jeremy Cohen, *The Friars and the Jews*, 97–98; Ram Ben-Shalom, "The Disputation of Tortosa: Vicente Ferrer and the Problem of the Conversos According to the Testimony of Isaac Nathan" (in Hebrew), *Zion* 56 (1991): 20–45.

20. Richard Kieckhefer, *Repression of Heresy in Medieval Germany* (Philadelphia: University of Pennsylvania Press, 1979), 53–73; Paul P. Bernard, "Heresy in Fourteenth Century Austria," *Medievalia et Humanistica* 110 (1956): 50–63; Siegfried Hoyer, "Die thüringische Kryptoflagellantenbewegung im 15. Jahrhundert," *Jahrbuch für Regionalgeschichte* 2 (1967): 148–74; Dietrich Kurze, "Zur Ketzergeschichte der Mark Brandenburg und Pommern vornehmlich im 14. Jahrhundert," *Jahrbuch für die Geschichte Mittel- und Ostdeutschlands* 16–17 (1968): 50–94; Martin Erbstoesser, *Sozialreligiöse*

Strömungen im späten Mittelalter: Geißler, Freigeister und Waldenser im 14. Jahrhundert (Berlin: Akademie-Verlag, 1970), 70–84; Alexander Patschovsky, "Ketzer und Ketzerverfolgung in Böhmen im Jahrhundert vor Hus," *Geschichte in Wissenschaft und Unterricht* 32 (1982): 70–77.

21. Bernard Guenée, *Histoire et culture historique dans l'occident médiéval* (Paris: Aubier Montaigne, 1980), 249–95.

22. Ora Limor, "The Epistle of Rabbi Samuel of Morocco: A Best-Seller in the World of Polemics," in *Contra Judaeos* (n. 5 above), 177–94.

23. Kaufmann, *Rabbi Yom-Tov Lipmann Mühlhausen*, 69, n. 72.

24. Yuval, *Scholars in Their Time*, 306; Kaufmann, *Rabbi Yom-Tov Lipmann Mühlhausen*, 92–93.

25. A good example is the fate of Nahmanides' report on the Barcelona disputation, which due to its wide dissemination in Jewish society raised anger among the Dominicans and drove them to take countermeasures both in the royal and papal courts. See Heinrich Denifle, "Quellen zur Disputation Pablos Christiani mit Moses Nachmani zu Barcelona 1263," *Historisches Jahrbuch* 8 (1887): 225–44; Robert Chazan, *Barcelona and Beyond: The Disputation of 1263 and Its Aftermath* (Berkeley and Los Angeles: University of California Press, 1992), 80–99.

26. Annette Wigger, *Stephan Bodeker, O. Praem., Bischof von Brandenburg, 1421–1459: Leben, Wirken, und ausgewählte Werke* (Frankfurt: Peter Lang, 1992), 114–66.

27. For a detailed discussion on the Antilipmanniana literature, see Kaufmann, *Rabbi Yom-Tov Lipmann Mühlhausen*, 91–109.

28. On this anecdote: Iohann Christoph Wolf, *Bibliothecae Hebraeae*, vol. 4 (Hamburg, 1733), 893–95; Kaufmann, *Rabbi Yom-Tov Lipmann Mühlhausen*, 64–66.

29. *Liber Nizachon Rabbi Lipmanni*, ed. Theodor Hackspan (Nürnberg, Ger., 1644 [reprinted in Jerusalem, 1984]). Hackspan's edition is the standard edition in use until this day. The three Jewish editions that appeared in the eighteenth and nineteenth centuries are also based on it and are not superior to it. We are now preparing a new critical edition of the book based on the oldest existing manuscript, which is now in the Staats- und Universitätsbibliothek in Hamburg, copied in the year 1425. The handwriting is clear, and the manuscript holds the entire text. It is even plausible that it was copied from the original itself. Two other manuscripts which represent two other families of manuscripts, as well as Hackspan's edition, will be collated, and the variants will be included in the apparatus criticus.

30. Iohann Christoph Wagenseil, *Carminis R. Lipmanni Confutatio, Tela ignea Satanae* (Altdorf, Switz., 1681), 118–635. The *correctiones* were included in the 1984 reprinted edition.

31. *Sefer ha-Nizzahon*, par. 262.

32. Johann Jacob Schudt, *Jüdische Merkwürdigkeiten* (Frankfurt, 1714–18), 2, 311–14.

33. Oxford, Bodleian Library, MS. Oppenheim 93 (Catalogue Adolf Neubauer, no. 973), fol. 109v.

34. *Sefer ha-Nizzahon*, par. 22.

35. *Sefer ha-Nizzahon*, par. 234.

36. *Sefer ha-Nizzahon*, par. 239; Elliott Horowitz, "The Unlikely Career of the Second Commandment: The People of the Image," *New Republic*: 25 September 2000, 41–49.

37. *Sefer ha-Nizzahon*, par. 334.

38. *Sefer ha-Nizzahon*, par. 348.

39. The first to notice this coincidence was Salo Baron, *A Social and Religious History of the Jews*, vol. 9 (New York: Columbia University Press, 1965), 336 n. 9.

40. Frantiek Graus, *Struktur und Geschichte. Drei Volksaufstände im mittelalterlichen Prag* (Sigmaringen, Ger.: Jan Thorbecke Verlag, 1971), 58.

41. Israel J. Yuval, "Juden, Hussiten und Deutschen nach einer hebräischen Chronik," *Zeitschrift für Historische Forschung*, Beiheft 13: *Juden in der christlichen Umwelt während des späten Mittelalters*, ed. Alfred Haverkamp and Franz-Josef Ziwes (Berlin: Duncker and Humblot, 1992), 59–102.

42. Eliyahu ben Elqana Capsali, *Seder Eliyahu Zuta*, vol. 2, ed. Aryeh Shmuelevitz et al. (Jerusalem: Ben Zvi Institute, 1977), 240–44.

43. A shining example of such a conversion is told by Herman of Cologne. See Karl F. Morrison, *Conversion and Text: The Case of Augustine of Hippo, Herman-Judah, and Constantine Tsatsos* (Charlottesville: University Press of Virginia, 1992), 39–113; Friedrich Lotter, "Ist Hermann von Schedas Opusculum de conversione sua eine Falschung?" *Aschkenas* 2 (1992): 207–18.

44. Printed in *Otzar Nechmad* 4 (Vienna, 1863), 177–214. The historical background of *Alilot Devarim* was studied by Reuven Bonfil, "Sefer Alilot Devarim: A Chapter in Fourteenth-Century Ashkenazic Thought" (in Hebrew), *Eshel Beer-Sheva* 2 (BeerSheba, Isr., 1980): 229–64.

45. Michael H. Shank, *"Unless You Believe You Shall Not Understand": Logic, University, and Society in Late Medieval Vienna* (Princeton: Princeton University Press, 1988).

46. Funkenstein, "Changes in the Patterns of Christian Anti-Jewish Polemics in the 12th Century"; idem, "Basic Types of Christian Anti-Jewish Polemics in the Later Middle Ages."

47. Daniel Lasker, "Jewish Philosophical Polemics in Ashkenaz."

48. On the Prague philosophical circle, see Kupfer, "Concerning the Cultural Image of German Jewry and Its Rabbis in the Fourteenth and Fifteenth Centuries."

49. Kaufmann, *Rabbi Yom-Tov Lipmann Mühlhausen*, 71–74.

50. Shank, *"Unless You Believe You Shall Not Understand"*, 149–51.

51. *Sefer ha-Nizzahon*, pars. 179, 225, 290.

52. *Sefer ha-Nizzahon*, par. 225.

53. *Sefer ha-Nizzahon*, par. 218.

54. *Sefer ha-Nizzahon*, pars. 179, 225, 290.

55. Nigel F. Palmer, "Marquard von Lindau," *Verfasserlexikon*, Bd. 6 (Berlin: de Gruyter, 1987), 81–125. This identification was first suggested by Yacov Guggenheim.

8
Reassessing the "Basel-Wittenberg Conflict": Dimensions of the Reformation-Era Discussion of Hebrew Scholarship

Stephen G. Burnett

The study of Reformation-era Christian Hebraism has benefited from increased scholarly attention over the past fifty years.[1] Sebastian Münster, Paul Fagius, Wolfgang Capito, and Conrad Pellican have all been the subjects of biographies.[2] Luther scholars have analyzed not only Luther's use of Hebrew[3] but to a lesser extent the Hebrew scholarship of Melanchthon, Bugenhagen, and Goldhahn.[4] Historians of the book trade have provided analytic bibliographies and studies of prominent Christian Hebrew printers, including Heinrich Petri, Thomas Anselm, and Robert Estienne[5] as well as studies of the Hebrew book trade in Augsburg and Basel.[6] The role of Jewish scholars in facilitating the growth of Hebrew studies has received less attention but has been advanced through Weil's study of the life and works of Elias Levita.[7] Yet despite this intense scholarly activity, Christian Hebraism in the Reformation era still lacks a convincing synthetic study relating the activities of Christian Hebraists to wider trends.

In this essay I will offer such a synthesis, based upon publishing data of Christian Hebrew books and a study of leading German Hebraists of the Reformation era. I will identify the most important authorities on the Hebrew language and examine their close personal and professional connections. Christian Hebrew scholarship grew at a dramatic rate in Germany in this period, thanks to their activities, which grew out of a commitment to the humanist ideal of a return to the sources (*ad fontes*) and, in most cases, the Protestant theological doctrine of *sola Scriptura*. The spread of Hebrew studies inevitably provoked discussions about what Christians could profitably learn from Jewish scholarship. The utility of Jewish scholarship became an important concern for Reformation-era Christian Hebraists.

There have been three recent attempts to fill the conceptual gap in the scholarly literature: Jerome Friedman's *Most Ancient Testimony* (1984), a series of articles written by R. Gerald Hobbs and Bernard Roussel on the activities of the "Upper Rhineland School of Biblical Exegesis," conveniently summarized by Roussel in *Le Bible de Tous les Temps*, volume 5 (1989), and Karl Heinz Burmeister's little-known but programmatic article "Johannes Campensis und Sebastian Münster" (1970).[8] Each of these authors emphasizes the differences of opinion between scholars living in southern Germany and the Wittenberg Hebraists concerning the use of Jewish biblical and linguistic scholarship. Friedman emphasizes this contrast most sharply when he chooses Johannes Forster as a typical representative of Lutheran scholarship. Forster, he argues, adopted a warped approach to Hebrew philology under Luther's influence.[9] Friedman coins the phrase the Basel-Wittenberg Conflict, portraying the Hebraist "schools" of Basel and Wittenberg as irreconcilably opposing camps espousing fundamentally different approaches to Hebrew studies.[10] Friedman's schema masks a number of features of Hebrew studies that were common to Protestant Hebraists throughout Germany. The most important commonality was a discussion that took place in published books, correspondence, and in person on the value of Jewish scholarship for biblical translation and exegesis. This discussion took place between 1525, when Oecolampadius's *Isaiah* commentary appeared, and midcentury, by which time most of the generation of pioneering Hebraists had died. The Christian Hebraists who wrote and responded to the most important, trendsetting exegetical studies that appeared during these years received similar training in Hebrew language, read most of the same books, and often posed the same questions concerning the utility of Jewish sources. This scholarly conversation cut across geographical and confessional lines, often pitting some members of the Upper Rhineland sodality, such as Pellican, against others such as Bucer as well as against the Wittenbergers. This conversation took place largely in Latin and focused primarily on the exposition of biblical texts rather than on dramatic changes to the received Latin biblical text.[11]

The Hebraists of the German Reformation were a surprisingly small group of scholars, many of whom knew each other or had the same Hebrew teachers. I have defined the "community of the competent" for the early German Reformation primarily as those who taught Hebrew either at Louvain[12] or one of the German universities and those who wrote or edited Christian Hebrew books, such as grammars, dictionaries, portions of the Bible, and biblical introductions. I have limited my sample to those scholars whose careers began before 1535 because these men set the trends in Hebrew study that would endure through midcentury, both through the books they authored and edited and through their often critical reception of these works.

TABLE 8.1. PROFESSORS OF HEBREW IN LOUVAIN AND GERMAN UNIVERSITIES TO 1535

Professor[13]	University	Hebrew Instructor
Adrianus, Matthaeus	Wittenberg, Louvain	Jewish education
Arnold Halderen of Wesel	Cologne	unknown
Boeschenstein, Johannes	Wittenberg	R. Moshe Moellin, Reuchlin
Campensis, Johannes	Louvain	Adrianus
Capito, Wolfgang	Strasbourg	Adrianus
Cellarius, Johannes	Leipzig, Frankfurt/O	Reuchlin, Berselius[14]
Cleinmann, Valentin	Heidelberg	Heidelberg; Basel (Münster?)
Delius [Däle], Michael	Freiburg, Strasbourg	unknown
Forster, Johannes	Wittenberg	Reuchlin[15]
Gennep, Andre	Louvain	unknown
Goldhahn, Matthaeus	Wittenberg	Cellarius
Grossmann, Kaspar	Bern	Zurich (Ceporin? Pellican?)
Jonas, Jacob	Tübingen	Goldhahn
Leonard, David	Ingolstadt	Jewish education
Lonicerus, Johannes	Freiburg, Marburg	Wittenberg
Margaritha, Antonius	Leipzig, Vienna	Jewish education
Molitoris, Johann	Freiburg/Br	Freiburg/Br (unknown)
Münster, Sebastian	Heidelberg, Basel	Pellican, Adrianus
Nouzen, Sebastian	Marburg	Louvain/(Adrianus?)
Pellican, Conrad	Basel, Zurich	Adrianus, Reuchlin
Reuchlin, Johannes	Tübingen, Ingolstadt	Loans, Obadiah Sforno[16]
Siboldi, Georg	Heidelberg	Heidelberg (Münster?)
Uelin, Wilhelm	Tübingen	unknown
Werner Einhorn of Bacharach	Ingolstadt, Erfurt	Jewish education, Von Karben
Ziegler, Bernhard	Liegnitz, Leipzig	Cellarius or Novenianus?[17]

In addition to these new professors of Hebrew, a second group of capable Hebraists who wrote on Hebraica-related topics but who did not teach Hebrew at a university must be considered.[18]

TABLE 8.2. AUTHORS/EDITORS OF HEBREW BOOKS IN GERMANY, 1505–35

Author/Editor	Instructor
Bucer, Martin	unknown
Caesar, Bartholomaeus	Reuchlin
Fabricius, Theodor	Goldhahn[19]
Marschalk, Nicolaus	unknown
Oecolampadius, Johannes	Adrianus
Potken, Johannes	Bishop Robert of Lecce[20]
Uranius, Heinrich	unknown
Westheimer, Bartholomaeus	unknown

The two most important teachers of Hebrew prior to the Reformation were Johannes Reuchlin and Matthäus Adrianus. Adrianus's students, including Reuchlin, Capito, Pellican, and Münster, were the most enthusiastic users of Jewish biblical commentaries and other postbiblical Jewish literature of this period. Apart from the teacher-pupil relationship, ties of acquaintanceship bound many of these men together. Philipp Melanchthon was not a professional Hebraist but had been well trained in Hebrew, and Luther frequently asked his help when revising his German Bible translation. He was distantly related to Reuchlin, who helped to guide his academic career. Oecolampadius met Reuchlin through his friendship with Melanchthon. Both Pellican and Münster knew Reuchlin from their years in Pforzheim.[21] Reuchlin generously made his library available to other scholars. For example, he allowed Sebastian Münster to make a copy of his manuscript of *Sefer Nizzahon*, which Münster would go on to use throughout his career.[22] Reuchlin had not only studied with Adrianus but also used his influence to bring him to Tübingen in 1513.[23] When Elector Frederick of Saxony invited Reuchlin himself to become the first professor of Hebrew at the University of Wittenberg, he politely declined but suggested Oecolampadius and Pellican as well as Matthäus Lang and Paul Ricius as suitable candidates for the post.[24]

This small circle of Christian Hebrew scholars, active in Germany during the early Reformation, was closely knit through common, mainly Christian, teachers and acquaintances. By contrast only a few of the Christian Hebraists of the early German Reformation received direct help from Jews in the development of their field. Reuchlin, the fountainhead of Hebrew scholarship in Germany, studied with Jacob Loans, the German emperor's personal physician, and with Obadiah Sforno when he lived in Rome.[25] Johannes Boeschenstein learned some Hebrew from R. Moshe Moellin of Weissenburg.[26] Johannes Eck studied with Elias Levita when he lived in Rome (1520–23), and Paul Fagius would do so when Levita worked for the Isny Hebrew press in 1540–41.[27] Four of the twenty-three professors of Hebrew—Adrianus, Leonard, Margaritha, and Werner Einhorn—were converts from Judaism though only Adrianus had a major impact upon Christian Hebrew scholarship.[28] The most important role that professing Jews would play in the development of Reformation-era Hebrew studies was not as tutors but as Hebrew printers and authors.

The production and consumption of Hebrew texts was crucially important for the growth of Christian Hebrew scholarship. Basic Hebrew grammars and dictionaries, written in Latin rather than Hebrew, were essential for beginning students, as were Bibles and portions of the Bible to study. More advanced students and their instructors sometimes sought books printed primarily with a Jewish readership in mind, especially the Bomberg rabbinical Bibles of 1517 and 1525. The Hebrew presses of Germany (and Paris after 1535) dominated this trade to a remarkable degree during the Reformation era.[29]

TABLE 8.3. CHRISTIAN HEBREW BOOKS PRINTED IN GERMANY AND LOUVAIN, 1500–1555

	To 1525	1526–35	1536–45	1546–55	Total
Basel	22	23	29	21	95
Cologne	3	3	1	4	11
Wittenberg	7	3	0	0	10
Augsburg	9	0	3	0	12
Isny	0	0	10	0	10
Hagenau	9	2	0	0	11
Strasbourg	5	1	0	1	7
Leipzig	2	1	1	0	4
Tübingen	4	0	0	0	4
Vienna	0	0	0	4	4
Other[30]	6	3	5	1	15
	68	36	48	31	183

TABLE 8.4. CHRISTIAN HEBREW BOOKS PRINTED IN FRANCE AND LOUVAIN, 1500–1555

	To 1525	1526–35	1536–45	1546–55	Total
Louvain	2	2	0	2	6
Paris	8	20	75[31]	36	139
Lyons	0	7	0	3	10
					155

Between 1500 and 1555 I have identified 396 Hebrew books produced primarily with Christian customers in mind. Before 1536 German presses produced an astounding 56 percent of all Christian Hebraica books produced in Europe (104 of 186 imprints). French Hebrew presses did not begin producing large numbers of titles until after 1535 when the discussion of the appropriate use of Hebraica was already well advanced among German Christian Hebraists.[32] By 1555 over 85 percent of Christian Hebraica books printed in Europe (338) were produced either in Germany, Louvain, or France. During this same period Italian presses produced only 32 Christian Hebrew imprints and Spain produced 20 imprints. Among these was the Complutensian Polyglot, which had an important impact upon scholarship despite its limited circulation.[33] Clearly, German Christian Hebraist writers dominated academic and theological discussions through 1535 due to the sheer number of works that German Hebrew printers produced and distributed.

Because German scholars, beginning with Reuchlin and Pellican, began to write for publication much earlier than their counterparts in other countries, they helped to ensure German dominance in the field of Christian Hebrew printing. Reuchlin's *Rudimenta Linguae Hebraeae* (Pforzheim, 1506) was not the earliest Hebrew grammar available for purchase; it was preceded by several printings by Manutius of Adrianus's short introduction to Hebrew (Venice, 1500) and by Pellican's short grammatical sketch (Strasbourg, 1504).[34] Reuchlin's book, however, was complete in itself, since it contained both a Hebrew grammar and a Hebrew dictionary based upon David Kimhi's *Mikhlol*. Reuchlin's work was not only far more substantial than any other Christian Hebrew grammar that had yet appeared, it would remain in a class by itself until Pagninus's translation of Kimhi's *Mikhlol* was published in Lyons, 1526. Luther, Melanchthon, Zwingli, and Bucer all owned and used copies of Reuchlin's grammar.[35] Pagninus's dictionary was first printed in 1523, the same year that Sebastian Münster printed the first edition of his Hebrew dictionary. The Germans were also the first to produce portions of the Hebrew Bible with linguistic help for the student: Reuchlin's printing of *In septem psalmos poenitentiales interpretatio* (Tübingen, 1512) was followed by another edited by Johannes Boeschenstein (Augsburg, 1520) and by a whole series of works edited by Pellican and Münster, the latter for his students first in Heidelberg, then in Basel.[36]

Surprisingly, given the amount of attention that Friedman and others have devoted to it, Kabbalah apparently played only a modest role in the German discussion of Hebrew studies after 1525.[37] It had of course been the focus of sharp scholarly debate during the Reuchlin-Pfefferkorn controversy, but judging from the very modest amount of kabbalistic-related Hebraica, only five books in Germany during this period, and three of them by Reuchlin, there was clearly only limited demand for kabbalistic texts and aids that would help Christian readers understand these texts in their original language.[38] Capito, Pellican, and for a time even Johannes Forster utilized kabbalistic interpretations and collected kabbalistic texts. This remained a private interest, communicated in person and by letter rather than in print.[39] Those scholars who were interested in reading kabbalistic texts were also more likely to seek out Jewish tutors, especially in Italy but occasionally also in Germany. This phenomenon became common enough to spark a fierce debate among Jews about how much they could legitimately teach Christian pupils.[40]

Beginning with Reuchlin, a relatively small number of German Christian Hebraists came to dominate public discussion of Hebrew scholarship, as their impressive publication statistics indicate.

But mere statistics do not tell the entire story of whose works of Hebrew scholarship had a significant impact and whose did not. Adrianus's imprints were all exemplars of his small grammatical sketch of Hebrew, the first of which appeared in Constantine Lascaris's *De Octo partibus orationis Liber primus* (Venice: Manutius, 1500). Thereafter, Manutius often included the work

TABLE 8.5. AUTHORS/EDITORS OF HEBREW BOOKS PRINTED IN GERMANY BEFORE 1555[41]

	Author	Editor	Total
Münster, Sebastian	21	46	67
Reuchlin, Johannes	12	2	14
Boeschenstein, Johannes	10	4	14
Pellican, Conrad	5	8	13
Adrianus, Matthaeus	11	0	11[42]
Goldhahn, Matthaeus	7	0	7
Westheimer, Bartholomaeus	6	0	6
Uranius, Heinrich	4	0	4
Marschalk, Nicolaus	3	1	4
Capito, Wolfgang	3	0	3
Cellarius, Johannes	2	0	2
Fabricius, Theodor	1	0	1
Caesar, Bartholomaeus	1	0	1
Margaritha, Antonius	0	1	1
Nouzen, Sebastian	1	0	1
Potken, Johannes	0	1	1

as an appendix in the grammar books he printed. Boeschenstein's works were all pamphlet length. Münster's works were often Bible portions or translations of Elias Levita's books, published at his initiative in Basel. Nonetheless, the sheer volume of publications that Münster, Pellican, and Reuchlin, and the other most prolific writers, produced ensured that they had a reputation as Hebraists and that their ideas and approaches to Hebraica had a good chance of being heard.

German Christian Hebraists had a long start on their French and Italian counterparts, but they were quick to seize on new Hebrew scholarship from these regions as it became available, whether by written by Christian or Jewish authors. For example, Münster's old teacher Pellican gave him a copy of the first printing of Pagninus's lexicon.[43] Münster also had access to a rare copy of the Complutensian Polyglot for his studies.[44] Christian Hebraists also made considerable use of books intended primarily for Jewish readers, most famously the Bomberg rabbinical Bibles of 1517 and 1525. Sebastian Münster and Martin Bucer each owned copies of both of these monumental works.[45] Melanchthon purchased a first-edition Bomberg rabbinical Bible (1517) in 1518. His younger colleague Caspar Cruciger may have owned a Bomberg second-edition rabbinical Bible, as apparently did Luther himself.[46] Perhaps the most profound example of indebtedness to Jewish scholarship may be found in Münster's fifteen-year-long effort to translate and transmit the scholarship of his older Jewish contemporary Elias Levita to the scholarly public at large. Eventually, Münster corresponded with Levita in Venice, and no fewer than thirteen Levita imprints would ultimately be printed in Basel between 1525 and 1552.[47]

The holdings of the Wittenberg University Library in 1536 indicate that the Wittenbergers were reading much the same works as Bucer, Münster, and their colleagues and that they too followed the emerging Hebrew scholarship closely. The catalog contains references to twenty-five Hebrew books, seventeen written or edited by Sebastian Münster. The two most important non-German Christian Hebraist works were Pagninus's *Thesaurus linguae sanctae lexicon Hebraicum* (Lyons, 1529) and Giustiniani's famous polyglot Psalter (Genoa, 1516). Jewish imprints included a second-edition Bomberg rabbinical Bible (1525), Nathan b. Kalonymous's Hebrew Bible Concordance, and Abraham de Balmes's Grammar (1523).[48]

Wittenberg's scholars, then, were linked to the general discussion of Hebrew scholarship that had been initiated by Reuchlin and continued with great vigor by his and Adrianus's students. Reuchlin had greater influence in Wittenberg than Adrianus, both because of the latter's inauspicious attempt to teach there and because of Reuchlin's textbook, which Luther, Melanchthon, and Bugenhagen all used.[49] Eight of the sixteen German Hebraist authors and editors lived either in Wittenberg or in nearby Leipzig: Boeschenstein, Adrianus, Goldhahn, Fabricius, and Marschalk had all taught at Wittenberg for varying lengths of time, and Cellarius and Caesar were both invited to teach there; Cellarius and Margaritha both taught at Leipzig. While the Wittenbergers' relations with the churches of Zurich, Strasbourg, and Basel became strained, especially over eucharistic theology, they continued to read and study the linguistic and exegetical works of Oecolampadius, Bucer, and Münster just as they continued to read and use Erasmus's New Testament–related works, regardless of their theological differences with him.[50]

The most impressive evidence for a common conversation over Hebraica is the conscious, if often selective, way that Luther and his colleagues used exegetical studies of biblical books written by the Upper Rhinelanders. Their response to these books was similar to the reactions of Pellican and Zwingli. The responses of Protestant scholars to three books in particular, Oecolampadius's *Isaiah* commentary (1525), Bucer's *Psalms* commentary (1529), and Münster's annotated Hebrew Bible (1534–35) provides strong evidence that the discussion about the utility of Hebrew studies was general and not limited to Wittenberg. These three books demonstrate a progressively greater use of Jewish biblical scholarship. They also provoked an argument over the utility of Jewish scholarship for biblical interpretation throughout German Protestant scholarship.[51]

Oecolampadius's *Isaiah* commentary was the earliest and least controversial of the three. As letters from both Luther and Bugenhagen to Oecolampadius attest, the Wittenbergers eagerly anticipated it.[52] When it finally arrived in Wittenberg, the commentary did not disappoint its readers. Oecolampadius's approach to the translation and interpretation of the text matched Luther's needs and priorities quite well. Oecolampadius wrote, "Since a number of my listeners had begun Hebrew studies, I wished to be content with the Hebrew text and be tied to no other translation; even though I did not despise the others, but consulted and even on occasion adduced them by way of commentary. For this same reason anywhere that idioms of the Hebrew people sounding somewhat harsh in Latin have been retained, this was deliberate, consideration having been taken of the students who might thereby read Hebrew more easily."[53] Luther used Oecolampadius's literal translation as an aid to understanding the Hebrew text of Isaiah and as a resource for his lectures on Isaiah (1528–30).[54]

Bucer's commentary on the Psalms (1529) was less gladly received by Luther, but he used it in the third revision of his Psalms translation.[55] Luther's response to Bucer's Psalms commentary can best be adduced through his *Defense of the Translation of the Psalms* (1531).[56] In his *Defense* Luther made it clear that not only were he and his colleagues aware that Jewish biblical commentaries existed, but that they had consulted them in their work. Luther crossly added that his detractors would see that when he differed from the rabbis and Jewish grammarians, "we have not acted out of a misunderstanding of the languages or out of ignorance of the rabbinical commentaries, but knowingly and deliberately."[57] When Luther discussed how the rabbis interpreted Psalm 58:9 (10) and Psalm 118:27 in both his *Defense* and in the Psalms revision protocol, he closely followed Bucer's account of rabbinical opinion.[58]

Luther's statement of principle about using the rabbinical commentaries and Jewish scholarship in general "with care," though given in an ill-tempered tone, was precisely what Upper Rhineland scholars of all shades professed to do. These scholars differed among themselves, however, about what constituted "careful" use of these commentaries. In fact, Pellican's opinion of Bucer's use of Jewish biblical commentaries in the Psalms commentary, given in a private letter, was far more critical than Luther's. "I . . . have read almost all of the first book of Hymns [Ps. 1–41], and am compelled to approve your effort and your judgment, save that I am pained by your labors in searching out and sifting the opinions of the rabbis, which you repeat time and again while they disagree with one another both in grammar and in sense." He went on to comment that the Jews generally "though not always" have some wisdom where it concerns the grammatical sense of the Bible.[59] Rather than sounding a note of caution unique to Wittenberg and himself, Luther's concerns about the usefulness of Jewish Bible commentaries were shared by Pellican and also by Zwingli.[60]

While Luther could receive and use with relative equanimity the commentaries of Oecolampadius and Bucer, Münster's biblical annotations (1534–35) were quite another matter. Münster employed a far wider variety of Jewish biblical commentaries than his predecessors and, like Bucer before him, would sometimes quote several conflicting opinions, leaving the reader to decide which (if any) of the rabbis had understood the text correctly.[61] In his introduction Münster stressed that his role was that of a philologist, a language expert who sought to clarify the meaning of individual verses as Erasmus had for the New Testament, leaving the theological aspects of the text for others to clarify.[62] Münster's aloofness from theological interpretation gave his annotations a wide readership among Catholics and Protestants alike[63] but also raised Luther's ire since it contradicted one of his strongest held principles concerning an interpreter's responsibilities.

Luther began to discuss Münster's biblical annotations in his *Table Talk* in 1536, a year after they appeared in print, and he would continue to read them carefully, discuss them with his colleagues, and argue against some of them until the end of his life. Luther made particular use of the annotations in the revision of his German Bible from 1539 to 1541 and in his decade-long lectures on Genesis. Yet whenever Luther mentioned Münster, he would always mix praise with blame. In a *Table Talk* passage of December 1536 Luther called Münster "the best of the Hebraists" but then went on to criticize his interpretation of several passages in Genesis.[64]

Luther referred to Münster several times in *Table Talk* as employing "judaizing" or "rabbinizing" interpretations.[65] Luther did not mean by this that Münster was consciously in league with the Jews or in sympathy with Judaism. In the last of these passages (winter of 1542–43), Luther admitted that Münster was hostile to the Jews, but "he does not take it to heart as much as I do."[66] Luther considered Münster to be theologically naive and criticized him for his willingness to concede too much to the rabbis both in grammatical matters and in biblical interpretation.

Luther believed that Münster used "judaizing interpretation" for three distinct but closely related reasons: Münster frequently failed to relate the individual words of Scripture (*verba*) to their "subject matter" (*res*); he had too much naive optimism concerning the state of Hebrew knowledge among both Jewish and Christian scholars; and, finally, Münster was not always diligent in seeking to establish the single simple meaning of Scripture. All of these, according to Luther, were failings Münster shared with the rabbis. During his second series of lectures on the Psalms (1518–21) and in his attack on Erasmus, *The Bondage of the Will* (1525), Luther formulated his position on the relationship between philological investigation and theological perspective.[67] He argued for a distinction between the overall "subject matter" (*res*) of the Bible and the individual words of particular Bible verses (*verba*). While individual verses might contain obscurities "because of our ignorance of their vocabulary and grammar," the overall message of Scripture was clear. Much of the obscurity of Scripture was due to the "blindness or indolence" of those who refused to trouble themselves to learn from it, whether they be lazy Christians or the Jews.[68] Expressing the "subject matter" properly meant rendering Old Testament passages in light of the new, in light of Christ and the Gospel. The rabbis did not know the "subject matter" because they could not understand the Bible. Therefore their guidance in interpreting the biblical text was of severely limited value.[69]

Luther frequently criticized Münster in his Genesis lectures for failing to relate words and subject matter properly. In his memorable discussion of Cain's complaint to God that his sin was too great to bear (Gen. 4:7), Luther delivered a broadside against the rabbis and "those who pattern themselves after them." He wrote, "Gerondi [Moses Nahmanides] has an excellent knowledge of the words (just as there are many today who far surpass me in their knowledge of the Hebrew language); but because he does not understand the matter (*res*), he distorts the passage with which we are dealing." Luther learned what Nahmanides thought at this point through Münster's biblical annotations, making it clear whom he meant by the phrase "those who pattern themselves after the rabbis."[70]

Luther's second criticism of Münster was that he was too confident about the state of scholarship on the Hebrew language. Luther's comments on Hebrew grammar have sometimes been understood to mean he had a cavalier attitude toward Jewish grammarians and the Hebrew language itself.[71] But Luther understood the tasks of theologian and grammarian to be complementary. He believed that study of the theological and grammatical aspects of particular verses could not be separated.[72] The minutes of Luther's translation committee meetings of 1531 and 1539–41 attest to the struggles of the Wittenbergers with the grammatical difficulties of particular verses. They frequently consulted rabbinical Bible commentaries, whether directly in their copies of rabbinical Bibles or indirectly through works such as Bucer's Psalms commentary or Münster's biblical annotations, though they did so in a very selective fashion.[73] Through over twenty years of biblical interpretation and lecture preparation Luther had come to realize how woefully inadequate all existing Hebrew grammars and lexicons were in dealing with figures of speech and proverbs.[74] On several occasions Luther commented in the Genesis lectures that neither he nor the rabbis knew what particular words meant.[75] While Münster was prone to "beat" Luther with the "whip" of the fallible rules of grammar,[76] Luther's response was to question the authority of Jewish grammatical scholarship. Part of Luther's skepticism stemmed from his belief that the

Hebrew vowel points were a postbiblical addition made by the rabbis to the canonical biblical text and were a man-made aid for reading which was subject to human error.[77] Luther felt that the Jewish grammarians were not nearly as well informed as they thought they were and that to depend too much on rabbinical scholarship was ill advised on both theological and philological grounds.

Luther's final criticism of Münster involved the latter's unconcern for establishing the single simple meaning of each and every biblical passage. Luther's commitment to "single meaning" reflected not only his position on the necessary relationship between the grammatical and theological meaning of each passage but also his lifetime work of Bible translation. By quoting so many different, frequently conflicting rabbinical comments in his biblical annotations, Münster gave them credence as possible interpretive options. When commenting on the meaning of the Hebrew word *kibrat* (distance), Luther wrote that neither he nor the Jews knew what the word meant (Gen. 35:17) but that ignorance spurred rather than stifled rabbinical creativity. "When the Jews have doubts about a word, they resort to equivocation and multiply meanings and make it more obscure by their glosses."[78]

Luther's concern that the presence of Christ, the "subject matter" of Scripture, be absolutely clear in exposition of the Old Testament was shared by members of the Upper Rhineland school. Luther's practice of biblical translation and exegesis and his objections to aspects of Münster's annotations find echoes in the writings of Pellican, Capito, and even Bucer. Six years before Luther began his Genesis lectures Pellican had questioned Jewish Hebrew grammatical scholarship, and he criticized Bucer's habit of quoting contradictory rabbinical opinions for the same passage. In 1527 Capito asserted in the introduction to his German translation of Hosea that since Christ "is the end of the Law and the prophets; accordingly I have determined to expound a prophet, namely Hosea, in a Christian manner."[79] Bucer too, for all his concern to identify the historical setting and meaning of the Psalms text, did so with the goal of identifying those passages in the Psalms where Christ's coming is genuinely prophesied.[80] The Hebraists of Zurich and Strasbourg shared many of Luther's fundamental hermeneutical principles.

What set Luther apart from members of the Upper Rhineland school was not an unwillingness to use Jewish biblical commentaries or Jewish grammatical scholarship but an abrupt change in his understanding of the danger that Jews and Judaism posed for Christianity, brought about by what he interpreted as a direct attack upon the Christian faith by Jews in 1542. Luther had become increasingly worried about the growing popularity of what he termed "judaizing" forms of biblical interpretation, and he believed that, if unchecked, such scholarship would damage the church from within when it was already under external attack from the devil's minions, the pope, the Jews, and the Turks.[81] In both *Against the Sabbatarians* and frequently in his lectures on Genesis, Luther offered refutations of Jewish interpretation of particular passages in order to "strengthen the faith" of his hearers-readers.[82] Luther first linked Christian "misinterpretation" of the Old Testament with the activities of living Jews in his *Against the Sabbatarians* (1538) and would do so again in his anti-Jewish treatises of 1543.[83] By Luther's own account, his rejection of Jewish biblical scholarship did not occur until 1542 when he received a pamphlet that he described as "a little book in which a Jew engages in a dialogue with a Christian. He dares to pervert the scriptural passages which we cite in testimony to our faith, concerning our Lord Jesus Christ and Mary his mother, and to interpret them quite differently."[84] Luther took it as evidence that his fears expressed in *Against the Sabbatarians* had been realized: that Jews were taking advantage of the confusion surrounding the Reformation and seeking converts among Christians.

Although Luther had previously decided that he was not going to write any more anti-Jewish polemics, he changed his mind and took up the task with a vengeance. In Luther's mind Christian Hebraists were responsible for part of the problem because their works gave Jewish biblical interpretations a patina of respectability. In two of the three treatises, *On the Ineffable Name* and *On the Last Words of David,* Luther appealed to Christian Hebraists directly, urging them to stop following the lead of Jewish commentators and to remember that they were Christians first, Hebraists only second. Some Christian Hebraists, he complained, were more "rabbinical" than "Christian."[85] Indeed, he named two of these Christians in his seldom-read conclusion to *On the Ineffable Name* (1543). "The two fine men, Sanctes [Pagninus] and Münster, have translated the Bible with incredible zeal and matchless (*inimitabili*) diligence, accomplishing much good. But the rabbis were sometimes too powerful for them, so that they chipped away at the analogy of faith, and were too dependent upon the rabbinical glosses."[86] Before 1542 Luther had come to believe that Jewish scholarship had less to offer the Christian interpreter than Münster and others like him believed. After 1542 he consciously repudiated much of what he and his colleagues had done previously. In *On the Last Words of David* (1543) Luther stated at the outset that he regretted having paid too much attention to Jewish scholarship in his Bible translation.[87]

Luther's end-of-life rejection of Jewish biblical and Hebrew scholarship did not mean that all Lutheran Hebrew scholars would follow Luther's admonitions, and Christian Hebraism within the Lutheran tradition is still a relatively unexplored topic. The evidence of Hebrew printing, however, suggests that Lutheran scholars remained strongly committed to Hebrew studies. After 1560 Wittenberg would become the third largest Hebrew printing center in

Europe,[88] and Lutheran scholars continued to read, interpret, and write expositions of the Hebrew Bible text.

The Reformation-era discussion of Hebrew scholarship was narrowly focused upon interpreting the Hebrew Bible. Other uses of Jewish scholarship, including the composition of anti-Jewish polemical literature or in various nontheological pursuits, were never controversial. Jewish linguistic scholarship was clearly useful for Christian interpreters as were Jewish biblical commentaries. All Christian Hebraists from the most enthusiastic, like Münster, to the least, such as Luther, agreed that these commentaries had to be used with care and discretion, not haphazardly or thoughtlessly.[89] In many respects the readiness of Christian Hebraists to follow the lead of Jewish interpreters was proportional to how much help they felt was needed to interpret the text at hand. There was also no necessary correlation between an interpreter's skill as a Hebraist and his willingness to use Jewish biblical commentaries. Conrad Pellican translated a number of Jewish commentaries into Latin and German, yet he believed that Jewish biblical commentaries were of limited use to Christians. He even had reservations about Jewish philological scholarship. But there was room at Wittenberg as in Basel, Strasbourg, and Zurich for Jewish help until the very end of Luther's life. Johannes Mathesius recalled that when the translation committee would meet in 1540, when he lived as a boarder in Luther's household, "Dr. Martin Luther came . . . with the Old Latin and new German Bible in addition to the Hebrew text. Herr Philip [Melanchthon] brought the Greek text, and Dr. Cruciger both the Hebrew Bible and the Targum. The professors all brought their rabbis."[90] The Wittenberg Sanhedrin (as Luther called his colleagues who advised him in translating the Hebrew Bible) met to advise Luther on how to understand the Hebrew Bible text and to translate it into German, using the most current scholarship to support their efforts.

Like their colleagues in the Upper Rhineland, Luther and his circle were participants in a single conversation on Hebrew studies. Thanks to the dominance of German Hebrew printers before 1535, German authorities and German texts defined the terms of this discussion and supported it philologically. The Wittenbergers were trained directly or indirectly by Reuchlin and Adrianus and were equipped with the same linguistic tools and texts as their colleagues in the Upper Rhineland. They faced many of the same interpretive challenges as their colleagues in southern Germany and often used the same hermeneutical principles to resolve these challenges. The Bible translations of Luther and Münster both incorporated the findings of Jewish scholarship, if to different degrees. The Basel-Wittenberg Conflict can best be understood as the Reformation-era discussion of the value of Jewish scholarship, a discussion that took place not only in Basel and Wittenberg but also among German Protestant Hebraists generally.

Notes

Research for this essay has been supported by grants from the Memorial Foundation for Jewish Culture, the American Council of Learned Societies, the Center for Advanced Judaic Studies of the University of Pennsylvania, the Friends of the University of Wisconsin–Madison Libraries, and the American Philosophical Society. I would especially like to acknowledge the professional support I have received from the Norman and Bernice Harris Center for Judaic Studies, University of Nebraska–Lincoln.

1. The following abbreviations have been used in this essay: WA = *D. Martin Luthers Werke; kritische Gesamtausgabe* (Weimar, Ger.: H. Bohlau, 1883–2001), 104 vols. (in all four series); WA Br = *Briefwechsel;* WA TR = *Tischreden;* WA DB = *Deutsche Bibel;* LW = *Luther's Works,* 55 vols., ed. Jaroslav J. Pelikan, Hilton C. Oswald, and Helmut T. Lehman (Saint Louis: Concordia Pub. House, 1955–86).

2. Karl Heinz Burmeister, *Sebastian Münster: Versuch eines biographischen Gesamtbildes* (Basel: Helbing & Lichtenhahn, 1963); R. Raubenheimer, *Paul Fagius aus Rheinzabern* (Grunstadt, Ger.: Verein fuer Pfaelzische Kirchengeschichte, 1957); James M. Kittelson, *Wolfgang Capito: From Humanist to Reformer* (Leiden, Neth.: E. J. Brill, 1975); Christoph Zürcher, *Konrad Pellikans Wirken in Zürich, 1526–1556* (Zürich: Theologischer Verlag, 1975).

3. Gerhard Krause, *Studien zu Luthers Auslegung der Kleinen Propheten* (Tübingen, Ger.: J. C. B. Mohr [P. Siebeck], 1962); and the works of Siegfried Raeder, especially his *Grammatica Theologica: Studien zu Luthers Operationes in Psalmos* (Tübingen, Ger.: J. C. B. Mohr [P. Siebeck], 1977).

4. Hans Volz, "Melanchthons Anteil an der Lutherbibel," *Archiv für Reformationsgeschichte* 45 (1954): 196–233; Volker Gummelt, *Lex et Evangelium: Untersuchungen zur Jesajavorlesung von Johannes Bugenhagen* (Berlin: Walter de Gruyter, 1994); Hans Hermann Holfelder, "Matthäus Aurogallus (ca. 1490–1543)," *Zeitschrift für Kirchengeschichte* 85 (1974): 383–88; and Otto Eissfeldt, "Des Matthäus Aurigallus Hebräische Grammatik von 1523," *Wissenschaftliche Zeitschrift der Martin-Luther-Universität Halle-Wittenberg,* Ges. Sprachw. ser., vol. 7, no. 4 (1958): 885–89.

5. Frank Hieronymus, *1478 Petri-Schwabe 1998: Eine traditionsreiche Basler Offizin im Spiegel ihrer frühen Drucke,* 2 vols. (Basel: Schwabe Verlag, 1997); Hildegard Alberts, "Reuchlins Drucker, Thomas Anselm, mit besonderer Berücksichtigung seiner Pforzheimer Presse," in *Johannes Reuchlin (1455–1522),* rev. ed., ed. Manfred Krebs, Hermann Kling, and Stefan Rhein (Sigmaringen, Ger.: Jan Thorbecke Verlag, 1994), 205–65; Elizabeth Tyler Armstrong, *Robert Estienne, Royal Printer: An Historical Study of the Elder Stephanus* (Cambridge: Cambridge University Press, 1954).

6. Hans-Jörg Künast, "Hebräisch-jüdischer Buchdruck in Schwaben in der ersten Hälfte des 16. Jahrhunderts," in *Landjudentum im deutschen Südwesten während der Frühen Neuzeit,* ed. Rolf Kiessling and Sabine Ullmann (Berlin: Akademie Verlag, 1999), 277–303; Moshe Rosenfeld, *Der jüdischer Buchdruck in Augsburg in der ersten Hälfte des 16. Jahrhunderts* (London: Rosenfeld, 1985); Joseph Prijs, *Die Basler hebräischen Drucke, 1492–1886* (Olten, Switz.: Urs Graf, 1965).

7. G. E. Weil, *Élie Lévita humaniste et massorète, 1469–1549* (Leiden, Neth.: E. J. Brill, 1963).

8. Jerome Friedman, *The Most Ancient Testimony: Sixteenth-Century Christian-Hebraica in the Age of Renaissance Nostalgia* (Athens: Ohio University Press, 1983); Bernard Roussel, "Des auteurs," in *Le temps des Réformes et la Bible* (Paris: Beauchesne, 1989): 215–34, and the literature cited at 744–46; Karl Heinz Burmeister, "Johannes Campensis und Sebastian Münster: Ihre Stellung in der Geschichte der Hebräischen Sprachstudien," *Ephemerides Theologicae Lovanienses* 46 (1970): 441–60.

9. Friedman, *Testimony*, 168–73. See also R. Gerald Hobbs, "How Firm a Foundation: Martin Bucer's Historical Exegesis of the Psalms," *Church History* 53 (1984): 490 n. 54; and Burmeister, "Campensis," 455.

10. Friedman, *Testimony*, 165–76.

11. I have followed a distinction proposed by Friedman in *Testimony*, 122. The actual revisions made to the received Latin biblical text were far less drastic than the rhetoric employed by Protestant scholars would suggest. See Martin Brecht, *Martin Luther*, vol. 3: *The Preservation of the Church*, trans. James L. Schaaf (Minneapolis: Fortress, 1993), 102; Hobbs, "Conrad Pellican," 90; and Benjamin Keder-Kopfstein, "Sebastian Münsters lateinische Psalmenübersetzung," *Theologische Zeitschrift* 53, nos. 1–2 (1997): 52.

12. I have included Louvain professors of Hebrew because of their connection with Erasmus and his connection with a number of other Hebraists, such as Capito, Pellican, and Oecolampadius, but also because several German Hebraists were trained there and because Campensis had important German connections, especially with Sebastian Münster. It was the only non-German university whose alumni figured in the pre-1535 discussion of Hebrew.

13. A further nine Hebrew instructors taught at German universities for less than a year. They were Johann Andernach (Ingolstadt, Ger., 1523 only), Gregor Casel (Strasbourg, Fr., 1525), Jacob Ceporin (Zurich, 1525), Antonius Foelix (Frankfurt, 1524), Bernhard Gibbingen (Wittenberg, part of 1519–20), Sebastian Hoffmeister (Bern, 1528), Philipp Melanchthon (Wittenberg, Ger., 1519), Philipp Novenianus (Leipzig, Ger., 1520), and Robert Wakefield (Tübingen, Ger., 1520–21). Wakefield (1519) and Robert Shirwood (1519) also taught at Louvain, each for less than a year. Apart from Melanchthon and Wakefield, all of them are marginal figures who were unimportant for developing trends in Reformation-era Hebrew studies.

14. Berselius was a humanist in Liege and a correspondent of Erasmus: Gustav Bauch, "Die Einführung des Hebräischen in Wittenberg," *Monatsschrift für Geschichte und Wissenschaft des Judentums* 48 (1905): 287. Bauch's seven-part article (all published in volume 48) remains one of the finest studies of Hebraists, not only in Wittenberg but elsewhere in Germany at this time.

15. On Forster's earlier stay in Wittenberg and activity as a lecturer, see Wilhelm Germann, *D. Johann Forster der Hennebergische Reformator. Festschrift zum 350jährige Hennebergischen Reformationsjubiläum* ([Wasungen]: published by the author, [1894]), 31–48.

16. According to Bauch, "Einführung," pt. 6, 332. Adrianus also taught Reuchlin for a time.

17. Ziegler was a member of the arts faculty at Leipzig from 14 January 1521 through at least 1524, possibly later. There was no professor of Hebrew on the faculty when he studied at Leipzig as a student or after Novenianus ceased to teach Hebrew in

1520 or 1521. He could conceivably have studied with either Cellarius (1519–20) or his student Novenianus (fl. 1520). On Ziegler, see WA Br 5: 119 n. 1.

18. A small third category of participants in the conversation over Hebrew included those such as Andreas Osiander, a student of Boeschenstein, who did not publish in the field but whose expertise was recognized: Gerhard Philipp Wolf, "Osiander und die Juden im Kontext seiner Theologie," *Zeitschrift für Bayerische Kirchengeschichte* 53 (1984): 52.

19. Robert Stupperich, "Theodor Fabricius," *Westfälische Lebensbilder* 15 (1990): 32, commented that the Hebrew teachers changed frequently during Fabricius's stay there, but Goldhahn was already teaching there by the time Fabricius had arrived.

20. Anna Dorothee v. den Brincken, "Johann Potken aus Schwerte, Propst von St. Georg in Köln. Der erste Äthiopologe des Abendlandes," in *Aus kölnischer und rheinischer Geschichte: Festgabe Arnold Güttsches zum 65. Geburtstag gewidmet,* ed. Hans Blum (Köln: Buchhandlung H. Wamper, 1969), 85.

21. Burmeister, *Münster,* 26–27; and Heinz Scheible, *Melanchthon, Eine Biographie* (München: C. H. Beck, 1997), 22.

22. Stephen G. Burnett, "A Dialogue of the Deaf: Hebrew Pedagogy and Anti-Jewish Polemic in Sebastian Münster's *Messiahs of the Christians and the Jews* (1529/39)," *Archiv für Reformationsgeschichte* 91 (2000): 176. More generally, see Heinz Scheible, "Reuchlins Einfluss auf Melanchthon," in *Reuchlin und die Juden,* ed. Arno Herzig and Julius H. Schoeps (Sigmaringen, Ger.: Jan Thorbecke, 1993), 125.

23. Bauch, "Einführung," 332–33.

24. Johann Reuchlin to Frederick of Saxony, Stuttgart, Ger., 7 May 1518; summarized by Bauch, "Einführung," 150.

25. Friedman, *Testimony,* 21, 24.

26. Bauch, "Einführung," 156.

27. Weil, *Lévita,* 90, 133–35.

28. Margaritha, of course, would be best remembered for his polemical portrayal of Judaism, *The Entire Jewish Faith.* See Stephen G. Burnett, "Distorted Mirrors: Antonius Margaritha, Johann Buxtorf, and Christian Ethnographies of Judaism," *Sixteenth-Century Journal* 25 (1994): 275–87.

29. The Hebrew printing statistics I have provided are based upon standard bibliographies and online library and union catalogues. See Stephen G. Burnett, "Christian Hebrew Printing in the Sixteenth Century: Printers, Humanism, and the Impact of the Reformation," *Helmantica* vol. 51, no. 154 (April 2000): 15–16 n. 9, 40–42.

30. "Other" includes German cities where three or fewer Hebrew books were printed during this period: Rostock, Constance, Solingen, Dortmund, Erfurt, Marburg, Nuremberg, Pforzheim, Worms, and Zurich.

31. Forty of these imprints are complete Hebrew Bibles or portions of Bibles printed by the Estienne (Stephanus) printing house. See Antoine August Renouard, *Annales de L'Imprimerie des Estienne ou Histoire de la Famille des Estienne et de ses Editions,* vol. 1 (Reprint, New York: Burt Franklin, n.d.).

32. The Collège Royale would become a remarkable center for Hebrew studies later in the sixteenth century but was founded in 1530. Agathius Guidacerius (1530–40) and Pierre Paradis (1530–49), two of its first three professors of Hebrew, began their careers in Italy. Paradis was a Jewish convert. They used the grammars of Campensis and Münster for at least some of their instruction. See Sophie Kessler Mesguich, "L'enseignement de l'hébreu et de l'araméen à Paris," in *Les origines du Collège de France (1500–1560),* ed. Marc Fumaroli (Paris: Collège de France, 1998), 360–61.

33. The Polyglot, printed by 1517, did not receive papal permission to be sold until March of 1520. Only six hundred exemplars of the Bible were printed, and a number of them were destroyed in a shipwreck off the coast of Italy, making the surviving copies more costly still, and severely limiting its impact upon the development of Hebrew scholarship: Basil Hall, "The Trilingual College of San Ildefonso and the Making of the Complutensian Polyglot," *Studies in Church History* 5 (1969): 144–46.

34. Hobbs, "Pellican," 73; and Bauch, "Einführung," 332.

35. Bucer: personal communication from R. Gerald Hobbs, 6 March 2001, summarizing his discussion of the reference books Bucer used in his Psalms commentary (1529), which will appear in his forthcoming introduction to the critical edition of Bucer's Psalms commentary.

36. On Luther, see Hans Ulrich Delius, *Die Quellen von Martin Luthers Genesisvorlesung* (München: Chr. Kaiser, 1992), 50–56; Melanchthon: Scheible, "Reuchlins Einfluss," 132; Zwingli: E. Egli, "Zwingli als Hebräer," *Zwingliana*, vol. 1, no. 2 (1900): 1; Bucer: Hobbs, personal communication to the author.

37. Christian Kabbalah, both in Catholic and Protestant Europe before 1650, is another topic within the sphere of Christian Hebraism that lacks a comprehensive, synthetic treatment. Provisionally, see François Secret, *Les Kabbalistes Chrétiens de la Renaissance* (Paris: Dunod, 1964); and J. Dan, ed., *The Christian Kabbalah: Jewish Mystical Books and Their Christian Interpreters* (Cambridge: Harvard College Library, 1997).

38. Reuchlin, *De Arte Cabalistica Libri Tres* (Hagenau, Ger.: Anselm, 1517; Hagenau, Ger.: Setzer, 1530); idem, *De Verbo Mirifico libri tres* (Cologne: Cervicornus, Eucharius, 1532); Pietro Galatinus, *Opus de Arcanis Catholicae Veritatis* (Basel: Herwagen, 1550); and Paulus Ricius, *De coelesti agricultura* (Augsburg: Steiner [Stayner], Heinrich, 1541). There were a number of other Ricius and Reuchlin imprints that discussed kabbalistic texts but that do not contain Hebrew type.

39. Zürcher, *Pellikan*, 182–89; and Germann, *Forster*, 46.

40. Eric Zimmer, "Jewish and Christian Hebraist Collaboration in Sixteenth-Century Germany," *Jewish Quarterly Review* 71 (1980): 70–71 n. 5.

41. For a discussion of my Christian Hebrew imprint database project, see section 2 below.

42. This figure does not include the twenty-five printings of his small grammatical sketch in Italy and one in France during these years.

43. Burmeister, *Münster*, 44, 47–48.

44. Prijs, *Drücke*, 489.

45. Bucer: Hobbs, personal communication to the author; Münster: Burmeister, *Münster*, 77; and Prijs, *Drucke*, 32 (second Bomberg Bible).

46. Hans Volz, "Anhang IV. Hebräische Handpsalter Luthers," WA DB 10, 290–320. Volz, "Melanchthons Anteil," 202 and n. 28 and, idem, introduction to Martin Luther, *Die gantze Heilige Schrifft Deudsch Wittenberg, 1545* (München: Rogner and Bernhard, 1972), 105; and Volz, Introduction, 43; and n. 32. Goldhahn provided a list of common abbreviations used in rabbinical Bible commentaries in his *Compendium Hebreae Grammatices* (Wittenberg, Ger., 1523), indicating the early interest of Wittenberg Hebraists in the use of these commentaries.

47. Weil, *Lévita*, 221–34.

48. Sachiko Kusukawa, *A Wittenberg University Library Catalogue of 1536*, Medieval and Renaissance Texts and Studies, vol. 142 (Binghamton, N.Y.: Medieval and Renaissance Texts and Studies, 1995), 1–3.

49. Siegfried Raeder, *Das Hebräische bei Luther, untersucht bis zum Ende der ersten Psalmenvorlesung* (Tübingen, Ger.: J. C. B. Mohr [Paul Siebeck], 1961), 169–74; Scheible, "Reuchlins Einfluss," 132; and Gummelt, *Lex et Evangelium*, 96.

50. Timothy J. Wengert, *Philipp Melanchthon's Annotationes in Johannem in Relation to its Predecssors and Contemporaries* (Geneva: Droz, 1987), 128–34.

51. Bernard Roussel has provided a typology for uses of Jewish biblical commentaries, using Rashi as his example commentator in "De Jean Oecolampade et Martin Bucer à Andreas Masius et Jean Mercier: Statut et fonction des références à Rashi dans les travaux d'exégètes chrétiens du XVIe siècle (v. 1525–v. 1575)," in *Rashi et la culture juive en France du Nord au moyen âge*, ed. Gilbert Dahan, Gerard Nahon, and Elie Nicolas (Paris-Louvain: E. Peeters, 1997), 396–76.

52. Wengert, *Philipp Melanchthon's Annotationes*, 40, and Dietrich Thyen, "Luthers Jesajavorlesung" (Ph.D. diss., Universität Heidelberg, 1964), 106.

53. Quoted and translated by R. Gerald Hobbs, "Exegetical Projects and Problems: A New Look at an Undated Letter from Bucer to Zwingli," in *Prophet, Pastor, Protestant: The Work of Huldrych Zwingli after Five Hundred Years*, ed. E. J. Furcha and H. Wayne Pipkin (Allen Park, Pa.: Pickwick, 1984), 94–95.

54. Thyen, "Luthers Jesajavorlesung," 105–9.

55. Luther was never entirely satisfied with his German translation of the Bible and spent considerable time over the course of his career revising parts of it or all of it. The process of revision involved returning to the Hebrew Bible text and reconsidering how it could be best translated into German. Luther revised his Psalms translation in 1531, the entire Bible in 1534, and again between 1539 and 1541. Melanchthon, Goldhahn, and other less regular members of Luther's "Sanhedrin" of Hebrew experts met regularly to discuss how best to render particular passages: Brecht, *Luther*, vol. 3, 104–5.

56. Brecht, *Luther*, 3: 107–8.

57. Luther, *Ursachen des Dolmetschens*, WA 38: 9, 9–14 = LW 35: 209.

58. Cf. Luther,*Ursachen des Dolmetschens*, WA 38: 9, 15–33 (Ps. 58:9) and 15, 11–20 (Ps. 118:27) and WA DB 3: 61, 16–28, 3: 147, 2–15 with Martin Bucer, *S. Psalmorum Libri Quinque ad Ebraicam Veritatem Versi et Familiari Explanatione Elucidati* (Strasbourg, Fr.: Georg Viricherus Andlanus Chalcographus, Sept. 1529); Oxford: Bodleian Library, SR 79. E. 1; Lutheran Brotherhood Reformation Library, microfiche, ff. 238b, 239b (Ps. 58:9) and 353b, 355a (Ps. 118:27).

59. Pellican to Bucer, 6 August 1529, quoted and translated by Hobbs, "Pellican," 97–98.

60. Hobbs, "Exegetical Projects," 94.

61. Burmeister, *Münster*, 91. On Münster's Jewish sources, see Erwin I. J. Rosenthal, "Sebastian Münster's Knowledge and Use of Jewish Exegesis," in *Studia Semitica*, vol. 1: *Jewish Themes* (Cambridge: Cambridge University Press, 1971), 127–45.

62. Burmeister, *Münster*, 90.

63. Ibid., 93–97.

64. WA TR 3: 362, 12–363, 6 (#3503), 12–16 December 1536.

65. WA TR 3: 362, 23 (#3503), 12–16 December 1536; TR 4: 478, 41 (#4764), "1530s"; TR 4: 608, 20 (#5003), 21 May–11 June 1540; TR 5: 212, 15 (winter 1542–43).

66. ". . . wie wol er den Juden auch feind ist, abr er nimbt sichs so hefftig nicht an als ich." TR 5: 218, 11–12 (#5533), winter 1542–3 = LW 54: 445.

67. Siegfried Raeder, *Grammatica Theologica*, 34–36.

68. Luther, *De servo arbitrio* (1525) WA 18: 606–9 = LW 33: 25–27; Armin Buch-

holz, *Schrift Gottes im Lehrstreit: Luthers Schriftverständnis und Schriftauslegung in seinen drei grossen Lehrstreitigkeiten der Jahre 1521–1528*, Europäische Hochschulschriften: Reihe 23, Theologie, Bd. 487 (Bern, Switz.: Lang, 1993), 85–91.

69. TR #312 (summer/fall 1532) = LW 54: 42–43.

70. Luther, *In Primum Librum Mose Enarrationes*, WA 42: 195, 22–24 = LW 1: 263–66 (Gen. 4:7).

71. Friedman, *Testimony*, 132.

72. Raeder, *Grammatica Theologica*, 34–36; and idem, "Voraussetzungen und Methode von Luthers Bibelübersetzung," in *Geist und Geschichte der Reformation: Festgabe Hanns Rückert zum 65. Geburtstag*, Arbeiten zur Kirchengeschichte, no. 38 (Berlin: Walter de Gruyter, 1966), 154.

73. We have already considered Luther's use of Bucer and Münster above. Several references to the rabbinical Bible in his translation protocols for 1539–41 include Psalm 68:27 where the notes read, "Sic exponunt Rabini Bibliam" (WA DB 3: 554, 10) and Psalm 127: "Rabbi Kimchi est deus Rabinorum" (WA DB 3: 574, 2).

74. See Gerhard Krause, *Studien zu Luthers Auslegung der Kleinen Propheten*, Beiträge zur Historischen Theologie, Bd. 33 (Tübingen, Ger.: JCB Mohr [Paul Siebeck], 1962), 71–72, 199–202; and Thyen, "Luthers Jesajavorlesung," 109, 170–86.

75. Luther, *Enarrationes*, WA 43: 206–7, 418–19, 659–60; 44: 101–2, 248 = LW 4: 99 (Gen. 22: 1–2), 393 (Gen. 25: 29–30); 5:335 (Gen. 30: 5–8); 6:136 (Gen. 32:25), 322 (Gen. 37: 9).

76. "Munsteri Hebraismus. 27 Martii fiebat mentio Munsteri et aliorum Hebraeorum, qui Lutherum flagellarunt in translatione bibliae omnia ad regulas grammaticas referentes: Grammatica quidem necessaria est in declinando, coniugando et construendo, sed in oratione sententiae et res considerandae non grammatica den die grammatica soll nicht gregnare super sententias." WA TR 3:619, 25–30, 27 March 1538.

77. Otto Kluge, "Die hebräische Sprachwissenschaft in Deutschland im Zeitalter des Humanismus," *Zeitschrift für die Geschichte der Juden in Deutschland* 3 (1931): 186 n. 93. See also Raeder, "Voraussetzungen," 160.

78. Luther, *Enarrationes*, WA 44: 197, 34–38 = LW 6: 266 (Gen. 35:17). Luther's source for Jewish opinion at this point, as in so many others, was Münster's annotations. See Münster, *Biblia Hebraica*, 37b, 49a.

79. Kittelson, *Capito*, 232.

80. R. Gerald Hobbs, "Martin Bucer on Psalm 22: A Study in the Application of Rabbinic Exegesis by a Christian Hebraist," in *Histoire de l'exégèse au XVIe siècle*, ed. Olivier Fatio and Pierre Fraenkel (Geneva: Droz, 1978), 161–62.

81. Heiko A. Oberman, *The Roots of Anti-Semitism in the Age of Renaissance and Reformation*, trans. James I. Porter (Philadelphia: Fortress, 1984), 117.

82. When commenting on circumcision in Genesis 17:1, Luther wrote, "Therefore this discussion concerning circumcision should not be slighted but should be carried on most diligently, not so much to confute the Jews as to strengthen and fortify our own people." *Enarrationes*, WA 42: 603 = LW 3: 77. In *Ein Brief D. Martini Luther. Wider die Sabbather an einen guten Freund*, Luther states that his purpose is to "refute" the rabbis and to "fortify" Christians. WA 50: 313, 6–11 = LW: 47: 65–66. In the Genesis lectures, see *Enarrationes*, WA 42: 448–51 = LW 2: 261–65; WA 42: 519, 13–14 = LW 2: 359; WA 42: 574, 24–25 = LW 3: 36.

83. Luther, *Wider die Sabbather*, WA 50: 321, 8–10.

84. Luther, *Von den Juden und Ihren Lügen*, WA 53: 417, 15–19 = LW 47: 137. Since

Luther's description of the passage involves a Jew in dialogue with a Christian, discussing key prophetic passages in the Old Testament, he might well have seen a copy of Münster's *Messiahs of the Christians and Jews*. It contains Jewish interpretations of Daniel 9:24, Haggai 2:6–10, and Isaiah 7:14, two of which Luther discussed at length in *On the Jews and their Lies*. WA 53: 476–511. For a summary of Münster's *Messiahs*, see Burnett, "Dialogue of the Deaf," 187–188.

85. Luther, *Vom Schem Hamphoras und vom Geschlecht Christi*, WA 53: 648. He made similar complaints in a letter to Elector Frederick. Luther to Elector Friedrich, (Wittenberg, Ger.), December 1543. WA Br 10: 461, 13–16.

86. Martin Luther, *Vom Schem Hamphoras*, WA 53: 647, 27–31 (my translation).

87. Martin Luther, *Von den letzten Worten Davids*, WA 54: 30, 21–26 = LW 15: 269.

88. Burnett, "Christian Hebrew Printing," 18.

89. Münster insisted in the Latin introduction to his *Biblia Hebraica* (1534–35) that he was not slavishly copying the Jewish biblical commentators but only did so "cum iudicio." Burmeister, "Campensis," 454.

90. Translation mine. Printed in WA DB 3: 15–16.

9
Polemical Ethnographies: Descriptions of Yom Kippur in the Writings of Christian Hebraists and Jewish Converts to Christianity in Early Modern Europe

Yaacov Deutsch

In the foreword to his 1785 *Yehudi mi-bachutz, das ist der äußerliche Jud*, Caspar Friedenheim, a Jewish convert to Christianity, observed that many Christians had great respect for the Jewish service on Yom Kippur: "I saw at this time, often with amazement, how frequently the Christians on the so called (*Jom Kipper*), or the long day, hurry to the synagogue in order to see the Jewish service and their ceremonies. They apparently believe that these prayers are really uplifting, reverential and pious, because on my walks near the Main I heard those returning from the synagogue saying to each other that the Jewish ceremonies should really not be despised, because their prayers, lasting all day long, the lighting of their synagogue, their white linen cloaks— all these arouse attention. The Jews themselves are proud to have such respectful observers, of both sexes, in their synagogue, and they believe that the *Goim* or the Christians derive special pleasure from their service and a few converts come back to the synagogue in order to celebrate this holiday with them once more."[1]

How accurate is Friedenheim's assessment? Were Christians really interested in going to the synagogues to watch the Jewish service? If they were, was it because they appreciated the Jewish way of observing this holiday, or did they have other interests and ideas in mind? In order to answer these and some other questions I will focus on Christian writings about one holiday—Yom Kippur (Day of Atonement)—as a case study for examining Christian approaches to Jewish ritual life. I have concentrated on Yom Kippur both because of its importance in the Jewish religion and because of the abundance of Christian writing about it. The discussion of Yom Kippur, more common than other holidays, also reveals its importance in Christian eyes. Those Christian authors who described Yom Kippur, however, chose to discuss some customs more than others, and it is noteworthy that these customs were usually of less importance in Jewish eyes. Concentrating on the descriptions of these customs, I will argue that they reveal four different types of motivations, all of them polemical and all aimed at discrediting Judaism.

Before turning to the specific descriptions of Yom Kippur a few words of introduction about Christian interest in the Jewish ceremonies and rituals are in order. Christian interest in and awareness of Jewish practice can be found in written sources from the very beginning of Christianity. Prior to the sixteenth century, however, there was no systematic discussion of the customs of the Jews; rather, we find fragmentary discussions of one or two specific Jewish customs or ceremonies.[2] The holiday of Yom Kippur was not different in this regard, and until the sixteenth century there are only a few Christian sources that refer to the ways in which this holiday was observed.[3] Most of the medieval authors who mentioned the holiday restricted their observations to the *shamta* prayer, which damned the Gentiles and was recited with a special ceremony specifically on this day.[4] Christians took this prayer as an example of Jewish anti-Christian sentiment. As the French inquisitor Bernard Gui wrote in his Inquisitor's Manual: "During the feast of expiation in September they have a special prayer that they offer against all enemies. This prayer is called 'cematha,' which means a ban or excommunication or a curse. And in this prayer they call Jesus the son of an illicit marriage and the blessed Virgin Mary a lustful or licentious woman, things that are not permitted to be said or thought."[5] In the sixteenth century these brief references gave way to books that are entirely devoted to descriptions of the rituals and ceremonies of contemporary Jews. This literary genre, which since the publication of R. Po-chia Hsia's article in 1994 has generally been described as "Christian Ethnographies of Jews,"[6] flourished between the sixteenth and the eighteenth centuries, and more than sixty books belonging to this genre were published during the period.[7]

Of these books describing the Jewish way of life, thirty-five discuss Yom Kippur. In some cases these are short discussions of one or two pages; in others, some thirty pages are devoted to the holiday; and in one case the holiday is the subject of almost an entire book of 110 pages.[8] Among the various books that describe other rituals and ceremonies, only the holiday of Passover is mentioned as often as Yom Kippur (also thirty-five times). Of the books that include descriptions of Yom Kippur, five were published in the sixteenth century, ten in the seventeenth, and twenty in the eighteenth century. Twenty-five books were written by converts from Judaism and only ten by Christians from birth. As we will see, this distinction between Christian authors and Jewish converts is important for appreciating the distinctive characteristics of the writings of these two groups as well as their motives for writing. In general it can be said that while Jewish converts stressed the anti-Christian nature of Jewish ceremonies and rituals and the absurd and superstitious nature of contemporary Jewish customs, the authors born and raised as Christians were more concerned with showing the nature of contemporary Jewish beliefs as contrary to biblical beliefs. The fact that both groups display a generally negative, if not actively hostile, attitude toward Judaism and that both groups wrote descriptions from a polemical perspective and as polemical tools suggests that Hsia's definition of this genre as "ethnographic" should be modified. Since the authors make no pretense of being impartial and objective, it would be more accurate to describe these writings as "polemical ethnographies of Judaism."

Jewish tradition includes many laws and customs that relate to Yom Kippur, but Christians writing about the holiday refer to relatively few of these (Fig. 9.1). I have listed the sixteen features that are most commonly described in the thirty-five texts. Since the decision to describe certain elements at the expense of others can help us better understand the focus of the different authors and their motives for writing, I have provided a table listing the features described by individual authors.[9]

As we can see from the table, one custom appears in almost all the descriptions of the holiday: Kapparot, the custom of discharging one's sins on a rooster, which appears in thirty-three descriptions.[10] The other widely mentioned customs were the Malkot (flagellation) and the lighting of the candles in the synagogue on Yom Kippur eve. Both appear in twenty-four descriptions. The next most frequently mentioned feature is the prayers of Yom Kippur, which appear in twenty-two cases. In order to explain the reasons for depicting these ceremonies and not others we need to turn to the observations made by these authors.

Johannes Pfefferkorn, a Jew who converted to Christianity in 1504, was the first to discuss Yom Kippur.[11] In his pamphlet *Ich heyß ain Büchlein der Iuden Peicht* (Booklet on the Jewish Confession), published in 1508,[12] Pfefferkorn describes both Rosh Hashana (New Year) and Yom Kippur. The chapter on Yom Kippur opens with the description of the Kapparot ritual and is accompanied by an engraving (Fig. 9.2):

On the ninth day of their atonement and penitence, they leave their synagogues and go home. All the Jewish men, young and old, have white roosters, and the women, married and unmarried, have white hens, if it is possible to get them. If the woman is pregnant she must take a rooster and a hen for herself and one for the unborn baby, who has not yet committed a sin but who was conceived from the lust of flesh. Everybody takes his rooster or her hen. The head of the family stands silently in the middle of the household for quite some time, contemplating his sins with great devotion. He then takes the rooster by its feet and waves it three times over his head so that the rooster has to flap its wings and put them together. Then he says to the rooster: "You

9.1. Johannes Bodenschatz, *Kirchliche Verfassung der heutigen Juden*, Frankfurt and Leipzig, 1748–49. Engraving of Yom Kippur customs. The central picture depicts the prayer in the synagogue. The vignettes depict some of the holiday ceremonies (from top left to right): flagellation, asking of forgiveness, asking forgiveness from the dead, Kapparot, visiting the cemetery. Photo courtesy of Jewish National and University Library, Jerusalem.

TABLE 9.1. YOM KIPPUR RITUALS DISCUSSED IN ETHNOGRAPHIC BOOKS

Ceremony Name	Kapparot	Immersion	Visiting cemetery	Flagellation	Confession	Candle lighting	Five banned activities	Eating on Yom Kippur eve	Request of forgiveness	"Al Da'at Hamakom" Prayer	"Kol Nidrey" Prayer	Birkat Cohanim	Liturgy	Blowing of Shofar	Blessing of Moon	Building of Sukkah
J. Pfefferkorn 1508	✓	✓		✓		✓							✓			
V. von Carben 1508	✓	✓														
A. Margaritha 1530	✓	✓	✓	✓	✓	✓			✓		✓		✓			
M. Lombardus 1573	✓														✓	
E. F. Hess 1598	✓	✓				✓							✓			
J. Buxtorf 1603	✓	✓	✓	✓	✓	✓	✓	✓	✓	✓	✓	✓	✓	✓		
A. Costerus 1608	✓	✓	✓	✓	✓	✓	✓			✓	✓	✓	✓			
S. Purchas 1613	✓		✓	✓	✓	✓					✓	✓	✓	✓		
H. Fabronius 1624	✓	✓	✓	✓	✓	✓										
T. Thumius 1624	✓	✓	✓	✓			✓				✓	✓	✓			
A. Ross 1653	✓	✓	✓	✓		✓	✓		✓			✓				
L. Addison 1675	✓			✓	✓	✓			✓	✓	✓		✓			

Author / Year	1	2	3	4	5	6	7	8	9	10	11	12	13
P. C. Majer 1678	♪												
G. Morosini 1683	♪			♪									
C. P. Mayer 1685		♪					♪						
M. P. M. Alberti 1703	♪		♪	♪	♪	♪	♪						
F. A. Christiani 1705	♪		♪	♪	♪	♪							
J. Schudt 1714	♪												
F. L. Fried 1715	♪				♪								
P. C. Kirchner 1717			♪	♪	♪	♪	♪		♪				
J.C. Salomon 1721	♪		♪	♪	♪	♪		♪					
M. Marcus 1723				♪	♪								
S. J. Jungendres 1724	♪		♪	♪	♪	♪	♪		♪	♪	♪	♪	
C. G. Seeligmann 1725	♪		♪	♪	♪	♪	♪		♪		♪		
C. G. Christian 1731	♪		♪			♪		♪		♪	♪	♪	♪
P. Christfelss 1735	♪		♪	♪	♪	♪	♪		♪		♪	♪	

TABLE 9.1. (CONTINUED)

Ceremony Name	Kapparot	Immersion	Visiting cemetery	Flagellation	Confession	Candle lighting	Five banned activities	Eating on Yom Kippur eve	Request of forgiveness	"Al Da'at Hamakom" Prayer	"Kol Nidrey" Prayer	Birkat Cohanim	Liturgy	Blowing of Shofar	Blessing of Moon	Building of Sukkah
P. Medici 1736	✓					✓		✓		✓			✓			
A. Mears 1738	✓		✓				✓	✓					✓			
J. F. Guthertz 1747	✓			✓				✓			✓		✓	✓		
J. C. G. Bodenschatz 1748	✓		✓	✓	✓	✓	✓	✓	✓	✓	✓		✓			
C. Anton 1752	✓	✓		✓	✓	✓	✓	✓	✓	✓	✓		✓			
A. R. G. C. Matthäi 1760	✓	✓	✓	✓	✓		✓	✓	✓	✓	✓		✓			
G. Selig 1768–1772	✓	✓	✓	✓	✓	✓	✓	✓	✓	✓	✓	✓	✓	✓	✓	✓
C. Dorville 1770–1771	✓	✓	✓			✓	✓		✓	✓	✓	✓	✓	✓	✓	
C. Friedenheim 1785	✓	✓		✓	✓	✓	✓	✓			✓		✓	✓	✓	✓
Total	33	18	19	24	14	24	17	13	13	13	16	8	24	11	9	6

Full titles of books appearing in table: Lancelot Addison, *The Present State of the Jews: (More Particularly Relating to Those in Barbary) Wherein Is Contained an Exact Account of Their Customs, Secular and Religious; to Which Is Added, a Summary Discourse of the Misna, Talmud, and Gemara* (London, 1675); M. Paul Martin Alberti, *Neuverfertigte Aus Gottes Wort und der Rabbinen Schrifften wolmeinend geflochtene Jüden-Geissel oder Gründliche Anführung derer zur Bekehrung der Jüden hauptsächlich dienenden Mittel, erstlich von einem bekehrten Juden Ernesto Ferdinando Heß, Med. Doct. herausgegeben; Nun aber mit einigen statt nützlicher Anmerckungen abgefasten Fragen und darauf ertheilten Antworten, welche zu desto nachdrücklicherer Überzeugung dieser blinden Leute, mehrentheils mit Anführung ihrer und ihrer Lehrer eigenen Worten hergeholet sind, erweitert und vermehrt* (Frankfurt: 1703,);[74] Carl Anton, *Kurzer Entwurf der Erklärung jüdischer Gebräuche sowol Geistlicher als Weltlicher zum Gebrauch Akademischer Vorlesungen entworfen* (Braunswick, 1751); Johannes Christoph Georg Bodenschatz, *Kirchliche Verfassung der heutigen Juden sonderlich derer in Deutschland in IV. Haupt-Theile abgefasset aus ihren eigenen und anderen Schriften umständlich dargethan und mit 30 saubern Kupfern erläutert* (Frankfurt, 1748–49); Johannes Buxtorf, *Synagoga Judaica: Das ist Juden Schul: Darinnen der gantz Jüdische Glaub und Glaubens-übung mit allen Ceremonien Satzungen Sitten und Gebräuchen* (Basel, Switz., 1603); Victor von Carben, *Dem durchleuchtigsten hochgebornen fursten und herren Herren Ludwigen Pfaltzgrauen bey Rein . . . Hier inne wirt gelesen wie Her Victor von Carben. Welicher eyn Rabi Jüde geweset ist, zu Cristlichem glauben komm. Weiter vindet man dar in eyn costliche disputatz eynes gelerten cristen und eyns gelerten Juden, dar inne alle irthumb der Juden durch yr aygen schrifft aufgelöst werden* (Köln, 1508);[75] Philipp Christfelss, *Emunah chadashah shel ha-yehudim oder das Neüe Judenthum Beedes Denen Juden und Christen zu nützlichem Gebauch, Nebst einer Vorrede Sr. Hochwürden, Hn. Gustav Georg Zeltners, Theil 1–6* (Onolzbach, Ger., 1735–38; C. G. C. (Christoph Gustav Christian),[76] *Entdeckung der gantzen Jüdischen Synagog, Oder immerwährender Ceremoniel-Calender: Darinnen erstlich zu finden, wie ordentlich die Juden durch das gantze Jahr ihre Feyer-Fest-Buss und Fast-Täge eingerichtet, woher dieselbe ihren Ursprung haben, und was auch ihre beutungen sind. Aus dem Hebr. Ins Teutsch über. Und zusammengetragen durch einen Proselyten* (Nürnberg, 1731); Friedrich Albert Christian, *Der Jüden Glaube und Aberglaube* (Leipzig, Ger., 1705); Abraham Costerus, *Historie der Joden* (Amsterdam, 1608); Contant André Guillaume Dorville, *Histoire des différens peuples du monde tenant les cérémonies religieuses et civiles, l'origine des religions, leurs sectes & superstitions, & les moeurs & usages de chacque nation* (Paris, 1770–71); Hermann Fabronius, *Bekehrung der Juden und von mancherley aberglaubischen Ceremonien unnd seltsamen Sitten so die zerstreweten Jüden haben: und wie sie in der Christenheit zu dulden seyn, neben Theologische und Historische Beschreibung der Göttlichen Weissagung Danielis von Verwüstung der Statt Jerusalem. Darinnen begriffen das der wahre Messias geboren sey. Alles aus heiliger Schrifft Flavio Iosepha, Ernst Ferdinando, Ioanne Buxdorffio und sonst zusammen geschrieben* (Erfurt, Ger., 1624); Franz Lothar Fried (Joseph Marcus), *Neupolierter und wohlgeschliffener Juden-Spiegel* (Mayntz, Ger., 1715); Caspar Friedenheim, *Yehudi mi-bachutz, das ist der äußerliche Jud in Ansehung ihres dermaligen vermeintlichen Gottesdienstes und besonders in Absicht auf das ihnen so wichtige Stück Jom Kipur, das ist der Versöhnungstag und dessen dermaligen Feyer und Begehung* (Würzburg, Ger., 1785); Johannes Friedrich Guthertz, *Beschreibung der Jüdischen Ceremonien und Gebräuche der heutigen Juden, dabey Gottes Gebot hindansetzen, und Die Aufsätze ihrer Väter weit höher achten: in einem kurtzen Auszuge* (Brieg, Ger., 1747); Ernst Ferdinand Hess, *Flagellum Iudeorum Juden Geissel, das ist ein neuwe sehr nütze und gründliche Erweisung, dass. Jesus Christus, Gottes und der H. Jungkfrauwen Marien Sohn der wahre verheissene und gesandte Messias sey* (s.l., 1598); Sebastian Jacob Jungendres and Paul Christian Kirchner, *Jüdisches Ceremoniel . . . nunmehro aber bey dieser neuen Auflage mit accuraten Kupfer versehen; Nicht weniger aus den besten Scribenten so wol, als aus Erzehlung glaubwürdiger Personen und selbst eigener Erfahrung, um vieles vermehrt und mit Anmerkungen erläutert* (Nürnberg, 1724);[77] Paul Christian Kirchner, *Jüdisches Ceremoniel* (Erfurt, 1717); Marcus Lombardus, *Gründlicher Bericht und Erklärung von der Juden Handlungen unnd Ceremonien* (Basel, Switz., 1573); Paul Christoph Majer, *Der heutigen Juden Ceremonien und Gebräuche* (Wittenberg, 1678); Moses Marcus, *The Ceremonies of the Present Jews* (London, 1723); Adam Rudolph Georg Christoph Matthäi, *Beschreibung des Jom Chippur* (Nürnberg, 1760); Christoph Paul Mayer,[78] *Der jüdische Narren Spiegel Worinne Sie sich spiegeln nach ihren weltlichen Messias der so ein grosser Herr sol sein als Moses gewesen ist der sie erlöset hat aus Egypten Land. Zum ander handelt diss Trachtätlein nicht allein von den Jüdischen Lebens Lauff sondern auch von Geistlich und weltlichen Dingen welches kürtzlich und Curiös zu lesen ist* (s.l., 1685); Abraham Mears (Gamliel Ben Pedahzur), *The Book of Religion, Ceremonies, and Prayers of the Jews. In their Synagogues and Families on all Occasions* (London, 1738); Paulo Medici, *Riti e customi degli Ebrei* (Florence, 1736); Giulio Morosini, *Via della Fede* (Roma, 1683); Johannes Pfefferkorn, *Ich heyß ain Büchlein der Juden Peicht* (Nürnberg, 1508); Samuel Purchas, *Purchas, His Pilgrimage; or, Relations of the World and the Religions Observed in All Ages and Places Discovered, from the Creation unto This Present* (London, 1613); Alexander Ross, *Pansebeia; or, A View of All Religions in the World* (London, 1653); Johannes Christian Salomon, *Sefer min'hagim shel yamim tovim v'nora'im das ist: Jüdisches Ceremonien Buch von der Jüden Feyer und Fest Tagen, Welche so wol ausser als in ihren Synagogen durch das gantze Jahr gebräuchlich sind: Auch was sie dabey von Aberglauben haben und wie solche von denen Feyer Tagen derer Christen unterschieden sind* (Halle, 1721); Johannes Schudt, *Jüdische Merckwürdigkeiten* (Frankfurt, 1714–18); Christian Gottlieb Seeligman, *Jüdische Ceremonien von der Jüden Hochzeiten/Fest und Feyer Tagen durchs gantze Jahr, nebst ihrem dabey habenden Aberglauben zum diens der Warheit vorgestellt* (Stockholm, 1725); Gottfried Selig, *Der Jude eine Wochenschrift*, vol. 1–9 (Leipzig, 1768–72); Theodor Thumius (Thumm), *Tractum de Festis Iudaeorum* (Tübingen, Ger., 1624).

9.2. Johannes Pfefferkorn, *Libellus de Judaica confessione* (Köln, 1508). Woodcut of Yom Kippur service. In the right corner a depiction of the flagellation ceremony. Photo courtesy of Jewish National and University Library, Jerusalem.

9.3. Gottfried Selig, *Der Jude, oder Altes und Neues Judenthum* (Leipzig, 1781–87). Engraving of the Kapparot ceremony. Note that the man holds a rooster and the woman holds a hen. Photo courtesy of Jewish National and University Library, Jerusalem.

are redeeming my sins which have gone from me to you. I am now free from my sins, but you are guilty for me. You will go to death and I will go to eternal life." Each member of the household follows with his own rooster and does what the father has done, showing great remorse for his sins and devotion to the mercy of God in his behavior and prayer. And they think and believe that in this manner their sins are forgiven.[13]

This description is an accurate one, verified by many Jewish custom books from the same period.[14] One notices that at the end of his description Pfefferkorn stresses the fact that the Jews think that their actions will free them from their sins, and it seems that he scorns this assumption. Another interesting aspect of Pfefferkorn's description is his remark about the need to perform the ritual for a fetus (Fig. 9.4), reflecting the Christian concept of original sin, which was thought to have been transmitted through the act of procreation. The idea that the *Kapparot* ritual should be applied to a fetus appears in Jewish sources for the first time in the beginning of the fifteenth century, a fact that calls for further examination. In contrast to the Christian sources, the Hebrew sources do not give a clear explanation for this practice.[15]

Pfefferkorn describes the purification performed in the Mikve (ritual bath) and the *Malkot* (flagellation) ritual (Fig. 9.5) as well as the lighting of the candles. He says of the first,

They go again to a place of running water, immerse once in the water so that nothing from their bodies can be seen. They go out and put on white linen robes and prepare themselves to eat. But he who thinks that he is still not clean from sins and feels pangs of conscience goes in the synagogue to a close friend or neighbor and kneels down, turning his face to the ground. The other person lifts his clothes and whips him with a strap from a belt or the like thirty-nine times. He whips him on his back, and if there are any sins kept and left they leave from behind and the man is completely pure and clean.[16]

Pfefferkorn writes that before the holiday starts each man takes a wax candle to the synagogue and lights it. On the next day, upon the conclusion of the holiday, each man looks at the light of his candle. If he sees that his candle is burning with a clear light, he is happy because this is a sign that God has accepted his prayers and has forgiven his sins.[17] In addition Pfefferkorn mentions that in the synagogue there was a Christian who watched over the candles because the Jews do not want to touch the candles and thus desecrate the holiday.[18] The figure of this Christian appears in the engraving that accompanies the booklet, and as Richard Cohen has suggested, it is probably the first visual evidence of the *Goy shel Shabbat* (Shabbos Goy).[19] The custom of candle lighting is found in contemporary Jewish sources as well; however, only one of them mentions that the way in which the candles burn is a sign of the future.[20]

9.4. Friedrich Albert Christiani, *Der Jüden Glaube und Aberglaube* (Leipzig, 1705). Engraving of the Kapparot ceremony and the flagellation ceremony. Note that the woman on the left is pregnant and holds two roosters, one for herself and one for the fetus. Photo courtesy of Jewish National and University Library, Jerusalem.

9.5. Johannes Pfefferkorn, *Libellus de Judaica confessione* (Köln, 1508). Woodcut of Yom Kippur customs. The upper part depicts the Kapparot ceremony; the bottom depicts the meal before the fast and the immersion in the ritual bath. Photo courtesy of Jewish National and University Library, Jerusalem.

The flagellation ceremony also appears in the Jewish sources although most of them do not mention stripping of the lashed person before the flagellation begins.[21]

There are also some additions in later descriptions of the candle lighting and flagellation rituals, but these are minor, and they all reflect an intimate awareness of Jewish practice. For example, some authors add that if a person looked at his candle and the light of it seemed clouded, he took it as a bad omen for the year to come. Other authors wrote that the candle is said to stand for the soul based on Proverbs 20:27, "The lifebreath of man is the lamp of the Lord," or that the numeric value of the word candle (*ner*) in Hebrew is 250, which is equal to the number of organs in the male body (248) together with the spirit and the soul.[22] In regard to the flagellation ritual, some authors claim that the Jews recite Psalm 78:38: "But He, being merciful, forgave iniquity and would not destroy; He restrained His wrath time and again and did not give full vent to His fury." This verse has thirteen words in the Hebrew original, and when repeated three times, it helps them count the thirty-nine lashings.[23] Others, such as Margaritha and Buxtorf, refer to the biblical basis of the flagellation ritual and point out that Paul says he was punished this way five times.[24] Buxtorf comments that there is no doubt that the lashings that Paul suffered were harder than those that the Jews undergo during the aforementioned ritual.[25]

In general, later descriptions of the Kapparot ritual are similar to Pfefferkorn's although there are some additions. For example, some report that after the Jews finished the Kapparot ceremony they tied the roosters with a rope, slit their throats, threw them to the ground, and burned them.[26] In doing this they were symbolically enacting the four different methods of the death penalty in the Jewish tradition—stoning, burning, decapitation, and suffocation—and thus the rooster suffered the death penalties intended for human sins. Others refer to the fact that the earlier custom was to give the rooster to the poor, but since it was not respectable for the poor people to eat the sins that were discharged upon the roosters, the custom was changed, and instead of receiving the roosters, the poor were given alms equal to the value of the rooster.[27]

The most interesting and controversial addition to Pfefferkorn's description is the claim that when the Jews could not afford to buy a rooster for Kapparot, they transferred their sins to a Christian. The first author who mentions this is Pfefferkorn's contemporary, the convert Victor von Carben. In his book *Dem durchleuchtigsten hochgebornen Fursten und Herren* (probably 1508), von Carben claims that some Jews could not afford to buy a rooster but they still wanted to purify themselves from sin. They therefore woke up early on Yom Kippur eve, went outside, and waited until they saw a Christian. Then they secretly said to him: "God grant that this year you must be or become my Kappara."[28] It seems from this description that the Christian was not aware of his function for the Jew.

This particular claim about the use of a Christian as a Kappara appears in elaborate forms in later descriptions of the Jewish religion and also in other types of polemical works against Judaism. According to later sources, such as Margaritha and Hess, the Jews went into the streets, waited until they saw a Christian, and then asked him, "Do you want to be my Kappara?" offering him a few pfennigs. They then said to the Christian, "You will receive my sins and you will die instead of me," adding the phrase "Kappara Mita Meshuna." This literally means "forgiveness, a strange death," but according to the Christian writers, the meaning was far more sinister: "You should enter into death for my sins and you should die." This claim also appears in other polemical works against Judaism, especially in books that list Jewish insults and prayers against Christianity. For example, it can be found in the anonymus *Verzeichniß Jüdischer Gottes Lästerung*, in Johannes Schmid's *Feuriger Drachen Gift* and in *Juden Spiegel*.[29] Not all the descriptions of the Kapparot ceremony mention this procedure. Some authors, like Buxtorf, Christiani, and Bodenschatz, do not mention the custom at all, and some, like Johannes Wülfer (1681), cite it as a false accusation.[30]

The most elaborate discussion on this point is to be found in Johannes Schudt's *Jüdische Merckwurdigkeiten* (1714).[31] Schudt opens his discussion by citing sources claiming that Jews use Christians as Kapparot. He then attacks Wülfer for denying this and for saying that he never met anyone who knew of such a practice. Schudt claims that on the contrary while he was in Hamburg in 1688 he actually saw a Jew giving bread and money to a Christian on the eve of Yom Kippur and saying in Hebrew that he transferred his sins to him.[32] Why, asked Schudt, should we not believe this claim when it is proven from other sources as well? After all, we know that the Jews claim the Christians are Edomites and that God transferred the sins of the Jews to Esau and to the Edomites. Schudt also refutes Wulfer's claim that Christians would never agree to take the Jews' sins upon themselves.[33] He argues that while this is a desecration, there are common people who are willing to give up their salvation for money. To prove his argument Schudt recounts the story of a servant in Lübeck who agreed to take his master's sins upon himself in order to obtain a nice piece of cloth.[34] He does not fail to mention this servant's fate: he was heard screaming and then found dead, his blood covering the walls,[35] a clear message for those who might consider serving as Kapparot for the Jews. Schudt continues his attack on Wülfer, adducing further counterexamples of Jews collectively and individually transferring their sins to Christians.[36]

Schudt's detailed discussion of this claim and the sources he cites (seven in number) as well as the account of his personal observation of the practice are all aimed at proving his claim.[37] One might conclude from Schudt's vehemence in this matter that he was motivated by an anti-Jewish approach, but this is an overly simplistic analysis. For example, at the end of his discussion of Yom Kippur, Schudt categorically denies that the Jews use Christian blood on Yom Kippur.[38] One therefore cannot characterize his motivations as purely anti-Jewish.[39] Rather, I would suggest that Schudt accepted the first claim because he believed his sources supported it, but he rejected the second for lack of evidence.[40]

These three ceremonies, Kapparot, Malkot, and candle lighting, receive by far the most attention in the thirty-five "Jewish ethnographies" that discuss Yom Kippur. This is true not only in terms of their frequent appearance in the various descriptions but also in terms of the length of these descriptions. Usually the longest account is devoted to the Kapparot ceremony, but the descriptions of the candle lighting and flagellation are also quite long.[41] Nevertheless, we should not ignore other details about Yom Kippur that appear in some of the descriptions and are an integral part of the way the holiday is portrayed. In certain cases we find general observations about the liturgy performed on the day. Most of these deal with the length of the prayers and describe the way they were recited with loud singing and crying. Some descriptions single out specific prayers, such as the prayers on Yom Kippur eve, *al da'at hamakom* and *Kol Nidrei*. In the first of these, the cantor summons everyone to join the community, even sinners, and then offers a prayer that Christians believed absolved Jews of any past and future vows they made. Another prayer that is mentioned on a few occasions is the blessing of the priests, which is recited in the afternoon. As can be seen from the chart, other frequently mentioned practices that are part of the Yom Kippur ritual are immersion in the ritual bath, which is mentioned fifteen times, and visiting the cemetery before the holiday, which is mentioned fourteen times.

All the customs and practices associated with Yom Kippur mentioned by Christian Hebraists and Jewish converts also appear in Jewish sources. But while most of the Jewish sources are devoted to descriptions of the prayers that should be said on this day and to the laws and customs regarding fasting and other prohibited activities, the Kapparot, flagellation, and candle lighting rituals are generally not the focus of the Jewish sources. For example, in Rabbi Eisik Tirna's custom book from the fifteenth century, a work that many Hebraists consulted, only five lines deal with the Kapparot ceremony, three lines with flagellation, and one line with candle lighting. In contrast, about 110 lines discuss the prayers of the holiday.[42] In Rabbi Juspa Kashman's custom and ruling book from the beginning of the eighteenth century 300 lines discuss the prayers while only 50 lines deal with the Kapparot, 5 lines with the flagellation, and 18 lines with candle lighting.[43]

On the basis of this comparison between Jewish and Christian sources we can conclude that Christian authors were not concerned with giving a full and complete account of Yom Kippur. They focused on those aspects of the Yom Kippur ritual that furthered their own Christian and anti-Jewish agenda. Altogether, I have distinguished four different motivations, related to one another but not identical: revealing the absurdity of Jewish ritual; revealing the superstitious character of Jewish ceremony; revealing the anti-Christian nature of Jewish practice; and showing the deviation of Judaism from the biblical text.

Pfefferkorn, who was among the first authors to describe the ritual life of the Jews and consequently one of the founders of this literary genre, makes his hostile intent clear in a chapter outlining his reasons for describing Jewish customs. As he says, "First, I have revealed here the unfounded bad habits of the Jews (so that everybody understands my point of view in this matter), in order to show them to them in a mocking light."[44] Pfefferkorn's desire to demonstrate the ridiculous character of the Jewish customs is dominant in the work of later authors as well and is revealed by their propensity for sarcasm. For example, they ridicule the traditional Jewish explanation for the use of a rooster to atone for the sins of a human on the grounds that a *Gever*, rooster in Aramaic, can replace a *Gever*, man in Hebrew. Buxtorf comments on this in his *Juden Schul*:

The reason for taking a rooster rather than any other animal is that a man is called *Gebher* in Hebrew. If a *Gebher* sins, a *Gebher* should be punished. But that punishment would be painful, therefore they take a rooster in place of themselves, a rooster, which is called in the Babylonian language of the Talmud *Gebher*. This is done because of the just treatment of God since a *Gebher* has sinned, a *Gebher*, meaning the rooster, will be punished. The blind and stupid Jews also believe that they can confuse God as they do the devil (as was shown in the previous chapter) and make him think that a rooster is a man.[45]

This sarcastic depiction of the Jewish ceremonies as absurd is also evident in the use of adjectives such as *seltsam* (strange) and *merckwürdig* (peculiar).[46] Margaritha's description of the flagellation ceremony is laced with sarcasm when he writes: "*Doch beyssen die Füchs anainander nit hart*"—that is, the Jewish "foxes . . . bite one another rather gently." As I already mentioned, Buxtorf claimed that the lashings endured by Paul were harder than those suffered by contemporary Jews during their ceremony. Sarcasm is especially prevalent in Christian descriptions of the customs of Kapparot and flagellation.

Another tendency among Christian authors is to emphasize the superstitious nature of Jewish customs. These accounts repeatedly resort to the words

Aberglauben and *abergläubisch* (superstition and superstitious).⁴⁷ In *Der Gantz Judisch Glaub* Margaritha describes the custom of lighting a candle on Yom Kippur eve. He mentions that each Jew takes a candle that will burn for at least twenty-four hours, and he writes that he himself saw a Jew who was so pious that he prepared a candle weighing thirty pounds. He emphasizes the superstitions the Jews have in regard to these candles and the way they are burnt.⁴⁸ The fact that Christian authors view the custom of lighting candles as superstitious explains why they refer to it so frequently even though it was not considered important from the Jewish point of view.⁴⁹

The Kapparot ceremony is also attacked as superstitious. For example, Johannes Christian Salomon, a converted Jew, writes that on the ninth of Tishri, in preparation for Yom Kippur, the Jews have an *erschrecklichen Aberglauben* (an appalling superstition), namely the Kapparot ceremony. In his description he mentions that after bestowing their sins upon their respective roosters the Jews take them, bind their feet, bring them to the slaughterer, and then eat them. In his opinion this is clear evidence of how superstitious Jews are.⁵⁰ It should be pointed out that during the same period this ceremony was attacked and condemned by Jewish rabbis as well. The criticism of the Kapparot ceremony started as early as the medieval period when some prominent Jewish figures such as Nahmanides and Rashba (Rabbi Shlomo ibn Aderet) said that it is the custom of the Gentiles, but later on some of these attacks referred to the Kapparot ceremony as superstitious without mentioning Christians.⁵¹

Criticism of the Kapparot ceremony is in some ways reminiscent of the criticism Protestants often voiced against Catholic practices. An examination of the authors who discussed the Jewish ceremonies reveals that most of the Christians authors who wrote descriptions of Jewish rituals and ceremonies were Protestants; only a few were Catholics. It is noteworthy, however, that the attacks on the Jewish rituals and their superstitious nature are common to both the Protestant and the Catholic authors. It is difficult to determine whether religious differences between the authors influenced their opinions in other matters. Thus, for example, the criticism on the candle lighting is common to both Protestants and Catholics although Protestant scholars tend to attack the Catholic practice of candle lighting as well.⁵² At the same time, although Protestants argued against the practices of flagellants, there is no hint that their criticism of the Jewish ceremony of flagellation was aimed at the Catholic practice.

A further reason Christians were inclined to describe the Kapparot ceremony and the different prayers for Yom Kippur is their anti-Christian character. Besides the long discussions about the use of Christians as Kapparot, there are references to the curses against Christians that, according to some descriptions, play an important role in the services of Yom Kippur. Authors like Margaritha and Hess refer to special prayers against Christians, and it is likely that they mean the *shamta*. Margaritha claims that Jews recite a very rare prayer against all the nations, including the Christians, but states that there are many reasons he prefers not to mention this prayer explicitly. Hess concludes his discussion of Yom Kippur with a prayer to God that he might help the poor Christians on this day by bringing it to an end since the Jews pray for the suffering of all Christians. Other parts of the service are singled out for their anti-Christian bias, for example, the prayer *'aleinu l'shabe'ach*. Although cited three times every day, it is accompanied on Yom Kippur (as well as on Rosh Hashana) with a special ceremony and was believed by many Christians to include insults against Jesus.[53] Christian writers also attacked the prayer *kol nidrei*. The basis for these attacks was the Christian claim that the Jews used this prayer to break promises they had previously made to Christians under oath. In his comments and additions to Hess's book, for example, Alberti claims Jews do this.[54]

Another example of the way Christian authors attack what they perceive as the anti-Christian character of some of the customs is found in Friedenheim, who claims that the custom of starting the building of the Sukkah immediately after the end of Yom Kippur reflects disdain for Christians. According to Friedenheim, one of the rabbis wrote:

During the time of the Temple, God ordered that on *Yom Kippur* two he-goats, which in Hebrew are called *se'irim*, will be sacrificed, one of them for God himself and the other one to *Azazel*, or according to their translation to Satan (Lev. 16:1). In the story of the patriarchs, however, we read (Gen. 33:16–7) that Esau chose the way to *Seir* and Jacob the way to *Sukkot*. Since *Seir* in the singular form means a he-goat, they claim that Esau went there to participate in the he-goat of Satan; Jacob in contrast went to *Sukkot* or the tabernacle to prepare for the holiday there. According to this also we, so ends this rabbi, can deal now with the laws of the feast of Tabernacle since we have sent the he-goat to Satan.[55]

Since for Jews, Esau was a symbol of Christianity, this passage, with its stark contrast between god-fearing Jacob and devil-worshiping Esau, clearly associates Christianity with the devil and Judaism with God.

I turn now to another aspect of the descriptions of Jewish customs, one that relates primarily to the motives of those authors who were Christian from birth. In his discussion of Yom Kippur, Buxtorf quotes the biblical verses that deal with this day. Buxtorf does not follow Luther's German translation but gives his own.[56] A comparison of the two translations shows that although there is no real difference between them, Buxtorf follows the word order of the Hebrew text more closely.[57] Buxtorf's concern with the exact translation of the Hebrew text arose from his conviction that the Jews had deviated from the biblical law. This claim appears in the first chapter of his book and again in the conclusion, where he writes: "It will be enough for the Christian reader to hear and understand from all of that, that the Jewish faith and their entire religion is not based on Moses, but on empty lies, false and ungrounded laws and fables that their rabbis and corrupted scholars invented, and thus among the Christians it should not be said any more that the Jews strongly adhere to the Mosaic law."[58] Buxtorf's literal translation of the Hebrew text is part of his attempt to show that while he understands the Hebrew text and follows it to the letter, the Jews do not, and they consequently deviate from the true meaning of the Bible.

A similar tactic of comparing the verses from the Bible that deal with Yom Kippur with a description of the holiday as it was performed by contemporary Jews is found in the work of Johannes Christoph Bodenschatz. Bodenschatz does not limit himself to citing the biblical verses about the holiday. In addition to these he provides a long description of the way in which Yom Kippur was observed during the biblical period. In this respect one of his central purposes is to highlight the discrepancies between the biblical and the rabbinic understanding of the holiday and to show the way the rabbis have distorted contemporary Jewish practice.[59] While Margaritha does not explicitly refer to Jewish deviations from specific biblical passages, as Buxtorf and Bodenschatz do, he does charge the rabbis with introducing customs and practices that are not mentioned in the Bible. As he says in the case of the Kapparot ceremony, "Listen to this, you blind Jew, and not to your Talmud which has blurred the truth with the rooster. A rooster cannot take over your sins. A man must redeem these sins again."[60]

These arguments belong to the theological sphere and are reminiscent of earlier Christian attacks on Judaism as a religion that no longer adheres to the Bible. As opposed to earlier attacks that concentrated mainly on the Jewish lack of understanding of the spiritual meaning of the biblical laws, the Christian focus in this case was on the way Jews have deviated from the meaning of the biblical text. This marks the first appearance of a systematic Christian attack on the Jewish law and on rabbinical Judaism as a different religion and on the Jews as a nation that no longer adheres to God's revelation but to a religion that is a human fabrication of fables and lies.[61] These theological arguments reveal that Christian interest in contemporary Judaism was an extension of the traditional theological polemics against the Jewish religion.

As we have seen, the different motives of the various authors discussed and the reasons they chose one way of presenting Jewish customs rather than another are varied. This is all the more true because later authors read the works of their predecessors and in many cases quote from them extensively.

Our ability to recognize the sources an author used gives us the opportunity to trace what he chose to transmit to his readers and what he chose to omit. For example, as Stephen Burnett has shown, Margaritha's *Der Gantz Judisch Glaub* was one of the main sources for Buxtorf's *Juden Schul*, as was Hess's *Juden Geissel*, although to a lesser degree.[62] Both Margaritha and Hess highlight different anti-Christian components in the ceremonies of Yom Kippur. Margaritha refers to the custom of using a Christian as a Kappara and to the special anti-Christian prayers that the Jews recite on this day. Both these customs appear in Hess's description; in addition he mentions the alleged custom that on Yom Kippur the Jews ask each other if they cheated Christians in business. Yet none of these details are mentioned by Buxtorf. This omission creates the impression that although Buxtorf employed sharp and sarcastic remarks about the Jews, he kept his focus on theological issues and refrained from depicting Judaism as an anti-Christian religion. A similar attitude can also be found in Fabronius's *Bekehrung der Juden und von mancherley abergläubischen Ceremonien*, which makes extensive use of Hess's *Juden Geissel*. Like Buxtorf, whose book he also used as a source, Fabronius does not mention the anti-Christian prayers or the questions that dealt with cheating Christians in business, and he also refrains from mentioning Hess's criticism of the Kapparot ceremony. The only anti-Christian element that he takes from Hess is the claim that the Jews use Christians as Kapparot.[63]

The Hess case shows us that not all later authors refrained from emphasizing the anti-Christian character of some of the Yom Kippur ceremonies. As Maria Diemling has shown, Hess made extensive use of Margaritha's book.[64] Not only does he mention the anti-Christian prayers and the use of Christians as Kapparot, but, as we have seen, he also adds another practice he viewed as an anti-Christian, namely that of questioning Jews about cheating Christians. The same is true for Lothar Fried who based his description on Margaritha and Hess and referred to the anti-Christian ceremonies they mentioned.[65]

The common denominator uniting the first group of authors I mentioned, namely Buxtorf and Fabronius,[66] is that they were Christians from birth while the other two authors, Hess and Fried, were converts. Those born Christian showed only a limited interest in discussing the anti-Christian character of the Jewish ceremonies. Their major concern was with proving that the Jewish ceremonies were ridiculous and absurd, and that from a theological perspective contemporary Judaism is no longer based on the Bible but on the fables of the rabbis. The approach of the converts was different: from their point of view the unveiling of the anti-Christian characteristics of the Jewish ceremonies was crucial. Thus those converts who used the works of their predecessors adopted the anti-Christian claims and even added to them.

From a historical perspective one can see that the references to the anti-

Christian character of the Jewish ceremonies, especially in regard to the claim that the Jews use Christians as Kapparot, are characteristic of the early literature that tended to be written by converts to Christianity. Three out of the four descriptions written in the sixteenth century, those of von Carben, Margaritha, and Hess, refer to this claim, and the fourth, Pfefferkorn, refers to the Jewish curses against Christians and Christianity during Yom Kippur. These authors were all converts.

In later descriptions, references to the anti-Christian character of Jewish ritual and practice are less extensive. For example, the claim that Jews use Christians as Kapparot appears only twice in the seventeenth century, and at least three out of the four references to it in the eighteenth century, those made by Fried in his *Juden Spiegel* (1715), by Jungendres in his notes to Kirchner's *Judisches Ceremoniel* (1724), and by Selig in his *Der Jude*, are based on Margaritha's description and not on their own experience.[67] It is still telling, however, that they raised this claim again after a century of silence. Although further study is necessary, it appears that there is a shift in the nature of the literature dealing with Jewish customs. The earlier works were written by converts, and their main focus was on revealing the anti-Christian character of Judaism. The books written in the seventeenth and eighteenth centuries, including those written by converts, are less concerned with this aspect of Judaism. They focus instead on the superstitious and ridiculous nature of the Jewish religion. Altogether we can see that both the origin of the authors, namely if they were Christian from birth or converts, and the change in time influenced the writings about Judaism in the early modern period.

I began this essay by noting the problems related to categorizing the literature under discussion as "Christian ethnographies of Jews." Hsia, who coined the term, points to the similarity between the rise of modern ethnography and the writings about the Jews.[68] While I agree with Hsia that there are parallels between the subjects discussed in books about the Jews and books about other nations and religions, there are also profound differences. One of the main tools of the ethnographer is firsthand observation, and this was the tool for most of the authors who wrote about other nations and religions. As we have seen, however, most of the writers examined in this essay based themselves on literary sources. This is especially true in the case of Christian authors, who rarely include their own observations, but it is also the case with most of the converts, who, in spite of their personal knowledge, often refer to the printed word. In addition we should remember that the converts are not typical outsiders who view another culture as strangers. They viewed Judaism from within and from without at the same time, a unique phenomenon that characterizes writings about Jews and has almost no parallels in the vast literature about other nations. In addition the literature about the Jews is characterized by religious and theological polemics, which are less prevalent in the writings about other nations.

In his article Hsia hints at the theological nature of the works about Jewish ritual life but fails to emphasize the crucial importance of either the polemical criticism of the Jews or of the actual relationships between Jews and Christians and the way they influenced the attitudes of the authors toward Jews.[69] As we have seen, the arguments in the works about Jews were *theological* inasmuch as they emphasize the deviation of contemporary Jewish customs from the original precepts of Mosaic law and their superstitious character and *social* when they underline the anti-Christian aspects of the Jewish way of life as it was expressed in Jewish prayers and ceremonies. But whichever aspect they singled out, it is clear that Christian authors had a defined polemical agenda.[70] Based on this conclusion, the use of the term *ethnography* to describe Christian writings about Jews is problematic because of the obvious religious bias shown by the authors. I would suggest that we describe this literature not simply as ethnographies but modify the term calling these texts polemical ethnographies.[71] In my opinion the use of this new term should not be limited to the literature about the Jews; it could be very useful in discussions of ethnographies about other nations as well.[72] This definition indicates that while much of the information in the books about the Jewish religion is ethnographic, namely it belongs to "the scientific description of nations or races of men, their customs, habits, and differences" (to quote the definition in the *Oxford English Dictionary*), most of them had a clearly polemical anti-Judaic agenda. Although today this definition seems a bit naive because we know that there is no "objective" ethnography, there is a difference between descriptions that focus on polemical aspects and descriptions that are biased due to their author's incapability to fully understand a different culture from outside.

However, one should notice that my definition of this literary genre as polemical ethnography does not imply that its consequences for European Jewry at the time were only negative. As mentioned before, this literary genre also fostered the process of disenchantment with Judaism and shifted the Christian interest from dealing with Judaism to dealing with Jews—a shift that later paved the road to the naturalization of the Jews. In addition one cannot ignore the influence of this literature, both directly and indirectly, on the internal Jewish process of abandoning customs that were considered by many as superstitious. Modena's work is one example of this approach.[73]

The quotation from Friedenheim's book with which I began recounted the interest and the impression that Yom Kippur made on the Christians. The numerous descriptions of Yom Kippur that were written by Christian authors as well as the fact that among the different holidays Yom Kippur (together with Passover) received the most attention prove the truth of the first part of Friedenheim's statement. The attitudes toward Yom Kippur as they were discussed here, however, show that it was not appreciation that induced Christians to write about the holiday but the polemical desire to discredit Judaism. Only at the end of the period we are dealing with, namely the second half of the eighteenth century, are there descriptions that not only criticize the Jews but also praise them.

Notes

1.

Ich sah diese Zeit hindurch oft mit Verwunderung, wie häufig die Christen an den sogenannten (Jom Kipper) oder langen Tage in die Synagogen eilen, um die jüdische Andacht und ihre Gebräuche mit anzusehen; sie glauben vielleicht dem Scheine nach wunder, wie auferbäulich, gottesfürchtig, und andächtig diese Gebräuchen seyen; denn ich hörte bey meinen Spaziergängen am Main, selbst von denen, die aus der Synagoge zurückkamen, daß sie zueinander sagten, die jüdischen Ceremonien seyen wirklich nicht zu verachten, denn ihr Gebeth, des den ganzen Tag über dauerte, die Beleuchtung ihrer Synagoge, ihre weissen leinenen Röcke, alles erregt Aufmerksamkeit. Die Juden selbst sind stolz darauf, so vornehme Zuschauer beyderley Geschlechts in ihren Synagogen zu haben; denn sie glauben die Goim oder Christen haben einen besondern Wohlgefallen an ihrem Gottesdienste, und einige Meschmodim oder Neugetaufte aber kämen in die Synagoge zurück, um dieses Fest noch einmal mitfeyern zu können.

Caspar Friedenheim, *Yehudi mi-bachutz, das ist der äußerliche Jud in Ansehung ihres dermaligen vermeintlichen Gottesdienstes und besonders in Absicht auf das ihnen so wichtige Stück Jom Kipur, das ist der Versöhnungstag und dessen dermaligen Feyer und Begehung* (Würzburg, Ger., 1785), Vorrede, first and second page (no pagination).

2. Yaacov Deutsch, "'A View of the Jewish Religion': Conceptions of Jewish Practice and Ritual in Early Modern Europe," *Archiv für Religionsgeschichte* 3 (2001): 273–95.

3. For a survey of earlier descriptions of Yom Kippur see Daniel Stökl, "The Impact of Yom Kippur on Early Christianity" (Ph.D. diss., Hebrew University, 2001), 65–75. Stökl mentions a number of authors who described Yom Kippur; however, as he writes, most of them did not go into detail about the rituals of the day.

4. On this prayer and on some of the Christian references to it, see Chen Merhavya, "The Caustic Poetic Rebuke (Shamta) in Medieval Christian Polemic Literature," *Tarbiz* 41 (1971): 95–115 (in Hebrew), and Israel J. Yuval, "Vengeance and Damnation, Blood Defamation: From Jewish Martyrdom to Blood Libel Accusations" (in Hebrew), *Zion* 58 (1993): 52–55.

5. "Item in festo propitiationum, in septembri, habent quamdam specialem orationem quam faciant contra omnes inimicos, quam orationem vocant 'cematha,' quod est dictum anathema vel separatio, vel maledictio. Et in illa oratione per circumlocutionem verborum vocant Christum spurium filium meretricis et beatam Mariam Virginem mulierem calefactionis seu luxurie, quod nephandum est loqui et etiam cogitare." Bernard Gui, *Manuel de l'inquisiteur*, vol. 2, ed. and trans. G. Mollat and G. Drioux (New York: AMS Press 1980), 16–18.

6. Ronnie Po-Chia Hsia, "Christian Ethnography of Jews in Early Modern Ger-

many," in *The Expulsion of the Jews: 1492 and After*, ed. Raymond B. Waddington and Arthur H. Williamson (New York: Garland, 1994), 223–35.

7. For a list of these books and a discussion of their content, see Deutsch, "'A View of the Jewish Religion.'"

8. See Friedenheim, *Yehudi mi-bachutz, das ist der äußerliche Jud*.

9. For practical reasons, I have mentioned in the table only the names of the authors. I have appended a list with full bibliographical references to the works.

10. On this custom and its history, see Jacob Z. Lauterbach, "The Ritual for the Kapparot Ceremony," in *Jewish Studies in Memory of George A. Kohut*, ed. Salo W. Baron and Alexander Marx (New York: Alexander Kohut Memorial Foundation 1935), 413–22 (reprinted in Jacob Z. Lauterbach, *Studies in Jewish Law, Custom, and Folklore*, selected with an introduction by Bernard J. Bamberger [New York: Ktav, 1970], 133–42); and idem, "Tashlik: A Study in Jewish Ceremonies," *HUCA* 11 (1936): 207–340.

11. On Pfefferkorn and his works, see Hans-Martin Kirn, *Das Bild vom Juden im Deutschland des frühen 16. Jahrhunderts: dargestellt an den Schriften Johannes Pfefferkorns*, Texts and Studies in Medieval and Early Modern Judaism 3 (Tübingen, Ger.: Mohr, 1989).

12. The pamphlet was printed six times during 1508, four times in German dialects and twice in Latin. See Kirn, *Das Bild vom Juden*, 202. The title above is that of the Nürnberg edition. In addition the booklet was published in 1516 in Danish. See Martin S. Lausten, "Jodernes hemmeligheder; den danske udgave af det antijodiske skrift *Libellus de Judaica confessione* (1516)," *Rambam* 31 (1991–92): 67–81.

13.

Uff den newenten tag yrer puß und penitentz, wan sy auß yrem tempel heym zu hauß kümen. So hant alle juden iunck und alt manß personen weyß hanen, die frawen und iunckfrawen sulch weyß hennen so vere als müglich ist die zu uber kümmen und zu kriegen. Ob aber ein fraw schwanger ist so müß sy ein hanen und ein hennen fur sich und die ungeborne frucht die noch kein sundt gethan hat, doch in wollust des fleysch entpfangen ist. Ein ytlicher nympt seinen hanen und hennen bey sich. Der herr des hauß stet mit seinem hannen in das mittel seins haußgesyndes mit grosser andach still schweigende ein güte weil bedencken sein sunden, wan die also bedacht seind, nympt er seinen hannen bey den füssen schwingt den drey mall umb sein haubt also das der hann mit seinem flügellen flattern und die zusamen flagen muß und spricht zu dem hannen, du pist ein vergeber meiner sund, welche von mir zu dir verwandelt und ubertragen und gesetzt werden. Ich byn nun vonn meynen sunden gefreyhet aber du pist schuldig fur mich, du geest in den todt und ich das ewig leben, dan kumpt ein ytlicher der ein nach dem andern mit seinen hannen und thut gleich wie der vater des haußgesins gethan hat mit gestalt und gepet gantzer grosser rew fur die sunden und andacht zu der barmhertzigkeyt gotz, meinen halden und glauben das gentzlich das in yre sunden verzyhen und vergeben sein.

Johannes Pfefferkorn, *Ich heyß ain Büchlein der Iuden Peicht* (Nürnberg, 1508), B1r–v.

14. See, for example, the description in the fifteenth–century *Book of Maharil: Customs by Rabbi Yaacov Mulin* (in Hebrew) (Jerusalem: Mifal Torath Chachmey Ashkenaz, Machon Yerushalayim, 1989), 313–15.

15. The first reference to taking a rooster for the fetus is found in the *Book of Maharil*, 314; and see the note of the editor in *Sefer Haminhagim (Rulings and Customs) of Rabbi Eisik Tirna* (Jerusalem: Mifal Torath Chachmey Ashkenaz, Machon Yerushalayim, 1979), 105 §139 n. 1.

16.

Geen darnach widerumb zu einen fliessenden wasser ducken sich aber ein mal darunder das nit von yrem leibe gesehen wirt, geen auß und thun weysse lynen kytel ann und rusten sich zu essen. Wer aber sach das sich eyner nit reyn von sunden bedeucht zu sein dannoch ein wydernagen leiner conscientz hette, der geet zu seinen negsten freunden aber nachtpawren in yr synagog knyet nyder, pucht sich mit dem haubte zu der erden so hebet im der ander die cleyder hynden uff und schlecht yn mit einem ryemen von einer gurtel oder sunst xxxix. Schlege fur das hynderst, wo dan noch eyniche sunde verhalten und geblieben gewest weren die faren also hynden auß dan ist der man gantz und gar lautter und reyn.

Pfefferkorn, *Iuden Peicht*, B1v.

17. "Und wer dan den selbigen tag umb die vesper zeyt wol nyesen mag aber dem sein kertz hell und clar geprant hat der erfrewet sich, wann sy halten das fur ein gewysses zeichen das got die selbigen erhort hab." Ibid., B3r.

18. "Darbey ein christen mensch sein unnd die verwarten müß das kein schad dar von uff stan, sy rüren die kertzen nit an uff das yr feyr nit gebrochen werde." Ibid., B2r.

19. Richard I. Cohen, *Jewish Icons: Art and Society in Modern Europe* (Berkeley and Los Angeles: University of California Press, 1998), 267 n. 33. This function of the Shabbos Goy appears also in Jewish sources, for example Yosef Juspa Hahn Neuerlingen, *Sefer Yosef Ometz* (in Hebrew) (Frankfurt: Hermon Verlag, 1928), 224.

20. For example, the description of Rabbi Eisik Tirna, who refers only to the blessing on the candles: *Sefer Haminhagim (Rulings and Customs) of Rabbi Eisik Tirna*, 107. The Maharil is the only one who refers to looking at the way the candles were burning as a sign for the future. See *The Book of Maharil*, 332.

21. For example, the description of Avraham Kleusner (d. ca. 1400), *Custom Book, according to the Trent edition printed on 1559* (in Hebrew), ed. Hayim Yehuda Ehrenreich (Deva, Rum., 1929), 12. The only reference to the stripping of the lashed person is found in the seventeenth-century description of Juspa Shammash who writes, "And they are accustomed to take the cloth at his waist." See *Wormser Minhagbuch des R. Jousep (Juspa) Schammes. Nach Handschriften des Verfassers zum ersten Male vollständig herausgegeben, Erläuterungen und Quellen von Benjamin Salomon Hamburger*, vol. 1 (in Hebrew) (Jerusalem: Machon Jeruschalajim, Mifal Torath Chachmey Aschkenaz, 1988), 173.

22. For example, see Johannes Buxtorf, *Synagoga Judaica: Das ist Juden Schul: Darinnen der gantz Jüdische Glaub und Glaubens ubung, mit allen Ceremonien, Satzungen, Sitten und Gebräuchen, wie sie bey ihnen offentlich und Heimlich im Brauche* (Basel, Switz., 1603), 517. According to this explanation, the female body has 252 organs, and therefore this explanation does not include her.

23. Johannes Christoph Georg Bodenschatz, *Kirchliche Verfassung der heutigen Juden sonderlich derer in Deutschland in IV. Haupt-Theile abgefasset aus ihren eigenen und anderen Schriften umständlich dargethan und mit 30 sauberen Kupfern erläutert* (Frankfurt, 1748–49), 215.

24. Anthonius Margaritha, *Der gantz Jüdisch Glaub* (Augsburg, 1530), F1r (note in the margins); Buxtorf, *Juden Schul*, 522.

25. "Dise strafe der, ein weniger denn viertzig schlägen, sagt der Apostel Paulus, daß er zum fünfften mal, von den Jüden erlitten habe, ohne zweiffel viel härter unnd

anderst, denn sie heutiges tages einander in der Kirchen schlagen." Buxtorf, *Juden Schul*, 522.

26. Johannes Jacob Schudt, *Jüdische Merckwürdigkeiten*, vol. 2, no. 2 (Frankfurt: 1714), 299.

27. Paul Christian Kirchner, *Jüdisches Ceremoniel . . . nunmehro aber bey dieser neuen Auflage mit accuraten Kupfer versehen; Nicht weniger aus den besten Scribenten so wol, als aus Erzehlung glaubwürdiger Personen und selbst eigener Erfahrung, um vieles vermehret und mit Anmerkungen erläutert*, ed. Sebastian Jacob Jungendres (Nürnberg, 1724), 118 n. b.

28. "Gott gebe dass du diss jair meyn Caporo must seyn oder werden." Victor von Carben, *Dem durchleuchtigsten hochgebornen fursten und herren Herren Ludwigen Phaltzgrauen bey Rein . . . Hier inne wirt gelesen wie Her Victor von Carben, welicher eyn Rabi der Juden gewest ist, zu cristlichem glauben komm. Weiter vindet man dar in eyn costliche disputatz eynes gelerten Cristen, und eyns gelerten Jude, dar inne alle Irthumb der Juden durch yr aygen schrifft aufgelost werden* (Köln?, probably 1508), Civ. Concerning the date and place of publication, see Maria Diemling, "Christliche Ethnographien über Juden und Judentum in der Frühen Neuzeit: Die Konvertiten Victor von Carben und Anthonius Margaritha und ihre Darstellung jüdischen Lebens und jüdischer Religion" (Ph.D. diss., Universität Wien, 1999), 14.

29. Johannes Schmid, *Feuriger Drachen Gift und wütiger Ottern Gall Mit welchem Des Teuffels Leibigen Juden Volck durch greuliches und abscheuliches Gotteslästern Schänden Fluchen Lügen Schrifftverkehren Betriegen und andere unmenschliche Boßheit Den Heiligen Drey-Einigen Gott frey speiset und trüncket . . . Nebst einem Anhang oder kurtzen Verlauff der Sabbats-Bedienung zu Hoerde* (Coburg, Ger., 1682), 35; *Verzeichniss und kurtzer Auszug aus etlicher Hochgelehrter (auch vieler anderer Gottseliger Menner und erfahrner der Hebrayschen Sprach) von den erschröcklichen Gotteslästerungen wieder unsern Herrn Christum die Jungfrau Maria wieder alle Christen und Weltliche Obrigkeit so von den Juden täglich geübet werden* (Leipzig, Ger., 1577), Aa3r + v; *Juden Spiegel in welchem kurz wahr und klärlich deren Juden herkommen jetziger Stand Glauben argerlicher Handel und Wandel Zur Gründlicher Nachricht und Freundlicher Warnung allen ihrer Seelen Heyl liebenden Christen aus bewehrten Christlichen und Judischen Schrifften Büchern und Exempelen fürgestellet werden* (Cölln, 1714), 73–75.

30. Johannes Wülfer, a Protestant preacher, published the book *Theriaca Judaica ad examen revocata* (Nürnberg) in 1681, in which he brought the text of Samuel Friedrich Brenz, *Jüdischer abgestreiffter Schlangen-Balg* (Nürnberg, Ger., 1614), and Solomon Zvi Aufhausen's response to it, *Jüdischer Theriak* (Hanau, Ger., 1615), and appended his remarks to both. Wülfer quotes the passage in Margaritha's book that mentions this claim and writes that he never saw or heard the claim. "Nec unquam vel oculis suis idipsum eos vidisse, vel ex aliis audivisse, deprehendi" (246).

31. Schudt, *Jüdische Merckwürdigkeiten*, vol. 2, no. 2 298–307.

32. "Allein ich bezeuge nochmalen mit Grund der Wahrheit, dass ich selbst An. 1688 zu Hamburg auf dem Ellern Steinweg Juden gesehen, so Geld und Brod an armen Christen, den Tag vor den Versöhnung Fest gegeben, und auff Hebräisch ihnen ihre Sünde auffgelegt." Schudt, *Jüdische Merckwürdigkeiten*, vol. 2, no. 2, 305.

33. Wülfer, *Theriaca Judaica*, 245.

34. Schudt, *Jüdische Merckwürdigkeiten*, vol. 2, no. 2, 304–5.

35. "Dabey sich dann dieser Diener gar lustig mit gemacht und umb seine Burgschafft sich wenig bekümmert, da er nun, gleich andern, zur Ruhe sich gelegt, ist in

des Dieners Kammer umb Mitternacht ein grosses Gepolter und Getümmel gehöret worden, daß da man aber bey anbrechenden Tage die Kammer eröffnet, hat man den Diener auf der Erden mit umgedreheten Halse und zerquetschten Fliedern erwürgt gefunden, daß man auch das an der Wand gesprützte Blut weder abwäschen noch mit Kalck übertünchen können." Schudt, *Jüdische Merckwürdigkeiten*, vol. 2, no. 2, 305.

36. Ibid., 306–7.

37. Altogether, Schudt mentions the following sources: Margaritha, *Der gantz Jüdisch Glaub*: E3r + v; *Verzeichniss und kurtzer Auszug*: Aa3r + v; Ernst Ferdinand Hess, *Flagellum Iudeorum, Juden Geissel, das ist ein neuwe sehr nütze und gründliche Erweisung, dass Jesus Christus, Gottes und der H. Jungkfrauwen Marien Sohn der wahre verheissene und gesandte Messias sey* (s.l., 1598), 92–93; Schmid, *Feuriger Drachen Gift*, 35; Johannes Andreas Eisenmenger, *Entdecktes Judenthum*, vol. 2 (Frankfurt: 1700), 150; Sigismund Hossman, *Das schwer zu bekehrende Juden Hertz* (Helmstädt, Ger., 1701), 311; Johannes Christian Harphstadt, *Das gottslästerliche Judenthum* (1701), 45. I could not find a library that holds a copy of this book. However, the author and the book are mentioned by Jöcher in his lexicon: Christian Gottlieb Jöcher, *Allgemeines Gelehrten-Lexicon*, vol. 2 (Leipzig, Ger., 1750), col. 1372.

38. "Daß aber die Juden an ihrem Versöhntag solten Christen Blut gebrauchen ist gantz irrig." Schudt, *Jüdische Merckwürdigkeiten*, vol. 2, no. 2, 307.

39. This is how he was described in Reuven Michael, "Schudt, Johann Jakob," *Encyclopedia Judaica*, vol. 14 (1971), cols. 1003–4.

40. In the preface to his work Schudt himself wrote that he tried to be impartial and objective: Schudt, *Jüdische Merckwürdigkeiten*, vol. 1, "Vorrede an der geneigten Leser," especially the third and fourth page (no pagination). Although Schudt was surely not impartial, we cannot ignore the fact that he supports many of his claims either by his own experience or by quoting from other people's works. For a different view of Schudt, see Allison P. Coudert, "Seventeenth-Century Christian Hebraists: Philosemites or Antisemites," in *Judaeo-Christian Intellectual Culture in the Seventeenth Century: A Celebration of the Library of Narcissus Marsh, 1638–1713*, ed. Allison P. Coudert et al. (Dordrecht, Neth., Boston: Kluwer Academic Publishers, 1999), 49–54.

41. For example, in Buxtorf's narrative the length of each part is as follows: *Kapparot*, 10 pages; going to the cemetery, 5 lines; immersion, 5 lines; candle lighting, 1 1/2 pages; request of forgiveness, 1 page; flagellation, 3 pages; eating on Yom Kippur eve, 1/2 page; 5 banned activities, 1 1/2 page; *al da'at hamakom*, 1/2 page; *kol nidrei*, almost a page; priestly blessing, 1 page; horn blowing, 1/2 page.

42. *Sefer Haminhagim (Rulings and Customs)* of Rabbi Eisik Tirna, 105–18.

43. Yosef Juspa Kashman Segal, *Sefer Noheg Ka'tzon Yosef*, Laws, Customs, and Addenda (in Hebrew) (Tel Aviv: H. Vagshal Publishing, 1969), 275–89.

44. "Zu dem ersten han ich der iuden ungegrunte Böse gewonhait geöffnet (Uff das ein ytlicher verstee mein meynung hier yn) darumb das solchs in gespötz weyse ynn fur gehalten werde." Pfefferkorn, *Iuden Peicht*, B3r.

45. "Ursuche daz sie ein Hanen lieber dann andere deir brauchen, ist, daz ein Mann auff Hebraeische *Gebher* genennt wird: wann nun ein *Gebher* sündiget, so soll auch ein *Gebher* umb die sünde gestrafft werden. Weil aber den Juden die Straft beschwärlich fallen wurde, so nemmen sie ein Hanen an ihr statt, der wird auch der Talmudischer oder Babylonischer Sprache *Gebher* gennent, und geschicht also der Gerechtigkeit Gottes genüg, dieweil ein *Gebher* gesündiget, so wird auch ein *Gebher* nemlich der Han, gestrafft. Vermeynen also die Blinden und Unvernünfftigen Juden, sie

wöllen auch also ihren Gott *Mebulbal*, irrig und verwirret machen, wie sie dem Teufel auch können thun (als im vorigen Capitel angezeigt), das er ein Hanen für ein Menschen ansehe." Buxtorf, *Juden Schul*, 511.

46. See, for example, the titles of Fabronius's and Schudt's books on p. 209.

47. See, for example, the titles of Friedrich Albrecht Christiani's, Salomon's, and Seeligmann's books on p. 209.

48. Margaritha, *Der gantz Jüdisch Glaub*, F1r.

49. As I mentioned above (note 20), only the Maharil relates to the futuristic omens that could be seen in the candles. In addition, not only does this custom not appear in other sources, but some of the contemporary Jewish sources do not mention the candle lighting at all. See, for example, Kleusner, *Custom Book*, 11–15.

50. "Hier siehest du nun lieber Christ, was das vor ein erschrecklicher Aberglaube ist." Johannes Christian Salomon, *Sefer min'hagim shel yamim tovim v'nora'im, das ist: Jüdisches Ceremonien Buch von der Jüden Feyer und Fest Tagen, Welche so wol ausser als in ihren Synagogen durch das gantze Jahr gebräuchlich sind: Auch was sie dabey voe Aberglauben haben und wie solche von denen Feyer Tagen derer Christen unterschieden sind* (Halle, Ger., 1721), 12.

51. On the attitudes of the rabbis, see Lauterbach, "The Ritual for the *Kapparot* Ceremony," esp. 418–22; Joshua Trachtenberg, *Jewish Magic and Superstition: A Study in Folk Religion* (Cleveland: Meridian and Jewish Publication Society of America, 1961), 163–65. Although I cannot expand on this point here, I think that at least in some cases there is a link between the Christian approach to the Jewish customs and the way in which they were perceived by Jewish figures. The most striking example is probably Leone Modena, *Historia de gli riti Hebraici* (Paris, 1637), which is a response to Buxtorf's *Juden Schul*, where Modena omits references to customs that Buxtorf described as superstitious or refers to them as false customs that should not be celebrated. See Mark R. Cohen, "Leone da Modena's *Riti*: A Seventeeth-Century Plea for Social Toleration of Jews," *Jewish Social Studies* 34 (1972): 287–319.

52. See, for example, Susan C. Karant-Nunn, *The Reformation of Ritual: An Interpretation of Early Modern Germany* (London: Routledge, 1997), 50–51.

53. The special ceremony that accompanied this prayer was probably the reason for referring to the prayer in the description of Yom Kippur and not in the description of the daily services.

54. Paul Martin M. Alberti, *Neuverfertigte Aus Gottes Wort und der Rabbinen Schrifften wolmeinend geflochtene Jüden-Geissel oder Gründliche Anführung derer zur Bekehrung der Jüden hauptsächlich dienenden Mittel, erstlich von einem bekehrten Juden Ernesto Ferdinando Heß, Med. Doct. herausgegeben; Nun aber mit einigen statt nützlicher Anmerckungen abgefasten Fragen und darauf ertheilten Antworten, welche zu desto nachdrücklicherer Uberzeugung dieser blinden Leute, mehrentheils mit Anführung ihrer und ihrer Lehrer eigenen Worten hergeholet sind, erweitert und vermehrt* (Frankfurt, 1703), 458.

55.

Der Hochgelobte Gott, heist es, hat zu Zeiten des Tempels am langen Tage gebothen, zween Böcke, die auf hebräisch Siirim heisen, zu opfern, einen Gott selbst, und den andern dem Asasel, oder nach ihrer Uebersetzung, dem Teufel. (3B. Mos. 16K. 1V). In der Geschichte der Patriarchen aber lesen wir (1B. Mos. 33Kap. 16–17V): Esau nahm seinen Weg gegen Seir; Jakob aber gegen Suchot. Da nun Seir in der einfachen Zahl einen Bock bedeuten soll, so sagen sie, Esau sey hingezogen, um an dem Bock des Teufels theil zu nehmen; Jakob habe sich aber nach Suchot, oder den

Lauberhütten begeben, um zu diesem Feste sich allda vorzubereiten; so wollen wir dann auch, schleist dieser Rabbi, da wir den Bock dem Teufel zugesendet haben, uns mit dem Gebothe des Lauberhüttensfestes beschäftigen.

Friedenheim, *Yehudi mi-bachutz, das ist der äußerliche Jud*, 96–97. According to Friedenheim, this explanation is found in a book called "Kaph Haiascher." This paragraph appears indeed in the book *Kav Hayashar*, which was first printed in 1705. See Rabbi Tzvi Hirsch Kaidenover, *The Complete Kav Hayashar*, vol. 2 (Jerusalem: Kav Hayashar Hashalem, 1999), 497–98.

56. Buxtorf, *Juden Schul*, 524.

57. For example, Luther translates Lev. 23:32 as, "Am Neundten Tage des Monden zu Abend solt ihr diesen Sabbath halten von Abend bis wieder zu Abend" while Buxtorf translates it as, "Am neundten tag desselben Monats zu abend, vom abend an biß wider zu abend solt ir disen eweren Feyrtag halten."

58. "Es wird aber der Christliche Läser genugsam auß diesem allem vernommen unnd verstanden haben, daß der Jüdisch Glaub und ihre gantze Religion nicht auff Mosen, sondern auff eitel Lügen, falsche und ungegründte Satzungen und Fabeln ihrer Rabbinen und weitverführten Schrifftgelehrten gegründet sey, und desshalben unter den Christen nicht mehr soll geredt werden, daß die Juden starck auff dem Gesetz Mosis halten." Buxtorf, *Juden Schul*, 663. For other places in the book where Buxtorf refers to the deviation of the Jews from the Bible, see Stephen Burnett, "Distorted Mirrors: Antonius Margaritha, Johannes Buxtorf, and Christian Ethnographies of the Jews," *Sixteenth Century Journal* 25 (1994): 281, n. 30–32.

59. Similar arguments are used by Schudt, who devotes his attention almost exclusively to the Kapparot ceremony. He attacks the blindness of the Jews, stating that there is no place in the Old Testament where such a precept is found. See Schudt, *Jüdische Merckwürdigkeiten*, vol. 2, no. 2, 299. Also see the same argument in Jungendres's opening remarks about the holiday: "Wie weit aber jene Ceremonien von den heutigen unterschieden sind, wird man bey Gegeneinanderhaltung derselbigen leicht sehen können." Jungendres, *Jüdisches Ceremoniel*, 116.

60. "Höre hie zu blinder Jude und nicht deinem Talmudt der dir hie mit dem hanen die warheit verstuncklet hatt. Ein han kan deine Sund nicht ertragen. Ein person mus sollich sund widerumb auffheben." Margaritha, *Der gantz Jüdisch Glaub*, E4r; and see Burnett, "Distorted Mirrors," 278. For a more detailed discussion of Margaritha's attacks on the differences between biblical and rabbinical Judaism, see Diemling, "'Christliche Ethnographien,'" 93–97.

61. Attacks on the abandoning of the Mosaic law and the preference of the sayings of the rabbis are found, probably for the first time, in the attacks on the Talmud from 1239, but there is no systematic discussion of particular precepts. See Chen Merhavya, *The Church versus Talmudic and Midrashic Literature (500–1248)* (in Hebrew) (Jerusalem: Bialik Institute, 1970), 251–52.

62. Stephen G. Burnett, *From Christian Hebraism to Jewish Studies: Johannes Buxtorf, 1564–1629, and Hebrew Learning in the Seventeenth Century* (Leiden, Neth.: Brill, 1996), 66–67.

63. Hermann Fabronius, *Bekehrung der Juden und von mancherley abergläubischen Ceremonien unnd seltsamen Sitten so die zerstreweten Jüden haben: und wie sie in der Christenheit zu dulden seyn, neben Theologische und Historische Beschreibung der Göttlichen Weissagung Danielis von Verwüstung der Stadt Jerusalem. Darinnen begriffen*

das der wahre Messias geboren sey. Alles aus heiliger Schrifft Flavio Iosepho, Ernst Ferdinando, Ioanne Buxdorffio und sonst zusammen geschrieben (Erfurt, Ger., 1624), 67–68. A similar attitude is found in Thumius who refers to the custom of using a Christian as a Kappara, but not to the other anti-Christian components that are mentioned by Margaritha. See Theodor Thumius (Thumm), *Tractatum de Festis Iudaeorum* (Tübingen, Ger., 1624), 61.

64. Diemling, "'Christliche Ethnographien,'" 213–14.

65. Lothar Franz Fried (Joseph Marcus), *Neupolierter und wohlgeschliffener Juden-Spiegel* (Mayntz, Ger., 1715), 15.

66. And Thumius as well. See note 63 above.

67. Lothar Franz Fried, *Neupolierter und wohlgeschliffener*, 15; Jungendres, *Jüdisches Ceremoniel*, 118; Gottfried Selig, *Der Jude eine Wochenschrift*, vol. 3 (Leipzig, Ger., 1769), 69–70. It should be noted that two of them, Fried and Selig, report that Margaritha wrote that the Jews use Christians for Kappara, but they themselves do not say that this is a true accusation.

68. Hsia, "Christian Ethnography," 233.

69. Idem, 226–27.

70. In his classic article Amos Funkenstein distinguished four types in the Jewish-Christian debate of the Middle Ages: the old pattern—proofs from the Bible for the truth of Christianity, the rationalistic polemic—a deduction of the Christian dogma, the attack against the Talmud—the accusation that it is heretical, and the use of Jewish tradition against the Jews—the use of postbiblical Jewish sources to prove the veracity of Christianity. See Amos Funkenstein, "Basic Types of Christian Anti-Jewish Polemics in the Later Middle Ages," *Viator* 2 (1971): 373–82. I suggest that this use of the Jewish ritual for polemical purposes is another phase in the history of the Jewish-Christian debate.

71. As far as I know the term has never been used in scholarly discussion of ethnography. Many works deal with the biased nature of Western ethnographies of other peoples, but usually they have emphasized the Eurocentric character of these ethnographies, and only rarely have they touched upon the polemical aspects of this literature. In my opinion the study of the ethnographic literature, especially that of the early modern period, with the focus on its polemical character, could be very fruitful.

72. Even if the term applies to ethnographic literature in general, there are, as I have shown, some crucial differences between the ethnographic literature about the Jews and the ethnographic literature about other nations that one needs to keep in mind while comparing them to each other.

73. See note 51.

74. Alberti's book brings the entire text of Hess's *Flagellum Iudeorum* but adds a lot of information to it. Altogether, Hess's book is only about a quarter of Alberti's book.

75. The title page of the book was lost, and this title is taken from the second page. The only known copy of the book is at the British Museum Library (1412. e. 19). I thank Maria Diemling for providing me a copy of the book. The book was published again in German in 1550 with the title *Juden Büchlein*. A Latin version appeared in 1509 under the title *Opus aureum*; and see Diemling, "'Christliche Ethnographien,'" 14–16.

76. On the title page only the initials C. G. C. appear, but according to the catalog of the library of Hebrew Union College in Cincinnati the author is Christian Gustav Christoph.

77. As the title of the book states, this is a revised and corrected edition of Kirchner's book. Since Jungendres not only added notes and references but also made extensive changes to Kirchner's work and discussed new subjects, I deal with it as a different book. For the differences between Kirchner's book and Jungendres' edition, see Elisheva Carlebach, *Divided Souls: Converts from Judaism in Germany, 1500–1750* (New Haven: Yale University Press, 2001), 205–10.

78. In this book the name of the author is written with a Y, Mayer. However, the same author wrote the book *Der heutigen Juden Ceremonien und Gebräuche,* but in the latter case the name that appears on the title page is Majer.

10
The "Jewish Quaker": Christian Perceptions of Sabbatai Zevi as an Enthusiast

Michael Heyd

In the spring of 1666, as reports concerning Sabbatai Zevi and the Sabbatian movement began to spread in Europe, several pamphlets appeared in German, Dutch, and later in Polish, that reported on the way Sabbatai Zevi was perceived by Christians and Moslems: "The Christians and Turks take him for an impostor, a Turkish [Moslem] or a Jewish Quaker and this whole affair as a temptation or a sign of the End of Days [The Day of Judgment] and although according to both, great things would happen, they nevertheless say that he is another Mohammed, Simon Magus or a Sorcerer."[1] It may not be surprising that Moslems and Christians viewed Sabbatai Zevi as an impostor though this designation also needs some comment, to which I shall return below.[2] More surprising is the characterization of Sabbatai Zevi as a "Jewish Quaker." The Quakers, one should remember, were, in the early stages of their development, a typical millenarian, indeed, radical and revolutionary movement. They continued to be seen as such by their opponents well after the end of the revolution in England. However, the very analogy drawn between Sabbatai Zevi and the Quakers is itself highly significant. It opens up a vista into the Christian perceptions of Sabbatai Zevi and the way he and his movement were linked with other Christian millenarian and "enthusiastic" movements in that period.

In the past twenty years historians have become increasingly aware of the links between Christian and Jewish millenarians, largely owing to the work of Michael McKeon, Richard Popkin, David Katz, Ernestine van der Wall, Jacob Barnai, and others.[3] In recent years some attention has also been paid to the Christian opponents of Sabbatai Zevi. Yet here one must make a distinction between two dimensions that will also underlie the present discussion: first the Jewish-Christian polemics and the role Sabbatai Zevi played in these polemics from 1666 onward, indeed, well into the eighteenth century; and second, the use of Sabbatai Zevi in intra-Christian debates, especially the ongoing polemics with the various radical sects, including the so-called enthusiasts, various Christian millenarians, and particularly the Quakers and Pietists. The first dimension, the role of Sabbatai Zevi in the Christian-Jewish debates, is fascinating and has already gained some attention.[4] Indeed, the Sabbatai Zevi phenomenon may in some respects have transformed the traditional Christian-Jewish debate. Yet my focus in this chapter will be on the second dimension, the role Sabbatai Zevi played in intra-Christian controversies. On this subject, apart from a few pertinent and important remarks by Richard Popkin, largely confined to the English scene, little has been studied so far.[5]

The central argument of this essay is that the extensive Christian references to Sabbatai Zevi and the Sabbatian phenomenon in the period between 1666 and the early eighteenth century should not be seen only in the context of Christian-Jewish debates. Christian reactions to Sabbatai Zevi were also part of another sort of debate within the Christian camp. This debate was conducted between established intellectuals and clergymen on the one hand and those who challenged their status—millenarians, mystics, and "enthusiasts" on the other. Since many of the millenarians and alleged messiahs of the time, including Sabbatai Zevi, also challenged the secular authorities, this was a confrontation with obvious political as well as purely religious connotations. The Jewish messiah from Smyrna thus played a role in both the religious and political discourse in Europe of that period.

Furthermore, as will become apparent in what follows, the association of Sabbatai Zevi and Christian "enthusiasts" was made by reporters, pamphlet writers, theologians, and church historians all over Europe, from England in the West to Poland and Russia in the East, and in Germany as well as in France and Italy.[6] The extent of the reporting and "press coverage" of the Sabbatai Zevi affair in 1666 was quite astounding, and recent scholarship has started to uncover some of it.[7] The newspaper reporting was usually more descriptive and less polemical in nature. Nevertheless the pamphlets with lasting influence, those that would be quoted or republished again and again in the next generation, contained explicit analogies between Sabbatai Zevi and the Quakers and other "enthusiastic" movements.

The German *Beschreibung* pamphlet from which I quoted at the beginning of this essay is one version of a text that circulated throughout Europe in the spring of 1666. Since the reference to Sabbtai Zevi as a "Jewish Quaker" is not identical in all versions of that text, and since some of these pamphlets also included a picture of Sabbatai and his prophet Nathan of Gaza, which is itself meaningful, it is worthwhile to look at them more closely.

All these pamphlets were anonymous, and there are no indications of the place of publication, or a date more exact than 1666. It is hard to establish their exact chronology, but for reasons that will be set forth below, I tend to think that the German *Beschreibung* was the original, although written on the basis of information coming from Amsterdam. In addition to the short biography of Sabbatai Zevi from his birth to his journey from Smyrna to Constantinople, the *Beschreibung* included in its second part a list of some ten previous Jewish false messiahs from Bar-Kochba in 133 C.E. down to David Reuveni in the sixteenth century.[8] This pamphlet was followed by a *Continuation*, which reproduced some of the accounts of the Sabbatai Zevi affair, including a report about the imminent return of the Jews to their promised land and their expected subsequent conversion to Christianity; various letters that arrived in Amsterdam in March 1666 from Jerusalem, Smyrna, and other places; as well as a report of the French ambassador in Constantinople.[9]

The *Beschreibung* was probably the basis for two Dutch versions, one a broadside, the other a more extensive version published under the title *Historis Verhael*.[10] The broadside included a picture of Sabbatai Zevi and Nathan (Fig. 10.1), which in the longer *Historis Verhael* was cut in half, the figure of Sabbatai appearing on the title page and that of Nathan on on page 4. I shall return to the picture and its significance below. The text of the broadside was mostly a translation of the first part of the *Beschreibung*: a short report of the life of Sabbatai from his birth, focusing on the events in 1665. It also included the same sentence concerning the Christian and Turkish description of Sabbatai Zevi as a "Jewish Quaker."[11] The Dutch broadside added, however, a few sentences to the German version, probably based on information that arrived in the interim in the spring of 1666. Most notably, toward the end, after the reference to Sabbatai Zevi as a "Jewish Quaker," it added the news about his capture by the Turks on the way to Constantinople at the beginning of February 1666.[12]

The *Historis Verhael* is more detailed than both the German *Beschreibung* and the Dutch broadside. It included an extended introductory paragraph, some additional biographical information about Sabbatai (including his three wives and his travels to Jerusalem and Egypt), further details concerning the various miracles Sabbatai performed, and a longer account of the Jewish reactions to Sabbatai Zevi. As for the Moslem and Christian views of Sabbatai Zevi, the *Historis Verhael* also departed from both the Dutch broadside version and the German *Beschreibung*. It dealt with the Moslem views separately from the Christian reactions. For the Turks the paramount danger of Sabbatai Zevi was obviously a political one.[13] In dealing with the Christian reactions the text interjected a detailed account of the prophesying phenomena among Sabbatai's adherents in the Ottoman Empire.[14] The opening and next-to-closing sentences of the paragraph, however, are almost exactly parallel to those of the German pamphlet and the Dutch broadside, only here the focus is exclusively

10.1. "A Picture of the imaginary [or awaited], new Jewish King SABETHA SEBI, with his accompanying Prophet." A Dutch broadside published in the spring of 1666. Bibliotheca Rosenthaliana, Amsterdam.

on the Christian views of Sabbatai Zevi: "The Christians hold him [Sabbatai] mostly for an impostor, a Turkish or Jewish Quaker. . . . Indeed they consider this whole work of the Jews either as a temptation or a fore-sign for the Last Day. Others call him the second Mohammed, another Simon Magus or magician."[15] The ambivalence in judging the phenomena is more clearly related here to different views within the Christian camp, regarding the movement either as a sign of the approaching end of days or as a temptation while "others" see him as a second Mohammed, another Simon Magus, or a witch.[16]

The ambivalence of the two Dutch pamphlets with respect to Sabbatai Zevi is most noticeable, perhaps, in the picture above the broadside (Fig. 10.1), which also appeared, as we have seen, in two separate parts, in the *Historis Verhael*. In the background, to the left, Sabbatai sits on his donkey alongside Nathan. At the center the scene seems to allude to the anointing of David by Samuel (I Sam. 16:13) with Nathan holding the horn and pouring oil on Sabbatai, who kneels in front of him. On the right-hand side one sees the Jewish soldiers, who were in those months reported to have gathered in Arabia.[17] What is important for our purposes, however, is that the picture is by no means hostile. Indeed it depicts the messianic hopes or fantasies from the point of view of the Jews. This is especially striking if one bears in mind the traditional theme of the *Judensau*, the Jewish sow, and the fact that from the Middle Ages onward Christians depicted the messiah of the Jews as riding on such a sow rather than on a donkey.[18] In fact it may not be accidental that a book carrying one of the most famous of these depictions, Dietrich Schwab's *Detectum velum Mosaicum*, was republished in that year.[19] Yet that engraving, titled "The Messianic Procession," contained no explicit reference to Sabbatai Zevi while the German and Dutch broadsheets which did refer to Sabbatai that year did not incorporate the theme of the *Judensau*.[20] This seems to indicate that in 1666 at least there were no demonological connotations to the Christian reactions to Sabbatai Zevi. Moreover, in texts such as the *Historis Verhael*, the possibility that Sabbatai's appearance may actually be a foresign of the coming millennium was not completely absent.[21]

The Dutch versions discussed above were not the only translations of the German *Beschreibung* and its *Umbständliche Continuation*. Three Polish pamphets on Sabbatai Zevi were recently discovered in the British Library by Hanna Swiderska and analyzed by Michal Galas. Two of these pamphlets are clearly based on the German ones. In the first of them, as in the German and Dutch versions, Sabbatai Zevi is described as "a Turkish impostor or a Jewish Quaker." The author hastens to add that he himself "cannot easily ignore and condemn them [the Jews] since many honourable men and martyrs shared the same belief" in the coming of the messianic kingdom on earth.[22] In the second part of the pamphlet, as in the *Beschreibung*, there is a list of Jewish messiahs from Bar-Kochba in 133 C.E. up to Sabbatai. The second pamphlet claims to be a continuation of the first and, like the German *Continuation*, includes various letters and writings about Sabbatai during late 1665 and early 1666. The third pamphlet is a combined German and Polish text, *Wunderlicher Anfang und Schmählicher Aussgang Des Jüdischen Königes Sabetha Sebi,* reporting on the events of the first few months of 1666 (including the battle between Sabbatai's forces and those of the Turks and his alleged excecution).[23] These pamphlets traveled still further east. As Daniel Clarke Waugh has shown, they were used by the Ukraine Orthodox monk Haliatovs'kyi in his anti-Jewish polemic, and parts of the *Beschreibung* were translated into Muscovite (Russian). Yet, significantly enough, the reference to Sabbatai Zevi as a "Jewish Quaker" was omitted from the Russian version.[24] Whereas for the Poles the analogy with the Quakers was apparently meaningful, this was not the case as far away as Moscow.

All these pamphlets, in their various versions and translations, not only testify to the widespread European reactions to Sabbatai Zevi in 1666, but they also indicate that the analogy between Sabbatai and the Quakers was geographically widespread. The purpose of the comparison seems to be to give the reader a better orientation concerning the phenomenon of Sabbatai Zevi by explaining the relatively faraway and exotic in terms of an association to a phenomenon closer to home, namely the Quakers. Nevertheless the criticism of the Quakers themselves implied by such a comparison is unmistakable. All over Europe, Sabbatianism was seen from the start as a sort of an "enthusiastic" movement, similar to contemporary Christian movements like the Quakers.

* * *

The term *enthusiasm* was ascribed to various millenarian, charismatic, and radical phenomena in the seventeenth century, and it is indeed highly significant that Sabbatai Zevi and the Sabbatian movement were seen as yet one more example of such "enthusiasm."[25] This becomes clear from another group of contemporary reports that drew an analogy between Sabbatai Zevi and his followers and various groups of Christian enthusiasts. The French Jesuit Jacques Becherand, stationed in Constantinople, wrote several letters in Italian and French during October–November 1666.[26] In these letters he described the earlier prophetic ecstasies of 120 (or 700–800!) Jewish women in the following words: . . . "It was a most amazing spectacle, and at the same time, a very ridiculous one, to see for many months some hundred and twenty Jewish women pretend to be filled with the spirit of this new prophet, and who, in order to prove that the more brilliantly, act as crazed, and affect to imitate the extravagant enthusiasms of our possessed, some of whom one had to bind and beat well and strong, in order to free them from that turbulent spirit, of which they claimed to have received the license for such madness."[27] While comparing these Jewish ecstasies to the features of Christian enthusiasm, Becherand nevertheless hinted at the faked character of the bodily symptoms of the Jewish pretenders to prophecy.[28] The element of imposture was indeed critical in most of the Christian perceptions of the Sabbatian movement. I shall return to this point below.

One of the more reliable although less widespread accounts of the Sabbatai Zevi story was that of the Dutch Reformed pastor in Smyrna, Thomas Coenen.[29] Writing in early 1667 but publishing only in 1669, Coenen made the comparison between the Sabbatian movement and the Quakers even more explicit than the pamphlets surveyed above. He made this comparison in connection with the prophesying movement in Smyrna in December 1665. His description of the prophesying phenomena is itself extremely interesting, especially in terms of the stress he put on the participation of women and children, a feature that was also emphasized in so many of the accounts of other prophesying movements in Europe at that time.[30] This description ends with an explicit comparison with the English Quakers: "To say the truth, at that time one heard nothing but of the multitude of prophets and prophetesses. And indeed, this work was nothing but a trick of the devil who took pleasure in hitting this stubborn and stiff-necked people with greater blindness, or [better say] that a seeming truth was mixed with much falsehood: one could notice enough the affectation, just as [in the case of] the Quakers in England."[31] Beyond the specific comparison to English Quakers, these lines are significant in the explanation they offer of the prophesying phenomena and their physical manifestations. Coenen gives a diabolical interpretation of these prophesying phenomena and at the same time sees them as artifice. Within one sentence he suggests two alternative explanations of the visions, convulsions, and other bodily symptoms of the prophets and prophetesses. The diabolical explanation was a standard one for the various symptoms of "enthusiasts" in the seventeenth century.[32] An alternative explanation was that of artificial "make-believe," an account to which Coenen seems to incline and which ties in with the designation of Sabbatai Zevi as an impostor. A third interpretation hinted at by Coenen a few lines earlier is the clinical explanation. Referring to Sabbatai's visit to Pegna's house and to the prophesying of Pegna's daughters, Coenen described their convulsions and the foam over their lips like mad persons ("schuym-betzten als besetene") in the manner of all other prophets ("nae de manier van alle de andere Propheten").[33] He did not mention explictily, however, the falling sickness, alluded to by the Dutch pamphlet, the *His-*

toris Verhael dealt with above, and on the whole seemed to prefer the impostor or diabolical explanation to the clinical one.

It is true that even within these paragraphs there is a clear anti-Jewish dimension along with an "anti-Quaker" or "anti-enthusiast" one. Coenen referred to the "stiff-necked and obdurate" people ("verstockte en de verherde volck"), whom Satan takes pleasure in deluding.[34] Nevertheless the analogies with Christian prophets and enthusiasts are unmistakable. No less important is another theme that is crucial to my argument: critical as Coenen was of the supporters of Sabbatai Zevi and even indebted as he was to traditional stereotypes concerning the Jews, Coenen did not hide his implied support of those rabbis and members of the Jewish establishment who opposed Sabbatai Zevi. Toward the end of chapter 4, after recounting the story about Sabbatai (by now a Moslem) promising to turn the Portuguese synagogue into a mosque, Coenen added these highly significant lines:

Whether these stories are true or not, I do not wish to determine. Yet his [Sabbatai's] innovative proposals and cunning tricks in order to attract the people to him, the reading of the Name of God, against the custom of the Jews, the sacrilegious breaking of the Sabbath, his promises to give a new Law, and finally, the lighthearted [rash] forsaking of the religion [God's worship] of his forefathers, all make it clear enough that he by no means was of a fine stock ("fijnste slagh"); also that in all this business he did not aim at [have before him] the honor of God, but at his own honor and greatness.[35]

Not only is this passage strikingly similar to many parallel pronouncements, *mutatis mutandis*, against prophets, Messiahs, and "enthusiasts" in the Christian world, but even more signficant is Coenen's implicit sympathy, not to say identification with, the point of view of the Jewish Orthodox establishment, including its insistence on the Torah, halakha, the Sabbath, and the religion of their forefathers. Alongside the explicit Christian-Jewish confrontation we have here an implicit but far more interesting confrontation of the viewpoint of a religious establishment—whether Christian or Jewish—and the charismatic, messianic, and antinomian forces that challenge it.

One further remark concerning Coenen: as Kaplan had shown, Coenen learned much of his anti-Jewish polemics from his former theology teacher at Leiden, Johannes Hoornbeek, whose book *Tesjubat Jehuda* was a fierce critique of Judaism in general and the Kabbalah in particular.[36] Less known is the fact that Hoornbeek also wrote a vast polemical treatise, *Summa Controversiarum Religionis*, against various theological opponents, in which he devoted the third book, close to two hundred pages, to a debate with various "enthusiasts."[37] From the Montanists of the first century to the Anabaptists of Münster, continuing with the Paracelsians, as well as Weigel and his disciples, Hoornbeek was concerned above all with millenarians like the Rosicrucians, who wished to establish a divine kingdom on earth. Writing in the mid-1650s, he was not yet cognizant of the challenge of the Quakers. As for the Jews, he was aware of their messianic expectations, eagerly waiting for the "coming of Elijah." Nevertheless he did not elaborate on this, not considering it a pressing danger.[38] Some ten years later the situation would change dramatically, and Hoornbeek's student Thomas Coenen picked up the challenge. Indeed, it was largely under Hoornbeek's instigation, just before he died, that Coenen decided to write his account of the Sabbatai Zevi affair.[39]

Yosef Kaplan has correctly noticed that Coenen was careful not to engage in explicit debate with the various enthusiasts in his own country, the United Provinces.[40] Therefore, in addition to the Jews and the Jewish followers of Sabbatai Zevi, he aimed his arrows at Roman Catholics (including monks and papal emissaries) who tended to be impressed by the Sabbatian claims. The only Protestants he mentioned, and to whom he compared Sabbatai's followers, were the English Quakers. However, the implicit debate with the enthusiasts in Holland itself is obvious throughout the text, and as a disciple of Hoornbeek and writing at his instigation, he clearly continued his mentor's polemics with the radical enthusiasts, even if the primary aim of the book was directed at the Jews.

The use of Sabbatai Zevi in the debate with the Quakers and enthusiasts was more explicit in the text that became the most widespread and quoted of the various accounts of Sabbatai Zevi, that of the famous English diarist and member of the Royal Society John Evelyn, who published in 1669 the account of the affair written by Paul Rycaut, the English consul in Smyrna.[41] Evelyn obtained the manuscript from Rycaut through the mediation of Lord Henry Howard and published it together with the accounts of two other impostors, Padre Ottomano and Mahomed Bei, written by Pietro Cesii.[42] The coupling of Sabbatai Zevi with two other impostors who converted either from Islam to Christianity or from Christianity to Islam is highly significant.[43] No less significant is the title of the publication, which clearly alludes to the legendary text *De tribus impostoribus*.[44] The term *impostor* (or *Betrüger*) had been previously used in various pamphlets published in 1666 (as has been shown above), but in Evelyn's text it is given obvious prominence and set within a political context that implies tacit identification with the legitimate authority of the Turkish Sultan, which all three impostors had either allegedly forsaken (Mahomet Bei) or openly challenged (Padre Ottomano and Sabbatai Zevi).[45]

In his preface "To the Reader," Evelyn ingeniously combined anti-Jewish motifs ("that *obstinate* and *miserable* People") with both the standard rhetoric about conversion and an explicit reference to contemporary "enthusiasts" in England:

You have at the end of the last Impostor *an* Account *of the* Jews Exile *out of that Vast* Empire *of* Persia, *happening but the other day; which, together with the miscarriage of their late* Messiah *(the* Twenty-Fifth *Pretender to it (as I am credibly inform'd, it stands in their own* Records)) *might, one would think, at last open the* Eyes, *and, turne the* hearts *of that* obstinate *and* miserable People: *But whil'st the* Time *not yet* Accomplish'd, *I could wish our modern* Enthusiasts, *and other prodigious* Sects *amongst us, who Dreame of the like* Carnal Expectations, *and a* Temporal Monarchy, *might seriously weigh how nearly their* Characters *approach the* Style *and* Design *of these* Deluded Wretches, *least they fall into the* same Condemnation, *and the Snare of the Devil.*[46]

The Sabbatai Zevi story itself was written by Rycaut, who was later to publish it in the 1680 edition of his *History of the Turkish Empire*. Rycaut in turn relied largely on Coenen for information, since he was in England during the critical months of the Sabbatai Zevi affair and returned to Smyrna only in May 1667. Rycaut similarly referred to contemporary Christian millenarians and, indeed, regarded them as relevant background and even as an explanation for the emergence of Sabbatai Zevi and his movement:

According to the Predictions of several *Christian* Writers, especially of such who Comment on the *Apocalyps,* or Revelations, this Year of 1666 was to prove a Year of Wonders, of strange Revolutions in the World, and particularly of Blessing to the *Jewes*, either in respect of their Conversion to the *Christian* Faith, or of their Restoration to their Temporal Kingdome: This Opinion was so dilated, and fixt in the Countreys of the Reformed Religion, and in the Heads of Phanatical *Enthusiasts*, who Dreamed of a Fift [sic] Monarchy, the downfall of the *Pope*, and *Antichrist*, and the Greatness of the *Jewes:* In so much, that this subtile People judged this Year the time to stir, and to fit their Motion according to the season of the Modern Prophesies.[47]

Like Coenen, Evelyn and Rycaut tended to give a demonological interpretation to the Sabbatian movement: "For thus farr had God permitted the devil to delude this people, that their very children were for a time possessed, and voices heard to sound from their stomacks, and intrails: those of riper years fell first into a trance, foamed at the mouth, and recounted the future prosperitie, and deliverance of the *Israelites,* their visions of the *Lion* of *Judah,* and the triumphs of *Sabatai,* all which were certainly true, being effects of *Diabolical* delusions: as the *Jews* themselves since have confessed unto me."[48] What is most significant for us, however, is Rycaut's suggestion in the last sentence that the Jews were themselves critical of Sabbatai Zevi and his followers and attributed diabolical origins to the movement. Indeed, Rycaut repeatedly stressed the distinction between the popular beliefs of the Jews and the opposition of the elite, the *Chochams,* as he called them: "In the heat of all this Talk and Rumor, comes *Sabatai Sevi* to *Smyrna,* the City of his Nativity, infinitely desir'd there by the common *Jewes*: but by the *Chochams,* or *Doctors* of their *Law,* who gave little or no credence to what he pretended, was ill receiv'd, not knowing what mischief or ruine this Doctrine and Prophesie of a New Kingdome might produce."[49] After recounting the events in Constantinople, following Sabbatai's imprisonment, Rycaut added: "However some of the *Jewes* remain'd in their Wits all this time, amongst which was a certain *Chochan* [sic] at *Smyrna*, one zealous of his Law, and of the good and safety of his Nation."[50] As in the case of Coenen, so with Evelyn and Rycaut, the thrust of the argument was not merely anti-Jewish but against millenarian and messianic expectations in both Christian and Jewish society. At one point, discussing Jewish beliefs concerning Elijah, Rycaut drew an analogy with popular beliefs and "superstitions" rather than with "enthusiasm": "This being the common Opinion amongst the *Jewes*, and that *Sabatai Sevi* was the *Messiah*, being become an Article of Faith, it was not hard to perswade them, that *Elias* was come already, that they met him in their Dishes, in the darke, in their Bedchambers, or anywhere else invisible, in the same manner as our common people in *England* believe of *Hobgoblins*, and *Fairies*."[51] Alongside the critique of popular beliefs among both Christians and Jews, one can identify in the Evelyn-Rycaut text an impicit sense of solidarity between the Christian elite (political, religious, and intellectual) and that part of the Jewish elite that opposed Sabbatai Zevi. As in the case of Coenen, the Sabbatai Zevi story served more than the purposes of Christian-Jewish controversy (with the accompanying traditional aim of converting the Jews). Though this may have been the primary purpose of both Coenen and Evelyn-Rycaut, another controversy served as a subtext, the controversy with the Quakers and various "enthusiasts" in the Christian camp itself. And as with Coenen, so with Evelyn and Rycaut, the dividing line on this issue cut across religious differences, separating the "establishment" (whether ministers, political authorities, or some of the rabbis) from the superstitious and fanatic crowd, who blindly followed the impostors, enthusiasts, false prophets, or false messiahs.

Evelyn-Rycaut's account of Sabbatai Sevi became the most widespread in the following generations; it was reprinted innumerable times, well into the eighteenth century.[52] In the years immediately after 1669, however, interest in Sabbatai Zevi seems to have subsided. With the exception of the French translation of Evelyn, which appeared in 1673, and Rycaut's *History of the Turkish Empire*, in which the Sabbatai Zevi story was included, little was published in the next fourteen years.[53] This lull might reflect an abatement of interest in millenarian phenomena in general in the 1670s. By the early 1680s, however, interest seems to have revived. This renewed interest in Sabbatai Zevi and in Jewish false messiahs may have been occasioned by the appearance of a new pretended messiah, Rabbi Mordechai of Eisenstadt, around 1682.[54] Thus Evelyn's text was republished in 1683. In Germany during that same year Sabbatai Zevi was included in the list of false messiahs in Johannes Lent's influential

*Schediasma historico-philologicum de Judaeorum Pseudo-mesiis.*⁵⁵ Indeed, Lent ended his list with Rabbi Mordechai.⁵⁶ A similar "list" of Jewish false messiahs appeared in Italy that year in Giulio Morosini's *Via Della Fede mostrata a'gli Ebrei*, but he focused only on Bar-Kochba as the first on the list and Sabbatai Sevi as the last.⁵⁷ Finally, Rocoles's well-known *Les imposteurs insignes*, which included a chapter on Sabbatai Zevi based both on Evelyn-Rycaut and on Coenen, was published in 1683 as well.⁵⁸ Yet, interestingly enough, in none of these writings was there an explicit connection made between Sabbatai Zevi and similar millenarian or "enthusiastic" movements in the Christian camp. Indeed, Rocoles mentioned the comparison of Sabbatai Zevi to Mahomet or to Simon Magus, but not to the Quakers.⁵⁹ Nevertheless the fact that Sabbatai was included in his long list of impostors (though in Rocoles's case, most of them were political in nature, rather than religious or messianic) indicates that Sabbatai continued to intrigue Christian intellectuals, and not only within the context of an anti-Jewish debate.

Sabbatai Zevi was brought back into the context of the intra-Christian controversies in the early years of the eighteenth century, first in Germany, and later, once again, in England. In Germany, the years around 1700 were the years when the controversies concerning Pietism reached a climax, particularly following the publication in 1699–1700 of Gottfried Arnold's *Unparteyische Kirchen- und Ketzer-Historie*, a history of the Christian church and its various heterodoxies, written from a clear, even radical, Pietist perspective. Arnold's *Historie*, together with his other publications, as well as the writings of millenarian "enthusiasts" like Johann Wilhelm Petersen, elicited sharp rebuttals. The controversies flared up in Quedlinburg, a hotbed of radical Pietism, where Arnold resided, spreading to the Electorate of Saxony itself and to its surroundings.⁶⁰ It is within this heated context that the next chapter in our story takes place: Johann Friedrich Corvinus, a conservative Lutheran minister from Hornburg in Halberstadt, not far from Quedlinburg, was one of Arnold's chief opponents.⁶¹ In 1702, a year after writing against Arnold, Corvinus published a vast compilation of texts titled *Anabaptisticum et Enthusiasticum Pantheon und Geistliches Rüst-Haus Wider die Alten Quacker/ und Neuen Frey-Geister*.⁶² It is indeed an arsenal of texts, many of them published before, against the Anabaptists, Millenarians, Weigelians, free spirits, and, above all, the Quakers and the Pietists. Within this collection Corvinus also published the Evelyn-Rycaut account of Sabbatai Zevi under the title "The History of the Great Impostor and False Messiah, Sabbatai Zevi, King of the Jews."⁶³ The text appears among the "special tracts" (Absonderliche Tractaten) at the end of the collection. Interestingly enough, it follows right after a tract dealing with four "new philosophers," Descartes, Hobbes, Spinoza, and Bekker, who were considered dangerous "free spirits."⁶⁴ As I have shown elsewhere, Descartes was indeed often regarded as an "enthusiast" by conservative critics in the second half of the seventeenth century.[65] The proximity of the Sabbatai Zevi story to accounts of these four philosophers, nowadays considered the founders of modern rationalist thought, is highly significant. In the eyes of conservative Lutheran theologians like Corvinus, they presented the same type of challenge to the religious order.

Corvinus added a few introductory lines at the beginning of Rycaut's text, in which he apologized for bringing up this well-known—more precisely "notorious" (*ruchbar*)—story once again. Nevertheless, he believed that the details and lessons one should draw from it justify its repetition.[66] The lessons were made explicit, indeed, in the verses that conclude the Rycaut account: "The Jewish example shows, how quickly half the world, when just one fool springs up, falls for that folly of his."[67] Then follow descriptions typical of the "enthusiasts" of the period: those who interpret dreams without the use of manuals, those who predict the future, claim to have direct divine revelations, pretend to be divine men (Göttes-Mann), perform miracles, and those who turn lies into seeming truth, carrying with them half the world. The warning to Christians is clearly not to follow such examples as that of Sabbatai Zevi:

When just a Sabatai comes now into the light
How many Christian people would he not seduce?
Oh! Christians! Don't go astray
Let the fools remain fools!
Leave this world to the Jews: You shall inherit heaven![68]

Sabbatianism was obviously viewed as a threat to Christians, a threat of which they had to beware.

Sabbatai Zevi figured in other texts in the Corvinus collection as well. Thus the fifth text among the "Special Tracts" in the volume was Johann Christoph Müller's *Greuel der Falschen Messien*.[69] As its title indicates, it included a list of sixty-four false messiahs since the beginning of the world, mostly Christian, but including Sabbatai Zevi (no. 61) as well as Moslem impostors. The last on the list was Oliger (or Holger) Pauli (or Paulli), a Dane by origin and a Christian "Judaizer," who claimed to have had a Jewish grandfather from the house of David. Paulli was active in Holland in the preceding years, claiming to be a messiah and king of the Jews and propagating his ideas about the imminent conversion of the Jews, the union between Jews and Christians, the establishment of a Jewish kingdom in Palestine, and the rebuilding of Jerusalem by 1720. Indeed, Paulli was the instigation for Müller in writing his tract.[70] The combination of a pretension to messianism with political, almost proto-Zionist, schemes made Paulli's case similar to that of

Sabbatai Zevi. Not by chance did Corvinus include Paulli's story right after the tract on Sabbatai Zevi and before the tract by Müller.[71] Once again we see how Sabbatai Zevi was viewed within the broader context of false messiahs, Christian, Moslem, and Jewish.

This point is made even more explicit in the next tract in the Corvinus collection, the anonymous *Erschröckliche Brüderschafft der Alten und Neuen Widertäuffer/Quäcker/Schwärmer und Frey-Geister/mit Denen Heil- und Gottlosen Juden* (1702).[72] Indeed, this text is a good example of the incorporation of the reactions to Sabbatai Zevi within intra-Christian polemics. It essentially consists of long lists of erroneous articles of faith of the Anabaptists, the Quakers, and, of course, the Jews, systematically comparing the errors of the Jews to those of the Quakers. The main focus, or at least the most interesting one for our purposes, is the similarity between the Jews and the Quakers in the expectations of a millenarian Kingdom of God here on earth. The Sabbatai Zevi phenomenon, and that of Jewish false messiahs in general, is taken as the epitome of the Jewish mixing of heaven and earth.[73] Yet, once again, the author of the text also mentions the Jewish rabbis who were critics of these false messiahs: "Their Rabbis put the target [date] of the coming of the Messiah very far from the present, by saying: God has indicated a certain time for the coming of the Messiah; the time, however, has not yet come, but, should this time come, the Messiah would arrive as well."[74] For all the strong anti-Jewish thrust of this tract, a distinction is nevertheless made between the false messiahs with their followers and the circumspect rabbis. Furthermore, the Jewish messianic expectations, as well as the Jewish false messiahs themselves, are mentioned in order to criticize the various Christian types of false messianisms, whether Quaker, Free-Spirits or others: "The Quakers, Free-Spirits and other Enthusiasts do not only give them [the Jewish false Messiahs] a good reason for that [claim], but pose themselves as the Messiah."[75] Included in the list of Christian false messiahs mentioned in the above text is the Quaker James Nayler. Indeed, one of the most interesting elements in the Corvinus Collection is a picture that precedes the above tract, showing Sabbatai Zevi side by side with Nayler, the famous Quaker revolutionary figure who allegedly claimed to be the Messiah in 1657 (Fig. 10.2).[76] The picture is titled "Die Grossen Ertz Betriger" (The Great Arch-Impostors). On the left side one sees "der falsche Messias Jacob Naylor, König der Quacker Im 1657 Jahr" (the false Messiah James Nayler, King of the Quakers in the year 1657). On the right hand side appears the figure of "der falsche Messias Sabatai-Sevi König der Juden Im 1666 Jahr" (the false Messiah Sabbatai Sevi, King of the Jews in the year 1666). In between them, there is a table covered with a cloth on which is written the significant term "Monarchia Nova" (New Monarchy) with the symbols of kingship associated with James Nayler. On the right sleeve of Nayler's coat is written, "Quäker

10.2. "The Great Arch-Impostors" Jacob Naylor and Sabatai Sevi. A woodcut print included in Johann Friedrich Corvinus, ed., *Anabaptisticum et Enthusiasticum Pantheon und Geistliches Rüst-Hauss Wider die Alten Quacker/ und Neuen Frey-Geister* (1702).

Bossheit" (Quaker Malice), on his left sleeve "Ehraetz" and "frey-geister" (ambitious and free spirit). On the right sleeve of Sabbatai Zevi's coat appears the word "Talmud" and on the left "Alcoran." The verse at the bottom reads:

This is how Nayler in his right costume looks,
Who in the Occident has been made the Quakers' King

and this is SABATAI whom in the Orient
the whole of Jewry, a Messiah made.⁷⁷

The coupling of Sabbatai Zevi and James Nayler is interesting for several reasons. Not only is it a dramatic illustration of the designation of Sabbatai Zevi as a "Jewish Quaker" with which I have started this essay. It also indicates how Sabbatai Zevi was used by Christian critics in order to further their own interpretation of "enthusiasm" in general and Quakerism in particular. The most recent historian of James Nayler argues that Nayler's famous entry into Bristol on a donkey in October 1656 was by no means intended as a messianic act.⁷⁸ Nayler acted the part of Christ rather than claiming to be the Messiah, the actual Christ, himself. Indeed, argued Nayler, every true Christian was Christ, in his suffering and regeneration. Nayler's opponents, however, did not understand or did not accept this interpretation of his actions. They saw him as a radical millenarian and a serious political threat.⁷⁹ The appearance of Sabbatai Zevi a few years later was linked with Nayler's entrance into Bristol precisely in order to confirm this political-messianic interpretation, according to which both Nayler and Sabbatai wished to establish "a New Monarchy" (Monarchia Nova) here on earth. In this respect Sabbatianism confirmed in a roundabout way the worst fears of mainstream Christians with respect to their fellow Christian "enthusiasts."

Thus, while the explicit theme in Christian discussions of Sabbatai Zevi was anti-Jewish polemics, a no less significant subtext running throughout the Corvinus volume was the warning to Christians themselves, and the placing of the Sabbatai Zevi story within this collection of anti-Anabaptist, anti-Quaker, and anti-Pietist texts makes this subtheme all the more significant historically speaking. In the eyes of conservative Lutherans like Corvinus, Sabbatai Zevi was seen, together with the Anabaptists, Quakers, Pietists, and even some new philosophers, as a serious danger to the religious as well as the sociopolitical order.

A few years later, across the Channel in England, the Sabbatai Zevi story was once again employed for the purpose of intra-Christian polemics, this time, against the so-called French Prophets, those enthusiasts among the Huguenot refugees who arrived in England in 1706, following the failure of the Camisard revolt.⁸⁰ I am referring to a tract titled "The Devil of Delphos; or, the Prophets of Baal" (1708).⁸¹ The text consisted once again of a list of some three dozen false prophets, false messiahs, and impostors, almost all of them Christian, beginning with Cerinthus and Montanus, including several Roman Catholic saints, Anabaptists like John of Leyden and David Joris, as well as Mahomet and some political impostors. The longest chapter, however, was devoted to Sabbatai Zevi and essentially reproduced the Evelyn-Rycaut text.⁸²

Yet the opening paragraph written by the anonymous author-compiler is worth quoting in full:

I the more willingly give the Reader the History of this Impostor, because it borders very much on the same Ground with the Pretensions of our *Prophets*. For the *Messiah* which the *Jews* expect, has been a great Snare to them, and produc'd as many Warnings of his Coming, as the *Christian* Notion of the Return of Christ to live and reign a Thousand Years on earth, and call home the *Jews,* and build a new *Jerusalem*. They both seem to have the same Source, and to be indeed the same Thing, and have both produc'd abundance of Impostors, that have for a while abus'd the People, and made a Noise in the World; among all which this of *Sabatai Sevi* is one of the most Famous.[83]

What is significant here is the explicit comparison of Jewish messianism and Christian millenarianism, which in the view of the author are "the same thing" and have the same source, namely the devil, and the place of Sabbatai Zevi as one of the most famous among such messianic impostors. By situating him within such a list, the anonymous author clearly placed him and the Sabbatian movement within a much broader religious context. The lesson to be drawn from his story was also explicitly aimed at Christian millenarians, such as the French "Prophets" and their English supporters in 1707–8. As in previous texts mentioned, an analogy was drawn between the prophesying that had taken place in Smyrna in December 1665—with their related physical symptoms—and the prophesying of the French prophets in 1707–08. The author's conclusion was clear: "This last Paragraph is worth the serious perusal of our Modern Prophets, and those who are inclin'd to give them any Credit; the Devil did the same in those *Jews*, which they wou'd persuade us is done by the Holy Spirit of God in them, tho' their Cause is much the same, and their Message extreamly like that of *Sabatai*."[84] Once again, in both the Sabbatian case and that of the French prophets the cause of the convulsions, visions, and prophesying was attributed to the devil. While the leaders (whether Sabbatai Zevi or the French prophets who came from the Cévennes) were impostors, the ecstasies of their followers, though genuine, were nevertheless diabolically induced.

This brings us to the question of the explanations given for the Sabbatai Zevi phenomenon by Christian critics. Indeed, the two predominant ones were those of imposture and demoniacal influences. The two were by no means mutually exclusive; as the various texts (from Coenen and Evelyn in 1669 to *The Devil of Delphos* in 1708) testify, Christian critics tended to combine the two explanations. In the case of the anonymous author of *The Devil of Delphos*, a distinction is implied between the imposture of Sabbatai Zevi himself and the delusions, convulsions, and prophesying of his supporters, which were caused by the devil. Seen in the broader context of the explanations given for the phenomenon of "enthusiasm" in the late seventeenth and early eighteenth centuries, several distinctive features emerge, which are worth noting. To begin with, while a medical account of enthusiasm, convulsions, and even alleged prophecy had become increasingly common during that period,[85] it is hardly manifest in the accounts concerning Sabbatai Zevi. On the other hand the demonological account, which by the late seventeenth century was on the decline,[86] plays a rather prominent role in the reports concerning Sabbatai Zevi and his followers, from the contemporary ones down to the early eighteenth century. Still the references to the devil may not have to be taken too seriously. It is worth bearing in mind, as has been noted above, that in the numerous visual depictions of Sabbatai and Nathan, there seem to be hardly any allusions to the devil, so far as I have managed to see, and that even a traditional theme like that of the *Judensau* is relatively absent (with the exception of the eighteenth-century etching depicting Sabbatai Zevi and Jacob Melstinius and perhaps also the Schwab print of 1666, which might have *implicitly* referred to Sabbatai Zevi).[87] Nevertheless the numerous textual references to the devil and the lack of extended clinical explanations of the Sabbatian "craze" on the part of Christian writers point to a significant distinction between their attitudes toward Christian and Jewish "enthusiasm." When accounting for the phenomenon of Sabbatianism, the current critique of enthusiasm in general was grafted onto traditional anti-Jewish polemics. However, when it came to the threats posed by the Sabbatian movement, the similarities between Jewish and Christian enthusiasm come to the fore. From 1666 to 1708 the messianic claims of Sabbatai Zevi and his prophet Nathan were seen as a threat both to the religious order and to political stability. In this respect Sabbatianism was indeed similar to Anabaptism, Quakerism, Pietism, and, indeed, to the "Free-Spirits," philosophers like Descartes, Hobbes, and Spinoza. By comparing or linking Sabbatai Zevi to such phenomena, Christain critics, beginning with the anonymous authors of the various 1666 pamphlets, continuing with Coenen, Evelyn, Rycaut, Corvinus, and the anonymous editor of *The Devil of Delphos*, all saw him as a threat to the Christian religious order as well as to the Jewish one. Especially in 1666 and immediately after, this may have been partly the result of concrete links between Christian millenarians and Sabbatians, links that have been increasingly pointed out by historians in recent years.[88] On a deeper level Sabbatianism posed a challenge to the Christian order by claiming to link heaven and earth and to realize the Kingdom of God here and now. Finally, of course, the tragic (or would it be better to say, farcical) end of Sabbatai Zevi, if not of his movement, served as potent proof of the vanity and hollowness of such messianic claims. Beyond the obvious, and by no means negligible, interest in affirming the uniqueness of the historical Christ as the Messiah vis-à-vis the Jews, it was important to prove the same point vis-à-vis the various Christian "enthusiasts."

Yet no less significant than the religious dimension in Christian interpretations of Sabbatai Zevi was the political one. Here it is important, almost ironic, to note that European Christians like Coenen, Evelyn, Rycaut, and the anonymous authors of the various broadsides and pamphlets tended to defend what they regarded as legitimate political authority even if it was that of the Turkish Sultan and even in a period when some European powers, like Venice, were at war with the Ottoman Empire. Evelyn's pamphlet *Three Late Famous Impostors* is the most obvious case in point. If Sabbatai Zevi and the Sabbatian movement may be taken as one of the manifestations of the "general crisis of the seventeenth century," critics like Evelyn were clearly expressing the "struggle for stability" in that period.[89] The very concept of "impostor," and the company in which Sabbatai was discussed, not only by Evelyn but in the "lists" of pretenders and impostors such as that of Rocoles, similarly point to the political dimension of the threat he was thought to pose. Sabbatai Zevi was regarded as one further challenger to legitimate authority, one further pretender who wished to subvert the political order. The political dimension is evident not just in the writings of lay critics like Evelyn, Rycaut, and Rocoles but also in those of a Lutheran minister like Johann Friedrich Corvinus. Indeed the *Pantheon* opens with the various Imperial constitutions and edicts against Anabaptists and enthusiasts from 1529 onward.[90]

It is an open and interesting question whether the political motivations for relating the Sabbatai Zevi story became increasingly important in the course of the eighteenth century. Until about 1710, however, political factors can hardly be disentangled from religious ones since church and state were still very closely linked. Sabbatai Zevi was seen as yet another "enthusiast" who posed a challenge to the religious and political order, primarily Christian, but by implication also to the Jewish religious and social order, as even some Christian critics have hinted.

One final question needs to be raised: how traditional were these Christian critics of Sabbatai Zevi? I have tried to point elsewhere to a significant transformation in the critique of enthusiasm in the late seventeenth and early eighteenth century. There was an increasing stress on medical explanations of enthusiasm and on the role of human reason and the new experimental science as effective "antidotes" to it.[91] The critics of Sabbatai Zevi, it should be said, were on the whole more conservative and relied mostly on traditional arguments. Indeed, they were defending a traditional religious and political order that was based on the separation of heaven and earth, and they reacted fiercely against any wish to constitute an ideal kingdom here on earth. In fact, they may have sensed that this order was no longer that secure, and from our modern perspective considering the numerous intervening attempts to establish a utopian or millenarian political order, their insight can hardly be regarded as misguided. Yet, in linking, even including, Sabbatai Zevi with Christian "enthusiastic" phenomena, these critics boldly overstepped traditional confessional boundaries. Realizing that the confrontation with "enthusiasm" was not confined to the Christian camp, intellectuals and theologians like Coenen, Evelyn, Rycaut, and Corvinus combined two traditional discourses, the anti-Jewish polemic and the critique of millenarianism and enthusiasm.[92]

Still there is no denying that the principal theme running through the Christian reactions to Sabbatai Zevi is anti-Jewish polemic. Indeed, much remains to be done along these lines since the extent, both geographical and chronological, of these reactions is much greater than previously suspected by historians. The various "lists" of Jewish false messiahs compiled in the course of the seventeenth and eighteenth centuries are just one facet of this polemic. Neither can one deny the missionary purpose of much of this anti-Jewish polemic, which, as Elisheva Carlebach has recently pointed out, may have had considerable success.[93]

Nevertheless the purpose of the present essay has been to highlight a subtheme that is no less important, indeed, which may be even more interesting and significant historically speaking: the incorporation of the Sabbatai Zevi movement within the broader and more general phenomenon of religious "enthusiasm" and prophetic and millenarian movements in this period.[94] Here a fascinating realignment of forces begins to emerge, even if implicitly more than explicitly: a sense of identification or, at least, solidarity, between Lutheran, Anglican, and Reformed ministers and intellectuals on the one hand and Jewish rabbis on the other.[95] They all faced a common challenge, that of individuals who claimed to be messiahs or prophets and who had a host of ardent followers. Faced with this challenge, established ministers, intellectuals, and rabbis fell back upon Scripture, law, and tradition, whether Christian or Jewish. They were aware of this affinity: all the more so should their historians be.

Notes

This essay was written during a stay at the Center for Advanced Judaic Studies in Philadelphia in the spring term of 2000. I wish to thank most heartily the director of the Center, Professor David Ruderman, for inviting me as a fellow to this wonderful place, a scholar's paradise in many ways. It was his initiative that prompted me to turn systematically to this topic. I also wish to thank the very helpful staff of the center, particularly Etty Lassman and the librarian, Judith Leifer. An earlier version of this essay was presented to the seminar on Christian Hebraists at the center. The comments and reactions of the participants were extremely helpful for improving the essay, and I am very grateful to all of them; some specific acknowledgments will be mentioned in the course of the essay. Some initial research on this subject was started many years ago in another very congenial institute, the Institute for Advanced Study of the Hebrew University, Jerusalem. I also wish to thank the following libraries for their courteous help: Scholem Collection at the National and University Library, Jerusalem; Herzog August Bibliothek, Wolfenbüttel; Staatsbibliothek zu Berlin; Bibliotheca Rosenthaliana at the University Library of Amsterdam; Royal Library in the Hague; University Library, Utrecht; Zentralbibliothek in Zurich; British Library, London; Historical Society of Pennsylvania Library and the Van Pelt Library, University of Pennsylvania, both in Philadelphia; Hebrew Union College, Cincinnati; Eisenhauer Library at Johns Hopkins University, Baltimore; and Princeton University Library. Finally, thanks are due to Professor Itta Shedletzky, Dr. Piet van Boxel, and Ms. Leontine Veerman-Kaplan for their help in verifying some of the translations from German and Dutch. All remaining inaccuracies are of course solely my responsibility.

1. "Die Christen und Türcken halten denselben für einen Betrieger / einen Türckischen oder Jüdischen Quäcker / und das gantze Werck für eine Verführung / oder Zeichen des jüngsten Tages / und ob wol von beyden grosse Dinge geschehen seind / so sagen sie doch / dass es ein ander Mahomet, Simon Magus oder Zauberer sey." *Beschreibung Des Newen Jüdischen Königs Sabetha Sebi/ Dessen Ursprung/ Alter/ Gestalt/ Thun/ Lassen/ Anhang und Wunderwercke/ Wie auch Der Christen/ Juden/ Türcken und anderer Urtheil hierüber/ und was sonsten aus unterschiedlichen Schrifften darvon bis dato kund worden* (n.l., 1666), A ii v°. Copy of the Bibliotheca Rosenthaliana, Amsterdam University Library. On the Dutch and Polish versions and the precise date (second half of March 1666), see below.

2. On the transformations of the term *impostor* in the seventeenth century, see the important essay by Sylvia Berti, "Unmasking the Truth: The Theme of Imposture in Early Modern European Culture, 1660–1730," in James E. Force and David S. Katz, *Everything Connects: In Conference with Richard H. Popkin* (Leiden, Neth.: Brill, 1999), 21–36.

3. Michael McKeon, "Sabbatai Sevi in England," *Association for Jewish Studies Review* 2 (1971): 131–69; Ernestine G. E. van der Wall, "A Precursor of Christ or a Jewish Impostor? Peter Serrarius and Jean de Labadie on the Jewish Messianic Movement around Sabbatai Sevi," *Pietismus und Neuzeit* 14 (1988): 109–24, as well as her dissertation, "De Mystieke Chiliast Petrus Serrarius (1600–1669) en zijn Wereld" (Leiden, 1987); Richard H. Popkin, "The End of the Career of a Great Seventeenth-Century Millenarian: John Dury," *Pietismus und Neuzeit* 14 (1988): 203–20; idem, "Jewish-Christian Relations in the Sixteenth and Seventeenth Centuries: The Conception of the Messiah," *Jewish History* 5 (1992): 153–77; idem, "Christian Interest and Concerns about Sabbatai Zevi," in *Jewish Messianism in the Early Modern World*, ed. idem and Matt D. Goldish (Dordrecht, Neth.: Kluwer, 2001), 159–84; David Katz, *Philo-Semitism and the Readmission of the Jews to England, 1603–1655* (Oxford: Oxford University Press, 1982); Jacob Barnai, "Christian Messianism and the Portuguese Marranos: The Emergence of Sabbateanism in Smyrna," *Jewish History* 7 (1993): 119–26.

4. Rich material on contemporary reactions along these Christian-Jewish polemical lines can be found in the vast "Thesaurus Hottingerianus" at the Zentralbibliothek in Zurich. Indeed, the Zurich theologian Johann Heinrich Hottinger, while in close

contact with the millenarist John Durie (himself rather ambivalent toward Sabbatai Zevi), has written quite a bit in traditional Christian terms against the messianic expectations of the Jews. I am grateful to Prof. Richard H. Popkin for directing my attention to this fascinating collection. A Dutch anonymous pamphlet along similar lines, written as a dialogue between a Christian and a Jew, was published in the spring of 1666: *Den gewaanden Joodsche Messias Sabatha Sebi Ontdeckt* (Amsterdam, 1666). See also G. Scholem, *Sabbatai Sevi: The Mystical Messiah*, trans. by R. J. Zwi Werblowsky (Princeton: Princeton University Press, 1973), 545 n. 197. For a later period, see especially Elisheva Carlebach, *Divided Souls: Jewish Converts to Christianity in Early Modern German Lands, 1550–1750* (New Haven: Yale University Press, 2001), ch. 8. Nils Roemer is currently working on Christian-Jewish polemics from the perspective of German historiography of Sabbatai Zevi in the late seventeenth and eighteenth centuries. See his essay in this volume, which immediately follows.

5. See Richard H. Popkin, "Three English Tellings of the Sabbatai Zevi Story," *Jewish History* 8 (1994): 43–54; and idem, "Christian Interest and Concerns about Sabbatai Zevi," mentioned in note 3 above.

6. There is of course another important dimension to the contextual history of Sabbatai Zevi and the Sabbatian movement that is beyond the scope of the present chapter (and beyond the competence of its author), namely possible connections with Moslem circles, whether similar mystical and messianic tendencies or political and religious opponents like the "ulamā." While there are, once again, first steps in researching possible links on the mystical-ecstatic side, there is none yet, as far as I know, on the side of the critics. See, for some initial possible examples and references, P. B. Fenton, "Shabbatay Sebi and His Muslim Contemporary Muhamad An-Niyazi," in *Approaches to Judaism in Medieval Times*, vol. 3, ed. D. Blumenthal (1988), 81–88; A. Elqayam, "Sabbatai Sevi's Manuscript Copy of the Zohar" (in Hebrew), *Kabbalah* 3 (1998): 345–78, esp. 367–69, 377–78; and Jacob Barnai, *Sabbateanism: Social Perspectives* (Jerusalem: Zalman Shazar Center for Jewish History, 2000), 30–38.

7. See especially the recent article by Jetteke van Wijk, "The Rise and Fall of Shabbatai Zevi as Reflected in Contemporary Press Reports," *Studia Rosenthaliana* 33 (1999): 7–27, which focuses mostly on the Dutch press, and her unpublished thesis, "Wachtend op de Wolk naar Jeruzalem: De Verslaglegging Rond Shabbatai Tsvi in Nederlandse Pamfletten en Couranten" (Amsterdam University, 1996), which includes also an extensive bibiliography. On the German press, see the thesis of Christiane Ahrens, "Sabbatai Zwi (1626–1676). Untersuchungen zu einer Messianischen Bewegung und ihrer Rezetin in deutschsprachigen zeitgenössischen Quellen" (Hamburg University, 1979).

8. This list was heavily based, often verbatim, on Christian Gerson, *Der Jüden Thalmud Fürnembster Inhalt und Widerlegung* (1st ed. Goslar, Ger., 1607). I have used the 1609 edition in which the "list" appears in part 2, chapter 9, pages 454–61. A later edition came out a few years before the breakout of the Sabbatai Zevi affair, in Erfurt, 1659, and another one was to appear in 1685. On Christian Gerson, a Jewish convert to Christianity, see Heinz Schreckenberg, *Die christlichen Adversus-Judaeos-Texte und ihr literarisches und historisches Umfeld (13.–20 Jh.)*, Europäische Hochschulschriften, Bd. 497 (Frankfurt: Peter Lang, 1994), 653–54. I shall return below to the issue of lists of Jewish (and Christian) false messiahs.

9. *Umbständliche Continuation, Darinnen enthalten Der fernere Verlauff . . . Von ihrem Gesalbten Könige und Propheten begeben . . .* (1666). A copy of this pamphlet

belongs to the Bibliotheca Rosenthaliana and may be found at the University Library in Amsterdam. This pamphlet seems to be more positive toward the messianic expectations of the Jews, including, as it does, texts written from an obvious apocalyptic perspective. The expectations for the Jews' conversion to Christianity, however, are a dominant theme in that pamphlet, as is obvious also from its opening verses titled "An die verirrete Judenschaft."

10. The broadside is titled *Afbeelding, van den gewaenden, nieuwen Joodschen Koning SABETHA SEBI, Met zijn byhebbende Profeet* . . . One copy is in the Bibliotheca Rosenthaliana in Amsterdam. It is also reprinted as plate 5 in Scholem, *Sabbatai Sevi*, between pages 546 and 547. The pamphlet is titled *Historis Verhael: Van den nieuwen gemeynden Koning der Joden; SABATHA SEBI, Als mede sijn by hebbende Propheet NATHAN LEVI* (1666). I have consulted the copy in the Royal Libraray in The Hague. Scholem did not notice the proximity between the two texts.

11. "Turken, en Christenen, houden den zelven meerendeel voor een bedrieger, Turksen oft Joodsen Quaker; en het geheele werk, een verleidinge, oft voor teeken van den Jongsten Dag; hoewel voor beide zeltzame dingen zijn vertoont, zeggen, hem, eenen anderen *Machumeth, Simon Magus* oft Tovenaer te wezen," *Afbeelding, van . . . Sabetha Sebi*.

12. Another addition that was not in the German version referred to Sabbatai's supporters: to Nathan of Gaza who was characterized as "a highly learned man, righteous, sincere, and very humble, possessed by the spirit" as well as to four or six other "distinguished" rabbis. On the basis of these additions, I tend to believe that the Dutch broadside was a translation of the German *Beschreibung* rather than vice versa although both texts are clearly reporting from Amsterdam. It is difficult to see why the German writer would choose to omit the additional sentences in the Dutch version, especially those characterizing Nathan of Gaza. Still it is possible that the *Afbeelding* broadside served as the original from which the German *Beschreibung* was translated.

13. *Historis Verhael*, 7.

14. This interjection, almost in the middle of a sentence, clearly indicates that the *Historis Verhael* is a later text in comparison to the *Beschreibung* or the broadside, adding to them rather than serving as a basis from which they abbreviated their account. The interpolated description is highly interesting in itself, however. It is strikingly similar to critical descriptions of prophesying phenomena among Christians, especially indeed the Quakers but also the *petits prophètes* in Southern France toward the end of the seventeenth century. Thus it included a reference to Joel's prophecy (Joel 3: 1–2), which was a recurrent verse in the debate with the enthusiasts and made an analogy between the physical manifestations of prophesying and the symptoms of the falling sickness, also a common analogy with respect to "enthusiastic" phenomena in the seventeenth century. Similar descriptions, including the reference to the falling sickness, were similarly made by other Dutch pamphlets at that time. See van Wijk, "The Rise and Fall of Shabbatai Zevi as Reflected in Contemporary Press Reports," 22. As far as actual developments were concerned, however, the text apparently is not very accurate, confusing events in Smyrna with those in Aleppo and Cairo. On events in Aleppo, see Scholem, *Sabbatai Sevi*, 255–59.

15. "De Christenen houden den selven meerendeel voor een bedrieger / Turcksen of Joodschen Quaker . . . Ja sy achten dit geheele werck der Joden / een verleydinge / oft voor-teecken van den Jongsten dagh. Andere noemen hem den tweeden *Mahometh*, eenen anderen *Symon Magus* ofte Tovenaer." *Historis Verhael*, 7, 8. I am deeply

indebted here to Dr. Piet van Boxel for his help in reading and translating this text. Whatever inaccuracies might remain are, of course, my responsiblility.

16. Unlike the broadside version, the *Historis Verhael* does not end with the account of Sabbatai's capture by the Turks, only with his departure for Constantinople, promising to report further details as they arrive. Nevertheless I still tend to believe that it is a later version than the broadside (see notes 12 and 14 above), especially given the fact that the picture on the broadside is here divided into two. The *Historis Verhael* might have omitted the story about Sabbatai's capture by the Turks since it seemed at that moment, perhaps, to be an unfounded rumor. On the conflicting rumors concerning his arrest, see Scholem, *Sabbatai Sevi*, 447–48.

17. These scenes of the anointment of Sabbatai as king and the gathering of a Jewish army are repeated in other broadsheets of the period. (See, for examples, Scholem, *Sabbatai Sevi*, plates 1, 6.) In deciphering the picture I was greatly aided by Prof. Israel Yuval and Prof. Ora Limor, to both of whom I am very grateful.

18. See on this subject, Isaiah Shahar, *The Judensau: A Medieval Anti-Jewish Motif and its History* (London: Warburg Institute, University of London, 1974). I am indebted to Prof. Israel Yuval for directing my attention to this important issue and to the related bibliography on this question.

19. The print appeared in a section on Jewish messianic hopes in the 1666 edition of Dietrich Schwab, *Detectum Velum Mosaicum Judaeorum nostri temporis*. The first edition of this book appeared in 1615 but without illustrations. See Shahar, *Judensau*, 60, 95 n. 306, plate 53. A colored print may be found in the Historisches Museum, Frankfurt, Inv. no. C 10154, and is also reprinted in Heinz Schreckenberg, *The Jews in Christian Art* (New York: Continuum, 1996), 239 plate 15.

20. The *Judensau* does appear in connection with Sabbatai Zevi in a later German broadsheet of the eighteenth century, depicting Sabbatai Zevi together with Jacob Melstinius (see Shahar, *Judensau*, plate 40 as well as page 50 and note 253 on page 89).

21. This is even clearer in the German text that purported to be a continuation of the *Beschreibung* pamphlet discussed above—the *Umbständliche Continuation*. As noted above (see note 9), it is a text that clearly expects the imminent conversion of the Jews and their return to their ancient land, and regards the Sabbatian movement as a means to this process. I shall return to the question of the demonological interpetation below.

22. Hanna Swiderska, "Three Polish Pamphlets on Pseudo-Messiah Sabbatai Sevi," *British Library Journal* 15 (1989): 212–16, quotations from 214. Michal Galas, "Sabbateanism in Polish Historiography," in *Jewish Studies in a New Europe*, Proceedings of the 5th Congress of Jewish Studies in Copenhagen 1994 under the auspices of the European Association for Jewish Studies (Copenhagen: C. A. Reitzel, 1998), 262–68. I have also relied on his unpublished lecture "Sabbateanism in the 17th Century Polish-Lithuanian Commonwealth: A Review of the Sources," given at a conference on Sabbatianism and Frankism in Jerusalem and Haifa, December 1997. I am grateful to Prof. Israel Bartal for directing my attention to Galas's work.

23. See Galas, "Sabbateanism in Polish Historiography." 266–67, and idem, "Sabbateanism in the 17th Century Polish-Lithuanian Commonwealth," 11. The third pamphlet in its original German edition included also an illustration. See Scholem, *Sabbatai Sevi*, plate 6.

24. Daniel Clarke Waugh, "News of the False Messiah: Reports on Shabbetai Zevi in Ukraine and Muscovy," *Jewish Social Studies* 41 (1979): 301–22, esp. 314 for the Rus-

sian text. I am very grateful to Prof. Israel Bartal who read and translated for me the relevant Russian paragraphs. Waugh was not aware of the printed Polish pamphlets, however, which were discovered after the publication of his article.

25. On the critique of "enthusiasm" in this period and the varieties of denotations and connotations of the term, see my book *"Be Sober and Reasonable": The Critique of Enthusiasm in the Seventeenth and Early Eighteenth Centuries* (Leiden, Neth.: Brill, 1995).

26. For the identification of the author of these texts as Jacobus Becherand or Beccaranda, see Shlomo Simonsohn, *The History of the Jews in the Duchy of Mantua* (New York: Kiryat Sepher: 1977), 563 n. 191; and his earlier article "A Christian Report from Constantinople Regarding Shabbethai Sevi (1666)," *Journal of Jewish Studies* 12 (1961): 33–58, esp. 33–34. There is also a Dutch translation of Becherand's letter, *Een seer perfecte Beschryvinge Van 't Leven en Bedrijf, mitsgaders het Turckx worden, van den gepretendeerden Joodsen Messias* (Haarlem, 1667).

27. "E stato un spettacolo da far stupire, & insieme far ridere, di vedere in circa di cento venti donne Ebree per molti mesi, le quali si spacciavano di esser piene dello sprito [sic] di quel nuovo profera [sic], le quali, per prova di ciò con più splendore, facevano le spiritate, e si sforzavano d'imitare que gli Entusiasmi stravaganti delle nostre Energumene, alcune delle quali è stato necessario legare, e battere ben bene, per liberarle di quello spirito turbolento, de cui si singevano haver ricevuto licanza di far la pazze [sic]." *Lettera mandata da Costantinopoli a Roma intorno al nuovo Messia de gli Ebrei* (Siena, It. 1667), 5. The French version of this letter did not refer to "*our* possessed" explicitly but made the same point: "Ca esté un spectacle des plus suprenans et à mesme temps des plus ridicules, de voir durant plusieurs mois dans un endroit de Constantinople nommé Balata [Galata], de voir dis-je sept ou huit cents femmes qui se disoient remplies de l'esprit de ce nouveau Prophete, et qui pour le prouver avec esclat faisoient les obsedées, et s'efforçoient d'imiter ces Antousiasmes [sic], et ces transports extravagans des personnes energumenes." *Relation de la veritable Imposture du faux Messie des JUIFS Nommé Sabbatai Sevi* (Avignon, Fr., 1667), 23.

28. The Dutch version of Becherand's letter tends, by contrast, to give a demonological interpretation to the prophesying phenomena in Constantinople:

Het was het allervremste spectakel, en self doen ter tijdt het aller-belacchelijckste te sien, gedurende eenige Maenden, aen een kant van Constantinopolen, genaemt Balata, 17 a 1800 Vrouwen, die seyden vervult te zijn met den Geest van dese nieuwen Propheet, en die, om dat te betoonen, haer aenstelden of beseten waren, en deden gewelt, om na te volgen die inwendige aenblasingen, en die uyt-sporige Verruckingen van op-getogen Persoonen. Men hadde wel moeten binden ende af-touwen eenighe van dese, om dien turbulenten Geest daer uyt te drijven, die hare harsenen hadden omgekeert, en van welke sy meynden, dat sy commissie hadden ontfangen, omme te moghen narren, en hen over te geven aen allerhande soorten van ongere-geltheden; het geen oock elders is gebeurt, niet alleenlijk aen Vrouwen, maer oock aen verscheyde kleyne Kinderen, die van den Duyvel scheenen beseten te zijn.

Een seer perfecte Beschryvinge, 13. Also, the Dutch text does not use the term *enthusiasm* but a Dutch equivalent, "die uyt-sporige Verruckingen van op-getogen Persoonen."

29. Thomas Coenen, *Ydele verwachtinge der Joden getoont in den Persoon van Sabethai Zevi, Haren laetsten vermeynden Messias* (Amsterdam, 1669). This text was published in several dozens of copies only and is rare today. A Hebrew translation with

an extensive scholarly introduction and notes by Yosef Kaplan was published in 1998 by Dinor Center in Jerusalem.

30. Coenen, *Ydele verwachtinge*, 39–41. On the events in Smyrna in December 1665, and the prophesying phenomena there, see Scholem, *Sabbatai Sevi*, 417–33.

31. "En om de waerheyt te seggen / in die tijt hoorde men anders niet dan van schare der Propheten en Prophetessen. Inder daet en is dit werck niet anders geweest / dan of een konst des Duyvels / die daer sijn vermaek in schepte / om 't verstockte ende verherde volck met een swaerder blintheyt te slaen / ofte een gemaeckten schijn / 't was met groote valscheyt vermenght: men koster genoegsaem een gemaecktheyt in mercken / gelijck in de Quakers van Engelandt." Coenen, *Ydele verwachtinge*, 41.

32. On the various accounts given by critics to the phenomena of enthusiasm, see my book *"Be Sober and Reasonable,"* passim.

33. Coenen, *Ydele verwachtinge*, 40–41.

34. Ibid., 41.

35. "Wat daer van is ofte niet / late ick daer immer / dese sijne nieuwe opwerpinge en sijn listigheydt om 't volck na sich te trecken / sijn lesen van de naem Godts tegen de gewoonte der Joden / sijn Sabbaths schendinghe / sijn beloften van een nieuwe Wet te willen gheven / en eyndelhck 't lichtveerdigh versaecken van sijn Vaderlijcke Godtsdienst / geven genoegh te kennen / dat hy geensins van de fijnste slagh was; oock dat hy in desen handel niet de eere Godts / maer sijn eyghen eer en grootheyt voor gehadt heeft." Ibid., 96.

36. See Yosef Kaplan's introduction to the Hebrew edition of Coenen, 7, 30 n. 6. Johannes Hoornbeek (1617–66) was a theology professor at the University of Leiden. His book *Tesjubat Jehuda sive pro convincendis et convertendis Judaeis Libri Octo* was published in Leiden in 1655. On Hoornbeek, see J. W. Hofmeyr, *Johannes Hoornbeek as Polemikus* (in Dutch, with English and German short summaries) (Kampen, Neth.: Kok, 1975).

37. Johannes Hoornbeek, *Summa Controversiarum Religionis*, 1st ed. 1653, 2d ed. 1658. Later editions were published in 1676 and 1697. I have used the 1697 Frankfurt edition. The section on the various enthusiasts is on pages 378–562. On this book, see Hofmeyr's study mentioned in the previous note, especially 118–30, which deals with Hoornbeek's polemics with the enthusiasts. See also Heyd, *"Be Sober and Reasonable,"* 21–22, 36–37.

38. *Summa Controversiarum Religionis*, 531.

39. See Kaplan's introduction to the Hebrew edition of Coenen's *Ydele verwachtinge*, 19. It is also worth noting that another colleague and great admirer of Hoornbeek (and like him, a student of Voetius), Andreas Essenius (1618–77), also wrote an extensive description of the Sabbatai Zevi movement in his *Heilzaem Bericht en Troost Aen de Joden, of Israëliten* (Utrecht, Neth., 1667), 42–62. On the relationship between Essenius and Hoornbeek, see Hofmeyr, *Johannes Hoornbeek as Polemikus*, 34, 76, 209–10.

40. See Kaplan, 19–20, in the introduction to the Hebrew edition of Coenen.

41. On Paul Rycaut, see Sonia P. Anderson, *An English Consul in Turkey: Paul Rycaut at Smyrna, 1667–1678* (Oxford: Clarendon Press, 1989).

42. *The History of the Three Late Famous Impostors viz. Padre Ottomano, Mahomed Bei, and Sabatai Sevi* (In the Savoy [London], 1669). A facsimile edition (of the letter "To the Reader" and "The History of Sabatai Sevi") has been published in 1968 by the Augustan Reprint Society (no. 131), William Andrews Clark Memorial Library, University of California, Los Angeles. On the circumstances leading to the

publication of this text, see Geoffrey Keynes, *John Evelyn: A Study in Bibliophily and a Bibliography of His Writings* (New York: Grolier Club, 1937), 194–97; and the more up-to-date work by Anderson, *An English Consul in Turkey*, 211–15. See also Michael Fixler, *Milton and the Kingdoms of God* (Evanston, Ill.: Northwestern University Press, 1964), 243–47, who examines Evelyn's pamphlet and the English reactions to Sabbatai Zevi in the context of Milton's writing of *Paradise Regained*. Fixler is also aware of the link that Evelyn made between Sabbatai Zevi and the contemporary English millenarians. I am indebted to Jeffrey Shoulson for directing my attention to Fixler's book.

43. Padre Ottomano was a son of a woman in the Turkish harem captured by the Knights of Malta, raised as a Christian, later to become a Dominican friar. The Maltese Order and the Dominicans claimed that he had been the brother of the Sultan Mehmed IV and during the siege of Candia in the summer of 1668 was present on one of the papal ships and allegedly claimed to be the legitimate heir to the Ottoman throne. See on this last point (not mentioned by Evelyn), J. de Hammer, *Histoire de l'Empire Ottoman depuis son origine jusqu'à nos jours*, vol. 11 (Paris, 1838), 311–12. Mahomed Bei was a Christian of Walachian origin who converted to Islam but pretended to be Joannes Michael Cigala, a descendent of the viscount of Cigala who was taken prisoner by the Turks and who married Sultan Murad's daughter. Evelyn's aim, based on Cesii's report, was to undermine the story this "Cigala" published under the title "The History of Mahomet Bei."

44. See, on this legendary text and on the issue of "imposture" in that period, Sylvia Berti, "Unmasking the Truth," referred to in note 2 above.

45. It is worth noting that while in the context of the war over Crete being waged in those years, the European powers were all officially supporting Venice; the English throughout the 1660s were in tacit contact with the Ottomans and at times even considered supporting them openly against the Spanish and the French. See Halil Inalcik, "The Heyday and Decline of the Ottoman Empire," in *Cambridge History of Islam*, vol. 1, 351. Nor should the English context be ignored. In the years following the Restoration, threats to legitimate political authority had obvious resonance. Indeed, Rycaut himself would hint at the similarities between the coup against Sultan Ibrahim in 1647 and the trial and execution of Charles I, a year and a half later (Rycaut, *History of the Turkish Empire*, 79a). In fact, the accounts of Padre Ottomano and Mahomed Bei were apparently written by Cesii at the request of King Charles II. See Anderson, *An English Consul in Turkey*, 213–14.

46. Evelyn, *The History of the Three Late Famous Impostors*, "To the Reader."

47. Evelyn-Rycaut, "The History of Sabatai Sevi, the Pretended *Messiah* of the Jewes," in *The History of the Three Late Famous Impostors*, 41–42. This view is in marked contrast to the account Gershom Scholem gave to the Sabbatian movement, seeing it primarily as an autonomous *Jewish* phenomenon although he was clearly aware of the broader context of Christian millenarianism at that period.

48. Ibid., 62–63.

49. Ibid., 56.

50. Ibid., 78. The Rabbi referred to may have been Solomon Algazi, or perhaps Aaron Lapapa. See Scholem, *Sabbatai Sevi*, 414–15, who also mentions a memorandum, now lost, that the opposing rabbis sent to Constantinople in February 1666.

51. *Impostors*, 82–83. The same sentence appeared also in Rycaut's *History of the Turkish Empire*, 1680, 212, but not in a German translation of 1700–1701 nor in a later English edition of 1708, to which I shall have occasion to return.

52. Sonia Anderson has a list of twenty-seven editions in English, German, French, and even Welsh. See *An English Consul in Turkey*, 25, and Appendix 1, 295–96. A German translation appeared in Hamburg already in 1669 and a French translation in 1673. Rycaut's *History*, which included that account, also appeared in many editions and translations, from its first 1680 edition onward. In addition there were various adaptations of Evelyn's and Rycaut's text, some of which will be mentioned in what follows as well as innumerable anonymous pirated versions.

53. De la Croix's account was originally written in 1679 but was published only in 1684. Chevalier De la Croix, *Memoire . . . contenant diverses Relations très curieuses de l"empire Ottoman* (Paris, 1684). The Sabbatai Zevi story appeared in volume 2, 259–398.

54. On Mordechai (or Mordecai) Ben Hayyim of Eisenstadt (1650–1729), see *Encyclopaedia Judaica* vol. 12 (1971), 311; G. Scholem, "Apocalyptic and Messianic Chapters Concerning Rabbi Mordechai of Eisenstadt" (in Hebrew), *Sepher Dinaburg* (Jerusalem, 1949), 237–62; and Jacob Leveen, "An Autograph Letter of the Pseudo-Messiah Mordecai ben Hayyim of Eisenstadt," in Samuel Löwinger and Joseph Somogyi, eds., *Ignace Goldziher Memorial Volume*, pt. 1 (Budapest, 1948), 393–99.

55. Johannes à Lent, *Schediasma historico-philologicum de Judaeorum Pseudo-messiis* (Herborn, Ger., 1683). This edition is rare. A second edition was published in 1697. There, two chapters (76–102) are devoted to Sabbatai Zevi. Lent was a doctor of theology and professor of oriental languages and church history in the Protestant Academy of Herborn, Germany. It is worth noting that two years later, in 1685, a new edition of Christian Gerson's book appeared, perhaps the earliest exponent of such a list, under the slightly different title, *Des Jüdischen Thalmuds fürnehmster Inhalt und Widerlegung* (see note 8 above).

56. Lent, *Schediasma*, 102–4.

57. Giulio Morosini, *Derekh Emunah, Via della Fede Mostrata a'gli Ebrei* (Rome, 1683), 76–78. Morosini was a Hebraist at the Vatican Library as well as lecturer of medicine in the Collegio de Propaganda Fide. I am indebted to Yaacov Deutsch for directing my attention to this work.

58. Jean-Baptiste de Rocoles, *Les Imposteurs insignes; ou, Histoires de plusieurs hommes de néant, de toutes Nations, qui ont usurpé la qualité d'Empereurs, Roys et Princes: Des Guerres qu'ils ont causé, accompagnées de plusieurs curieuses circonstances* (Amsterdam, 1683). Chapter 36 on Sabbatai Zevi is on pages 502–36. The following chapter, interestingly enough, seems to be a translation of Evelyn's final "Extirpation, Destruction, and Exile of the Jews out of the Empire of Persia." An abbreviated English translation of Rocoles appeared that same year, but included only twelve impostors, rather than thirty-six, and Sabbatai Zevi was not among them: *The History of Infamous Impostors; or, The Lives and Actions of Several Notorious Counterfeits . . .* (London, 1683, 1686). On the strange career of Rocoles (1620?–96), who converted twice back and forth from Roman Catholicism to Protestantism (he wrote the *Imposteurs insignes* while a Protestant in Holland in 1683), served as court historiographer in Berlin for a while and ended his life once again as a canon of Saint-Benoît. See *Biographie universelle*, vol. 36, (Paris, 1854), 268–69; *Nouvelle biographie générale*, vol. 42 (Paris, 1866), 472–73; *La France protestante*, vol. 7 (Paris, 1858), 463–64, which is naturally rather negative. See also on this text, Popkin, "Christian Interest and Concerns about Sabbatai Zevi," and Berti, "Unmasking the Truth" (see notes 2–3 above), especially 26, 32, where Rocoles is situated in the context of the issue of impostors in the second half of the seventeenth century.

59. Rocoles, *Les Imposteurs insgines*, 526. Rocoles seems to have relied here on the *Historis Verhael* mentioned above, as he refers earlier on to a "relation flamand" that served as one of his sources (ibid., 502). Indeed, he mentions the comparison to Mohammed and Simon Magus in the context of a report about Sabbatian phenomena in Aleppo, which is strikingly similar to a parallel story in the *Historis Verhael*, 7–8. Popkin suggests, in the article mentioned in the previous note, that the "Flemish" source had been Coenen, but Coenen did not make the comparison to Mohammed and Simon Magus nor relate the story about the hermit in Aleppo to whom the *Historis Verhael* referred and which Rocoles repeated word for word.

60. See on this subject, Peter C. Erb, *Pietists, Protestants, and Mysticism: The Use of Late Medieval Spiritual Texts in the Work of Gottfried Arnold (1666–1714)* (Metuchen, N.J.: Scarecrow Press, 1989), ch. 2. On Pietism in this period, the literature is enormous, but see especially Martin Brecht, *Geschichte des Pietismus*, 2 vols. (Göttingen, Ger.: Vandenhoeck and Ruprecht, 1993, 1995); and Martin Gierl, *Pietismus und Aufklärung* (Göttingen, Ger.: Vandenhoeck and Ruprecht, 1997).

61. On Corvinus, see C. G. Jöcher, *Allgemeines Gelehrten-Lexicon*, vol. 1 (rpt. ed. Hildesheim, Ger.: Georg Olms, 1960), col. 2127. Corvinus published in 1701 his *Corpus Doctrinae Oder Fürbildung der Lehre Von der wahren und falschen Pietät* (Frankfurt, 1701), which included in its second part a critical examination of Arnold's book: *Eine Gründliche Untersuchung Gottfried Arnolds Kirchen- und Ketzer-Historie*. On Corvinus's polemics with Arnold, see Erb, *Pietists, Protestants, and Mystics*, 41, 231 n. 56. Erb mistakenly calls Johann Friedrich Corvinus, Johann *Andreas* Corvinus.

62. *Anabaptisticum et Enthusiasticum Pantheon und Geistliches Rüst-Hauss Wider die Alten Quacker / und Neuen Frey-Geister* (1702). This big volume includes also other texts written against the Anabaptists, Quakers, Pietists, and various enthusiasts, with 1701 as their publication year, most of them under the title *Der Alten und Neuen Schwärmer Widertäufferischer Geist*. There are various copies of this collection in Europe and the United States, but the order of the texts differs in some of the copies.

63. *Die Geschichte von dem Grossen Betrieger oder Falschen Juden Könige Sabatai-Sevi von Smirna*, 18 pages, separate pagination. Evelyn was already translated into German in 1669; Rycaut was translated and published first in 1694 and published again in 1700 and 1701. Corvinus published Rycaut's account verbatim, except for a few additions noted below.

64. *Fürstellung Vier Neuer Welt = Weisen / Nahmentlich / I. Renati Des Cartes, II. Thomae Hobbes, III. Benedicti Spinoza, IV. Balthasar Beckers, Nach Ihrem Leben und Fürnehmsten Irrthümern* (1702).

65. Michael Heyd, "Be Sober and Reasonable," ch. 4.

66. "Es ist zwar nicht ohne / dass seine gantze Geschichte schon aller Orten genugsam ruchbar / jedoch wird es nicht gar übel gethan seyn / wann wir selbige hier auch anführen / und der General Historie / mit deren sie einiger massen eine Verwandschafft hat / einverleiben." *Die Geschichte von dem Sabatai-Sevi*, 1.

67. "Der Juden Beyspiel lehrt / wie bald die halbe Welt / Wenn sich ein Narr erhebt / auff dessen Thorheit fält." Ibid., 17.

68.

Wann nur ein SABATAI käm itzo an das Licht
Wie vieles Christen-Volck verführet' er wol nicht?
Ach! Christen! irrt euch nicht / last Narren Narren Seyn!
Lasst Juden diese Welt: Ihr solt zum Himmel ein! (Ibid.)

69. Johann Christoph Müller, *Greuel der Falschen Messien / wie auch / Shatz-Kammer des Wahren Messiae Jesu Christi, das ist: Eine ziemliche LISTA der Jenigen falschen MESSIEN, so von Anfang der Welt / bis auff diese ietzige Zeit haben können in Erfahrung gebracht werden* (1702). Johann Christoph Müller was rector of a school in Anhalt. The Sabbatai Zevi story appears on page 24.

70. See Müller's "To the Reader" ("Hochgeneigter und Christlicher Leser"). I am indebted to Dr. Nils Roemer for directing my attention to this fact. Paulli also appealed to Louis XIV and earlier to William III in order to further his schemes. His story appears on pages 24–25. On Paulli, see *The Jewish Encyclopedia* vol. 9 (1905), 563.

71. *Novus in Belgio Judæorum Rex Oliger Paulli . . . das ist Der Neue Juden = König / Oliger Paulli, In Niederland* (1702).

72. 1702. Anonymous.

73. *Erschröckliche Brüderschafft*, vol. 2, 9 left. The paragraph begins with a list of ten Jewish false messiahs, Sabbatai Zevi being the ninth, and Mordechai of Eisenstadt concluding the list though it stresses that there are many more. It refers to Christian Gerson, Johannes Lent, and Johann Christoph Müller as sources of such lists of Jewish false messiahs. The dates of many of them, however, is completely mistaken (Bar-Kochba is given the year 71, and David Elroi, the year 940).

74. "Ihre Rabbinen stecken das Ziel der Ankunfft des Messia sehr weit hinaus / indem sie sagen: Gott habe zwar eine gewisse Zeit des Messia Ankunfft auffzeichnen lassen / aber die Zeit sey noch nicht kommen / wenn aber dieselbe Zeit kähme / so würde der Messias auch Kommen." Ibid. The text goes on and quotes Kimchi in his commentary on Psalms 91:16 as well as the Targum Yerushalmi on Exodus 12:42 on this issue.

75. "Die Quäcker / Frey-Geister und andere Schwärmer geben ihnen hierzu nicht allein guten Anlass / sondern werffen sich selber für den Messiam auf . . ." Ibid. The text then goes on to mention some of the Christian pretenders to be the Messiah, among whom are John of Leiden, Jacob Nayler, and most recently, Oliger Paulli. Among its sources, it refers to Figk, *Historia Fanaticorum*, Johannes Müller's *Quäcker-Greuel*, and Johann-Christoph Müller, *Greuel der falschen Messien*, that were all also included in the Corvinus volume.

76. The exact date and provenance of this picture is not yet clear. A copy may be found in the Germanisches Museum, Nürenberg. See Georg Liebe, *Das Judentum in der deutschen Vergangenheit* (Leipzig, Ger., 1903), 74–75, and illust. no. 60, who dates it to the seventeenth century. Two similar (but not identical) pictures appear in other parts of the Corvinus collection. One, showing Nayler's portrait, appears at the beginning of one of the early tracts: Lassenius's *Historische und Schrifftmässige Erörterung . . . der Quacker*, opposite page 112, in part 3 of the collection whereas Sabbatai's portrait, referred to above, appears in front of the tract on Sabbatai Zevi. In both these portraits the term *Monarchia Nova* is written on the tablecloth next to them whereas the emblems of that new monarchy are situated on the table itself. The portraits, however, are clearly different.

77.

"So siehet Naylor aus, in seiner rechten Tracht,
Die ihn in Occident zum Quacker König macht
und dis ist SABATAI den in den Orient
die gantze Judenschafft Messias hat genennt.

78. Leo Damrosch, *The Sorrows of the Quaker Jesus: James Nayler and the Puritan Crackdown on the Free Spirit* (Cambridge: Harvard University Press, 1996). See especially ch. 3, 163–76. I am indebted to Prof. Jason Rosenblatt for drawing my attention to this important book.

79. See, for example, Richard Blome, *The Fanatick History; or, An Exact Relation and Account of the Old Anabaptists and New Quakers* (London, 1660). This tract was translated into German by Benedict Figk, *Historia Fanaticorum, Oder eine vollkommene Relation und Wissenschafft / von den Alten Anabaptisten und Neuen Quäkern* (Frankfurt, 1701), also included in the volume containing the Corvinus compilation. Other critics, on the other hand, like Richard Baxter, understood quite well the nature of Nayler's entry to Bristol as an "acting out" performance. See Damrosch, *Sorrows*, 172–73.

80. On the "French Prophets," see Hillel Schwartz, *The French Prophets: The History of a Millenarian Group in Eighteenth-Century England* (Berkeley and Los Angeles: University of California Press, 1980). On the various reactions to the French prophets, see idem, *Knaves, Fools, Madmen, and That Subtile Effluvium: A Study of the Opposition to the French Prophets in England, 1706–1710* (Gainesville: University Press of Florida, 1978); and Heyd, *"Be Sober and Reasonable,"* chs. 6, 7.

81. Anon., *The Devil of Delphos; or, The Prophets of Baal: Containing an Account of a Notorious Impostor, Call'd Sabatai Sevi, Pretended Messiah of the Jews, in 1666. Who Afterwards Turn'd Turk* (London, 1708). Richard Popkin has already noted the significance of this text in the context of English reactions to Sabbatai Zevi. See Popkin, "Three English Tellings of the Sabbatai Zevi Story," 49–51, and his recent article "Christian Interest and Concerns about Sabbatai Zevi" (see note 3 above).

82. *Devil of Delphos*, 56–73.

83. Ibid., 56.

84. Ibid., 64. At the end of the text the author also compared the reactions of some of the Jews to Sabbatai's apostasy—the claims that it was only his *shadow* that converted to Islam—to the probable reaction of the adherents of the French prophets in 1708 when they will see that the expected resurrection of Dr. Emes (due to occur on May 25, 1708) had not occurred: ibid., 72–73. This comment clearly situates the writing of the text between December 1707 and May 1708. On the expected resurrection of Dr. Emes, see Schwartz, *The French Prophets*, ch. 4, 113–25.

85. See Heyd, *"Be Sober and Reasonable,"* ch. 2, 7. See also Schwartz, *Knaves, Fools, Madmen*, ch. 2, esp. 43–56.

86. See Keith Thomas, *Religion and the Decline of Magic* (New York: Scribner's, 1971), 571–72; Heyd, *"Be Sober and Reasonable,"* 104–5, 238–39; Schwartz, *Knaves, Fools, Madmen*, 54–55.

87. See notes 18 and 20 above.

88. See note 3 above.

89. Theodore K. Rabb, *The Struggle for Stability in Early Modern Europe: A Post-Crisis Interpretation* (New York: Oxford University Press, 1975).

90. See note 62. In addition to the imperial edicts that open the volume (in most of its copies), the volume included eleven imperial, royal, and princely edicts under the title *Königliche / Chur- und Fürstliche Edicta und Verordnungen* (1701).

91. Heyd, *"Be Sober and Reasonable,"* esp. ch. 5 and 6.

92. Elisheva Carlebach has argued that Jewish reactions to Sabbatai Zevi foreshadow in many ways later Orthodox reactions to Hasidism and Reformed Judaism,

and in this respect were conservative but by no means traditional: Carlebach, *The Pursuit of Heresy* (New York: Columbia University Press, 1990), 277–78. To some extent this might be true for the *Christian* reactions too, but the subject requires further study.

93. See her recent book *Divided Souls: Converts from Judaism in Germany, 1500–1750* (New Haven: Yale University Press, 2001).

94. It is manifest, among other things, also in the incorporation of Sabbatai Zevi and other Jewish false messiahs within "lists" of Christian impostors and false messiahs, not only that of Rocoles (see note 58) but most noticeably, in Johann Christoph Müller's list of sixty-four false messiahs (see note 69 above), as well as in the list included in *The Devil of Delphos* (see note 81 above).

95. It should be stressed that at the height of the Sabbatian excitement in early 1666 the rabbis were divided in their attitudes, especially in places like Smyrna or Amsterdam. The implicit "solidarity" I am referring to regards those rabbis who opposed Sabbatai. After his conversion to Islam, the situation changed, of course. On Amsterdam, see Yosef Kaplan, "The Attitude of the Leadership of the Portuguese Community in Amsterdam to the Sabbatian Movement, 1665–1667" (in Hebrew), *Zion* 39 (1974): 198–216. On Smyrna and other communities in the Ottoman Empire, see Barnai, "Messianism and Leadership: The Sabbatean Movement and the Leadership of the Jewish Communities in the Ottoman Empire," in *Ottoman and Turkish Jewry: Community and Leadership,* ed. A. Rodrigue (Bloomington: Indiana University Press, 1996), 167–82.

11
Colliding Visions: Jewish Messianism and German Scholarship in the Eighteenth Century

Nils Roemer

In the public debate over Jewish civic improvement at the end of the eighteenth century the distinguished scholar Johann David Michaelis charged that "Jews will always see the state as a temporary home, which they will leave in the hour of their greatest happiness to return to Palestine."[1] For Michaelis, Jewish messianism did not pose a theological question but raised a sociopolitical issue. He viewed messianism as an obstacle to Jewish integration into the emerging civic societies and as an issue concerning primarily Jewish-German, not Jewish-Christian, relations.[2] Michaelis's reframing of the debate over Jewish messianism as a political concern reflected a larger German discourse about the process of Enlightenment and, above all, what is commonly described as the transformation of messianic expectations into a secularized model of historical progress.

Several decades ago Karl Löwith argued in his influential book *Meaning in History* (1949) that an intimate connection between all modern philosophies of history and Christian thought existed. Löwith noted that the belief in progress is "a sort of religion, derived from the Christian faith in a future goal, though substituting an indefinite and immanent *eschaton* for a definite and transcendent one."[3] Accordingly, the modern idea of progress appears as the transformed successor to Christian religious messianic expectations. Löwith stands within a long and fierce debate over Jewish messianism that took hold with the Sabbatian movement in the seventeenth century and never subsided. Against this prevailing view the German-Jewish philosopher Hermann Cohen asserted at the beginning of the twentieth century that the concept of a progressing history is a creation of the biblical prophets.[4]

Instead of engaging in the debate about origins and precedence, I would like to argue that the secularization of Christian beliefs entailed an intense discussion of Jewish messianic movements and doctrines. Löwith's swift characterization obliterates the fact that the presumed secularization involved the eradication of religious, political, and apocalyptic vestiges in modern thought. Moreover, proponents of the secularization theory, such as Löwith, have always relied on a model of historical continuity and have effaced the major paradigm shift that occurred during the late eighteenth century.[5] Whereas chiliastic movements sought to move incrementally and progressively from historical time into the messianic age, Immanuel Kant, for example, preserved the notion of redemption within the nontemporal realm as a genuine other and invisible future. In his disentangling of historical progress from redemption, Kant's emphasis on the incomprehensible nature of salvation marked indeed a substantial shift in enlightened perceptions of the messianic era. The fundamental uncertainty of the future encompassed even the question of the Jews' role in the messianic era. At the same time, however, this novel understanding once more denied Jewish messianism's universal significance and relegated it to the sphere of enlightened politics.

The continued virulence of enlightened debate on messianism reflects the central importance this issue received in Christian-Jewish debates in the aftermath of the Sabbatian movement in the seventeenth century. Whereas at first the perception of the movement became an issue in intra-Christian debates over religious dissenters, later commentators fully identified Jewish messianism with an outdated restorative political movement. They equated Christian notions of the end of the world with the universal idea of progress. According to these authors, Christianity had cleansed itself of this Jewish heritage while Judaism still clung to an outdated and parochial carnal vision of redemption.[6]

Messianism has always been a central point in Christian-Jewish polemics, as Gershom Scholem noted at the opening of his influential essay on the messianic idea in Judaism: "For it is here that the essential conflict between Judaism and Christianity has developed and continues to exist."[7] Central, however, to Christian commentators and disputants was not Jewish messianism as such but whether Jesus was the Messiah. With the increasing amount of literature produced by converts from Judaism during the early modern period, this situation, however, slowly started to change. Antonius Margaritha, the son of Jacob Margolioth of Regensburg, produced one of the most widely read books on Jewish customs and beliefs. He was influenced by the writings of other converts like Johannes Pfefferkorn and Victor von Carben. In his *Der gantz Jüdisch glaub* (The Entire Jewish Faith), which appeared in 1530, Margaritha spoke of how the Jews have "many excellent sayings about the redemption and the future of the Messiah" that formed a central component of their religious belief.[8] In light of the postulated centrality of messianic hopes, Margaritha suggested addressing the issue of messianism in attempts at converting the Jews.[9]

Martin Luther, who read Margaritha in 1539, mentioned only Genesis

49:10 ("The staff shall not depart from Yehuda, nor the scepter from between his feet, until Shilo comes") in his *Von den Jüden und iren Lügen* (On the Jews and Their Lies) in 1543. Luther asserted that the Messiah had arrived 1500 years earlier and that Judah had lost the scepter. Yet one year later in a short lecture Luther drew out the differences between Christian and Jewish messianic expectations. For Luther, Jews were still awaiting a messiah as an earthly ruler who would rebuild the temple and slay the Gentiles whereas Christians expected forgiveness of sins and resurrection.[10] By casting Jewish messianism as a politically restorative doctrine in combination with the motif of Jewish vengeance Luther foreshadowed later discussions, while Jewish messianic figures Asher Lemlein and Shlomoh Molkho served within the sixteenth century as contemporary examples for Jewish "gullibility."[11]

With these notable exceptions Jewish messianism remained overall only a minor concern in Jewish-Christian polemics during the sixteenth century.[12] The convert Christian Gerson, however, encouraged a renewed Christian interest in Jewish historical messianic figures when he provided a detailed list of various false Jewish messiahs and extensively elaborated on Jewish messianic doctrines.[13] Despite this initial interest in the history of Jewish messianic movements displayed in Gerson's publications, his contemporary, the Hebraist Johannes Buxtorf, while discussing Jewish messianic beliefs in great detail in his 1603 *Juden Schul* (Jewish Synagogue), nevertheless attributed to it no central role within his work. In Buxtorf's denunciation of Judaism, messianism was simply another illustration of Judaism being based on "false and unfounded statutes and fables."[14]

With the intensifying Jewish and Christian messianic activism of the mid-seventeenth century, however, perceptions started to change. A cluster of Christian and Jewish messianic speculation led to rumors about an alleged Council of the rabbis in 1650, which was to have debated whether the Messiah had already come.[15] These rumors, together with Menasseh ben Israel's promotion of the idea of the ten lost tribes living in America, and last but not least the Sabbatian movement, made Jewish messianism a central issue in Christian polemics.[16]

The virulence of messianic activism and speculation increased with the continued rise of print media. Travel literature brought with it reports about the ten lost tribes while newspaper articles, broadsides, and various books informed readers in great detail about the events surrounding Sabbatai Zevi and Nathan of Gaza.[17] The unabated interest in Sabbatai Zevi continued into the eighteenth century, even after his apostasy. John Evelyn, a member of the Royal Society of England, composed *The History of the Three Late Famous Impostors* (1669) based on the account of the affair by Paul Rycaut, the English consul in Smyrna. Evelyn combined the account of Sabbatai Zevi with a discussion of the impostors Padre Ottomano and Mohamed Bei. By bringing these various episodes together, Evelyn aimed to undermine the confidence in contemporary English millenarians. Linking Sabbatai Zevi, Padre Ottomano, and Mohamed Bei allowed him to highlight the potential political danger of active messianism. Evelyn branded Sabbatai Zevi a political leader and emphasized that the movement itself was rather of an earthly nature. The Jews, opined Evelyn, were "so deeply possessed with a beliefe of their new Kingdome, and Riches, and many of them with promotion to Offices of Government, Renown, and Greatness."[18] Evelyn was not alone in associating the Sabbatian movement with political upheaval. Paul Rycaut similarly denounced the delusional political Sabbatian movement as well as contemporary Christian millenarism in his *History of the Turkish Empire* (1680).[19]

In the Germanic lands, reports were not significantly different. Both Evelyn and Rycaut appeared in German translation, and the first periodicals and broadsides included detailed stories about fictitious military battles. Examples of such stories included Sabbatai Zevi as the leader of a Jewish army that was eventually crushed by the Sultan's forces.[20] Along these lines the popular German writer Grimmelshausen asserted that the Jews expected "an earthly king" who would usher in the destruction and annihilation of all their enemies.[21]

The 1680s witnessed new Jewish messianic contenders like Mordechai of Eisenstadt as well as Christian millenarians who magnified the debate and led to a stepped-up campaign against Judaizers. As the Sabbatian movement unfolded, the theologian Michael Buchenröder had already claimed that Christians were in doubt about the true faith.[22] Subsequently, Christian theologians had to confront substantial groups of religious dissenters, mystics, and "enthusiasts" within Christianity.[23] The renowned theologian Martin Diefenbach charged, for example, that Pietists strengthened the Jewish cause with their assertion that the Messiah was still to come.[24] He reported that Jews referred in their defense to Christian messianic expectations.[25] Several Pietists indeed believed that the end of the world was imminent and that Jews were destined to play a major role in the final drama. Johann Wilhelm Petersen, for example, expected the approaching conversion of the Jews, which would usher in the end of days.[26] More radical in the application of this idea was the theologian Johann Jakob Zimmermann who lost his office in 1689 in Württemberg because of his heightened expectations of the Jews' conversion as part of his chiliastic hopes.[27]

It was probably in response to these events that German scholars started compiling lists of false messiahs whereby Jewish messianism became entangled with internal Christian debates, as Michael Heyd's richly documented essay illustrates.[28] Already, one of the first extensive pamphlets on Sabbetai Zevi not only denounced the "king Sabbatai Zevi" but augmented the presentation of the impostors with an extensive list of Jewish messiahs beginning with Bar Kokhba down to David Reubeni in the sixteenth century based on Christian Gerson.[29] The republication of Gerson's 1607 *Der Jüden Talmud fürnebmster inhalt* (The Jew's Talmud Primary Content) in 1668 and 1685 further supplied the reading public with substantial accounts of false messiahs.[30] On the heels of this increased interest in impostors, Johannes Lent, assisted in his task by the Hebraist Johann Christoph Wagenseil, listed a total of nineteen messianic figures from Bar Kochba to Mordechai of Eisenstadt at the end of the seventeenth century. Lent's compilation appeared first in 1683 and was republished in 1697, and functioned subsequently as the basis for many other authors.[31]

Following Lent, Johannes Christian Müller arranged an even more extensive list of sixty-four false messiahs in his *Greuel der falschen Messien wie auch Schatz-Kammer des wahren Messien* (Horror of the False Messiahs and the Treasure Chamber of the True Messiah, 1702). Müller's list entails both Jewish and Christian impostors like Sabbatai Zevi, the Quaker James Nayler, and the self-proclaimed Christian messiah Oliger Paulli.[32] Current messianic contenders fueled Müller's interest, and he applied himself to this task of compiling this exhaustive list in particular to refute Oliger Paulli and to commemorate the true Messiah, Jesus.[33]

These various debates and textual traditions formed the backdrop against which the work of eighteenth-century Christian Hebraists emerged, who extensively utilized the accounts of false messiahs.[34] Whereas the clandestine literature presented Moses, Jesus, and Mohammed as frauds, these authors differentiated between the true messiah and impostors.[35] Within the context of these religious debates the categorization of false Messiahs as impostors elevated their deceitful character and portrayed them as political leaders and legislators.[36] The English bishop Richard Kidder (1633–1703) called Jewish messiahs "false Christs" and "impostors" while Jacob Schudt included a poem addressed to the Jews that labeled Sabbatai Zevi a "false Christ."[37] Following Müller, Schudt counted sixty-four false messiahs in his vast book on Jewish history and lore titled *Jüdische Merkwürdigkeiten* (Jewish Curiosities).[38] Other Christian commentators saw the Sabbatian movement as a plot for a Jewish "uprising" (*Aufstand*).[39] Along similar lines Sabbatai Zevi introduces himself in a fictional conversation with the court Jew and financial adviser to the duke of Württemberg, Jud Süß, as, "I am a descendent of Bar Kohkba, Rabbi David, El David, Moses Cretensis, the Messiah of Worms and other particular illustrious people of our nation."[40] Sabbatai Zevi and Jud Süß go on to compete against each other in their respective importance as impostors.[41] Only in the realm of Christian imagination could Sabbatai Zevi be comparable to Jud Süß,[42] who embodied the image of Jewish usurpation for his contemporaries.[43]

In their elaborate accounts of Jewish messianic beliefs Christian Hebraists focused on usurpation of power, deceit, vengeance, and notions of Jews yearning for a tyrannical reign. Johannes Eisenmenger charged that Jews intended to murder all Christians during the reign of the messiah, including those in Germany. By citing the medieval Spanish-Jewish exegete David Kimhi on Obadiah 1:20, Eisenmenger argued that the German Christians were descendants of the Canaanites, and therefore Deuteronomy 7:16 ("And thou shall consume all the peoples which the Lord thy God will deliver to thee; thy eye shall have no pity upon them") applied to them.[44] For Eisenmenger a Jewish messiah would bring war against the people of the earth and establish an earthly reign over them.[45] While Eisenmenger may strike one as a particularly vitriolic writer, Schudt's *Jüdische Merkwürdigkeiten* reiterated his presentation of the messianic era as a period of Jewish vengeance.[46]

Underlying the unremitting interest in Jewish messianism was the continuation of concepts of the future that remained essentially theological in nature. Protestant theologians like Wagenseil shared with Christian millenarians the belief that the conversion of the Jews would usher in the end of the world. He condemned the church for neglecting to pursue Jews' conversion more vigorously and contended that in contrast to the rapid development in the field of sciences and art, Jews' conversion was progressing much more slowly. Nevertheless, Wagenseil remained convinced of the approaching conversion as it had been prophesied in the Bible.[47] Within the framework of the missionary activities, dismantling Jewish messianism served therefore not simply to reassert the veracity of Christianity for Christians and Jews; the Hebraists also believed that their attacks on Jewish messianism would lead to Jews' conversion and universal salvation.[48] The increasing importance of messianic expectations for Christian-Jewish polemics and conversion attempts is supported by various publicized accounts of Jewish converts. Albert Christiani related that he converted in the aftermath of the Sabbatian movement when he realized that Scripture had prophesied not an earthly messiah but a spiritual reign.[49] Upon Sabbatai Zevi's conversion, Jacob Melammed from Cornitz turned to the Lutheran pastor at the Michaeliskirche in Hamburg, Esras Edzard, who had already attempted to convince Jews and Christians in Hamburg that Sabbatai Zevi was a false messiah. Consequently, Melammed converted to Christianity.[50] Conversely, other Jewish converts listed various false Jewish messiahs in order to explain why it was difficult for Jews of the time to believe in Jesus. Too often they had believed in a false messiah and had therefore lost the ability to put their hopes in yet another.[51]

Responding to the potential danger of manifestations of Jewish messianism for Jewish-Christian relations, the ma'amad of the Sephardic community in Hamburg had already interceded at the height of the Sabbatian movement and collected the printed version of Moses Gideon Abudiente's *Fin de los Dias*

(End of Days). It was felt that the book, which deals with "the end of days," could harm Jews' reputation among Christians.[52] A few decades later Tobias Cohn (1652–1729) in his scientific anthology *Ma'aseh Tuviyyah* (*The Work of Tobias*, 1707) asserted that the deception of false Jewish messiahs had given Christians an opportunity to ridicule and defame the Jews.[53]

By the middle of the eighteenth century the situation had not changed markedly but was revitalized in response to several events. In England, David Hartley gave his readers assurance of the expected restoration of the Jews in his *Observation on Man* (1749)[54] while within the German context Thomas Sherlock's messianic speculations appeared in 1749.[55] At the same time, the internal debates between the rabbis of Hamburg, Jonathan Eybeschütz and Jacob Emden, seemed to have been responsible for a renewed interest in Sabbatai Zevi. Karl Anton, a convert and former student of Eybeschütz, composed a lengthy defense on behalf of his former teacher that encapsulated a description of the Sabbatian movement.[56] Aside from these various publications, the Protestant theologian David Friederich Megerlin urged both Christians and Jews to live in the realm of the messiah and appealed to the rabbis to organize a rabbinical assembly to discuss the question of the messiah.[57]

These renewed speculations triggered responses from the Protestant theologians, who once again dismissed Jewish messianic hopes.[58] The Christian Hebraist Johann Wolfgang Bodenschatz restated Eisenmenger's presentation of Jewish messianism that aimed to establish a Jewish reign on earth. In line with the carnal portrayal, Bodenschatz cast Jewish messianic contenders as insidious individuals who had a disruptive impact on society because they wanted to retaliate against the enemies of the Jews.[59] Bodenschatz's reiteration of Eisenmenger notwithstanding, the firmness with which the future was envisioned significantly waned in the second half of the eighteenth century. In his *Aussichten in die Ewigkeit* (Views into Eternity) Johann Christian Lavater (1741–1801) reasserted the fundamental difference between the present and an unknown future, and posited the arbitrariness of speculating about the future.[60] Similarly, Gotthold Ephraim Lessing, who is commonly credited with writing comprehensive philosophy of history, refrained from sketching, deducing, or delineating a possible future in his 1780 *Die Erziehung des Menschengeschlechts* (The Education of Humanity).[61]

The increasing incomprehensibility of the future reshaped enlightened concepts about the messianic era and restructured the debate on Jewish messianism. Bodenschatz still clearly regarded the current situation of the Jews as a token of their just and divine punishment. Yet even he asserted that "it is concealed from our eyes, what the eternal providence has decided about them for the future."[62] When Johann Semler continued Siegmund Jacob Baumgarten's universal history, he grouped the history of the Ottomans together with an elaborate account of Jewish history from the destruction of the Second Temple to the end of the seventeenth century. The survival of Jews in exile led Semler to conclude that God not only watched over Israel but also ensured they were spared and protected for a particular divine purpose. Yet he refrained from speculating about the nature of this divine purpose and only referred the reader to the messianic works of Joseph Mede, Pierre Jurieau, Bishop Scherlock, among others.[63]

The growing uncertainty was shared by some of the eminent enlightened theologians of the period. Johann Christoph Döderlein, for example, did not see in his *Giebt uns die Bibel Hoffnung zu einer künftigen allgemeinen Judenbekehrung* (Does the Bible give Us Hope Regarding the Complete Future Conversion of the Jews?, 1781) "why . . . the conviction about the generally expected conversion of the Jews be also necessary for the peace and improvement of humanity."[64] He differentiated between the hope in the political restoration of the Jews and the expectation in the universal spiritual transformation of modern society.[65] Ultimately he could not discern unambiguous biblical references that pointed to the Jews' ensuing conversion.[66] As Döderlein noted, even one of the key texts (Rom. 11:26, 27) did not provide certainty for these expectations.[67] Along these lines Hosea 3:5 ("Afterwards the children of Yisra'el shall return, and seek the Lord their God, and David their king: and shall come trembling to the Lord and his goodness in the latter days") did not predict Jews' conversion but described a historical reality.[68]

Döderlein's careful evaluation of the biblical evidence was part of a larger critical reworking of the chiliastic Christian and Jewish legacies that revealed the fundamental refashioning of future expectations.[69] Michaelis's calm review of Moses Mendelssohn's translation of Menasseh's *Hope of Israel* that, roughly a hundred years ago, still had unnerved many Christian scholars, is indicative of the change.[70] Predicting the Jews' conversion, these *Aufklärer* argued, would be tantamount to knowing God's providence. Like Döderlein, Michaelis could not confidently decipher the future and forecast Jews' conversion based on biblical prophecies. In his commentary on Isaiah he declared that no human could name the ways and time of their conversion.[71]

The growing skepticism resulted in a new understanding of the future that differentiated between a more or less well known tomorrow and the absolute incomprehensibility of the transcendent messianic age. Immanuel Kant, in his *Ideen zur einer allgemeinen Geschichte in weltbürgerlicher Absicht* (Ideas for a Universal History with a Cosmopolitan Intention), simply imagined a state of humanity that is fully unfolded and developed in the creation of a proper state constitution.[72] Yet in his *Das Ende aller Dinge* (The End of all Things) Kant, more clearly than Michaelis, transferred the *eschaton* to the present while envisioning the future as genuine transcendence breaking into the realm of historical time. He contended that it was impossible to know the future. Luke 17:31–22 ("The kingdom of God does not come in a visible fashion. There will be no saying, look, here it is or there. See, the kingdom of God is among you") served Kant to illustrate his point.[73] However, by excluding the *eschaton* from the temporal realm Kant presented the future as solely dependent on the past and present.[74]

These transformations turned Jewish messianism into an issue in the here and now that related to the general process of the emerging civic society and the spread of the Enlightenment. Within the Germanic lands Christian Wilhelm Dohm's *Ueber die bürglicher Verbesserung der Juden* (On the Civic Improvement of the Jews) in 1781 brought the discussion to new heights. Dohm addressed the topic of the Jews from a secular point of view, which was predicated on bracketing speculations about a transcendent future. His goal was not salvation or redemption but enlightenment and improvement. Unlike his predecessors, Dohm did not address the question of the Jews within the framework of his own messianic hopes but from the point of view of present politics. Thus in his seminal work he explored "if and by what means the Jews can become morally and politically better than they are now."[75] Dohm argued that once civic improvement set in Jews would undoubtedly reform their religious practices as well.[76]

In response to Dohm, Michaelis opined that Jews would never integrate themselves into German society because their hopes would continue to be directed at their return to Palestine. Jews could hardly be convinced otherwise, claimed Michaelis, since their rabbinic authorities predicted it this way, as did Isaac Newton and John Locke. Michaelis was apparently thinking here of Locke's *Commentaries on St. Paul's Epistles* from 1705 and Newton's *Dissertation on the Prophecies* (1754).[77]

Dohm agreed first of all with Michaelis's understanding of Jewish messianism as a political ideal. Yet he doubted that this represented a serious threat to the stability of the state: "The idea that the Jews still expect a savior who will save them from the present misery, and will erect a kingdom for them should not give us concern about the peace of our states."[78] Like other Enlighteners, he continued to ascribe a political nature to Jewish messianism. He differed, however, from others in comparing it to similar developments within early Christianity and contemporary Germany. In an interesting twist Dohm went on to postulate that the early church also believed in a messiah who would come and destroy empires and erect a thousand-year rule.[79] He asserted that this idea eventually waned but had at least remained with Christianity up to the time of Justin Martyr. Eventually the church embraced a spiritual understanding of the messianic era.[80] In order to buttress this view Dohm referred to Michaelis and extensively quoted from Lavater's *Aussichten in die*

Ewigkeit (Prospects of Eternity).[81] While Judaism still succumbed to this understanding, its messianic expectation, however, did not disturb the stability of the states. Most often only the lower classes become enchanted with these expectations, as Dohm explained in reference to the Christian messianic contenders of the second half of the eighteenth century.[82]

For the Enlighteners the self-proclaimed contemporary messiahs like Rosenfeld and Philipp Jakob Bekker were manic and delusional, and the state had the responsibility to act against them for the common good.[83] Rosenfeld and Bekker regarded the New Testament, the Sacraments, and the church service as works of the devil and Saturday as the true Sabbath. They saw themselves as divinely elected prophets. Drawing out a comparison between these "messiahs" and their Jewish counterparts, Dohm claimed that while David Alroi, David Reubeni, and Sabbatai Zevi caused the greatest stir among the Jews, it nevertheless took very little effort on the part of the government to suppress their movement.[84] Moreover, various rabbis no longer regarded the belief in the messiah as a fundamental principle. Finally, Dohm contended that messianism is a function of oppression and that every government that treats Jews well will undoubtedly quell these yearnings.[85] Despite Dohm's pervasive style of argumentation, Jewish messianism continued to be regarded by many as an obstacle for Jews' social and civil integration.[86]

Among German Jews the unrelenting criticism of Jewish messianism did not go unnoticed. In his rejoinder to the Dohm debate Moses Mendelssohn denied the importance of messianic hope for contemporary Jews and reminded Michaelis that the Jewish tradition prohibits speculating about the end of days.[87] Mendelssohn likewise countered the pervasive representation of Jewish messianism as a political platform when, basing himself on the Bible, he envisioned the ultimate fusion of all religion along with Isaiah 11:9 ("For the earth shall be full of the knowledge of the Lord, as the waters cover the sea"): "All the prophets of the Old Testament agree and reason is pleased in this expectation that the differences between the religions will not exist for an eternity and that the recognition of the true God will cover the whole earth, like the water the ocean."[88] At the same time, Mendelssohn also reiterated the belief in the messiah, who will restore the Jewish nation and liberate it from political oppression so that all nations can unite and pray to one God.[89] These two statements are, however, not at odds. Mendelssohn seems to suggest that Judaism anticipated first a messiah who will restore the Jews and consequently a new age that will unite all the nations. In between these two stages Mendelssohn anticipated a second revelation that would alter Jewish religious law.[90] In his 1783 *Jerusalem, oder über die religiöse Macht des Judentums* (Jerusalem; or, on the Religious Power of Judaism) he expected the principles of natural religion to have gained universal currency by 2240.[91]

The polemical edge of these statements becomes apparent if we remember that for Mendelssohn, Judaism encapsulated the true religion. If Dohm and others conceived of religion as an institution developed by reforming legislators, Mendelssohn upheld the view that an eternal legislator, who was not superseded by subsequent legislators, created Judaism. In light of this the messianic era was attainable not within historical progress but only through God. History would come to completion only at divinity's whim. For this reason Mendelssohn also staunchly opposed this idea when he attacked Lessing with "You want to divine what designs Providence has for Mankind?"[92]

In his defense of Judaism, Mendelssohn adopted the enlightened transcendental conception of a future in order to refute the Enlighteners' notion of progress. He presented a well-crafted critique of a fairly simplistic secularized philosophy of history that relegated Judaism to the distant past. In response to Mendelssohn, Kant once more denied Jewish messianism any universal significance and could not help but view Mendelssohn's opposition as tantamount to a new version of the Sisyphus myth.[93] Differentiating now more clearly between Jewish and Christian concepts of the messianic era, Kant embraced a model of a historical continuity. He faulted the Jews as having "sought to create a political and not a moral concept of the Messiah."[94] For Kant, only the "church belief" (*Kirchenglaube*) created evidence for "*Universalhistorie des menschlichen Geschlechts*" (universal history of humanity). With this secularized philosophy of history "the Jewish belief with its church belief" had no connection at all since it is only a collection of political legislation and not a genuine religion.[95] In line with this argument, Kant stressed that Christianity was a genuine new beginning and not a creation that continued to develop out of Judaism.[96] The future thus unfolds from the "kernel of true religious belief . . . in order to constantly approach the expected church that unites all of humanity, which makes up the visible vision of an invisible kingdom on earth."[97]

Kant based this secularized vision of historical progress and improvement on the postulated universalistic vision of Christianity. This understanding was predicated on a novel understanding of Christian messianism that eventually had overcome its "Jewish heritage." Historicizing Christian messianism thus helped to reclaim a Christian origin of the ideal of universal progress while leaving the question of ultimate redemption as an untouched and incomprehensible event. At the same time, this new conception of historical progress and salvation continued to displace Jewish messianism as an outdated concept that lacked the important spiritual dimension. In the eyes of the Enlighteners, Jewish messianism no longer competed with Christian eschatological anticipation but raised only a social question. Dohm, Michaelis, and Kant transferred the issue of Jews' conversion from the theological framework of redemption and religious polemics to this-worldly debates on social and cultural improvement and integration. Secularization represented here, therefore, more than a transformation of religious concepts. It entailed a complex process of displacement and discontinuity and, to use Blumenberg's formulations, a functional reoccupation of religious concepts.[98]

Notes

I want to thank my wife, Jennifer Roemer, for her unlimited patience and help in preparing this article as well as the editors of this volume, Allison Coudert and Jeffrey Shoulson, and the anonymous readers of the University of Pennsylvania Press for their helpful comments and suggestions. Last but not least, I want to thank Stephen Burnett and Michael Heyd for their generosity in sharing ideas and sources with me, and the staff of the Center for Advanced Judaic Studies and David Ruderman for their assistance and hospitality.

1. Christian Wilhelm Dohm, *Ueber die bürgerliche Verbesserung der Juden*, vol. 2 (Berlin, 1781–83), 42.

2. Dohm, *Ueber die bürgerliche Verbesserung der Juden*, vol. 2, 75. On French Enlightened debates about Jewish messianism, see Bertram E. Schwarzbach, "Le messianisme juif des divers écrits du siècle de lumières," *La Lettre Clandestine* 5 (1996): 291–331.

3. Karl Löwith, *Meaning in History: The Theological Implications of the Philosophy of History* (Chicago: University of Chicago Press, 1949), 114. See also W. Warren Wagar, "Modern Views of the Origins of the Idea of Progress," *Journal of the History of Ideas* 28 (1967): 55–70.

4. Hermann Cohen, *Religion of Reason Out of the Sources of Judaism*, trans. Simon Kaplan (New York: F. Ungar, 1972), 261.

5. Hans Blumenberg has forcefully argued against the secularization model. See his *Legitimacy of the Modern Age*, trans. Robert M. Wallace (Cambridge: MIT Press, 1983), 31–32, 64–65, 145. See also Alice Kuzniar, "Philosophic Chiliasm: Generating the Future or Delaying the End?" *Eighteenth-Century Studies* 19 (1985): 1–20.

6. The best guide for the discussion about Jewish messianism during this period remains the (unfortunately) never published or translated dissertation by Barukh Mevorah, *She'elat ha-mashiah be-pulmusey ha-emanzipaziah veha-reforma, 1781–1819* (The Problem of the Messiah in the Emancipation and Reform Controversies, 1781–1819) (Ph.D. diss., Hebrew University, 1966).

7. Gershom Scholem, "Toward an Understanding of the Messianic Idea in Judaism," in *The Messianic Idea in Judaism and Other Essays on Jewish Spirituality* (New York: Schocken, 1995), 1.

8. Antonius Margaritha, *Der gantz Jüdisch Glaub mit sampt eyner gründtlichenn und warhafftigen anzeygunge / aller satzungen / Ceremonien / gebetten / heymliche und öffentliche Gebreuch / deren sich die Juden halten, durch das gantz Jar / mit schönen unnd gegründeten Argumente wider iren glauben*, vol. 2 (Augsburg, 1531), B2, C2.

9. Ibid., vol. 2, B2, C1, C4. See also Elisheva Carlebach, "Jews, Christians, and the Endtime in Early Modern Germany," *Jewish History* 14 (2000): 331–44.

10. Martin Brecht, *Martin Luther: The Preservation of the Church, 1532–1546*, trans.

James L. Schaaf (Minneapolis: Fortress, 1993), 334–51 and Heiko A. Oberman, *Luther: Man Between God and the Devil,* trans. Eileen Walliser-Schwarzbart (New Haven: Yale University Press, 1982), 57–64.

11. Elisheva Carlebach, "Between History and Hope: Jewish Messianism in Ashkenaz and Sepharad" (Selmanowitz Lecture, Touro College, New York, 1998). The popular Till Eulenspiegel, for example, described how Jews of Frankfurt believed that they had acquired mystical berries that enabled them to prophesize the coming of the messiah. See Oskar Frankl, *Der Jude in der deutschen Dichtungen des 15., 16. und 17. Jahrhunderts* (Mähr.-Ostrau, Czech., 1905), 66.

12. Haim Hillel Ben-Sasson, "Jewish-Christian Disputations in the Setting of Humanism and Reformation in the German Empire," *Harvard Theological Review* 59 (1966): 369–90; and Elisheva Carlebach, "Between History and Hope: Jewish Messianism in Ashkenaz and Sepharad."

13. Christian Gerson, *Der Juden Thalmud fuernembster innhalt / und Widerlegung. In zwey Bücher verfasset. Im Ersten wird die gantze jüdische Religion und falsche Gottesdienst beschrieben. Im Andern werden dieselbe / beydes durch die Schrifft des Alten Testaments / und des Thalmuds selbst / gründlich widerlegt* (Goslar, Ger., 1609), 453–64; and Christian Gerson, *Chelec Oder Thalmudischer Jüdenschatz, Ist ein Capittel des Jüdischen Thalmuds* (Helmstedt, Ger., 1610).

14. Johann Buxtorf, *Synagoga Iudaica* (Basel, Switz., 1603), 641–91, esp. 645, 646–89. See Stephen Burnett, "Distorted Mirrors: Antonius Margaritha, Johann Buxtorf, and Christian Ethnographies of Judaism," *Sixteenth Century Journal* 25 (1994): 275–87.

15. Richard H. Popkin, "The Fictional Jewish Council of 1650: A Great English Pipedream," *Jewish History* 5 (1991): 7–22.

16. On Menasseh ben Israel's messianic thinking see Harold Fisch, "The Messianic Politics of Menasseh ben Israel," in *Menasseh ben Israel and His World,* ed. Yosef Kaplan et al. (Leiden, Neth.: E. J. Brill, 1989), 228–39; and Rivka Schatz-Uffenheimer, "Menasseh ben Israel's Approach to Messianism in the Jewish-Christian Context," in ibid., 244–61. On the ten lost tribes, see Richard H. Popkin, "The Rise and Fall of the Jewish Indian Theory," in ibid., 63–82.

17. Michael Buchenröder actually held these accounts partially responsible for the pervasive spread of the movement. See Michael Buchenröder, *Eilende Messias Juden-Post / Oder gründliche Widerlegung des heutigen Gedichts von den neu- / standenen Messia der Juden / und seine Propheten Nathans: Wie auch / von anderen dergleichen sich mehrmahls entbörenden jüdischen Rebellen: Dem einigen / rechten und wahren Messia / JESU CHRISTO zu Ehren; Denen Christen allerseits / und ins gemein zu Staerckung ihres Glaubens; Denen Juden und Juden-Genossen aber / zur Warnung fuer Schaden mit GOTT / aus Treuen wohmeindem Hertzen An alle Hohe und Nidere / zu sonder-barem Belieben und Nachdencken aufgesetzet* (Nürnberg, 1666), F4v. See also Richard H. Popkin, "Three English Tellings of the Sabbatai Zevi Story," *Jewish History* 8 (1994): 43–54; Michael McKeon, "Sabbatai Sevi in England," *Association of Jewish Studies Review* 3 (1977): 131–69; Jetteke van Wijk, "The Rise and Fall of Sabbati Zevi as Reflected in Contemporary Press Reports," *Studia Rosenthaliana* 33 (1999): 7–27; Christiane Ahrens, "Sabbatai Zevi (1626–1676), Untersuchungen zu einer messianischen Bewegung und ihrer Rezeption in deutschsprachigen zeitgenössischen Quellen" (diss., Hamburg University, 1979); Michal Galas, "Sabbateanism in Polish Historiography," in *Jewish Studies in a New Europe* (Copenhagen: C. A. Reitzel, 1998), 262–68; and S. Simonsohn, "A Christian Report from Constantinople Regarding Sabbethai Sevi (1666)," *Jewish Social Studies* 12 (1961): 33–58.

18. John Evelyn, *The History of the Three Late Famous Impostors: Padre Ottomano, Mohamed Bei, and Sabatai Sevi* (London, 1669), 43.

19. Paul Rycaut, *The History of the Turkish Empire from the Year 1623 to the Year 1677: Containing the Reigns of the Three Last Emperours, viz. Sultan Morat or Amurat IV. Sultan Ibrahim, and Sultan Mahomet IV. His Son, the XIII. Emperour Now Reigning* (London, 1680). A German translation of this work appeared in *Die neu-eröffnete Ottomanische Pforte* (Augsburg, Ger., 1700).

20. Ahrens, "Sabbatai Zevi (1626–1676), Untersuchungen zu einer messianischen Bewegung und ihrer Rezeption in deutschsprachigen zeitgenössischen Quellen," 79–80.

21. Grimmelshausen, *Das wunderliche Vogelnest*, ed. Rolf Tarot (Tübingen, Ger.: Max Niemeyer, 1970), 228–29.

22. Buchenröder, *Eilende Messias Juden-Post*, A2v, A3r.

23. See the article by Michael Heyd, "The 'Jewish Quaker': Christian Perceptions of Sabbatai Zevi as an Enthusiast," in this volume as well as idem, "*Be Sober and Reasonable*": *The Critique of Enthusiasm in the Seventeenth and Early Eighteenth Centuries* (Leiden, Neth.: E. J. Brill, 1995).

24. Martin Diefenbach, *Judaeus Convertendus, oder verschiedene Urtheile und Vorschläge Führnehmer Theologen und anderer Gelehrten wie die Bekehrung eines Juden durch Gottes Gnade zu suchen und zu befördern seye / aus ihrem Schrifften mit beygefügten Anmerckungen* (Frankfurt, 1696), 65; idem, *Judaeus Conversus, Oder: Umständliche und glaubhafte Erzehlung / was sich vormahls mit einem allhier im Hospital Dieb-Stahls halben / gefänglich gesessen / und auff sein instendiges Begehren im Christenthumb wohl unterwiesenen / darauf gehörig getaufften und so nochmals am Hoch-Gericht in Glauben an CHR Jesum selig Bekehrten Juden begeben. Sammt fernen Erläuterungen und weitlauffigen Ausführungen des von Ihm allbereit Anno 1696 herauß gegebenen Judaei Convertendi. Zu Endt findet sich: Die Nachricht wegen des vor 5. Jahren allhier geschehenen Tauffe / Asel zum Hinter-Hecht / hiesigen geschaften Juden Sohns / nochmals Johann Zacharias Heylwart genanndt / und der mit Ihm seithero vorgefallenen bedencklichen Begebenheiten. Mit Zweyen dahin gehörigen Juden-Predigten / und behorigen Register* (Frankfurt, 1709), 78. On Pietism, see Martin Schmidt, "Judentum und Christentum im Pietismus des 17. und 18. Jahrhunderts," in *Kirche und Synagoge: Handbuch zur Geschichte von Christen und Juden. Darstellung mit Quellen*, vol. 2, ed. Karl Heinrich Rengstorf and Siegfried von Kortzfleisch (Stuttgart, Ger.: Klett, 1968), 87–128.

25. Diefenbach, *Judaeus Convertendus*, 65–66. In 1708, for example, the University of Giessen brought two Judaizers to trial, who had apparently confused Christians and simultaneously reassured Jews in their beliefs. Johann Jacob Schudt reprinted the testimonial in his *Jüdische Merkwürdigkeiten Vorstellende was sich Curieuses und denckwürdiges in den neuern Zeiten bey einigen Jahr-hunderten mit denen in alle IV. Theile der Welt / sonderlich durch Teutschland / zerstreuten Juden zugetragen. Sammt einer vollständigen Frankfurter Juden-Chronik / Darinnen der zu Franckfurt am Mayn wohnenden Juden / von eingen Jahr-hunderten / bis auff unsere Zeiten merckwürdigste Begebenheiten enthaltend. Benebst eingen / zur Erläuterung beygefügten Kupffern und Figuren*, vol. 1 (Frankfurt, 1714–18), 562–69.

26. Johann Wilhelm Petersen, *Bekenntnis von dem Zukünfftigen herrlichen Reich Jesu Christi Und Der damit verbundenen ersten Aufferstehung: Zum Unterrichte aus den unmittelbaren Worten der heiligen Schrifften und nach dem Zeugnüß der Wahrheit in Frag und Antwort gestellet* (Magdeburg, Ger., 1693).

27. He fled with his followers to Pennsylvania but died on the way. See J. F. A. de le Roi, *Die evangelische Christenheit und die Juden in der Zeit der Herrschaft christlicher Lebensanschauungen unter den Völkern. Von der Reformation bis zur Mitte des 18. Jahrhunderts* (Karlsruhe, Ger., 1884), 100.

28. See his contribution in this volume.

29. *Beschreibung des newen Jüdischen Königs Sabetha Sebi / Dessen Ursprung / Alter / Gestalt / Thun / Lassen / Anhang und Wunderwerke. Wie auch der Christen / Juden / Türcken und anderer Urtheil hierüber / und was sonsten aus unterschiedlichen Schrifften dar von bis dato kund worden. Wobey dann auch des Königs eigentliche Gestalt / in Kupffer gestochen ist* (1666), A2r–B4v. Grimmelshausen posited that Sabbatai Zevi was the nineteenth false messiah. See Grimmelshausen, *Das wunderliche Vogelnest*, 241.

30. Gerson, *Der Juden Thalmud fuernembster inhalt*, 453–64. This work appeared originally in 1607 and subsequently in 1609, 1613, 1618, 1659, 1668, and 1685.

31. Johann à Lent, *Schediasma Philologicum de Judaeorum Pseudo-Messiis* (Herbornae, Ger., 1697). See, for example, Sigismund Hosmann, *Das schwer zu bekehrende Juden-Hertz nebst einigen Vorbereitungs-Mittel zu der Juden-Bekehrung. Auf Veranlassung des erschröcklichen Gottes-Lästerung / welche der Juden Jonas Meyer von Wunschtorff / als er vor der Fürstl. Residentz-Stadt Zelle / nebst anderen hochberüchtigten Dieben den 21 Martii. An 1699 abgethan / und nach dem Oberbalcken des Gerichts / behuff einer Wände hierauf gezogen ward. Zu vieler tausend Zuschauer höchster Bestürzung öffentlich in der Lufft schwerbend ausgerufen* (Zelle, Ger., 1699), 92–127; Richard Kidder, *A Demonstration of the Messias: In Which the Truth of the Christian Religion Is Proved, Against All the Enemies Thereof; But Especially against the Jews*, vol. 3 (London, 1684–1700), 389–425; and Johann Andreas Eisenmenger, *Entdecktes Judenthum, Oder Gründlicher und wahrhaffter Bericht, welchergestalt die verstockten Juden die hochheilige Dreyeinigkeit, GOtt Vater, Sohn und Heiligen Geist, erschrecklicher Weise lästern und verunehren, die Heil. Mutter Christi verschmähen, das Neue Testament, die Evangelisten und Aposteln, die Christliche Religion spöttlich durchziehen, und die gantze Christenheit auff das äusserste verachten und verfluchen; dabey noch viele andere, bishero unter den Christen entweder gar nicht, oder nur zum Theil bekant-gewesene Dinge und grosse Irrthüme der Jüdischen Religion und Theologie, wie auch Viel lächerliche und kurtzweilige Fabeln, und andere ungereimte Sachen an den Tag kommen; Alles aus ihren eigenen, und zwar sehr vielen, mit grosser Mühe und unverdrossenen Fleiß durchgelesenen Büchern, mit Anziehung der Hebräischen Worte, und deren treuen Uebersetzung in die teutsche Sprach, kräfftiglich erwiesen, und in Zweyen Theilen verfasset, deren jeder seine behörige allemal von einer gewissenen Materie außführlich handelnde Capitel enthält. Allen Christen zur treuhertzigen Nachricht verfertiget, und mit vollkommenen Registern versehen*, vol. 2 (Königsberg, Ger., 1700), 654–68.

32. Johann Christoph Müller, *Greuel der falschen Messien / wie auch / Schatz-Kammer des wahren Messiae Jesu Christi* (1702), 23–25. On Oliger Paulli, see Hans Joachim Schoeps, *Philosemitismus im Barock: Religionsgeschichtliche Untersuchungen* (Tübingen, Ger., J. C. Mohr, 1952), 53–67; and Wolfgang Philipp, "Spätbarock and frühe Aufklärung. Das Zeitalter des Philosemitismus," ed. Karl Heinrich Regnstorf and Siegfried von Kortzfleisch, *Kirche und Synagoge: Handbuch zur Geschichte von Christen und Juden. Darstellung mit Quellen*, vol. 2 (Stuttgart, Ger., Ernst Klett Verlag, 1970), 65–67.

33. Müller, Introduction to *Greuel der falschen Messien wie auch Schatz-Kammer des wahren Messiae Jesu Christi*.

34. Jacques Basnage devoted a substantial section to Sabbatai Zevi as well as to other messianic contenders like Mordechai of Eisenstadt. See Berek Laurent, "Vision du Messianisme juif et apologétique chrétienne dans l'histoire des juifs de Jacques Basnage," *Dix-Septième Siècle* 45 (1993): 247–71. The influential Zedler encyclopedia features a long entry on Sabbatai Zevi that summarized previous scholarship. See "Sevi" in Johann Heinrich Zedler, *Grosses vollständiges Universal-Lexikon*, vol. 35 (Halle, Ger., 1743), 713–15.

35. Schudt, *Jüdische Merkwürdigkeiten*, vol. 2: pt. 2, 43–47; and Johann Eisenmenger, *Entdecktes Judenthum*, 666–67.

36. Silvia Berti, "Unmasking the Truth: The Theme of Imposture in Early European Culture, 1660–1730," in *Everything Connects: In Conference with Richard H. Popkin. Essays in His Honor*, ed. James E. Force and David S. Katz (Leiden, Neth.: Brill, 1999), 21–36.

37. Kidder, *A Demonstration of the Messias*, vol. 3, 389–424; and Schudt, *Jüdische Merkwürdigkeiten*, introduction to vol. 4.

38. Schudt, *Jüdische Merkwürdigkeiten*, vol. 2, pt. 2, 55–63; and Johann Andreas Eisenmenger, *Entdecktes Judenthum*, vol. 2, 667–68. The works of Abraham Franckenburg of Silesia (1593–1652), John Mochinger of Danzig (1603–52), and Paul Felgenhauer (1593–1600) of Bohemia became well known in Germany. See Abba Hillel Silver, *A History of Messianic Speculation in Israel: From the First through the Seventeenth Centuries* (New York: Macmillan, 1927), 161–83.

39. Hosmann, *Das schwer zu bekehrende Juden-Hertz*, 101.

40. *Curieuser Nachrichten aus dem Reich der Beschnittenen, 1. Theil zwischen Sabathai Sevi einem im vorigen Seculo in den Morgenländern höchst-berichtigt gewesenen jüdischen Ertz-Betrüger, und dem Fameusen Würtenberg. Advanturier, Jud Joseph Süß Oppenheimer worinnen dieser beyden beschnittenen Spitzbuben Leben und Begebenheiten entdecket, und noch andere, zur Erkänntniß jüdischer Geschichte, Gebräuche, Ceremonien dienlichen und Lebenswürdigen Sachen mit angebracht werden* (Frankfurt, 1738), 19.

41. *Curieuser Nachrichten aus dem Reich der Beschnittenen*, 21.

42. On Jud Süss, see Barbara Gerber, *Jud Süss Aufstieg und Fall im frühen 18. Jahrhundert. Ein Beitrag zur historischen Antisemitismus- und Rezeptionsforschung* (Hamburg, Ger.: H. Christians, 1990).

43. *Curieuser Nachrichten aus dem Reich der Beschnittenen*, 21.

44. Eisenmenger, *Entdecktes Judenthum*, vol. 2, 202.

45. Ibid., 747–48, 755–74.

46. Ibid., vol. 3, 237–38.

47. Johann Christoph Wagenseil, *Hoffnung der Erlösung Israels oder klarer Beweis des annoch bevorstehenden / und / wie es scheinet / allgemach-herannahenden großen Juden-Bekehrung / sammt unvorgreifflichen Gedancken / wie solche nächst Verleihung göttlicher Hülfe zu befördern* (Nürnberg, 1707), 1–15.

48. Johann Wolfgang Bodenschatz, *Kirchliche Verfassung der heutigen Juden sonderlich derer in Deutschland in IV. Haupt-Theile abgefasset aus ihren eigenen und anderen Schriften umständlich dargethan und mit 30 sauberen Kupfern erläutert*, vol. 3 (Frankfurt, 1748–49), 181–216, esp. 182.

49. Albrecht Friedrich Christiani, *Der Jüden Glaube und Aberglaube: Ehemals auff Verlangen seiner Auditorum zu mehrer Gewissheit beschrieben* (Leipzig, Ger., 1705), 65–80; Christoph Paulo Meyer, *Der jüdische Narren-Spigel / Worinne sie sich Spiegeln nach ihren weltlichen Messias / der so ein grosser Herr soll sein / als Mosis gewesen ist /*

der sie erlöset hat aus Egypten-Land. Zum andern handelt diß Tractätlein / nicht alleine von den Jüdischen Lebens-Lauff / sondern auch von Geistlichen und Weltlichen Dingen / welches kürtzlich und Curieus zu lesen ist (1685), and Friedrich Christian Mayer, *Davidisches Blümlein aus dem 91. Psalm darinnen die Eigenschafften des Herren Messiae aus denen Rabbinen und caballistischen Büchern angeführet worden / auch wie die Juden in der Succa unter den Schatten deren Bäume annoch sitzen / Aber die Gläubigen Christen / unter den Schatten Gottes / Nebst gewisser Ursache ihrer Verstockung / daß sie den HERRN Christum nicht vor den wahren Messiam erkenne wollen* (Jena, Ger., 1715). For additional references, see Elisheva Carlebach, "Sabbatianism and the Jewish-Christian Polemic," in *Proceedings of the World Congress of Jewish Studies*, Division C2 (1989): 1–7; Richard Popkin, "Christian Jews and Jewish Christians in the Seventeenth Century," in *Jewish Christians and Christian Jews: From the Renaissance to the Enlightenment*, ed. idem and Gordon M. Weiner (Dordrecht, Neth.: Kluwer Academic Publishers, 1993), 57–72; and Jehuda Libes, "A Crypto Judaeo-Christian Sect of Sabbatean Origin" (in Hebrew), *Tarbiz* 77 (1988): 349–84.

50. de le Roi, *Die evangelische Christenheit und die Juden*, 108.

51. Johann Friedrich Mentes, *Buch des Glaubens des Messias. Buch des wahren Glaubens des warhafftigen Messiä und Heylandes Jesu Christu* (Hamburg, Ger., 1720), 27–30.

52. See Gershom Scholem, *Sabbatai Sevi: The Mystical Messiah* (Princeton: Princeton University Press, 1973), 584–88; and in general on Jewish opposition to active messianism during this period, see Elisheva Carlebach, *The Pursuit of Heresy: Rabbi Moses Hagiz and the Sabbatian Controversies* (New York: Columbia University Press, 1990).

53. Tobias Cohen, *Ma'aseh Tuviyyah* (Venice, 1707), 17b–19b; and David B. Ruderman, *Jewish Thought and Scientific Discovery in Early Modern Europe* (New Haven: Yale University Press, 1995), 242–43.

54. D. Hartley, *Observations on Man, His Fame, His Duty, and His Expectations in Two Parts*, 2d ed. (London, 1791), 526–628. The work was also translated into German and appeared as David Hartley, *Betrachtungen über den Menschen, seine Natur, seine Pflicht und Erwartungen*, 2 vols. (Rostock, Ger., 1772–73).

55. D. Thomas Scherlock, *Abhandlungen vom Zweck und Gebrauch der Weissagungen*, trans. Friedrich Eberhard Rambach (Lemgo, Ger., 1749).

56. Carl Anton, *Kurze Nachricht von dem falschen Messias Sabbatai Zebbi, und den neulich seinetwegen in Hamburg und Altona entstandenen Bewegungen zu besserer Beurteilung derer bisher in den Zeitungen und andern Schriften davon bekandt gewordenen Erzählungen* (Wolfenbüttel, Ger., 1752); Carl Anton, *Nachlese zu seiner letztern Nachricht von Sabbatai Zebbi worin zugleich das Ende dieser Streitigkeiten erzählet wird* (Braunschweig, Ger., 1753); and *Leben und Thaten des berufenen Verführers und falschen Messias Sabathai Sevi oder Schabsasvi. Bey Gelegenheit der Streitigkeiten, so seit einiger Zeit unter den Juden hervorgethan, aus dem Französischen übersetzt von R. R.* (Frankfurt, 1752). At the same time, the seventeenth-century French account of Sabbatai Zevi by the historian Jean-Baptiste de Rocoles appeared in a German translation. See Jean-Baptiste de Rocoles, *Der Erzbetrüger Sabbatai Sevi, der letzte falsche Messias der Juden unter Leopolds I. Regierung. Im Jahr der 5666 und 1666sten nach Christi Geburt. Mit allergnädigsten Privilegien* (Halle, Ger., 1760). Apparently this is an offprint of Jean Baptista de Rocoles, *Königlich Französicher und Churfürstlich Brandenburgischer Geschichtsschreiber, Begebenheiten ausnehmender Betrüger. In zwei Theilen. Mit Anmerkungen und einer Vorrede herausgegeben von D. Carl Friedrich Pauli* (Halle, Ger., 1760).

57. David Friedrich Megerlin, *Bedenkliche Lehren der zwey vornehmsten Jüdischen Rabbinen, Abarbanels und Maimonidis, von dem gesetzlichen Jubel-Jahr und dessen sonderbaren Absichten, wie auch von denen Kennzeichen des Königs Meßiä und dem heiligen Verlangen nach ihm aus dem Rabbinischen neu übersezt, und zu erbaulichem Gebrauch der Christen und Juden, sonderlich der leztern Überzeugung von der Wahrheit Jesu des Welt-Heilandes auf Begehren ans Licht gegeben* (Frankfurt, 1751). See the partial reprint of this work in Friedrich Niewöhner, *Aufklärung und Toleranz in Mittelalter* (Heidelberg, 1988), 43–54. David Megerlin also cites the reports about the fictional rabbinical council by S. Brett in his *Geheime Zeugnisse, vor die Wahrheit der Christlichen Religion, aus vier und zwanzig neuen und seltenen Jüdischen Amuleten, oder Anhäng-Zetteln gezogen: welche, samt dabey stehenden Siglen oder Davids-Schilden, nach Cabbalistischen Reglen aufgeschlossen, in eine allenfaßliche teutsche Übersetzung gebracht, und mit nöthigen und erbaulichen Anmerckungen versehen worden, zu Rettung der Ehre des Christlichen Lehr-Begriffs, von der H. H. Dreyeinigkeit, und dem Königreich Jesu Christi, wider die neueste Jüdische Einwendungen* (Frankfurt, 1756), 64.

58. J. F. A. de le Roi, *Geschichte der evangelischen Juden-Mission seit Entstehung des neueren Judentums* (Leipzig, Ger., 1889), 23.

59. Bodenschatz, *Kirchliche Verfassung der heutigen Juden*, vol. 3, 182, 197–204.

60. Christian Janetzky, *Lavaters Sturm und Drang in Zusammenhang seines religiösen Bewußtseins* (Halle, Ger.: Niemeyer, 1916), 30, 64.

61. Gotthold Ephraim Lessing, *Erziehung des Menschengeschlechts*, in *Gotthold Ephraim Lessing. Werke*, vol. 8, ed. Herbert G. Göpfert (Darmstadt, Ger.: Wissenschaftliche Buchgesellschaft, 1996), 489–510.

62. Bodenschatz, *Kirchliche Verfassung der heutigen Juden*, vol. 1.

63. Johann Jacob Semler, *Uebersetzung der Algemeinen Welthistorie der Neuen Zeiten die in England durch eine Gesellschaft von Gelehrten ausgefertigt worden* (Halle, Ger., 1765), 308–09. See also Anton Friedrich Büsching, *Geschichte der jüdischen Religion oder des Gesetzes. Ein Grundriß* (Berlin, 1779), 246.

64. Johann Christoph Döderlein, *Giebt uns die Bibel Hoffnung zu einer künftigen allgemeinen Judenbekehrung* (Nürnberg, 1781), 8.

65. Ibid., 11.

66. Ibid., 20.

67. Ibid., 30–42.

68. Ibid., 44.

69. Heinrich Corrodi, *Kritische Geschichte des Chiliasmus*, 2 vols. (Frankfurt, 1781–1783); and Reinhart Koselleck, "'Space of Experience' and 'Horizon of Expectation': Two Historical Categories," in *Futures Past: On the Semantics of Historical Time*, trans. Keith Tribe (Cambridge: MIT Press, 1985), 267–88.

70. Dohm, *Ueber die bürgerliche Verbesserung der Juden*, vol. 2, 77–88.

71. Johann David Michaelis, *Deutsche Übersetzung des Alten Testaments* (Göttingen, Ger., 1779), 297.

72. Immanuel Kant, *Ideen zur einer allgemeinen Geschichte in weltbürgerlicher Absicht*, in *Immanuel Kant: Werkausgabe*, vol. 6, ed. Wilhelm Weischedel (Frankfurt: Suhrkamp, 1993), 45: A 404.

73. Immanuel Kant, *Die Religion innerhalb der Grenzen der blossen Vernunft*, in *Immanuel Kant: Werkausgabe*, vol. 6, ed. Weischedel, 802–3: A 195–96.

74. Immanuel Kant, *Das Ende aller Dinge*, in *Immanuel Kant: Werkausgabe*, vol. 6, ed. Weischedel, 175–76; A 495–A 498, and Kant, *Die Religion innerhalb der Grenzen der*

blossen Vernunft, 800–803: A 192–96. See also Johann Gottfried Herder, "Vom Wissen und Nichtwissen der Zukunft," in *Herders Sämmtliche Werke*, ed. Bernhard Suphan (Berlin, 1887), 16:368–81.

75. Dohm, *Ueber die bürgerliche Verbesserung der Juden*, vol. 2, 152.

76. Ibid. vol. 1, 143–44.

77. Ibid., vol. 2, 42–43. Thomas Newton also appeared in a German translation as *Abhandlungen über die Weissagungen, die merkwürdig erfüllt sind, und noch bis auf den heutigen Tag in ihre Erfüllung gehen*, 3 vols. (Leipzig, Ger., 1757–63).

78. Dohm, *Ueber die bürgerliche Verbesserung der Juden*, vol. 2, 215.

79. Dohm is here referring to Justin Martyr's *Dialogue with Trypho*, chapter 80, titled "The Opinion of Justin with Regard to the Reign of a Thousand Years. Several Catholics Reject It." Along these lines the German poet Christoph Martin Wieland presented Jesus in 1799 as still wavering between the political and spiritual forms of messianism, an ambiguity, however, that Jesus overcame toward the end of his life. See Christoph Martin Wieland, *Agathodaemon. In sieben Büchern*, ed. Fritz Martini and Hans Werner Seiffert, vol. 2, bk. 7, no. 3 of *Werke* (Munich, 1966), 2: 673.

80. Dohm pointed to the scholarship of Lavater and Michaelis to buttress this point. This, however, could also have been based on Reimarus, who contended that Jesus was still sharing the political understanding of messianism before the Apostles spiritualized it. This idea can also be found in some of the clandestine literature. See Winfried Schröder, *Ursprünge des Atheismus, Untersuchungen zur Metaphysik- und Religionskritik des 17. und 18. Jahrhunderts* (Stuttgart-Bad-Canstatt, Ger.: Friedrich Frommann Verlag, 1998), 103.

81. Dohm, *Ueber die bürgerliche Verbesserung der Juden*, vol. 2, 215.

82. Ibid., 218.

83. J. E. Biester, "Der vorgebliche Messias in Berlin," *Berlinische Monatsschrift*, vol. 1 (1783), 43–79; J. M. Schwager, "Noch ein neuer Messias. An die Herausgeber der Berlinischen Monatsschrift," *Berlinische Monatsschrift* (1783), 266–76; and J. E. Biester, "Ein neuer Messias," *Berlinische Monatsschrift* (1784), 438–41.

84. Dohm, *Ueber die bürgerliche Verbesserung der Juden*, vol. 2, 218.

85. Ibid., 218–20.

86. L. Kahle, *Anmerkungen zu dem Buch ueber die bürgerliche Verbesserung der Juden* (Berlin, 1789), 75, postulated that the messianic belief had remained an essential component of Judaism and that Jews could easily again be fooled into believing in a messiah.

87. Mendelssohn illustrates this by quoting the Song of Songs 2:77 and 3:5. See Dohm, *Ueber die bürgerliche Verbesserung der Juden*, vol. 2, 42–43.

88. Moses Mendelssohn, "Gegenbetrachtungen über Bonnets Palingenesie," ed. Alexander Altmann et al., in vol. 7 of *Moses Mendelssohn. Gesammelte Schriften. Jubiläumsausgabe* (Stuttgart-Bad-Canstatt: Friedrich Frommann Verlag, 1974), 98.

89. Mendelssohn, "Gegenbetrachtungen über Bonnets Palingenesie," 102.

90. Ibid., 97.

91. Moses Mendelssohn, "Jerusalem oder über religiöse Macht und Judentum," in vol. 8 of *Moses Mendelssohn. Gesammelte Schriften. Jubiläumsausgabe*, ed. Alexander Altmann et al. (Stuttgart-Bad-Canstatt, Ger.: Friedrich Frommann Verlag, 1983), 127. Mendelssohn was apparently basing himself here on Avoda zarah 9a–b and Sanhedrin 97a–b.

92. Mendelssohn, "Jerusalem oder über religiöse Macht und Judentum," 163.

93. Immanuel Kant, *Ueber den Gemeinspruch: Das mag in der Theorie richtig sein, taugt aber nicht fuer die Praxis* (1793), in vol. 6 of *Immanuel Kant: Werkausgabe*, ed. Weischedel, 166; A 273. See also Alexander Altmann, *Moses Mendelssohn: A Biographical Study* (London: Routledge and Kegan Paul, 1973), 542–43.

94. Kant, *Die Religion innerhalb der Grenzen der blossen Vernunft*, 788–89, A 174–76.

95. Ibid., 791, A 179.

96. Ibid., 792, A 180.

97. Ibid., 797, A 188.

98. Blumenberg, *Legitimacy of the Modern Age*, 31–32, 64–65, 145.

12
Five Seventeenth-Century Christian Hebraists

Allison P. Coudert

This essay is addressed to those "modern scavengers" who, to cite Frank Manuel's colorful rhetoric, have begun to "pick the bones" of Christian Hebraists, whose vast and largely unread tomes occupy "a corner in the cemetery of baroque learning."[1] The disinterring of these largely forgotten works, which began only recently, has made it clear that bone-picking can be a lively and exciting business that involves far more than a confrontation between Christians and Jews, or Judaism and Christianity. No single thread runs through the works of Christian Hebraists. Their responses to Jews and Judaism were as varied as their own religious and cultural backgrounds, perspectives, and even professions. From the Renaissance through the Enlightenment, Jewish-Christian encounters became a key element in defining attitudes toward personal, national, and religious identity, and these definitions, in turn, involved debates about the nature and basis of language, history, religion, morality, and truth in general. The goal of this essay is to substantiate this claim by analyzing the work of five seventeenth-century Christian Hebraists, whose varied responses to Judaism reflect assumptions about God, nature, and man that were anything but settled at the time. The Christian Hebraists I shall deal with are Johan Jacob Schudt (1644–1722), Christian Knorr von Rosenroth (1636–89), Francis Mercury van Helmont (1614–98), Johann Georg Wachter (1673–1757), and Johann Peter Späth (1642/5–1701).[2] I have chosen these five because they were among the most influential Christian Hebraists of the period, they knew each other, and they were all deeply involved in a scandalous event that quickly became a cause célèbre, the conversion of one of them, namely Späth, to Judaism. Describing the reasons for Späth's conversion and the reactions to it is a bit like creating a seventeenth-century Christian Hebraist "Rashomon": there are multiple stories and multiple truths depending on who tells the tale. For Johann Jacob Schudt, a sincere and dedicated Lutheran apologist, Späth's conversion was an unmitigated disaster, which reinforced the dangers of Judaism and the need for Lutherans to shore up their identity as the new "Chosen People" and legitimate successors to the Jews. For Christian Kabbalists like Knorr von Rosenroth and van Helmont, Späth's conversion represented a failure of nerve and a retreat into the kind of divisive, combative religious particularism they worked tirelessly to overcome. From Johann Georg Wachter's perspective Späth's conversion represented something quite different. It was enticing evidence of the utter bankruptcy of confessional Christianity of every variety and of revealed religion in general, including Judaism. For Späth himself, however, converting to Judaism was the only logical and possible choice for someone who had tried a smorgasbord of Christianities—Catholicism, Lutheranism, Socinianism, Quakerism—and found them all wanting. These very different reactions to a single event illustrate the crucial role that Jewish-Christian encounters had in raising and answering uncomfortable questions about the nature of religious identity and religious truth.

But before discussing the causes and repercussions of Späth's conversion it is important to understand that these Christian Hebraists were part of a more inclusive network of Christian scholars, theologians, scientists, and sectarians, all of whom were Christian Hebraists to some degree and many of whom had personal and professional contacts with Jewish scholars, tradesmen, and artisans. I have tried to give some idea of the extent and intricacy of these connections in the appendix at the end of this essay. I have placed van Helmont and his friend and collaborator Knorr von Rosenroth at the head of the appendix along with their patron, Prince Christian August of Sulzbach, who was himself a passionate Christian Hebraist, to emphasize the little-known fact that Sulzbach was a center of Christian Hebraism at the time. The connections between these Christian Hebraists and their contemporaries are extensive and cut across both geographical lines and, more importantly, those neat intellectual categories largely and inaccurately drawn by nineteenth- and twentieth-century scholars. Gottfried Wilhelm Leibniz may not seem such an anomaly on this list because everyone is aware of his diverse philosophical interests though not the extent of his knowledge and use of Kabbalah.[3] But what is John Locke, that alleged champion of reason and foremost exponent of British empiricism, doing on the same page as rabbis, Kabbalists, Quakers, and Collegiants? The answer is that Locke's interests and acquaintances were more varied than commonly imagined. He was a close friend of van Helmont, had a number of van Helmont's kabbalistic works in his library, and copied passages from kabbalistic texts that are preserved among his manuscripts in the Bodleian Library. In addition he was intimately acquainted with Benjamin Furly, a leading Dutch Quaker and an accomplished Christian Hebraist, who was also a close friend of van Helmont and accepted his kabbalistic theories.[4] From the Dutch and English columns in the appendix it is apparent that Furly was not the only Quaker linked to the Sulzbach Christian Hebraists. This is because van Helmont actually became a Quaker himself on the assumption that the Quakers would accept his brand of Lurianic Kabbalah. Indeed, a number of Quakers did accept it, and a group of Helmontian-Quaker-Kabbalists emerged, who caused considerable controversy among Quakers in Europe and America.[5] The fact that Jews appear on this list—for example, rabbis like Menasseh ben Israel and Jacob Juda Leon, famous for his reconstruction of the Temple, as well as Jewish printers and teachers—is evidence that Jews were key players and not passive onlookers in the religious debates of the period. Even more surprising, perhaps, is the inclusion of Spinoza and his placement between Jews, Collegiants, and Quakers. The actual extent of Spinoza's relationship with the last two groups is still a matter of conjecture. Richard Popkin is convinced that Spinoza translated two Quaker tracts into Hebrew. Popkin has also argued that Spinoza's *Tractatus Theologico-Politicus* reflects the influence of the Quaker Samuel Fisher.[6]

But to return to Späth and his conversion to Judaism. Späth had a long history of conversion and reconversion before he took the decisive and dangerous step of abandoning Christianity for Judaism. Born a Catholic, he apparently first had doubts about his faith while employed as a tutor by a Protestant family, whose members challenged him to defend his beliefs. He subsequently had occasion to meet and debate with Lutherans, and at some point—the date is uncertain—he went to Tübingen, where he converted. But this was only the beginning of Späth's religious odyssey. Remarking on the bitter divisions within the ranks of Lutherans, he became increasingly disillusioned with his new faith, regretted his conversion, and returned to the Catholic fold. Still his doubts continued, and he moved to Amsterdam, where he came in contact with Mennonites, Collegiants, and Socinians, such as Peter Serrarius and Adam Boreel, who were themselves in touch with Jews and, indeed, with Spinoza. Johan Jacob Schudt reports that Späth became a Quaker.[7] It was at this juncture that he met Francis Mercury van Helmont and moved to Sulzbach to help with the printing and publication of the *Kabbala denudata*, the largest collection of kabbalistic, especially Lurianic, texts published in Latin up to that time. The exact chronology of subsequent events is hazy, but for some years before his official conversion to Judaism in 1696 Späth resided in Amsterdam, where he assumed the name Moses Germanus. After being initially rebuffed by the leaders of the Portuguese synagogue, Späth was officially converted and circumcised. He married a Jewish woman, started a family, and found employment as a teacher. According to the reports of Christians, which will be discussed below, he lived in dire poverty and died under mysterious circumstances.[8]

The most complete account of Späth's life and conversion is found in

Johann Jacob Schudt's imposing multivolume work *Jüdische Merkwürdigkeiten*, a title that is difficult to translate because *Merkwürdigkeiten* can be taken in the pejorative sense of curiosities, peculiarities, oddness, or strangeness but can at the same time imply things that are exceptional and worth noticing or pointing out.[9] This huge work was published in Frankfurt and Leipzig in 1714–18.[10] If any work can claim to be an ethnography of the Jews, this is surely it. Schudt is clearly intrigued by Jews. In the preface to his work he is anxious to establish his impartiality and objectivity. He claims that he knows Jews well and that most of his information comes from what he has seen with his own eyes. When he includes secondhand information, he promises the reader that he has carefully evaluated it in the light of other sources. He insists that unlike all too many other Christians, his intention is not to attack or insult Jews with harsh words or scolding harangues but simply to describe their customs and beliefs with the hope of encouraging their conversion to Christianity. He assures the reader that his approach is fair and evenhanded: where there are good things to point out about Jewish traditions and practices, he will assuredly do so; but he will be equally certain to point out bad aspects, and in this case sharp words are appropriate. He also insists that he has no wish to attack the "whole Nation" of Jews nor to stir up Christian hatred against them.

Schudt's claim to objectivity is deeply suspect. Yes, on occasion he does say positive things about Jews. For example, he praises Jews for their religious fervor and for praying, as he says, "more diligently than we Christians are in the habit of doing."[11] But each time Schudt makes a favorable remark he undercuts it, in this case by objecting to the "ridiculous and strange" demeanor of Jews when they pray.[12] The same ambivalence occurs in his discussion of usury. Schudt provides a good example of a Christian Hebraist whose actual knowledge of Jews and Judaism sets up a conflict in his thinking. While he is aware, as ordinary, uneducated Christians were not, of precisely the kind of historical discrimination practiced against Jews and the way this forced them into money lending, he still has to look for deeper and darker motives to explain why Jews engage in the nefarious business practices he claims they do. And these motives lie in the peculiar, innate character of Jews, which, in turn, explains their rejection of Jesus and the curse that God laid upon them because of this rejection:

> The reason the Jews practice usury so readily is partly due to Christians and partly to Jews. Christians are responsible because they do not allow them to practice any trades and because they do not allow them to possess any real estate or till the land or raise livestock. So, all that remains is trading, haggling, and usury. One of the greatest obstacles to their conversion is probably that they generally grow up and spend most of their lives in idleness and commonly earn their living through trading and haggling

and yet really do not work. This is not altogether their fault since they do not have land to farm and in most places they are not allowed to learn or practice trades. *Yet they can be faulted because even if they were allowed to work, they would not know how to go about it because of their laziness.* Regarding those who are poor among them, whose number, as among Christians, is always the greater part, it is a sheer impossibility that anyone who has very little money can through trading turn this into enough to make ends meet and support a family without shady practices and fraud. As a consequence, these miserable people can ponder and think of nothing but how to maintain their poor lives through cunning, intrigue, fraud, and theft. . . .

It is on this account that the famous jurist from Halle, D. Böhmer . . . and some others are of the opinion that one should, on the contrary, encourage the Jews to learn trades so that they will have to earn their bread by the sweat of their brow. But since Christian craftsmen would hardly allow them to enter the guilds and to work with them, one should let them practice trades on their own. *But, according to my humble opinion, this would cause many problems since the Jews would ruin the trades with their bungling as much as they have bungled trading* [emphasis added].[13]

The highlighted portions of the text illustrate Schudt's need to locate some essential feature in Jews themselves to explain their behavior regardless of how Christians treat them. Schudt, the self-proclaimed objective ethnographer, is in conflict with Schudt the Lutheran theologian and apologist. It is this tension that explains the "polemical" nature of his ethnography, to employ the adjective insisted upon by Yaacov Deutsch when it comes to describing Christian ethnographies of Jews.[14]

One of the prime examples Schudt gives of Jewish "bungling" brings us back to Späth, for Schudt takes obvious (and one might suggest sadistic) pleasure in the fact that Späth's circumcision was poorly done, causing him intense and prolonged pain. As Schudt says: "Some Jews practice trades in Holland and it happened that a certain Jewish carpenter circumcised the apostate Speeth, but rather unfortunately, as both Herr Diefenbach . . . and I were told by a learned and noble friend, who heard from Speeth's own mouth what great pain he had to suffer for a long time on account of such a botched circumcision. It serves the apostate right!"[15] One would have thought that Christians might be more respectful when it came to the profession of Jewish carpentry. In a further passage Schudt again blames the Jews' own laziness for their predicament and in doing so equates them with fleas and lice, an analogy that had a long history and would enjoy a robust future, culminating in *Mein Kampf*:

From the point of view of the Jews, their poverty comes from the fact that they are prohibited from practicing handicrafts, trades, or farming, and yet they wish to live and feed themselves. In addition to this is the fact that for over three hundred years their young people were not used to working. Add to that the pleasure of idleness and laziness compels them to practice usury, and like lice and fleas they have the bread from the sweat and blood of others. Add to that their misconception that it is a sign of God's care, love, and grace that other people work hard and toil, while they can live in idleness and peace and have enough to eat. As it says in the Talmud (*Tract. Jebamot*, page 63): "With 100 florins made through trade, one can enjoy meat and wine daily; but 100 florins made from farming hardly buys salt and cabbage."[16]

Such a passage belies Schudt's claim to evenhandedness, a claim that becomes even more suspect when one realizes that he had read Johann Andreas Eisenmenger, the "arch Jew-hater," as Ettinger has called him, whose work *Entdecktes Judenthum* (Judaism Discovered) was used by nineteenth-century antisemites and republished during the Nazi era.[17] Schudt quotes Eisenmenger's examples showing the dreadful consequences of allowing the Jews "too great freedom," and he adds examples of his own. Holland, of course, provided Schudt with the worst case of such freedom. The fact that Jews were allowed to practice their religion openly there is something Schudt totally opposes because he is convinced this openness encourages Christians to convert to Judaism.[18] Schudt's palpable worry about the effect such conversions have in undermining Christian beliefs is a leitmotif throughout his enormous work.[19] At one point he says he had intended to reprint Späth's own account of the reasons for his conversion, but he decided not to because they had already been printed once and had proven to have a deleterious effect on wavering Christians.[20]

The fear that Christians will convert to Judaism unless Jews are prohibited from proselytizing is a constant theme in the work of many other Christians and Christian Hebraists as well. It is difficult to comprehend why this fear should have been so pronounced since the number of such conversions was actually minuscule. Such fear is understandable, however, as a sign of the anxieties and doubts Christians had about a religion that had become so fragmented and divisive. It is also understandable in terms of the increasing fluidity of religious identity that was paradoxically fostered by the growing intolerance of early modern regimes. This intolerance had a similar effect on many Jews and Christians. The streamlining of states along religious lines led to conversions among both groups, which meant that many Christians and Jews shared the experience of what Peter Berger has described as "alternation." In many cases, like Späth's, this led to a crisis of identity and sense of rootlessness.[21] In other cases forced conversions and reconversions created the distrust for religious institutions and skepticism about religious beliefs described by Kolakowski, Kaplan, Méchoulan, Popkin, and others.[22]

Schudt returns to Späth's conversion a number of times. The way the story escalates as he retells it is especially interesting in psychological terms. The first time Schudt mentions Späth, he stresses the miserable conditions in which Späth lives, attributing this to the Jews' disregard and contempt for him and contrasting this with the Christian charity of his former friends. More tellingly, Schudt suggests that the Jews poisoned Späth because he had doubts about Judaism:

Speeth married an honest German Jewess and had children by her (since a noble friend saw a little son at his home). He led a miserably poor life because the Portuguese and other Jews cared little about him. Not only did he make very little money teaching Jewish children but he also begged in writing for a single gulden from a good Christian friend, who had visited him previously in Amsterdam to alleviate his extreme poverty, which he received. This friend assured me that, as one could clearly see from his conversion, the new Moses Germanus suffered from uncertainty, doubt, and anxiety, which caused the Jews, having certainly observed this, to worry about his return to Christianity. And because it happened that he was so opportunely plucked from the earth, having taken to his bed on April 26, 1701, dying on the 27th and having been buried by the Jews on the 28th, it is understandable that doubt arose as to whether he died so quickly naturally, or took his own life, or whether his life was made shorter by the Jews.[23]

When Schudt returns to this point later, Späth's murder has become a reality, which proves that even such a reprobate as Späth finally recognized the truth of Christianity: "Some years after his apostasy the Jews got him out of the way with poison because he would not condone all their Talmudic fables."[24]

Schudt was a Lutheran, and his work is characteristic of the attitude of most Lutherans toward Jews in the seventeenth century. As we have learned from Stephen Burnett's essay in this volume, many of the most prolific Christian Hebraists in the sixteenth and seventeenth centuries were Lutherans. But as Burnett and a number of other scholars argue, their interest in Judaism is not a sign that Lutherans as a whole were interested in Jews or particularly sympathetic to them. R. P. Hsia contends that Jewish ethnographies were simply one more way—in addition to religious polemics—of proving that Jews were no longer the "Chosen People" because they had been superseded by Lutherans.[25] Thus reverence for Judaism and the Old Testament could coexist nicely with disdain for actual Jews because they had been effectively removed from their own history.[26] Martin Friedrich claims that for the most part seventeenth-century Lutherans had no real respect for Jews and little concern with converting them, and he rejects the notion that Pietism introduced a more positive attitude.[27] Elisheva Carlebach disputes this conclusion to some extent. Citing the Pietists at Halle, she contends that they did manifest greater interest than earlier German Lutherans in attracting Jewish converts, but the difficulties these converts had in assimilating into mainstream German society often resulted in their retaining an identity distinct from the larger Christian community. For example, the fact that Jews spoke Yiddish rather than "pure" German and continued for the most part to use Jewish forms of language and speech even after becoming Christian was taken as a clear sign of their distinctiveness and inability to fully convert.[28] As this last example reveals, there was considerable doubt among Lutherans and among Christians in general about whether Jewish converts could ever fully lose their Jewishness. It is interesting to point out that Yosef Kaplan documents the same wariness among Jews about Christian converts.[29] Thus at the very time when religious identity had become more fluid than ever, opposition to this fluidity arose in the form of essentialist theories. Friedrich argues that the degree to which Lutherans believed in the possibility of Jewish conversion readily correlates with their view of Jews as a whole. Those who thought conversion unlikely, if not out of the question—and these were the majority—were overtly hostile to Jews. Schudt was definitely conflicted on this point. As much as he wanted Jews to convert, he comes back time and again to whether Jewish conversions could really ever be genuine.

When we turn from Schudt to Knorr von Rosenroth and van Helmont, we find a radically different attitude toward Jews and Judaism. While also a Lutheran, Knorr was a Lutheran of a decidedly different stripe. Part of this can be attributed to the fact that he was not a university professor and consequently did not have to wear two hats, one as a researcher and the other as a professor expected to subscribe to and teach the religion embraced by the university. But more important for understanding Knorr's basic ecumenism was his association with van Helmont and through van Helmont with the Kabbalah.

Schudt refers to the fact that Späth had worked in Sulzbach on the *Kabbala denudata*, suggesting that his infection with Judaism began there. Others also attributed Späth's conversion to his association with van Helmont and Knorr. Leibniz was among these, as was Wachter, as we shall see, and Späth himself. It is somewhat ironic that Späth should have attributed his conversion to van Helmont, for the very idea of identifying with a single religion to the exclusion of all others was something van Helmont fought against his entire life. Ecumenism, not exclusivity, was van Helmont's lifelong and constantly reiterated message. Although called a "Judaizer" and considered by many to be a secret Jew, van Helmont was neither. He described himself as a "seeker," who, for all his wanderings across Europe during the many years of his long life, remained intensely curious. Not many eighty-year-olds plan, as van Helmont did, to travel to India to consult the Brahmins in the hope of obtaining new and better answers to life's great existential questions.[30] Späth's conversion was thus the very antithesis of what van Helmont would have wanted or expected, for to quote one of the Inquisition's charges against van Helmont, "occasionally he was heard to say that anyone is able to be saved in his own faith according to his own inner light and the light of conscience."[31]

As I have argued elsewhere, Sulzbach was perhaps the only place where true philosemitism flourished, for here Jews were accepted as Jews and there was no agenda of conversion in the usual sense of rejecting one religion and embracing a new and superior one.[32] Conversion was not an issue among the Kabbalists at Sulzbach because they firmly believed that the Kabbalah represented the true core of every religion. In other words, these seventeenth-century Kabbalists stuck to the notion of a *philosophia perennis* that provided the means for uniting every kind of Christian with every kind of Jew, Moslem, and pagan under the umbrella of a single universal truth.[33] It was on this basis that Knorr defended his interest in the Kabbalah. As he says: "In the Cabalist writings of the Jews I hoped I would be able to discover what remained of the ancient Barbaric-Judaic philosophy. . . . I had no greater wish than that I might be permitted to enjoy the sun itself and its brighter light once all the clouds of obstructions and hindrances were scattered. I scarcely hoped I would be able to catch sight of this light unless I followed in the footsteps of that river and arrived at the spring itself. I believed that I would discover this spring in these very ancient books."[34] As Moshe Idel pointed out, this way of thinking is not necessarily tolerant—one man's *philosophia perennis* might well be another man's poison.[35] One might even say that when Christians like Knorr and van Helmont embraced the Kabbalah as an essentially Christian perennial philosophy, they effectively invalidated Judaism as a religion historically practiced by actual Jews. There is certainly truth in this, but only if it is recognized that in the case of van Helmont the same rejection of particularism applied to Christianity as well. The nondogmatic variety of kabbalistic perennial philosophy offered by Knorr and van Helmont appealed to a number of people precisely because it rejected the divisive Christian doctrines of predestination, the Trinity, original sin, and eternal damnation, and it minimized or allegorized the role of Christ in the redemptive process. It offered instead a belief in universal salvation, which would be attained by every human being (as well as every other created thing from the very dirt of the earth on up) through repeated reincarnation and as a result of individual effort. In all these respects the vision of the Sulzbach Christian Hebraists was closer to Isaac Luria than to Catholicism, Lutheranism, or Calvinism. This Christian kabbalistic vision of a universe that would eventually be restored to is original perfection through human effort provided the basis for a radically optimistic philosophy predicated on the conviction that progress is inevitable, an idea that became the hallmark of the scientific revolution and the Enlightenment.[36]

I would suggest that it was in the tolerant atmosphere of Sulzbach that Späth gained the positive attitude toward Jews that eventually led to his conversion. Christian August's policy toward the Jews was highly unusual for the time. Not only did he encourage Jewish immigration into the Sulzbach territories, but he offered Jewish immigrants liberal terms and protection without making this a means of extortion like so many other Christian rulers. Christian August was so taken with Hebrew and Hebrew learning that he joined van Helmont and Knorr in establishing several presses in Sulzbach, one devoted to Hebrew, Latin, and vernacular works and a second solely devoted to printing texts in Hebrew, Syriac, and Aramaic. This latter press became extremely famous in the eighteenth and nineteenth centuries and, indeed, continued in existence until 1933 when it was closed by the Nazis.[37] The last building in which it was housed still stands.

As Stephen Burnett points out, Hebrew printing was a complicated and costly business that required considerable investment in expensive type and the hiring and paying of skilled compositors, editors, and knowledgeable readers, who would ensure that each printed book passed the censor.[38] The fact that Christian August, van Helmont, and Knorr continued to fund the Sulzbach presses even after several false starts, temporary shutdowns, and changes of management is evidence of their commitment to the publication of quality Hebrew books. Among the Hebrew books printed during their lifetimes were the *Kabbala denudata*, the largest collection of kabbalistic texts published in Latin translation to that time; a Syriac Bible printed in Hebrew letters; a Hebrew grammar; a book on Hebrew accents; and van Helmont's *Natural Hebrew Alphabet*, in which he argues that Hebrew letters are entirely "natural" because in their written form they are composed of the movements made by the tongue pronouncing them.[39] One of the most important books produced at Sulzbach was the 1684 edition of the *Sohar*. Van Helmont, whom Leibniz described as a master of many arts and crafts in his epitaph for his friend, taught Moses Bloch, the founder of the first successful Hebrew press, how to cut Hebrew type.[40]

It is difficult to know with any certainty exactly what relationships between Christians and Jews were like in Sulzbach. Among the members of Christian August's court the situation appears to have been extremely positive. Knorr read the Kabbalah under the guidance of two members of the Sulzbach Jewish community, R. Moses Hauser and his son R. Joseph, Polish Jews, who also read Hebrew texts with Christian August and his daughters, who were proficient in Hebrew as well.[41] Hebrew was actually spoken in the homes of several members of Christian August's court,[42] and there are reports, emanating from a hostile source to be sure (the Inquisition), that Hebrew lessons were offered on a daily basis to the young people in Sulzbach.[43] This, of course, does not tell us to what extent Jews took part in these events. But from another source, the Christian Hebraist Johann Christoph Wagenseil, we know that Jews in Sulzbach were better off than just about anywhere else in Germany. He gives a glowing picture of Christian August's relations with his Jewish subjects. From his account one can see that Christian August's approach to his Jewish subjects was unusual enough to rate special mention, especially because of his dismissal of the charge of ritual murder as an outright lie and his threat to punish any subject who spread such rumors:

> In this context we especially need to mention that the illustrious Prince Christian August of Pfaltz-Sulzbach, etc. has perfectly learned the sacred Hebrew language together with all the Jewish secrets, even the Cabbala, and that he delighted in such studies daily. Also after the rumor started for the second time in his territory, in 1682 and 1692, that the Jews had hanged Christian children, a rumor which was investigated and found to be totally false, he also had official proclamations nailed up everywhere to the effect that his subjects and inhabitants were strictly admonished under pain of mandatory corporal punishment not to believe this aforementioned vain fiction and lying rumor, much less to spread it further or to command or allow their children, servants [gebrodeten Leuten] or tenants [Hintersaßen] to speak of it, let alone to verbally attack a Jew or ask, or allow, someone to attack a Jew because of these rumors.[44]

But all was not sweetness and light. From a passionate statement made by Knorr in the *Kabbala denudata* we learn that he refrained from acknowledging and thanking his Hebrew teacher for his instruction and help because Jews and Christians alike were deeply suspicious of their friendship—so suspicious indeed that they attributed the death of two of his Hebrew teacher's children and two of his own to their collaboration. Knorr refers to this mutual distrust in his preface to the reader:

> From this you will know with how much devotion, indeed with what danger to my own health and life I am borne towards you—I say nothing about the expenses. Nor did I allow myself to be discouraged when towards the beginning (of my work) two of my teacher's children died (my teacher, who was already old and whose name I omit on account of the hatred of his relatives and co-religionists, otherwise he ought not to be deprived of praise); soon the same number were lost to me, which my teacher interpreted as a punishment for the publication of this doctrine. Neither was I deterred by so many warnings of all my friends. I persevered with one aim alone, that I might be of service to you; so that the knowledge of Hebrew matters should no longer be concerned with mere ritual, still less with grammar, but should reach to the things themselves which should then be compared with the phrases and doctrines of the new covenant, to see if by chance by this means it would be possible to facilitate the conversion of the Jewish race to the faith of Jesus Christ.[45]

Clearly profound distrust and superstition existed on both sides of the religious divide.

The first two parts of the *Kabbala denudata* were published in 1677 and 1678 and the last part in 1684. Späth did not officially convert to Judaism until 1696. It is therefore impossible to argue that Späth's experiences in Sulzbach were directly responsible for his later conversion, especially since his conversion involved his complete rejection of the *Kabbala denudata* and the Kabbalah in general as a patchwork of "pagan delusions and misunderstood Rabbinical texts."[46] In fact, from the letter he wrote to van Helmont after his conversion, it is clear that while he was in Sulzbach and under the influence of van Helmont and Knorr he continued to believe that their kind of kabbalistic Christianity was the true religion. But it would not be farfetched to suggest that the ecumenism and positive attitude toward Jews and Judaism that Späth found in Sulzbach, together with the tendency of the Christian Kabbalists there to attenuate Christian doctrine by either explaining it allegorically or dismissing it altogether, further undermined Späth's Christian convictions. The leader of the early Pietists Philipp Jakob Spener certainly believed this to have been the case. He singled out van Helmont as responsible for Späth's conversion on the grounds that he had made Späth's belief in Christianity "lukewarm."[47] Späth eventually came to the conclusion that if Christians disagreed so fundamentally among themselves and if Christian kabbalists appropriated Jewish philosophy for their own purposes while discarding Christian fundamentals, perhaps the real kernel of truth lay in Judaism, from which Christianity arose. Herman van der Hardt, professor of oriental languages and librarian at Helmstadt, suggested that this was indeed Späth's reasoning when he described him as concluding after a long internal battle that "everything is uncertain except this: God is certainly one."[48]

Späth, whom we must from now on call Moses Germanus, provides an example of the way increasing contact between Christians and Jews in the early modern period contributed to religious skepticism. In important respects his critique of Christianity anticipated ideas that became commonplace in the following century. With his dual background he was able to attack Christianity from the perspectives of both its Christian and Jewish critics. From the Jewish perspective he repeatedly argues that Christians have misunderstood and misinterpreted the messianic prophecies in the Hebrew Bible. By showing that these prophecies are not fulfilled in the New Testament he, along with other Jewish critics of Christianity, effectively separated the Old and New Testaments, thus removing the historical and theological rationale for Christianity as the fulfillment of Judaism and not a new religion. Once this was done it was possible for other questions to be asked. For example, what was the historical and theological basis of the New Testament? Did Jesus really exist? And was he anything more than a Jewish prophet preaching to messianically inclined Jews?[49]

Moses Germanus makes all these points in his self-appointed role as Christian critic and Jewish apologist. He indicted Christianity on the basis of both doctrine and practice. He dismissed the Christian church as a gross fraud and invention from the period of Constantine. The core of Jesus' teaching in the New Testament came from Jewish oral tradition, which was deposited in the Talmud. Therefore everything valid in Christianity originated in Judaism. What was invalid—for example, the cult of saints, the adoration of the host, and the worship of a human being—came from idolatrous paganism.[50] Moses Germanus accused the Catholic Church of being a "God-maker" (*Gottermacherin*) and dismissed the papal throne as a "seat of pestilence" (*Stuhl der Pestilenz*).[51] In his opinion the Christian martyrs of the early centuries were really Jews. Moses Germanus drew on the work of other biblical critics to corroborate his own critique of Christianity. In all probability it was from reading Richard Simon that he came to reject the passage in 1 John 5:7–8 on the Trinity as a later interpolation because it was not found in the oldest Vatican Bible manuscript.[52] It is interesting to note that Newton and Locke came to the same conclusion, which explains why both were crypto-Arians. In fact, Newton sent Locke a manuscript on just this point, which he and Locke intended to publish. At the last minute, however, Newton requested the manuscript back, fearing that its publication could lead to legal prosecution and loss of employment under the English Act for the "Suppression of Blasphemy." This act stipulated that "whoever by printing, teaching, or advisedly speaking, denied one of the persons of the Holy Trinity to be God" should "for the first offence be disabled to have any office or employment, ecclesiastical, civil, or military, or any profit appertaining thereunto."[53] Thomas Aikenhead, an eighteen-year-old Scotsman, had been hanged in 1696 for denying the Trinity, a capital offense in Scotland. This case was avidly followed by Locke and, one suspects, Newton as well.[54]

Moses Germanus also rejected the incident of the adulterous woman in John 7:53–8:11 as a later addition, probably on the basis of information he received from Johannes Leusden (1624–99), professor of Middle Eastern languages at the University of Utrecht and one of his correspondents.[55] Moses Germanus also realized that all the signs Jesus mentioned concerning the imminent apocalypse were modeled on accounts of the destruction of the Temple in 70 CE, and he also argued that the author of the Book of Revelation interpreted the destruction of the Temple as the beginning of the millennium.[56] He took the position of many modern scholars, namely that early Christianity represented a special form of Jewish eschatology.[57] Only when millenarianism was renounced did Christianity become a separate religion. It was for this reason that he regarded millenarian groups among Christians as essentially Jewish since they expected the millennium to occur on earth.

Späth's conversion to Judaism was completely genuine. Only after many years of deep and anguished thought did he finally take the momentous step of converting to a religion that offered virtually nothing in antisemitic Europe except, perhaps, his own peace of mind.

In his book *Spinozismus im Judenthum* Johann Georg Wachter made the preposterous claim that Moses Germanus did not convert to "real" Judaism but to a disguised form of Spinozism as a result of van Helmont's influence and the mistaken assumption that Spinoza's philosophy was the closest thing possible to the Kabbalah. Wachter also dates Moses Germanus's conversion to 1682. Wachter was wrong on all counts. As we have seen, Moses Germanus repudiated the Kabbalah. He also repudiated Spinoza for his betrayal of the Jewish belief in human free will and for his conviction that reason, not revelation, was the source of all knowledge.[58] What I want to stress here is not so much the elements of Wachter's argument but his overall intention in making it in the first place. Wachter's book is much more than an anti-Jewish polemic, although it certainly is that. It is essentially an attack on all revealed religion. Winfried Schröder describes Wachter as one of the earliest German freethinkers. The subversive nature of Wachter's text lies in the fact that he provided a public forum in which Moses Germanus could air his criticisms of Christianity while Wachter, the very person who allowed him to do this, ostensibly defends Christianity against this attack. But Wachter does not so much defend Christianity as attack Judaism on precisely the same grounds that Moses Germanus attacks Christianity, namely that it is not revealed. Wachter's further attack on the Old Testament as full of pagan and Egyptian laws and on Moses as a miserable self-deceiver was also as bad for Christianity as Judaism; it effectively severed Christianity from its source and undermined the idea that Christianity represented the continuation and completion of a single ancient divine revelation. Wachter's argument that the Jews were not the only ones to whom God revealed himself was acceptable to Christians, but it could and did lead to the Enlightenment idea found, for example, in Lessing's Reimarus fragments, that no single revelation was valid for all people.[59] The conflict between Wachter and Moses Germanus made Wachter articulate a position close to what Schröder describes as deism.[60] Schudt certainly considered Wachter in this light. As he says of Wachter, "He is tied to no religion; he follows his own reason."[61]

In his introduction Wachter says that his controversy with Moses Germanus is "the latest thing" in Holland and that it has wide-ranging implications about the nature of God, the nature of the world, and the nature of the Jewish religion. I think we can all agree. Späth's conversion to Judaism and his outspoken attack on Christianity provides one admittedly extreme illustration of the effects the encounter between Christian and Jews had through the work of Christian Hebraists. Johann Jacob Schudt's reaction was entirely different. He was confirmed in his distrust of Judaism and retreated behind the ramparts of orthodox Lutheranism. Wachter took the radical step of abandoning Lutheranism and revealed religion altogether. Van Helmont—at this point Knorr was dead—reaffirmed his commitment to his brand of ecumenical

Christian Kabbalah. In fact, it was during the years around Späth's conversion that van Helmont had his closest contacts with Leibniz, spending considerable time at Hanover, where Leibniz reports that van Helmont gave lessons in Christian Kabbalah to himself and his patron, the inimitable Sophie, duchess of Hanover. As I have suggested, Leibniz was influenced by these discussions to a much greater extent than people generally realize.[62] I cannot say the same for the duchess. Levelheaded Sophie was an old friend of van Helmont. From her correspondence it is clear that she had been privy to van Helmont's kabbalistic philosophy with his belief in reincarnation and universal salvation for some thirty years. On a number of occasions she admits, however, that it is too speculative for her and she is not certain how the idea of reincarnation can do any good if you cannot remember whether you were previously a pig or a Roman emperor. But the long friendship between van Helmont and Sophie and, indeed, between van Helmont and Leibniz rested in good part on their ecumenical outlook and tolerance. It was therefore a surprise but not a shock when I found a book describing a religious debate held in the presence of Sophie at the court of Hanover in 1704. The debate was between a certain R. Joseph and a Jewish convert to Christianity. It began at 3:30 and ended at 7:00 PM. After it was over Sophie remained behind. According to the report, she turned to the Jewish convert and said, "You have proved nothing" (*Ihr habt doch noch nix bewiesen*). When R. Joseph took his leave, Sophie said to him, "I am thankful that we all have one God." (*Ich bedanke mich, wir haben doch alle Einen Gott*).[63] That idea was, of course, the guiding force in van Helmont's life and the whole point of the *Kabbala denudata*.

I hope my Rashomon approach to the conversion of Johann Peter Späth to Judaism has provided further evidence that picking the bones of Christian Hebraist tomes is a fruitful enterprise that, in this case, offers insights into changing religious sensibilities on the eve of the Enlightenment.

Appendix 12.1
Christian Hebraism at Sulzbach: European Links

Francis Mercury van Helmont (1614–98)	Christian Knorr von Rosenroth (1636–89)	Prince Christian August (1622–1708)

Hebrew Press
Moses ben Uri Schraga Bloch
Feustel & Samuel Bloch
Ahron Fränkel

R. Moses Hauser
R. Joseph Hauser
Johann Peter Späth (Moses Germanus)

Additional Christian Hebraists at Sulzbach
Johann Jacob Fabricius
Clamerus Florinus
Justus Brawe
Tobias Ludwig Kohlhans

CONNECTIONS BETWEEN SULZBACH, HOLLAND, ENGLAND, AND GERMANY

Holland	England	Germany
Isaac Orobio de Castro	Henry More	Duchess Sophie of Hanover
R. Menasseh ben Israel	Anne, Viscountess Conway	G. W. Leibniz
R. Jacob Juda Leon	Robert Boyle	J. C. Wagenseil
Baruch Spinoza	Isaac Newton	J. J. Schudt
Peter Serrarius (Collegiant)	John Locke	J. G. Wachter
Adam Boreel (Collegiant)	Damaris Masham	Karl Ludwig, Elector Palatine
Abraham Galenus (Collegiant)	Samuel Hartlib	Elizabeth, Abbess of Hereford
William Ames (Quaker)	Henry Oldenburg	
Samuel Fisher (Quaker)	Prince Rupert	
Peter Balling (Quaker)		
Benjamin Furly (Quaker)	George Fox (Quaker)	
	William Penn (Quaker)	
John Locke	Robert Barclay (Quaker)	
Philippe van Limborch	George Keith (Quaker)	
Jean Le Clerc	William Clarke (Helmontian-Quaker)	
William Popple		
J. G. Graevius	Abendana Brothers	

Notes

1. Frank E. Manuel, "Israel and the Enlightenment," *Daedalus* 111 (1982): 33–52.
2. Späth's name has been spelled various ways—Späth, Speeth, Speath—but he preferred Späth. Cf. J. J. Schudt, *Jüdische Merkwürdigkeiten. vorstellende was sich Curiouses und denckwürdiges in den neuen Zeiten bey einigen Jahr-hunderten mit denen in alle IV. Theile der Welt / sonderlich durch Teutschland / zerstrueten Juden augetragen . . .* (Frankfurt, 1714). *Jüdischer Merckwürdigkeiten Vierdter Theil. Als eine weitere Continuation dessen / so in denen drey vorhergehenden Theilen vorgestellet worden . . .* (Frankfurt: Matthias Andreae, 1718), vol. 4, 198.
3. Allison P. Coudert, *Leibniz and the Kabbalah* (Dordrecht, Neth.: Kluwer, 1995).
4. Allison P. Coudert, *The Impact of the Kabbalah in the Seventeenth Century: The Life and Thought of Francis Mercury van Helmont, 1614–1698* (Leiden, Neth.: E. J. Brill, 1999), ch. 12.
5. Coudert, *Impact of the Kabbalah*, ch. 11.
6. R. H. Popkin and Michael A. Signer, eds., *Spinoza's Earliest Publication? The Hebrew Translation of Margaret Fell's A loving salutation to the seed of Abraham among the Jews, wherever they are scattered up and down upon the face of the earth* (Assen, Neth.: Van Gorcum, 1987); Popkin, "Samuel Fisher and Spinoza," *Philosophia* 15 (1985): 219–36.
7. Schudt, *Jüdische Merkwürdigkeiten*, vol. 1, 273, par. 5.
8. Schudt, *Jüdische Merkwürdigkeiten*, vol. 4, 198. For a discussion of Späth's life and conversion, see N. Samter, "Johann Peter Späth (Moses Germanus), der Proselyt," *Monatsschrift für Geschichte und Wissenschaft des Judenthums* (1895): 178ff, 221ff; H. J. Schoeps, *Philosemitismus im Barock* (Tübingen: J. C. B. Mohr, 1952), 67ff.
9. On the theme of curiosity as the condition that drives people to reexamine accepted truth and as an essential aspect of modernity, see Hans Blumeberg, *The Legitimacy of the Modern Age*, trans. Robert M. Wallace (Cambridge: Harvard University Press, 1983).
10. In his encyclopedia, *Großes vollständiges universal-Lexikon aller Wissenschafften und Künste* (Leipzig, Ger. 1743), 1328–29, Johann Heinrich Zedler gives a glowing account of Schudt as a man of great learning with a prodigious skill in languages.
11. Schudt, *Jüdische Merkwürdigkeiten*, vol. 5, 6, 218, 22.
12. This is a constant charge against Jews. See Elisheva Carlebach, *Divided Souls: Converts from Judaism in Germany, 1500–1750* (New Haven: Yale University Press, 2001), 157.
13. Schudt, *Jüdische Merkwürdigkeiten*, vol. 2, 6, 16–170:

2. Die Veranlassung / daß die Juden so gern wuchern / ist enstanden theils von denen Christen / theils von denen Juden; Von denen Christen kommt die Veranlassung her / weil man ihnen keine Handwercke zu treiben erlaubet / und weil sie keine eigenthümliche unbewegliche Güther besitzen dürffen / können sie keinen Ackerbau noch Viehzucht treiben / bleibet also nichts als die Handlung / Schacherei und Wucher übrig; Eines der grössen Hindernüssen (ihrer Bekehrung) ist wol / daß sie insgemein alle von Jugend auf in Müßiggang aufwachsen / das Leben meistens in solchem zubringen / und sich insgemein alle von handeln und schachern nähren / hingegen zu keiner Arbeit kommen. Das theils ohne ihre Schuld geschiehet / indem sie eignes Land zu bauen nicht haben / auch an meisten Orten zu Handwercken / sie zu lernen / oder zu treiben / nicht gelassen werden / theils aber ists nicht ohne eigene Schuld / da ob sie zu arbeiten gelassen / aus Faulheit sich nicht darzu verstehen würden. Was nun arme unter ihnen sind / dero Anzahl so wol

als bey den Christen allezeit den grössensten Theil machet / ists eine pure Unmöglichkeit / daß einer ohne Practiquen und Betrug / da er kaum wenige Thaler zum Capital hat / dieses durch Handlung also umsetzen könnte / dass er davon / wie genau er sich behilfft / mit einer Famille solte leben können; Daher die elende Leute Tag und Nacht auf nichts anders sinnen und dencken können / als wie sie mit List / Ränken / Betrug und also Diebstahl ihr armes Leben hinbringen.
3. Dahero der berühmte Hallische Jurist Herr D. Böhmer . . . und andere mehr / der Meynung sind / man solle die Juden allerdings anhalten / daß sie Handwercker erlernen / und im Schweiß der Angesichts ihr Brod verdienen müssen / und da die Christl. Handwercker dieselbige wohl schwerlich für zünfftig passiren und als Mitmeister unter sich leyden würden / so solte man sie die Handwercker für sich treiben lassen; welches aber / meines wenigen Erachtens / eben so wol viele Beschwehrden würde nach sich ziehen / und durfften die Juden mit ihre Stümperey die Handwercker eben so sehr verderben / wie sie die Handlung verstümpeln.

14. See Deutsch's essay in this volume.
15. Schudt, *Jüdische Merkwürdigkeiten*, vol. 2, 6, 170: "Gleichwol treiben einige Juden in Holland Handwercker / wie dann ein jüdischer Schreiner es gewesen / der den abgefallenen Speeth beschnitten / aber ziemlich unglücklich / davon Herr Diefenbach Jud. Convers. 15. p. 154 und mir aus des Speeth Mund ein gelährter vornehmer Freund hier erzehlet / was große Schmertzen er lange Zeit von solcher übel verrichteten Beschneidung ausgestanden; ist dem abtrünnigen Vogel recht geschehen."
16. Ibid., 173–74:

5. Von Seiten der Juden kommt die Noth / weil sie keine andere Handthierung haben / Handwercker und Ackerbau ist ihnen versagt / und wollen doch leben und ihre Nahrung haben; es kommt darzu die lange Gewohnheit von so vielen 300 Jahren und daß sie von Jugend an zu keiner Arbeit gewöhnet; es kommt darzu die Annehmlichkeit dess Müßiggangs und Faulheit / daß sie bey dem Wucher müßig gehen / und wie Läuss und Flöh / von anderer Schweiß und Blut ihre Nahrung haben; es kommt darzu die falsche Einbildung / daß solches ein Zeichen Göttl. Vorsorge / Liebe und Huld gegen sie seye / daß ander Völcker hart und sauer arbeiten / sie aber in Müßiggang und Ruhe leben könten / und doch gleichwol vergnüglich ernehret würden / wie dann im Talmud Tract. *Jebamot* p. 63 stehet: . . . 100 fl.in Handlung machen / daß man täglich Fleisch und Wein genießen kan aber 100 fl. auf Ackerbau / verschaffen kaum Saltz und Kraut.

17. S. Ettinger, "The Beginning of the Change in the Attitude of European Society Towards the Jews," *Scripta Hierosolymitana* 7 (1961): 208.
18. Schudt, *Jüdische Merkwürdigkeiten*, vol. 1, 4, 270ff:

Von den Juden in Holland und Friesland: Eine allzu grosse Juden-Freiheit in Holland ist es / II. daß in Holland / sonderlich zu Amsterdam / die Christen öffentlich und ohne Scheu den Jüdischen Glauben annehmen und sich beschneiden lassen / welches im Römischen Reich nicht gelidten / sondern am Leben gestrafft wird; Ob wohl solches Herr Wülffer *Animadvers. ad Theo. Jud.* C. 3. para 16. p. 211 seq. für zu hart und einen Gewissens-Zwang hält / ist es doch allerdings billig und recht / weil der Abfall vom Christlichen Glauben zu dem Judenthum nicht ohne Gotteslästerung der Hochheiligen Dreyeinigkeit / und schandliche Schmähung des gebennedeyten-Heylandes JESU CHRIST (so ja allerdings / sonderlich bey einem Christen / den Todt verdienet) geschehen kan / dahero auch so gar die Rechte denen Juden / die einen Christen zum Judenthum verführen / die Todtes-Straffe setzen davon unterschiedlicher Juristen Zeugnüss anführen / Herr Diefenbach im *Jud. Convers.* para 14. p. 128. So ist Nicol Antonius, ein Reformirter Prediger in Genffer-Gebieth / als er ein Jud worden / anno 1632 erstlich gehenckt und hernach verbrandt worden.

19. For example, he refers to Eisenmenger's description of the conversion of three Chistians and immediately after to a legal case in Frankfurt against one Abraham zum Drachen, who was responsible for converting—through bribery, according to Eisenmenter—a Christian tailor from Bergen, by the name of Philipp Heyland, and his wife (ibid., vol. 2, 18, 997).

20. Ibid., vol. 2, 4, 273:

Ein Brief / den er an Herrn D. Petersens Ehliebste / seines Abfalls wegen geschrieben / ist von Herrn Bücher aus Dantzig anno 1699 in 4 herausgegeben worden / welchen ich anfänglich hier mit einzurucken vorhabens war / allein wegen der ärgerlichen Reden von Christo / so der Böswicht ausgegossen / aus Furcht eines Anstosses bey Schwachgläubigen / billig habe unterlassen.... Herrn M. Bücher sehr verdacht worden / daß er den gottlosen Brief in Dantzig drucken und in Sachsen divulgiren lassen / alldieweil sowohl an andern Orten / als vornehmlich in Dantzig / wahrhafftig geschehen seye / dass unterschiedliche Menschen dadurch nicht nur an ihrem Christenthum irre gemacht worden / sondern auch die Christlicher Religion zu verläugnen im Sinne gehabt hätten / denen aber durch andere fromme Christen wieder seye zurecht geholffen / und ein besserer Grund angewiesen worden. Diefenbach Jud. Convers. para 15, p. 139.

21. On this point, see Stephen Sharot's description of the effect of alternation on Marranos in *Messianism, Mysticism, and Magic: A Sociological Analysis of Jewish Religious Movements* (Chapel Hill: University of North Carolina Press, 1982), 108:

They had passed between logically contradictory intellectual universes. What was peculiar about the former Marranos was that they experienced alternation in a largely traditional society, a society of closed and binding worldviews in which people were assigned definite and permanent identities. The Christian and Jewish worlds in the seventeenth century were separated by legal, cultural, and social barriers; Jews and Christians had little contact beyond formal economic and political relationships, and each group regarded the other as another species of being. In such a society alternation caused acute problems of identity and location in society. Many former Marranos retained a nostalgia for the land of their births, and a few returned despite the dangers. Some retained a fondness for Catholicism, a few returning to the religion of their childhood. Others, identifying strongly with Judaism, felt an overwhelming sense of guilt and sought pardon for their Catholic past by such practices as wearing hair shirts.

22. L. Kolakowski, *Chrétiens sans église: La conscience religieuse et le confessionnel au xvii siècle* (Paris: Gallimard, 1969); Y. Kaplan, *From Christianity to Judaism: The Story of Isaac Orobio de Castro* (New York: Oxford University Press, 1989); H. Méchoulan, "Morteira et Spinoza au carrefour du Socinianisme," *Revue des études juives* 135 (1976): 51–65; R. H. Popkin, *The History of Skepticism from Erasmus to Spinoza*, rev. ed. (Berkeley and Los Angeles: University of California Press, 1979); idem, "Jewish Anti-Christian Arguments as a Source of Irreligion from the Seventeenth to the Early Nineteenth Century," in *Atheism from the Reformation to the Enlightenment*, ed. M. Hunter and D. Wootton (Oxford: Oxford University Press, 1992).

23. Schudt, *Jüdische Merkwürdigkeiten*, vol. 1, 4, 273:

Es hat der Speeth auch eine saubere Teutsche Jüdin geheirathet / und mit ihr Kinder gezeuget / wie dann ein Christlicher vornehmer Freund bey ihm ein Söhngen gesehen; Er hat aber sein Leben / weil die Portugiesische und andere Juden sich seiner wenig angenommen / in solcher kümmerlichen Dürfftigkeit zubringenmüssen / daß er nicht nur um ein gar geringes der Juden Kinder informiret / sondern auch von einem Christlichen guten Freund allhier / der ihn vormahls in Amsterdam besucht gehabt / durch Schreiben um einen eintzigen Gulden / zu Sublevirung seiner äußersten Armuth gebetten / und auch erhalten / welcher Freund dann mich versicherte / daß der neue Moses Germanus, wie man aus seinen Reden deutlich abnehmen können / in lauter Ungewißheit / Zweiffel und Gewissens-Angst gewesen / welches dann die Juden wohl an ihm gemercket / und seinen Rücktritt zu der Christlichen Religion werden besorgen haben; und weil er . . . so gelingen von der Erden weggerafft / indem er den 26. April 1701 sich zu Bette gelegt / den 27 gestorben / und den 28. von den Juden begraben worden / so ist billig ein Zweifel entstanden / ob er natürlich / oder durch seine / oder der Juden Verkürtzung / so geschwind davon gefahren.

24. Ibid., vol. 4, 192: "Es hätten ihn auch die Juden / einige Jahr nach seinem Abfall / mit Gifft aus dem Weeg [sic] geräumet / weil er alle ihre Talmudische-Fabeln nicht billigen wollen / wie sich Heer [sic] D. Spener bemühet / den Menschen von denen Papisten / und nachmahls von denen Juden wieder abzuziehen / ist in seinen Teutschen *Consiliis Theolog.* P. III. p. 534. f. 961. f. P. IV. p. 623. und in *Consiliis Latinis Theol.* P. III. p. 430 zu lesen."

25. R. P. Hsia, "Christian Ethnography of Jews in Early Modern Germany," in *The Expulsion of the Jews: 1492 and After,* ed. R. B. Waddington and A. H. Williamson (New York: Garland, 1994), 229: "The intense interest in matters Jewish was but a prelude to the cultural appropriation that would result in a parallel construction of Lutheran and Jewish identities. In claiming its identity as the New Israel, the evangelical church had first to deprive the Jews of their claim as the 'Chosen People.' The same is also true of Calvinists like Jacques Basnage, who also identified with the ancient Jews and saw Calvinists as the new Chosen People."

26. Hsia, "The Usurious Jew," in *In and Out of the Ghetto: Jewish-Gentile Relations in Late Medieval and Early Modern Germany,* ed. R. P. Hsia and H. Lehmann (New York: Columbia University Press, 1995), 173–74.

27. Martin Friedrich, *Zwischen Abwehr und Bekehrung: Die Stellung der deutschen evangelischen Theologie zum Judenthum in siebzehnten Jahrhundert* (Tübingen, Ger.: J. C. B. Mohr, 1988).

28. Carlebach, *Divided Souls,* 159. Carlebach discusses other aspects of supposed "Jewish identity" that made their conversion suspect in the eyes of many Christians.

29. Yosef Kaplan, "Political Concepts in the World of the Portuguese Jews of Amsterdam during the Seventeenth Century: The Problem of Exclusion and the Boundaries of Self-Idenity," in *Menasseh ben Israel and His World,* ed. idem, Henry Méchoulan, and Richard H. Popkin (Leiden, Neth.: E. J. Brill, 1989), 45–62. Jacob Katz thinks that on the whole a positive view of conversion outweighed the negative. See *Exclusiveness and Tolerance: Studies in Jewish-Gentile Relations in Medieval and Modern Times* (New York: Behrman, Inc., 1961), 81.

30. Furly reports this in a letter to Locke, 19–29 May 1694, in *The Correspondence of John Locke,* ed. E. S. De Beer, vol. 5 (Oxford: Clarendon Press, 1976–89), 54–55.

31. "Informatio de Helmontio, May–June 1662; The Errors and Teachings of Helmont" (Archivio Segreto Vaticano, Archivio della Nunziatura di Colonia 81, n. 4). Inquisitorial documents relating to van Helmont's case were printed as an appendix to Klaus Jaitner, "Der Pfalz-Sulzbacher Hof in der europäischen Ideengeschichte des 17. Jahrhunderts," in *Wolfenbüttler Beiträge,* ed. Paul Raabe (Frankfurt: Vittorio Klostermann, 1988). I have included them (with a translation) in *The Impact of the Kabbalah in the Seventeenth Century,* Appendix 1.

32. Allison P. Coudert, "The *Kabbala Denudata:* Converting Jews or Seducing

Christians?" in *Christian-Jews and Jewish-Christians,* ed. Richard H. Popkin and Gordon M. Weiner (Dordrecht, Neth.: Kluwer, 1994), 73–96.

33. This interpretation appears to be belied by the fact that von Rosenroth emphasizes his missionary intent in the second part of the *Kabbala denudata,* where he offers a systematic outline of the doctrines of the Zohar, to which he appends parallel passages from the New Testament. The same technique is used in the *Adumbratio Kabbalae Christianae,* the last treatise in the *Kabbala denudata,* which was written by van Helmont and published separately because of its alleged importance in the task of converting Jews to Christianity. However, a careful reading of these texts reveals that the Christianity proffered to the potential Jewish convert seems far more Jewish than Christian.

34. "Amica Responsio," *Kabbala denudata,* vol. 1, pt. 2, 75, 76.

35. He made this point in one of the seminars on Christian Hebraism held at the Center for Advanced Judaic Studies (1999–2000).

36. Coudert, *Impact of the Kabbalah in the Seventeenth Century,* ch. 7.

37. M. Weinberg, *Geschichte der Juden in der Oberpfalz,* vol. 5, *Herzogtum Sulzbach* (München: Kommissions-Verlag der Ewer-Buchhandlung, 1927); idem, "Die Hebräischen Druckereien in Sulzbach (1669–1851): Ihre Geschichte; ihre Drucke; ihr Personal," in *Sonderabdruck aus dem Jahrbuche der Jüdisch-Literarischen Gesellschaft* (Frankfurt: Commissionsverlag von A. L. Hofmann, 1904), 1–186.

38. Stephen G. Burnett, *From Christian Hebraism to Jewish Studies: Johannes Buxtorf (1564–1629) and Hebrew Learning in the Seventeenth Century* (Leiden, Neth.: E. J. Brill, 1996).

39. For a fuller discussion of van Helmont's theory of a natural language and the part it played in the seventeenth-century debate about language and the nature of Hebrew, see Coudert, *Impact of the Kabbalah in the Seventeenth Century,* chs. 4–5.

40. Niedersächsische Landesbibliothek, LBr. 389, f. 125: "Nil patre inferior jacet hic Helmontius alter, / Qui junxit varias mentis et artis opes; / Per quem Pythagoras et Cabbala sacra revixit, / Elausque potest qui dare cuncta sibi. / Quod si Graja virum tellus, et prisca tulissent / Secula, nunc inter lumina prima foret." In a note Leibniz explains the reference to Elaus: "Hippias patria Elaus, professione philosophus, qui omnia quibus opus, manu sua elaborare poterat."

41. Manfred Finke and Erni Handschur, "Christian Knorr von Rosenroth Lebenslauf aus dem Jahre 1718," *Morgen-Glantz: Zeitschrift der Christian Knorr von Rosenroth Gesellschaft* 1 (1991): 45.

42. Volker Wappmann, *Durchburch zur Toleranz: Die Religionspolitik des Pfalzgrafen Christian August von Sulzbach, 1622–1708* (Neustadt, Ger.: Verlag Degener and Co., 1995), 175 n. 79.

43. Archivo Segreto Vaticano, Archivo della Nunziatura di Colona 81, "Informatio de Helmontio": "In order that the appearance of the old religion might remain, since the greater part of the Bible is written in the Hebrew language, they learn and teach the Hebrew language, in which both the prince and his daughters are steeped, first in the early morning for one or two hours" (cited in Coudert, *Impact of the Kabbalah in the Seventeenth Century,* 352–53).

44. J. C. Wagenseil, *Benachrichtigungen wegen einiger die Judenschafft angehende wichtigen Sachen. Erste Theil worinnen 1. Die Hoffnung der Erlösung Israelis oder klarer Beweiß der grossen und wie es scheinet / allgemach herannahenden Juden-Bekehrung / sammt vorgreifflichen Gedancken / wie solche nechst Verheißung Göttlicher Hülffe / zu*

befordern. 2. Wiederlegung der Unwahrheit daß die Juden zu ihrer Bedürfniß Christen-Blut haben müssen. 3. Anzeigung / wie leicht es dahin zu bringen / dass die Juden forthin abstehen müssen / die Christen mit Wuchern und Schinden zu plagen (Leipzig: bei Johann Heinrichens Wittwe, 1705), 32–33:

Hieher gehöret absonderlich / daß der Durchlauchtigste Fürst Christianus Augustus von Pfaltz-Sulzbach etc. die heilige Hebräische Sprach / sammt allen der Jüden Geheimnüssen / auch so gar der Cabbala, vollkommen erlernet / und mit solchen Studien sich täglich ergetzet. Er hat auch / nachdem in seinem Land zum zweyten mahl / als 1682 und 1692 der Ruf auskommen / als wenn die Juden Christen-Kinder aufgehangen hätten / nach genau untersuchter und Grund-falsch befundener Sache allenthalben öffentliche Mandata anschlagen lassen / durch welche Dero Hochfürstliche Durchl. Landes-Unterthanen und Ingesessenen bey unausbleiblicher Leibes-Straffe ernstlich geboten worden / den eitel erdichteten und lügenhafften Ausstreuen keinen Glauben beyzumessen / vielweniger aber davon weiter Ausbreitung zu thun / noch ihren Kindern und gebrodeten Leuten / oder Hintersaßen davon zu reden / geschweig einen Juden deswegen anzufechten oder fürzuwerffen heissen oder gestatten. Wer wolte diese hohe Begebnüssen für schlecht / gering und nicht würdig achten / dass ihnen beygeschrieben werde / was der weisseste König [p. 33] unter den Juden Prov. xxi. i. gesagt: Des Königs (und Fürsten) Hertz ist in der Hand des Herrn / wie Wasser-Bäche / und er neigets wohin er will.

45. "Lectori Philebraeo Salutem!," *Kabbala denudata*, vol. 2, pt. 1, 18–19.

46. This is how Moses Germanus described the *Kabbala denudata* in a letter to Francis Mercury van Helmont (Hamburg, Staats- und Universitätsbibliothek, Suppellex. Epistolica Uffenbaccii, v. 26, f. 71 [157], quoted by permission of the Staats- und Universitätsbibliothek, Hamburg. The letter was probably written in 1698–99. Späth refers to this letter in his third letter to Johann Georg Wachter, which Wachter printed in his *Der Spinozismus im Judenthumb, oder, Die von dem heütigen Jüdenthumb und dessen Geheimen Kabbala vergötterte Welt: an Moses Germano sonsten Johan Peter Speeth von Augspurg gebürtig / befunden und widerleget von Johann Georg Wachter* (Amsterdam: Bey J. Wolter, 1699).

47. P. J. Spener, *Consilia et judicia theologica Latina* (1709), vol. 3, 430.

48. Van der Hardt made this observation in a conversation he had with Stolle. See G. E. Guhrauer, "Beiträge zur Kenntnis des 17. u. 18. Jahrhunderts aus den handschriftlichen Aufzeichnungen Gottlieb Stolle's," *Allgemeine Zeitschrift für Geschichte* 7 (1847): 403.

49. See Popkin, "Jewish Anti-Christian Arguments as a Source of Irreligion from the Seventeenth to the Early Nineteenth Century."

50. Hamburg, Staats- und Universitätsbibliothek, Suppellex. Epistolica Uffenbaccii, v. 26. Cf. J. J. Schudt, *Compendium Historiae Judaicae . . .*, vol. 1 (Frankfurt, 1700), 694; Wachter, *Der Spinozismus im Judenthumb*, 30.

51. Hamburg, Staats- undUniversitätsbibliothek, Suppellex. Epistolica Uffenbaccii, vol. 26, f. 57.

52. The passage, which has been removed from modern scholarly translations of the Bible, reads as follows in the King James version: "For there are three that bear record in heaven, the Father, the Word, and the Holy Ghost: and these three are one. And there are three that bear witness in the earth, the spirit, and the water, and the blood: and these three agree in one."

53. In a letter to Locke, which Edmund De Beer thinks may have been written by James Johnstoun, the writer quotes the Scottish Law on Blasphemy against the Trinity:

The Correspondence of John Locke, ed. E. S. De Beer, vol. 6 (Oxford: Clarendon Press, 1976–89), 17–19.

54. Michael Hunter, "'Aikenhead the Atheist': The Context and Consequences of Articulate Irreligion in the Late Seventeenth Century," in *Atheism from the Reformation to the Enlightenment*, ed. M. Hunter and D. Wootton (Oxford: Oxford University Press, 1992).

55. Letters between Moses Germanus and Leusden are to be found in Hamburg, Staats- und Universitätsbibliothek, Suppellex. Epistolica Uffenbaccii, v. 26.

56. Schudt, *Compendium Historiae Judaicae*, vol. 1, 695; vol. 4, 195.

57. *T'Groote Hosianna selfs von Joden uytgeroepen* (Amsterdam, 1701), 30ff.

58. Moses Germanus's refutation of Spinoza appears in *Sapientia in Israele*, which appeared as the second volume of *Diatribe de Ortu et Progressu Facultatis* . . . (1697), which Späth published anonymously. (The first volume is titled *Salus ex Iudaeis*.) The date 1670 appears on the title page, but this refers to the publication date of Spinoza's *Tractatus Theologico-Politicus*, not to Späth's critique of it.

59. Hermann Samuel Reimarus (1694–1768) was author of the "Wolfenbüttel Fragments," which were published by Gotthold Ephraim Lessing as *Fragmente einer Ungenannten* (1774–78).

60. See Schröder's introduction to *Johann Georg Wachter: Der Spinozismus im Jüdenthumb, 1699*. Mit einer Einleitung herausgegeben von Winfried Schröder (Stuttgart-Bad-Cannstatt: Friedrich Frommann Verlag/Günther Holzboog, 1994).

61. Schudt, *Jüdische Merkwürdigkeiten*, vol. 5, 4, 201.

62. Coudert, *Leibniz and the Kabbalah*.

63. *Religionsgespräch gehalten am kurfürstlichen Hofe zu Hannover 1704 nach einer hebräischen Handschrift herausgegeben und übersetzt von A. Berliner* (Berlin: Louis Lamm, 1914), 16–17.

Contributors

Stephen G. Burnett is Assistant Professor of Classics and Religious Studies and of History at the University of Nebraska–Lincoln. In addition to his book, *From Christian Hebraism to Jewish Studies: Johannes Buxtorf, 1564–1629, and Hebrew Learning in the Seventeenth Century* (1996), he has written numerous articles on Christian Hebrew scholarship in the Reformation era and on Hebrew printing by both Jewish and Christian printers in early modern Europe.

Allison P. Coudert is Professor of Religious Studies at Arizona State University. She is the author of numerous articles and books on early modern religious and esoteric thought, including *The Impact of the Kabbalah in the Seventeenth Century: The Life and Thought of Francis Mercury van Helmont, 1614–1698* (Leiden: Brill, 1999), and the editor and translator of Anne Conway's *The Principles of the Most Ancient and Modern Philosophy,* Cambridge Texts in the History of Philosophy (Cambridge: Cambridge University Press, 1996).

Yaacov Deutsch is a Ph.D. candidate at the Hebrew University in Jerusalem, where he also teaches in the School of History. His research focuses on Christian-Jewish relations in the medieval and early modern period and especially on Christian Hebraism. He has published several articles in Hebrew, English, and German on topics related to his areas of interest.

Michael Heyd is Professor of History at the Hebrew University, Jerusalem. He specialized in early modern intellectual and religious history and is interested particularly in problems of secularization and changing religious sensibilities on the eve of the Enlightenment. His chapter in this volume is an offshoot of a previous study on the critique of enthusiasm in that period, published as a book, *Be Sober and Reasonable: The Critique of Enthusiasm in the Seventeenth and Early Eighteenth Centuries* (Leiden: Brill, 1995). He is currently working on changing attitudes toward original sin in the Protestant world before the Enlightenment.

Moshe Idel is Max Cooper Professor of Jewish Thought at the Hebrew University and senior researcher at the Shalom Hartman Institute. He is the author of numerous studies on Jewish mysticism, including *Kabbalah: New Perspectives* (New Haven: Yale University Press, 1988) and *Absorbing Perfections* (New Haven: Yale University Press, 2002).

Fabrizio Lelli is currently a lecturer at the University of Lecce, where he teaches Hebrew Language and Literature. His research focuses on the philosophical and mystical literature of Italian Jews in the early Renaissance. He has published numerous articles on the history of the transmission of Hermetic texts in medieval Jewish philosophy.

Ora Limor is a professor at the Open University of Israel, where she teaches medieval history. Her main fields of research are Christian-Jewish dialogue and polemic, and sacred space, pilgrimage, and ritual behavior in medieval Christianity. Her publications include *Contra Judaeos: Ancient and medieval polemics between Christians and Jews* (Tübingen: J. C. B. Mohr, 1996), which she co-edited with Guy G. Stroumsa.

Peter N. Miller is Professor of Cultural History at the Bard Graduate Center in New York City. He has written several books, including *Peiresc's Europe: Learning and Virtue in the Seventeenth Century* (New Haven: Yale University Press, 2000), and is currently finishing *Peiresc's Orient: The Antiquarian Imagination*.

Amnon Raz-Krakotzkin is a lecturer in the Department of History at Ben Gurion University of the Negev, where he teaches and writes on Jewish historiography and historical consciousness in the Middle Ages, Jews and Christians in medieval Europe, and secularization and nationalism. He has published numerous articles and is currently completing a book titled *Zionist Historians and Medieval Jewry: The Zionist Narration of the Jewish Past*.

Nils Roemer received his Ph.D. from Columbia University in 2000. He currently teaches Jewish history at the James Parkes Centre at the University of Southampton. He has published several articles on German-Jewish history during the modern period and is finishing a book on Jewish historiography and popular culture in nineteenth-century Germany.

Jason P. Rosenblatt, Professor of English at Georgetown University, has published numerous essays on seventeenth-century England and Milton. He is coeditor of *"Not in Heaven": Coherence and Complexity in Biblical Narrative* (Bloomington: Indiana University Press, 1991) and author of *Torah and Law in*

Paradise Lost (Princeton: Princeton University Press, 1994). He is completing a book on Christian Hebraism in the English literary Renaissance.

Jeffrey S. Shoulson is Associate Professor of English and Director of the Program in Judaic Studies at the University of Miami. His book, *Milton and the Rabbis: Hebraism, Hellenism, and Christianity* (New York: Columbia University Press, 2001) was awarded the 2001 Salo W. Baron Prize by the American Academy of Jewish Research. He is currently completing a book tentatively titled *Fictions of Conversion: Community, Identity, and Instability in Early Modern England*.

Michael A. Signer is Abrams Professor of Jewish Thought and Culture in the Department of Theology at the University of Notre Dame. He is the coeditor with John van Engen of *Jews and Christians in the Twelfth-Century Renaissance* (Notre Dame: University of Notre Dame Press, 2001).

Israel Jacob Yuval is Professor of Jewish History at the Hebrew University in Jerusalem. He is the author of two books in Hebrew, *Scholars in Their Time: The Religious Leadership of German Jewry in the Late Middle Ages* and *Two Nations in Your Womb: Perceptions of Jews and Christians*.

Index

Abraham ibn Ezra, 34, 42
Abulafia, Abraham, 37, 40
Alan of Lille, 21
Alemanno, Yohanan, 7, 35, 37, 38–43, 53, 55, 57, 58, 59, 61, 66
Alfonsi, Petrus, 21, 165
Andrew of St. Victor, 22, 23, 25, 26
apocalypticism, 2, 11, 130. *See also* messianism; millenarianism; Sabbatai Sevi
Arabic language, 57, 58, 79, 82, 91, 130
Aramaic, knowledge of, 5, 295
Arias Montano, Benito, 91
Aristotle, 33, 36, 37, 42, 51, 58
Ashkenazim, 1, 142, 165, 173, 174, 175
assimilation, 4, 8, 224, 266, 274, 275, 292
Augustine, 21, 25, 28, 58, 164, 169
Averroes, 55
Avigdor of Fano, 60–66
Azubi, Salomon, 7, 71–101; on astronomy, 84–86, 89, 90, 92; correspondence with Kircher, 86–88; encomium on Christian bishop, 72–74, 92; on Jewish culture, 77–78, 79–84; visiting Peiresc, 77, 84, 92, 93

Baldini, Baccio, 51
Baron, Salo W., 2
al-Batalyawsi, Ibn al-Sid, 34–35, 37, 39
Benjamin of Tudela, 79
biblical studies, 1, 5, 6, 7, 10, 12, 21–32, 51, 82, 84, 104, 110, 118, 134, 174, 176, 221; with contemporary Jews, 21–23, 24, 26, 52, 81; Enlightenment, 273, 274, 297–98; by Jews (*see* Azubi; Mühlhausen); medieval Christian, 21–32, 159 (*see also* Hugh of St. Victor); Reformation Christian, 181, 182, 185, 187, 188, 189, 192
Boccaccio, Giovanni, 60
Bohemia, Jews in, 170–73
Bucer, Martin, 182, 183, 186–90, 192
Buxtorf, Johannes, 135, 166, 215, 216, 218, 220–21, 222, 268

Calvinism, 5, 12, 294
von Carben, Victor, 166, 176, 215–16, 223, 267

censorship, 5, 8, 125–55, 295; by Christians, 125, 126–27, 134–35, 136, 139, 143, 165; by Jews, 128, 136, 139, 140–42; impact on literature, 126–28, 133, 134, 142–43, 145
Clement VIII, 134
Cohen, Jeremy, 21–22
conversion: within Christianity, 11, 287; of Christians to Judaism, 12, 286–87, 288–89, 291, 293, 296–300 (*see also* Späth); to Islam, 241, 242 (*see also* Sabbatai Sevi); of Jews to Christianity, 4, 5, 7, 8, 9, 10, 21, 126, 130, 172–73, 246, 267, 271, 276, 292–93, 300
Conversos, converts, 7, 9, 12, 129, 130, 135, 136, 160, 166, 172, 176, 184, 202, 204, 215, 218–22, 267, 268, 292. *See also names of individual figures*; "ethnographies"; Yom Kippur
Coptic, knowledge of, 72, 91
Counter-Reformation, 8, 9, 127, 128, 142
creation, 27, 36, 51
Crescas, Hasdai, 38
Crusades, 2, 3

Dante, 49
Descartes, René, 245, 251
devil and diabolism, 5, 8, 39, 111, 131, 132, 238, 240, 243, 250–51, 275
diaspora, Jewish, 3, 12, 102–3, 162, 170, 173, 266, 273

Enlightenment, 1, 9, 10, 11, 12, 266, 267, 273–76, 286, 294, 299, 300
Erasmus, Desiderius, 129, 188, 190
"ethnographies," of Jews, 10–11, 202–33; by Christians, 202–3, 223–24, 225, 289–90, 292; by converts, 202, 204, 212, 215–16, 223–24
Eucharist, doctrine, 2; and Jews, 163–64, 170, 172
Evelyn, John, 242–44, 249, 250–53, 268–69

Ficino, Marsilio, 33, 34, 50–51, 52, 55, 57, 58

Gassendi, Pierre, 71–72, 77, 82, 84, 86, 88, 93
Giacomo da Bergamo, 60, 62

Giorgione, 54–55, 58, 59, 66
Grotius, Hugo, 91, 111

Halakha, 10, 12, 133, 143, 144, 145, 161, 168, 173, 176, 241
Harding, Stephen, 21, 23–24
Hayyim, Elijah, 57
Hebrew language, 3, 5, 26, 27, 91, 295; from Christian teachers, 10; Christians' study of, 5, 6, 10, 21–32, 130, 174, 181, 191, 194–95, 287, 296; from Jewish teachers, 21–23, 24, 26, 181, 182, 184, 187, 194, 287, 295–96. *See also* biblical studies; Peiresc; Reformation
van Helmont, Francis Mercury, 286, 287, 288, 293, 294, 295, 297, 299, 300, 301
Herbert of Bosham, 23, 26–27
Hermetic Corpus, 33, 42–43, 50–51, 55–57
holidays, Jewish, 203, 204, 220. *See also* Passover; Sukkoth; Yom Kippur
Holocaust, 2
Hugh of St. Victor, 3, 23, 25–26, 27; *De Scripturis*, 25; *Didascalicon*, 23, 25; *Notulae*, 25–26
Humanism, 1, 5, 6, 7, 49–50, 52, 58, 66, 129, 130

Ibn Verga, 143–44
identity, 3, 12; Christian, 1, 4, 11–12, 103, 140, 286, 287, 291, 293; Jewish, 1, 4, 8, 12, 138, 140, 142–45, 291, 293
Index (of prohibited books), 125, 129, 132, 134, 135, 142, 165
Innocent III, 3
Inquisition, 4, 125, 128, 129, 134, 145, 164, 203, 293, 295
Isaac of Acco, 58
Islam, 3, 241, 242, 246, 247, 252, 269, 294
Israel, Jonathan, 5
Istanbul (Constantinople), 78, 236, 239–40, 244
Italy, 6–7, 38–39, 49–70; Florence, art in, 51–52, 53, 61–62; Siena, art in, 50–51, 56, 61; Venice, printing in, 130, 135, 136. *See also names of individual figures*; Renaissance

Jerome, 23, 24, 25, 27, 28
Judah Leon, 52–53, 288, 301
Julius III, 125, 134

Kabbalah, 5, 6, 7, 33–38, 41, 51, 161, 241, 299; Christians' study of, 10, 41, 43, 57, 186, 287–88, 293–97, 300
Kant, Immanuel, 267, 273–74, 276–77
Karaites, 161, 164
Karo, Joseph, 133
Kimhi, David, 186, 271

Kircher, Athanasius, 72, 86–88, 92, 93
Knorr von Rosenroth, Christian, 286, 287, 293–97, 299, 301

legislation, anti-Jewish, 3, 125, 126
Leibniz, Gottfried Wilhelm, 287, 295, 300, 301
Leone Ebreo, 41
Lessing, Gotthold Ephraim, 272, 299
Levita, Elias, 181, 184, 187–88
Locke, John, 117, 287, 298, 301
Luria, Isaac, 288, 294
Luther, Martin, 3, 10, 181, 182, 184, 186–89, 190–94, 267–68
Lutheranism, 8, 153, 246, 249, 286–87, 288, 290, 292, 293, 294, 299

magic, 5, 33–34, 39, 42, 50, 51, 129
Maimonides, 34, 40, 42, 57–58, 79, 107, 118, 133
man, doctrine of, 33–48; in Christian thought, 33–34, 43, 286; in Ficino, 43, 55; in Jewish thought, 34–41
Manetti, Giannozzo, 51–52, 55
Manjacoria, Nicolas, 23, 24
Margaritha, Antonius, 166, 176, 183, 184, 187, 188, 215, 216, 218–23, 267
Marranos, 4, 9, 130
medicine, Jews in, 3, 5
Melanchthon, Philipp, 181, 184, 186, 187, 188, 194
Menasseh Ben Israel, 91, 105, 107, 268, 273, 288, 301
Mendelssohn, Moses, 273, 275–76
messianism, 11, 27, 162, 235–36, 238, 241, 242, 244–45, 246–47, 249, 250, 253, 266–77, 297; and secularism, 266, 267, 274–77. *See also* millenarianism; Sabbatai Sevi
microcosm, 35–38, 39
millenarianism, 8, 11, 234–35, 239–45, 247, 250, 253, 273, 298. *See also* messianism; Sabbatai Sevi
Milton, John, 104, 108, 112, 115–16, 117–18
Mithridates, Flavius, 7, 40, 41
Modena, Leon, 74, 224
Mordechai of Eisenstadt, 244–45, 269
Moses, representations of, 51–55, 58, 66
Mühlhausen, Yom Tov Lippman (*Sefer ha-Nizzahon*), 9, 159–80, 184; awareness of Christianity, 174–76; on biblical studies, 161–63; Christians' study of, 166–68; transmission of, 164–66; on violence against Jews, 162, 163–64
Münster, Sebastian, 166, 181–84, 186–88, 190–94

Nahmanides, 166, 191, 219
Nayler, James, 11, 247–49, 270
Neoplatonism, 33, 36–37, 43, 57
Newton, Isaac, 112, 298

Oberman, Heiko, 2, 8
Oecolampadius, Johannes, 182, 183, 184, 188–89, 190
Orpheus, figure of, 50–51

paganism, 3, 25, 27, 49–52, 107, 294, 298, 299
Passover, described by Christians, 203; by Jews, 170
Paul IV, 125, 126, 129, 130
de Peiresc, Nicolas-Claude Fabri, 7, 71–101; defense of Azubi, 88; knowledge of Hebrew, 92–93; on Samaritans, 77, 78–79, 82, 84, 85; studies on Jewish culture, 74–77, 79, 84, 90
Pellican, Conrad, 181–87, 194
Pfefferkorn, Johann, 165, 166, 186, 204, 212, 218, 223, 267
Pico della Mirandola, 5, 7, 33, 34, 35, 37, 39, 40–41, 43, 52, 57, 58
Pietists, 245, 269, 292, 297
Pius V, 132
Plato, 25, 52, 55. *See also* Neoplatonism
Plotinus, 37
polemics: against Christianity, 9, 137–41, 142, 144, 159–63, 169, 174, 176, 192, 216, 219–20 (*see also* Mühlhausen); intra-Christian, 219, 235, 242, 245–50, 253, 267, 269, 298 (*see also* Protestantism); against Judaism, 8, 9, 10–11, 93, 103, 115, 143, 159–60, 193, 194, 204, 218, 241, 249, 253, 267, 271
printing trade, 3, 4, 181, 185–87, 295; Christians in, 7–8, 103, 119, 129, 135–37, 181, 193–94; converts in, 136–37, 141, 184; Jews in, 3, 5, 7–8, 10, 82, 129, 135–37, 184, 295, 301. *See also* censorship
prisca philosophia/theologia, 5, 50–51, 53, 57, 294
Protestantism, 10, 11–12, 93, 103, 106, 113, 118, 129, 131, 137, 143, 145, 181, 188, 190, 195, 219, 271, 272, 288. *See also* Calvinism; Lutheranism; polemics, intra-Christian; Reformation

Quakers, 11, 234, 235, 239, 240–41, 242, 244, 245, 247–49, 251, 270, 287, 288, 302

rabbinic Judaism, 7, 11, 103, 104, 111, 114, 118, 131, 134, 137, 141, 159, 175, 191, 221, 222. *See also* biblical studies; polemics
Rashba, 219

Rashi, 22, 25, 26, 81, 82, 118
reciprocity, between communities, 1–4, 5–6, 10, 145, 160, 202, 297
Reformation, 1, 8, 9, 10, 130, 131, 181–201; biblical studies in, 181, 182, 184, 187, 191; study of Hebrew in, 188–94. *See also names of individual figures*
Renaissance, 1, 5–6, 7, 33–48, 104, 142, 286. *See also* Italy
Reuchlin, Johannes, 166, 183–88, 194
Roman law, 7
Russian Orthodoxy, 239
Rycaut, Paul, 242–44, 246, 249, 251, 252, 253, 268–69

Sabbatai Sevi, 3, 11, 234–65; conversion to Islam, 241, 242, 268; Christians' view of, 234–35, 236, 238–44, 246, 250–53, 267, 268–70, 271; converts' view of, 272; Jews' view of, 236, 241, 242, 246, 266, 275; Moslems' view of, 234, 236
Scaliger, Joseph, 78, 91
scholasticism, 2, 27
Scholem, Gershom, 1, 11, 267
Schudt, Johannes Jacob, 168, 216–17, 270–71, 286–87, 288–93, 299, 301
Selden, John, 7, 92, 102–24; on Jewish chronology, 103; on Jewish law, 104; on natural law, 104–5, 107, 108, 111–12, 115–19; on Sanhedrin, 103, 104, 106
Sephardim, 271–72
Shem Tov b. Shem Tov, 35–38
Sixtus V, 132
skepticism, 1, 9, 159–80, 287, 291, 297, 299; among Jews, 161, 163, 164, 170, 172, 173, 175
Smalley, Beryl, 22, 26
Solomon, representations of, 58, 59–60, 66
Spain, 3, 6, 24, 34–36, 38
Späth, Johann Peter, 12, 286–93, 296–301
Spinoza, Baruch, 288, 299, 301
Sukkoth, 220
Sulzbach, Germany, 287, 293–97, 301
Syriac, knowledge of, 5, 295

Talmud, 22; attacks on, 2, 125, 126, 129–31, 132, 136, 141, 144; Christian study of, 79, 83, 92, 104, 107–10, 114, 118, 125, 126, 130, 132, 139, 159, 221 (*see also* Selden); Jewish study of, 58, 79, 86, 106, 130, 132, 133, 173; printings of, 132, 141
toleration, 1, 2, 12, 93, 110, 111, 115, 119, 291, 294, 296
trade, 4, 5, 287
travel, 4, 79
Trent, Council of, 132, 133–34

violence, against Jews, 2, 143, 162, 163–64, 170, 172, 289

Wachter, Johann Georg, 286, 287, 299–300, 301
Wenceslas, King, 171–72
women, role of, 59–66, 161

Yates, Frances, 33–34, 43

Yehuda ha-Levi, 34, 37
Yiddish, 292–93
Yom Kippur: described by Christians, 202–3, 218, 222; described by converts, 163, 202, 203, 204, 212, 215–16, 218, 219, 222; described by Jews, 217–18
Ysagoge in Theologiam, 23, 27–28

Acknowledgments

This volume of essays owes its existence to David Ruderman, director of the University of Pennsylvania's Center for Advanced Judaic Studies, Anthony Grafton, Moshe Idel, and Guy Stroumsa, who together determined that the subject of Christian Hebraism was important enough to merit a year-long seminar. As the moving force behind the Center, we are especially grateful to David Ruderman, whose enormous energy, enthusiasm, and knowledge made our time at the Center truly memorable and rewarding. Organizing and running such a seminar, however, required the combined forces of the entire staff. We thank Sheila Allen and Sam Cardillo for being such efficient and welcoming administrators. We are grateful to Etty Lassman for helping us deal with things as diverse as computer problems and theater tickets and to Bonnie Blankenship, who took time from her job as managing editor of *The Jewish Quarterly Review* to ensure that we ate well at the weekly seminar lunches. Our hours in the library were greatly enhanced by the expert assistance provided by Arthur Kiron, Seth Jerchower, and Judith Leifer.

Each of the essays in this volume was enriched by the thoughtful discussions among all the participants in the year-long seminar and its culminating colloquium. While not all the members of the seminar are represented in the table of contents, in a very real sense they all are contributors to the project. In a similar vein, we would like to thank the anonymous readers of the manuscript, whose comments and suggestions were all valuable. Jerry Singerman, at the University of Pennsylvania Press, has been an enthusiastic supporter of this volume since its beginning. Rebecca Rich and Ted Mann, editorial assistants at the Press, deserve our thanks for their skilled and meticulous oversight of the editorial process. We also thank Erica Ginsburg, Associate Managing Editor, for her assistance in preparing the manuscript for publication.

Book Shelves
PJ4509 .H4 2004
Hebraica veritas? :
Christian Hebraists and the
study of Judaism in early
modern Europe